Word Sense Disambiguation

Text, Speech and Language Technology

VOLUME 33

The titles published in this series are listed on www.springer.com.

Eneko Agirre · Philip Edmonds
Editors

Word Sense Disambiguation
Algorithms and Applications

 Springer

Eneko Agirre
University of the Basque Country
Basque Country
Spain

Philip Edmonds
Sharp Laboratories of Europe
Oxford
U.K.

ISBN 978-1-4020-6870-6   e-ISBN 978-1-4020-4809-2

Library of Congress Control Number: 2007938211

9 8 7 6 5 4 3 2 1

springer.com

Contents

10 Domain-Specific WSD 275

Paul Buitelaar, Bernardo Magnini, Carlo Strapparava, Piek Vossen

11 WSD in NLP Applications 299

Philip Resnik

Contributors

Eneko Agirre is an Associate Professor in the University of the Basque Country, where he is member of the IXA NLP group. He organized the Basque tasks for Senseval and coordinates the construction of the Basque WordNet and Semcor. Department of Computer Science, University of the Basque Country, Manuel de Lardizabal 1, E-20018 Donostia, Basque Country, Spain.

Paul Buitelaar is a Senior Researcher in the Language Technology Lab and co-chair of the Competence Center Semantic Web at DFKI (German Research Center for Artificial Intelligence) GmbH. He was organizer of several international workshops and has been an invited speaker at panels and workshops on topics in semantic annotation and ontology development. DFKI GmbH Language Technology Department, Stuhlsatzen-hausweg 3, Saarbrücken, Germany.

Hoa Trang Dang is a Computer Scientist at the National Institute of Standards and Technology (NIST), where she coordinates evaluations of automatic question answering and summarization systems in TREC and DUC. National Institute of Standards and Technology, 100 Bureau Drive, Mailstop 8940, Gaithersburg, MD 20899-8940, U.S.A.

Philip Edmonds is a Research Scientist at Sharp Laboratories of Europe. He was chair of Senseval, 2001–2004, and is the author of the entry on lexical disambiguation in the *Elsevier Encyclopedia of Language and Linguistics, 2nd Ed.* Sharp Laboratories of Europe Limited, Oxford Science Park, Oxford OX4 4GB, United Kingdom.

Gerard Escudero is an Assistant Professor at the Universitat Politècnica de Catalunya. He was a participant in Senseval-2 and Senseval-3. He also participated in the MEANING project, funded by the EU. EUETIB, Urgell 187, E-08036 Barcelona, Catalonia, Spain.

Julio Gonzalo is an Assistant Professor at the UNED School of Computer Science. He is co-editor of the CLEF (Cross-Language Evaluation Forum) proceedings on multilingual information access published by Springer. In 2006, he is co-chair of the Programme Committee of the European

Conference on Advanced Research and Development for Digital Libraries. Dep. Lenguajes y Sistemas Informáticos, ETSI Informática – UNED, Ciudad Universitaria, c/ Juan del Rosal 16, 28040 Madrid, Spain.

Nancy Ide is a Professor of Computer Science at Vassar College and chair of the Computer Science Department. She is founder of the Text Encoding Initiative (TEI) and creator of the Corpus Encoding Standard. Currently she is directing the development of the American National Corpus. Department of Computer Science, Vassar College, 124 Raymond Avenue, Poughkeepsie, New York 12604-0520, U.S.A.

Adam Kilgarriff is Director of Lexical Computing Ltd. and Visiting Research Fellow at the University of Sussex, U.K. He works on both the theory and the practice, at the intersection of language corpora, language technologies and practical dictionary-making. Lexical Computing Ltd., 71 Freshfield Road, Brighton BN2 0BL, U.K.

Bernardo Magnini is a Senior Researcher at ITC-irst, where he coordinates the research group on Text Technologies. He is the local organizer co-chair of EACL-06, the 11th Conference of the European Chapter of the Association for Computational Linguistics. ITC-irst, Via Sommarive 18, I-38050, Povo-Trento, Italy.

Lluís Màrquez is an Associate Professor at the Polytechnical University of Catalunya (UPC). He organized two shared tasks on semantic role labeling at the Conference on Natural Language Learning (CoNLL) in 2004 and 2005, and led the team that organized the Catalan and Spanish lexical sample tasks at Senseval-3. In 2006, he will be the co-chair of the CoNLL conference. Despatx S120 - Edifici Omega, Campus Nord UPC, C/ Jordi Girona Salgado 1-3, E-08034 Barcelona, Catalonia, Spain.

David Martínez is a post-doc researcher in the NLP group of the University of Sheffield. Natural Language Processing Group, Department of Computer Science, University of Sheffield, Sheffield, S1 4DP, United Kingdom.

Rada Mihalcea is an Assistant Professor of Computer Science at University of North Texas. She is the president of ACL SIGLEX and was a co-chair of Senseval-3. Department of Computer Science, University of North Texas, PO Box 311366, Denton, TX 76203, U.S.A.

Hwee Tou Ng is an Associate Professor of Computer Science at the National University of Singapore. He is on the editorial board of *Computational Linguistics*, was program co-chair of the ACL-2005 conference, and has served on the program committees of many past conferences including ACL, SIGIR, AAAI, and IJCAI. Department of Computer Science, School of Computing, National University of Singapore, 3 Science Drive 2, Singapore 117543.

Martha Palmer is an Associate Professor in the Departments of Linguistics and Computer Science and a Faculty Fellow of the Institute of Cognitive Science at the University of Colorado at Boulder. She has been a member of the Advisory Committee for the DARPA TIDES program, chair of ACL SIGLEX and ACL SIGHAN, and is currently Past-President of the Association for Computational Linguistics. Department of Linguistics, 295 UCB - Hellems 295, Boulder, CO 80309, U.S.A.

Ted Pedersen is an Associate Professor in the Department of Computer Science at the University of Minnesota, Duluth. He is the recipient of a National Science Foundation (NSF, USA) Faculty Early Career Development (CAREER) Award. Department of Computer Science, 1114 Kirby Drive, University of Minnesota, Duluth, MN 55812, U.S.A.

Philip Resnik is an associate professor at the University of Maryland, College Park, in the Department of Linguistics and the Institute for Advanced Computer Studies. He is on the editorial board of *Cognitive Linguistics*. 1401 Marie Mount Hall, University of Maryland, College Park, MD 20742, U.S.A.

German Rigau is an Associate Professor in the Department of Computer Science of the Basque Country University. He coordinated the EU's 5th framework MEANING project. He has also participated in Senseval-2 and Senseval-3. Department of Computer Science, University of the Basque Country, Manuel de Lardizabal 1, E-20018 Donostia, Basque Country, Spain.

Mark Stevenson is a Lecturer in Computer Science at the University of Sheffield. He is author of the monograph *Word Sense Disambiguation: Combining Knowledge Sources for Sense Resolution* (2003) based on his Ph.D. thesis. Natural Language Processing Group, Department of Computer Science, University of Sheffield, Sheffield, S1 4DP, United Kingdom.

Carlo Strapparava is a Senior Researcher at ITC-irst in the Communication and Cognitive Technologies Division. He is author of over ninety published papers on topics including artificial intelligence, natural language processing, and word sense disambiguation. ITC-irst, Via Sommarive, 18 I-38050, Povo-Trento, Italy.

M. Felisa Verdejo is Full Professor and head of the department Lenguajes y Sistemas Informáticos (LSI) at National Distance Learning University (UNED). She has been involved in several large-scale EU-funded projects such as EuroWordNet and CLEF. Dep. Lenguajes y Sistemas Informáticos, ETSI Informática – UNED, Ciudad Universitaria, c/ Juan del Rosal 16, 28040 Madrid, Spain.

Piek Vossen is CTO of Irion Technologies. He worked on several EU projects: Acquilex, Sift, EAGLES, EuroWordNet, EuroTerm, BalkaNet and MEANING and most recently on an American project to develop an Arabic wordnet. He is also founder and president of the Global Wordnet Association (GWA). Irion Technologies BV., Delftechpark 26, 2628 XH Delft, PO Box 2849, 2601 CV Delft, The Netherlands.

Yorick Wilks is Professor of Computer Science at the University of Sheffield. He is author of numerous articles and six books including *Electric Words: Dictionaries, Computers and Meanings* (1996 with Brian Slator and Louise Guthrie). He is a Fellow of the American and European Associations for Artificial Intelligence, and on the boards of some fifteen AI-related journals. Department of Computer Science, University of Sheffield, Sheffield S1 4DP, United Kingdom.

Foreword

Graeme Hirst

University of Toronto

Of the many kinds of ambiguity in language, the two that have received the most attention in computational linguistics are those of word senses and those of syntactic structure, and the reasons for this are clear: these ambiguities are overt, their resolution is seemingly essential for any practical application, and they seem to require a wide variety of methods and knowledge-sources with no pattern apparent in what any particular instance requires.

Right at the birth of artificial intelligence, in his 1950 paper "Computing machinery and intelligence", Alan Turing saw the ability to understand language as an essential test of intelligence, and an essential test of language understanding was an ability to disambiguate; his example involved deciding between the generic and specific readings of the phrase *a winter's day*. The first generations of AI researchers found it easy to construct examples of ambiguities whose resolution seemed to require vast knowledge and deep understanding of the world and complex inference on this knowledge; for example, *Pharmacists dispense with accuracy*. The disambiguation problem was, in a way, nothing less than the artificial intelligence problem itself. No use was seen for a disambiguation method that was less than 100% perfect; either it worked or it didn't. Lexical resources, such as they were, were considered secondary to non-linguistic common-sense knowledge of the world.

And because the methods that were developed required a resource whose eventual existence was merely hypothesized – a knowledge base containing everything a typical adult knows – and because there were no test data available, it was not possible to empirically test them or quantitatively evaluate them or their underlying ideas in any serious way. Rather, systems and methods were presented like theorems whose truth or correctness could be demonstrated by a rational argument bolstered by hand-waving and a 'toy' demonstration: a knowledge source would be built for a few words and facts, and the system would be run on a few "interesting" constructed examples to show that it did "the right thing". This approach to evaluation was quite normal in the milieu in which this research was carried out and didn't seem to worry anyone at the time: computational linguistics had not yet achieved its empirical orientation.

Contemporary approaches have turned all that upside-down. Statistical and machine-learning methods and methodologies that have been adopted in the last decade have revolutionized our view of ambiguity resolution. It is now understood that imperfect methods that rely on rich lexical resources but limited additional knowledge have great use in the world; and that systems must undergo rigorous evaluation. The present volume demonstrates this in particular for word sense disambiguation – both the strengths and the inherent limitations of these approaches.[1] In particular, contemporary methods are less ambitious and have lower expectations. Unlike the earlier research, they don't worry about case roles, about helping a parser with attachment decisions, or about working with a semantic interpretation process aimed at a deep level of "understanding". Rather than aiming for a complete solution and hypothesizing a resource that this necessitates, they rely on an existing resource and try to see how much can be done with it. And yet they still have enormous application in NLP (see Chap. 11).

One issue that has remained constant is what kinds of information in the text may be drawn upon as cues for disambiguation, and how near in the text to the target word those cues should be. In my own early work (Hirst 1987), restrictions on communication between disambiguating processes arose from two competing principles: any particular word or structural cue for disambiguation has quite a limited sphere of influence, and yet almost anything in a text or discourse is potentially a cue for disambiguation (cf. McRoy 1992). In contemporary systems, the analogous dilemma is in the choice of features and the window size (see Chap. 8).

The other thing that hasn't changed is how hard the lexical disambiguation problem is. Many sophisticated systems struggle merely to reach the modest accuracy of simple baseline algorithms such as that of Lesk (1986) (see Chap. 5) or just choosing the most frequent sense. But what is a poor computer to do when humans themselves frequently disagree on what the correct answer is supposed to be (see Chaps. 2–4)?

Although it is an edited volume, this book is not an anthology of "recent advances" papers by individual authors on their own research, requiring

---

[1] A similar revolution has occurred in parsing and structural disambiguation; see Manning and Schütze (2000, Chaps. 11–12) for an overview.

each reader to synthesize a view of the overall situation in a research topic. Rather, editors Agirre and Edmonds have enlisted the leading researchers of the field to do the hard work. Each chapter of this book presents an overview and synthesis of one facet of current research. The result is a clear and well-organized presentation of the state of the art in word sense disambiguation that can be read, like a textbook, from start to finish. I commend it to you.

Graeme Hirst is the author of Semantic Interpretation and the Resolution of Ambiguity *(Cambridge University Press, 1987), which presents an integrated theory of lexical disambiguation, structural disambiguation, and semantic interpretation.*

References

Hirst, Graeme. 1987. *Semantic Interpretation and the Resolution of Ambiguity.* Cambridge University Press.

Lesk, Michael. 1986. Automatic sense disambiguation using machine readable dictionaries: How to tell a pine cone from an ice cream cone. *Proceedings of SIGDOC-86: 5th International Conference on Systems Documentation*, Toronto, Canada, 24–26.

Manning, Christopher D. & Hinrich Schütze. 2000. *Foundations of Statistical Natural Language Processing.* Cambridge, MA: The MIT Press.

McRoy, Susan. 1992. Using multiple knowledge sources for word sense discrimination. *Computational Linguistics*, 19(1):1–30.

Turing, Alan M. 1950. Computing machinery and intelligence. *Mind*, 59:433–460. Reprinted in: Stuart Shieber, ed. 2004. *The Turing Test: Verbal Behavior as the Hallmark of Intelligence.* Cambridge, MA: The MIT Press.

Preface

Word sense disambiguation is a core research problem in computational linguistics, which was recognized at the beginning of the scientific interest in machine translation and artificial intelligence. And yet no book has been fully devoted to review the wide variety of approaches to solving the problem. The time is right for such a book.

This book had its genesis over five years ago when Nancy Ide, series co-editor of then Kluwer's, now Springer's, *Text, Speech, and Language Technology* series, approached us with the project. Word sense disambiguation is an active and quickly progressing research field, so we thought it far more beneficial to the research community if we were to enlist the main experts to each give their own view of the field.

Being the first major book on the topic, and with the hope of it becoming the definitive reference, we endeavoured to fashion a coherent, consistent, critical, and readable survey of the current state of the art. We started by sketching an overview of the main topics that should be covered, and then approached experts in the field with desiderata for each chapter. We requested that authors give a general overview of their topic and proceed with a thorough exposition of the theory, methodology, algorithms, critical analysis, experimentation, results, and open issues. We are indebted to all of the authors, who worked with us most patiently.

The manuscript has taken time to produce, having been through numerous reviews and revisions along the way. Many difficult decisions were made in the attempt to best embrace all of the important research in the field, and to keep up with new developments. We apologize if we have missed something.

Please visit the book website, www.wsdbook.org, for the latest information updates, and a book search interface.

Word sense disambiguation is a fascinating topic; we hope you enjoy reading this book as much as we did creating it!

Acknowledgments

First all, it is the chapter authors who created the book; we thank them all for exceeding their remits and for their patience during the lengthy reviewing cycles. We owe the existence of this book to Nancy Ide, the series co-editor.

A few people gave us encouragement and feedback at various stages about the content and organization of the book. We are grateful to Robert Dale, David Farwell, Graeme Hirst, Eduard Hovy, Inderjeet Mani, Pete Whitelock, and David Yarowsky.

Three anonymous reviewers helped us get around the weak points. We also thank the team at Kluwer and Springer for their support: Tamara Welschot, Jacqueline Bergsma, Helen van der Stelt, and Jolanda Voogd (Associate Publishing Editor).

Phil was supported by Sharp Laboratories of Europe, and Eneko by the IXA research group.

Finally, this book is dedicated to our families, who had to sacrifice their time with us for the sake of this book.

Phil Edmonds and Eneko Agirre
27 January 2006

1 Introduction

Eneko Agirre[1] and Philip Edmonds[2]

[1]University of the Basque Country
[2]Sharp Laboratories of Europe Limited

1.1 Word Sense Disambiguation

Anyone who gets the joke when they hear a pun will realize that lexical ambiguity is a fundamental characteristic of language: Words can have more than one distinct meaning. So why is it that text doesn't seem like one long string of puns? After all, lexical ambiguity is pervasive. The 121 most frequent English nouns, which account for about one in five word occurrences in real text, have on average 7.8 meanings each (in the Princeton WordNet (Miller 1990), tabulated by Ng and Lee (1996)). But the potential for ambiguous readings tends to go completely unnoticed in normal text and flowing conversation. The effect is so strong that some people will even miss a pun (a real ambiguity) obvious to others. Words may be polysemous in principle, but in actual text there is very little real ambiguity – to a person.

Lexical disambiguation in its broadest definition is nothing less than determining the meaning of every word in context, which appears to be a largely unconscious process in people. As a computational problem it is often described as "AI-complete", that is, a problem whose solution presupposes a solution to complete natural-language understanding or common-sense reasoning (Ide and Véronis 1998).

In the field of computational linguistics, the problem is generally called word sense disambiguation (WSD), and is defined as the problem of computationally determining which "sense" of a word is activated by the use of the word in a particular context. WSD is essentially a task of classification:

E. Agirre and P. Edmonds (eds.), Word Sense Disambiguation: Algorithms and Applications, 1–28.
© 2007 *Springer.*

word senses are the classes, the context provides the evidence, and each occurrence of a word is assigned to one or more of its possible classes based on the evidence. This is the traditional and common characterization of WSD that sees it as an explicit process of disambiguation with respect to a fixed inventory of word senses. Words are assumed to have a finite and discrete set of senses from a dictionary, a lexical knowledge base, or an ontology (in the latter, senses correspond to concepts that a word lexicalizes). Application-specific inventories can also be used. For instance, in a machine translation (MT) setting, one can treat word translations as word senses, an approach that is becoming increasingly feasible because of the availability of large multi-lingual parallel corpora that can serve as training data. The fixed inventory of traditional WSD reduces the complexity of the problem, making it tractable, but alternatives exist, as we will see below.

WSD has obvious relationships to other fields such as lexical semantics, whose main endeavour is to define, analyze, and ultimately understand the relationships between "word", "meaning", and "context". But even though word meaning is at the heart of the problem, WSD has never really found a home in lexical semantics. It could be that lexical semantics has always been more concerned with representational issues (see, for example, Lyons 1995) and models of word meaning and polysemy so far too complex for WSD (Cruse 1986; Ravin and Leacock 2000). And so, the obvious procedural or computational nature of WSD paired with its early invocation in the context of machine translation (Weaver 1949) has allied it more closely with language technology and thus computational linguistics. In fact, WSD has more in common with modern lexicography, with its intuitive premise that word uses group into coherent semantic units and its empirical corpus-based approaches, than with lexical semantics (Wilks et al. 1993).

The importance of WSD has been widely acknowledged in computational linguistics; some 700 papers in the ACL Anthology mention the term "word sense disambiguation".[1] Of course, WSD is not thought of as an end in itself, but as an enabler for other tasks and applications of computational linguistics and natural language processing (NLP) such as parsing, semantic interpretation, machine translation, information retrieval, text

---

[1] To compare, "anaphora resolution" occurs in 438 papers; however, such statistics should not be taken too seriously. The ACL Anthology is a digital archive of research papers in computational linguistics, covering conferences and workshops from 1979 to the present, maintained by the Association for Computational Linguistics (www.aclweb.org/anthology). Our statistics were gathered in November 2005.

mining, and (lexical) knowledge acquisition. However, in counterpoint to its theoretical importance, explicit WSD has not always demonstrated benefits in real applications.

A long-standing and central debate is whether WSD should be researched as a generic or as an integrated component. In the generic setting, the WSD component is a black box encompassing an explicit process of WSD that can be dropped into any application, much like a part-of-speech tagger or a syntactic parser. The alternative is to include WSD as a task-specific "component" of a particular application in a specific domain and integrated so completely into a system that it is difficult to separate out. Research into explicit WSD, having received the bulk of effort, has progressed steadily and successfully to a point where some people now question if the upper limit in accuracy (low as it is on fine-grained sense distinctions) has been attained (Section 1.6 gives current performance levels). And yet, explicit WSD has not yet been convincingly demonstrated to have a significant positive effect on any application. Only the integrated approach has been successful, with disambiguation often occurring implicitly by virtue of other operations, for example, in the language and translation models of statistical machine translation. The former conception is easier to define, experiment with, and evaluate, and is thus more amenable to the scientific method; the latter is more applicable and puts the need for explicit WSD into question.

Despite uncertain results on real applications, the effort on explicit WSD has produced a solid legacy of research results, methodology, and insights for computational semantics. For example, local contextual features (i.e., other words near the target word) provide better evidence in general than wider topical features (Yarowsky 2000). Indeed, the role of context in WSD is much better understood: Compared to other classification tasks in NLP (such as part-of-speech tagging), WSD requires a wide range of contextual knowledge to be modeled from fixed patterns of part-of-speech tags around a topic word to syntactic relations to topical and domain associations. Each part-of-speech and even each word relies on different types of knowledge for disambiguation. For instance, nouns benefit from a wide context and local collocations, whereas verbs benefit from syntactic features. Some words can be disambiguated by a single feature in the right position, benefiting from a "discriminative" method; others require an aggregation of many features. Homographs are generally much easier to disambiguate than polysemous words?[2] An evaluation methodology has been defined by Senseval (Kilgarriff and Palmer 2000) and many resources in several languages are now available. Finally, for a small sample of tested words, that have sufficient training data, the performance of WSD systems is comparable to that of humans (measured as the inter-tagger agreement among two or more humans), as demonstrated by the recent Senseval results (see Sect. 1.6 below).

Two "spin offs" worth mentioning include the development of explicit WSD as a benchmark application for machine learning research, because of the clear problem definition and methodology, the variety of problem spaces (each word is a separate classification task), the high-dimensional feature space, and the skewed nature of word sense distributions. And second, WSD research is helping in the development of popular lexical resources such as WordNet (Fellbaum 1998; Palmer et al. 2001, 2006) and the multilingual lexicons of the MEANING project (Vossen et al. 2006).

To introduce the topic of WSD, we begin with a brief history. Then, in Section 1.3 we discuss the central theoretical issues of "word sense" and the sense inventory. In Sections 1.4–1.6 we summarize several practical aspects including applicability to NLP tasks, the three basic approaches to WSD, and current performance achievements. Finally, Section 1.7 gathers our thoughts on emerging and future research into WSD.

1.2 A Brief History of WSD Research

In order to introduce current WSD research, reported in the book, we provide here a brief review of the history of WSD research.[3]

WSD was first formulated as a distinct computational task during the early days of machine translation in the late 1940s, making it one of the oldest problems in computational linguistics. Weaver (1949) introduced the problem in his now famous memorandum on machine translation:

> If one examines the words in a book, one at a time through an opaque mask with a hole in it one word wide, then it is obviously impossible to determine,

---

[2] For the present purposes, a homograph is a coarse-grained sense distinction between often completely unrelated meanings of the same word string (e.g., *bank* as a financial institution or a river side). Polysemy involves a finer-grained sense distinction in which the senses can be related in different ways (e.g., *bank* as a physical building or as an institution). See Section 1.3 for further details.

[3] See Ide and Véronis (1998) for a more extensive history (up to 1998, of course.)

one at a time, the meaning of words. "Fast" may mean "rapid"; or it may mean "motionless"; and there is no way of telling which.

But, if one lengthens the slit in the opaque mask, until one can see not only the central word in question but also say N words on either side, then, if N is large enough one can unambiguously decide the meaning ...

In addition to formulating the general methodology still applied today (see also Kaplan (1950) and Reifler (1955)), Weaver acknowledged that context is crucial, and recognized the basic statistical character of the problem in proposing that "statistical semantic studies should be undertaken, as a necessary primary step."

The 1950s then saw much work in estimating the degree of ambiguity in texts and bilingual dictionaries, and applying simple statistical models. Zipf (1949) published his "Law of Meaning"[4] that accounts for the skewed distribution of words by number of senses, that is, that more frequent words have more senses than less frequent words in a power-law relationship; the relationship has been confirmed for the *British National Corpus* (Edmonds 2005). Kaplan (1950) determined that two words of context on either side of an ambiguous word was equivalent to a whole sentence of context in resolving power.

Some early work set the stage for methods still pursued today. Masterman (1957), for instance, used the headings of the categories in *Roget's International Thesaurus* (Chapman 1977) to represent the different senses of a word, and then chose the heading whose contained words were most prominent in the context. Madhu and Lytle (1965) calculated sense frequencies of words in different domains – observing early on that domain constrains sense – and then applied Bayes formula to choose the most probable sense given a context.

Early researchers well understood the significance and difficulty of WSD. In fact, this difficulty was one of the reasons why most of MT was abandoned in the 1960s due to the unfavorable ALPAC report (1966). For example, Bar-Hillel (1960) argued that "no existing or imaginable program will enable an electronic computer to determine that the word *pen*" is used in its 'enclosure' sense in the passage below, because of the need to model, in general, all world knowledge like, for example, the relative sizes of objects:

---

[4] Zipf's "Law of Meaning" is different from his well known "Zipf's Law" about the power-law distribution of word frequencies.

> Little John was looking for his toy box. Finally he found it. The box was in the *pen*. John was very happy.

Ironically, the very "statistical semantics" that Weaver proposed might have applied in cases such as this: Yarowsky (2000) notes that the trigram *in the pen* is very strongly indicative of the enclosure sense, since one almost never refers to what is in a writing pen, except for ink.

WSD was resurrected in the 1970s within artificial intelligence (AI) research on full natural language understanding. In this spirit, Wilks (1975) developed "preference semantics", one of the first systems to explicitly account for WSD. The system used selectional restrictions and a frame-based lexical semantics to find a consistent set of word senses for the words in a sentence. The idea of individual "word experts" evolved over this time (Rieger and Small 1979). For example, in Hirst's (1987) system, a word was gradually disambiguated as information was passed between the various modules (including a lexicon, parser, and semantic interpreter) in a process he called "Polaroid Words". "Proper" knowledge representation was important in the AI paradigm. Knowledge sources had to be handcrafted, so the ensuing knowledge acquisition bottleneck inevitably led to limited lexical coverage of narrow domains and would not scale.

The 1980s were a turning point for WSD. Large-scale lexical resources and corpora became available so handcrafting could be replaced with knowledge extracted automatically from the resources (Wilks et al. 1990). Lesk's (1986) short but extremely seminal paper used the overlap of word sense definitions in the *Oxford Advanced Learner's Dictionary of Current English* (OALD) to resolve word senses. Given two (or more) target words in a sentence, the pair of senses whose definitions have the greatest lexical overlap are chosen (see Chap. 5 (Sect. 5.2)). Dictionary-based WSD had begun and the relationship of WSD to lexicography became explicit. For example, Guthrie et al. (1991) used the subject codes (e.g., Economics, Engineering, etc.) in the *Longman Dictionary of Contemporary English* (LDOCE) (Procter 1978) on top of Lesk's method. Yarowsky (1992) combined the information in *Roget's International Thesaurus* with co-occurrence data from large corpora in order to learn disambiguation rules for Roget's classes, which could then be applied to words in a manner reminiscent of Masterman (1957) (see Chap. 10 (Sect. 10.2.1)). Although dictionary methods are useful for some cases of word sense ambiguity (such as homographs), they are not robust since dictionaries lack complete coverage of information on sense distinctions.

The 1990s saw three major developments: WordNet became available, the statistical revolution in NLP swept through, and Senseval began.

WordNet (Miller 1990) pushed research forward because it was both computationally accessible and hierarchically organized into word senses called synsets. Today, English WordNet (together with wordnets for other languages) is the most-used general sense inventory in WSD research.

Statistical and machine learning methods have been successfully applied to the sense classification problem. Today, methods that train on manually sense-tagged corpora (i.e., supervised learning methods) have become the mainstream approach to WSD, with the best results in all tasks of the Senseval competitions. Weaver had recognized the statistical nature of the problem as early as 1949 and early corpus-based work by Weiss (1973), Kelley and Stone (1975), and Black (1988) presaged the statistical revolution by demonstrating the potential of empirical methods to extract disambiguation clues from manually-tagged corpora. Brown et al. (1991) were the first to use corpus-based WSD in statistical MT.

Before Senseval, it was extremely difficult to compare and evaluate different systems because of disparities in test words, annotators, sense inventories, and corpora. For instance, Gale et al. (1992:252) noted that "the literature on word sense disambiguation fails to offer a clear model that we might follow in order to quantify the performance of our disambiguation algorithms," and so they introduced lower bounds (choosing the most frequent sense) and upper bounds (the performance of human annotators). However, these could not be used effectively until sufficiently large test corpora were generated. Senseval was first discussed in 1997 (Resnik and Yarowsky 1999; Kilgarriff and Palmer 2000) and now after hosting three evaluation exercises has grown into the primary forum for researchers to discuss and advance the field. Its main contribution was to establish a framework for WSD evaluation that includes standardized task descriptions and an evaluation methodology. It has also focused research, enabled scientific rigor, produced benchmarks, and generated substantial resources in many languages (e.g., sense-annotated corpora), thus enabling research in languages other than English.

Recently, at the Senseval-3 workshop (Mihalcea and Edmonds 2004) there was a general consensus (and a sense of unease) that the traditional explicit WSD task, so effective at driving research, had reached a plateau and was not likely to lead to fundamentally new research. This could indicate the need to look for new research directions in the field, some of which may already be emerging, for instance the use of parallel bilingual corpora. Section 1.7 explores the emerging research, but let's first review the issue at the center of it all: word senses.

1.3 What is a Word Sense?

Word meaning is in principle infinitely variable and context sensitive. It does not divide up easily into distinct sub-meanings or senses. Lexicographers frequently discover in corpus data loose and overlapping word meanings, and standard or conventional meanings extended, modulated, and exploited in a bewildering variety of ways (Kilgarriff 1997; Hanks 2000; also Chap. 2). In lexical semantics, this phenomenon is often addressed in theories that model sense extension and semantic vagueness, but such theories are at a very early stage in explaining the complexities of word meaning (e.g., Cruse 1986; Tuggy 1993; Lyons 1995).

"Polysemy" means to have multiple meanings. It is an intrinsic property of words (in isolation from text), whereas "ambiguity" is a property of text. Whenever there is uncertainty as to the meaning that a speaker or writer intends, there is ambiguity. So, polysemy indicates only potential ambiguity, and context works to remove ambiguity.

At a coarse grain a word often has a small number of senses that are clearly different and probably completely unrelated to each other, usually called *homographs*. Such senses are just "accidentally" collected under the same word string. As one moves to finer-grained distinctions the coarse-grained senses break up into a complex structure of interrelated senses, involving phenomena such as general polysemy, regular polysemy, and metaphorical extension. Thus, most sense distinctions are not as clear as the distinction between *bank* as 'financial institution' and *bank* as 'river side'. For example, *bank* as financial institution splits into the following cloud of related senses: the company or institution, the building itself, the counter where money is exchanged, a fund or reserve of money, a money box (*piggy bank*), the funds in a gambling house, the dealer in a gambling house, and a supply of something held in reserve (*blood bank*) (WordNet 2.1).

Even rare and seemingly innocuous words such as *quoin* offer a rich structure of meanings. *The American Heritage Dictionary of the English Language* lists three related noun-senses: the outer angle or corner of a wall, a brick forming such an angle (a cornerstone), and a wedge-shaped block. As a verb, it can mean to build a corner with distinctive blocks, or, in the printing domain, to secure metal type with a quoin.

Given the range of sense distinctions in examples such as these, which represent the norm, one might start to wonder if the very idea of word-sense is suspect. Some argue that task-independent senses simply cannot be enumerated in a list (Kilgarriff 1997; others that words are monosemous, having a have only a single, abstract meaning (Ruhl 1989). And perhaps the only tenable position is that a word must have a different meaning in each distinct context in which it occurs. But a strong word-in-context position ignores the intuition that word usages seem to cluster together into coherent sets, which could be called senses, even if the sets cannot be satisfactorily described or labeled. The work on sense discovery or induction gives some empirical evidence for this intuition, however such "senses" are more aptly called "word uses" (see Chap. 6 (Sect. 6.3)).

Concerns about the theoretical, linguistic, or psychological reality of word senses notwithstanding, the field of WSD has successfully established itself by largely ignoring them, much as lexicographers do in order to produce dictionaries. Except, Kilgarriff (Chap. 2) suggests that it *is* time to take notice.

In practice, the need for a sense inventory has driven WSD research. In the common conception, a sense inventory is an exhaustive and fixed list of the senses of every word of concern in an application. The nature of the sense inventory depends on the application, and the nature of the disambiguation task depends on the inventory. The three Cs of sense inventories are: clarity, consistency, and complete coverage of the range of meaning distinctions that matter. Sense granularity is actually a key consideration: too coarse and some critical senses may be missed, too fine and unnecessary errors may occur. For example, the ambiguity of *mouse* (animal or device) is not relevant in English-Basque machine translation, where *sagu* is the only translation, but is relevant in (English and Basque) information retrieval. The opposite is true of *sister*, which is translated differently into Basque depending on the gender of the other sibling: *ahizpa* for 'sister of a girl' and *arreba* for 'sister of a boy'. In fact, Ide and Wilks (Chap. 3) argue that coarse-level distinctions are the only ones that humans and machines can reliably discriminate (and that they are *the* distinctions of concern to applications). There is evidence (see Chap. 4) that if senses are too fine or unclear, human annotators also have difficulty assigning them.

The "sense inventory" has been the most contentious issue in the WSD community, and it surfaced during the formation of Senseval, which required agreement on a common standard. The main inventories used in English research have included LDOCE, *Roget's International Thesaurus*, Hector, and WordNet. For other languages a variety of dictionaries have been used, together with local WordNet versions. Each resource has its pros and cons, which will become clear throughout the book (especially Chaps. 2, 3, and 4). For example, Hector (Atkins 1991) is lexicographically sound and detailed, but lacks coverage; LDOCE has subject codes and a structure such that homographs are part-of-speech-homogeneous, but is not freely available; WordNet is an open and very popular resource, but is too fine-grained in many cases. Senseval eventually settled on WordNet, mainly because of its availability and coverage. Of course, this choice sidesteps the greater debate of explicit versus implicit WSD, which brings the challenge that entirely different kinds of inventory would be required for applications such as MT (translation equivalences) and IR (induced clusters of usages).

1.4 Applications of WSD

Machine translation is the original and most obvious application for WSD but disambiguation has been considered in almost every NLP application, and is becoming increasingly important in recent areas such as bioinformatics and the Semantic Web.

Machine translation (MT). WSD is required for lexical choice in MT for words that have different translations for different senses and that are potentially ambiguous within a given domain (since non-domain senses could be removed during lexicon development). For example, in an English-French financial news translator, the English noun *change* could translate to either *changement* ('transformation') or *monnaie* ('pocket money'). In MT, the senses are often represented directly as words in the target language. However, most MT models do not use explicit WSD. Either the lexicon is pre-disambiguated for a given domain, hand-crafted rules are devised, or WSD is folded into a statistical translation model (Brown et al. 1991).

Information retrieval (IR). Ambiguity has to be resolved in some queries. For instance, given the query "*depression*" should the system return documents about illness, weather systems, or economics? A similar problem arises for proper nouns such as *Raleigh* (bicycle, person, city, etc.). Current IR systems do not use explicit WSD, and rely on the user typing enough context in the query to only retrieve documents relevant to the intended sense (e.g., "*tropical depression*"). Early experiments suggested that reliable IR would require at least 90% disambiguation accuracy for explicit WSD to be of benefit (Sanderson 1994). More recently, WSD has been shown to improve cross-lingual IR and document classification (Vossen et al. 2006; Bloehdorn and Hotho 2004; Clough and Stevenson 2004). Besides document classification and cross-lingual IR, related applications include news recommendation and alerting, topic tracking, and automatic advertisement placement.

Information extraction (IE) and text mining. WSD is required for the accurate analysis of text in many applications. For instance, an intelligence gathering system might require the flagging of, say, all the references to illegal *drugs*, rather than medical *drugs*. Bioinformatics research requires the relationships between genes and gene products to be catalogued from the vast scientific literature; however, genes and their proteins often have the same name. More generally, the Semantic Web requires automatic annotation of documents according to a reference ontology: all textual references must be resolved to the right concepts and event structures in the ontology (Dill et al. 2003). Named-entity classification, co-reference determination, and acronym expansion (*MG* as *magnesium* or *milligram*) can also be cast as WSD problems for proper names. WSD is only beginning to be applied in these areas.

Lexicography. Modern lexicography is corpus-based, thus WSD and lexicography can work in a loop, with WSD providing rough empirical sense groupings and statistically significant contextual indicators of sense to lexicographers, who provide better sense inventories and sense-annotated corpora to WSD. Furthermore, intelligent dictionaries and thesauri might one day provide us with a semantically-cross-referenced dictionary as well as better contextual look-up facilities.

Despite this range of applications where WSD shows a great potential to be useful, WSD has not yet been shown to make a decisive difference in any application. There are various isolated results that show minor improvements, but just as often WSD can hurt performance, as is the case in one experiment on information retrieval (Sanderson 1994). There are several possible reasons for this. First, the domain of an application often constrains strains the number of senses a word can have (e.g., one would not expect to see the 'river side' sense of *bank* in a financial application), and so lexicons can be constructed accordingly. Second, WSD might not be accurate enough yet to show an effect. Third, treating WSD as an explicit component, as the majority of research does, means that it cannot be properly integrated into a particular application or appropriately trained on the domain. main. Most applications, such as MT, do not have a place for a WSD module (but see Carpuat and Wu (2005)), so either the application or the WSD would have to be redesigned. Research is just beginning on domain-specific WSD (see Chap. 10).

Nevertheless, it's clear that applications do require WSD in some form – perhaps through an *implicit* encoding of the same contextual models used in explicit WSD. For example in IR, a two-word query can disambiguate itself, implicitly, since both words are often used in text together in the senses intended by the user (e.g., *tropical depression*, above), and we've already mentioned the modeling of WSD in MT. The work on explicit WSD can serve to explore and highlight the particular features that provide the best evidence for accurate disambiguation, implicit or explicit.

1.5 Basic Approaches to WSD

Approaches to WSD are often classified according to the main source of knowledge used in sense differentiation. Methods that rely primarily on dictionaries, thesauri, and lexical knowledge bases, without using any corpus evidence, are termed *dictionary-based* or *knowledge-based*. Methods that eschew (almost) completely external information and work directly from raw unannotated corpora are termed *unsupervised* methods (adopting terminology from machine learning). Included in this category are methods that use word-aligned corpora to gather cross-linguistic evidence for sense discrimination. Finally, *supervised* and *semi-supervised* WSD make use of annotated corpora to train from, or as seed data in a bootstrapping process.

Almost every approach to supervised learning has now been applied to WSD, including aggregative and discriminative algorithms and associated techniques such as feature selection, parameter optimization, and ensemble learning (see Chap. 7).

Unsupervised learning methods have the potential to overcome the new knowledge acquisition bottleneck (manual sense-tagging) and have achieved good results (Schütze 1998). These methods are able to induce word senses from training text by clustering word occurrences, and then classifying new occurrences into the induced clusters/senses (see Chap. 6).

The knowledge-based proposals of the 1970s and 80s are still a matter of current research. The main techniques use selectional restrictions, the overlap of definition text, and semantic similarity measures (see Chap. 5). Ultimately, the goal is to do general semantic inference using knowledge bases, with WSD as a by-product.

Table 1.1 is our attempt to be systematic in covering the main approaches to WSD in this book, but it was not always easy. For instance, Chapters 9 and 10 cover some techniques that did not fit very well in other chapters. Indeed, drawing a line between current systems is difficult, not

Table 1.1. A variety of approaches to word sense disambiguation are discussed in this book.

Approach	Technique	Chapter
Knowledge-based	Hand-crafted disambiguation rules	Not covered
	Selectional restrictions (or preferences), used to filter out inconsistent senses	5
	Comparing dictionary definitions to the context (Lesk's method)	5
	The sense most similar to its context, using semantic similarity measures	5
	"One-sense-per-discourse" and other heuristics	5
Unsupervised corpus-based	Unsupervised methods that cluster word occurrences or contexts, thus inducing senses	6
	Using an aligned parallel corpus to infer cross-language sense distinctions	6, 9, 11
Supervised corpus-based	Supervised machine learning, trained on a manually-tagged corpus	7
	Bootstrapping from seed data (semi-supervised)	7
Combinations	Unsupervised clustering techniques combined with knowledge base similarities	6
	Using knowledge bases to search for examples for training in supervised WSD	9
	Using an aligned parallel corpus, combined with knowledge-based methods	9
	Using domain knowledge and subject codes	10

least because recent research is exploring novel combinations of already existing techniques. For instance, cross-linguistic evidence gathered from word-aligned corpora can be used to train supervised systems, and then be combined with knowledge bases; unsupervised clustering techniques can be combined with knowledge-base similarities to produce sense preferences; and the information in knowledge-bases can be used to search for training examples which are then fed into supervised WSD.

Regardless of the approach, all WSD systems extract contextual features of a target word (in text) and compare them against the sense differentiation information stored for that word. A natural classification problem, WSD is characterized by its very high-dimensional feature space. Almost every type of local and topical feature has been shown to be useful including part-of-speech, word (as written and lemma), collocation, semantic class, subject or domain code, and syntactic dependency (see Chap. 8).

1.6 State-of-the-Art Performance

We will briefly summarize the performance achieved by state-of-the-art WSD systems. First, homographs are often considered to be a solved problem. Accuracy above 95% is routinely achieved using very little input knowledge: for example, Yarowsky (1995) used a semi-supervised approach evaluated on 12 words (96.5%), and Stevenson and Wilks (2001) used part-of-speech data (and other knowledge sources) on all words using LDOCE (94.7%).

Accurate WSD on general polysemy has been more difficult to achieve, but has improved over time. In 1997, Senseval-1 (Kilgarriff and Palmer 2000) found accuracy of 77% on the English lexical sample task,[5] just below the 80% level of human performance (estimated by inter-tagger agreement; however, human replicability was estimated at 95%; see Chap. 4). In 2001, scores at Senseval-2 (Edmonds and Cotton 2001) appeared to be lower, but the task was more difficult, as it was based on the finer-grained senses of WordNet. The best accuracy on the English lexical sample task at Senseval-2 was 64% (to an inter-tagger agreement of 86%). Table 1.2 gives the results for all evaluated languages. Previous to Senseval-2, there was debate over whether a knowledge-based or machine learning approach was better, but Senseval-2 showed that supervised approaches had the best overall performance. However, the best unsupervised system on the English lexical sample task performed at 40%, well below the most-frequent-sense baseline of 48%, but better than the random baseline of 16%.

By 2004, the top systems on the English lexical sample task at Senseval-3 (Mihalcea and Edmonds 2004) were performing at human levels according to inter-tagger agreement (see Table 1.3). The ten top systems, all supervised, made between 71.8% and 72.9% correct disambiguations compared to an inter-tagger agreement of 67%.[6] The best unsupervised system overcame the most-frequent-sense baseline achieving 66% accuracy. The score on the

---

[5] A "lexical sample" task involves tagging a few occurrences of a sample of words for which hand-annotated training data is provided. An "all-words" task involves tagging all words occurring in running text. See Chapter 4.

[6] This low agreement is perhaps explained because the annotators in this case were non-experts at the task – they were merely self-selected participants in the Open Mind Word Expert project (Chlovski & Mihalcea 2002) – rather than linguistically trained lexicographers and students as employed previously. Systems can beat human ITA because adjudication for the gold standard occurs after inter-tagger agreement is calculated (see Chap. 4). This means that the systems could be

Table 1.2. Performance of WSD systems in the Senseval-2 evaluation (Edmonds and Kilgarriff 2002).

Language	Task[a]	Systems	Lemmas	Instances	ITA[b]	Baseline[d]	Best score
English	AW	21	1,082	2,473	75%	57%/–[e]	69%/55%
Estonian	AW	2	4,608	11,504	72	85	67
Basque	LS	3	40	5,284	75	65	76
English	LS	26	73	12,939	86[c]	48/16	64/40
Italian	LS	2	83	3,900	21	–	39
Japanese	LS	7	100	10,000	86	72	78
Korean	LS	2	11	1,733	–	71	74
Spanish	LS	12	39	6,705	64	48	65
Swedish	LS	8	40	10,241	95	–	70
Japanese	TM	9	40	1,200	81	37	79

[a] *AW* all-words, *LS* lexical sample, *TM* translation memory.
[b] ITA is inter-tagger agreement, which is deemed as upper bound for the task.
[c] The ITA for English nouns and adjectives is reported. Verbs had an ITA of 71%.
[d] The baseline is most-frequent sense.
[e] Scores separated by a slash are supervised/unsupervised methods; supervised when there is no slash.

all-words task was lower than for Senseval-2, probably because of a more difficult text. Senseval-3 also brought the complete domination of supervised approaches over pure knowledge-based approaches.

1.7 Promising Directions

Martin Kay, in his acceptance speech for the 2005 ACL Lifetime Achievement Award, made a distinction between "computational linguistics" (CL), the use of computers to investigate and further linguistic theory, and "natural language processing" (NLP), engineering technologies for speech and text processing. Although much of the recent work in computational WSD falls squarely in the latter, solving the WSD problem is actually a prototypical endeavor for the former.

performing more like linguistically trained individuals, having learned from the adjudicated corpus. Notice that other languages had higher agreements.

Table 1.3. Performance of WSD systems in the Senseval-3 evaluation (Mihalcea and Edmonds 2004).

Language	Task[a]	Systems	Lemmas	Instances	ITA[b]	Baseline[c]	Best score
English	AW	26	–	2,081	62%	62%/–[d]	65%/58%
Basque	LS	8	40	7,362	78	59	70
Catalan	LS	7	27	6,721	93	66	85
English	LS	47	57	–	67	55/–	73/66
Italian	LS	6	45	7,584	89	18	53
Romanian	LS	7	39	11,532	–	58	73
Spanish	LS	9	46	12,625	83–90	67	84
Hindi	TM	8	41	11,984	–	56	67
English	GL	10	–	42,491	–	–	68

Copyright © 2004, Association for Computational Linguistics. Reproduced with permission of the Association for Computational Linguistics and Mihalcea and Edmonds.
[a]*AW* all-words, *LS* lexical sample, *TM* translation memory, *GL* gloss task.
[b]ITA is inter-tagger agreement.
[c]The baseline is most-frequent sense.
[d]Scores separated by a slash are supervised/unsupervised methods; supervised when there is no slash.

Thus, the field finds itself in a strange position. The problem of resolving lexical ambiguity itself is one of the oldest problems in CL/NLP and MT research, acknowledged as both difficult and necessary. So difficult that it was partially responsible for the cessation of funding to MT research in the 1960s following the ALPAC report. Nevertheless, researchers have made great strides in solving one constrained version of the problem: the traditional conception as an explicit task of resolving fine-grained and coarse-grained ambiguity to a fixed inventory of senses. The three evaluation exercises run by Senseval show that over a variety of word types, word frequencies, and sense distributions, explicit WSD systems are achieving consistent and respectable accuracy levels. And yet, this success has not translated into better performance or utility in real applications. Ironically, research into WSD has become separate from research into NLP applications, despite several efforts to investigate and demonstrate utility.

As we mentioned in Section 1.2, there is a growing feeling in the community that change is necessary. The route taken to reach the state-of-the-art systems – explicit WSD solved by supervised learning approaches – may not lead to future performance increases or to fundamentally new research results.

We believe that there are two complementary routes forward. The first is to become more theoretical, to return to computational linguistics, to work on WSD embracing more realistic models of word sense (including non-discreteness, vagueness, and analogy), thus drawing on and feeding theories of word meaning and context from (computational) lexical semantics and lexicography. While not obviously immediately applicable, this research has defensible goals. Can we look to WSD research to provide a practical computational lexical semantics?

The second route is to focus on making WSD applicable whatever it takes. Can any of the results to date be applied in real applications? Why doesn't explicit WSD work in applications when other generic NLP components do? Does WSD have to be more accurate? Are homographs the best level of granularity? Is domain-based WSD the answer?

Both routes could lead to better applications and a better understanding of meaning and language – surely the two main goals of NLP and computational linguistics.

It is worth revisiting the three main open problems of 1998, as put forth by Ide and Véronis (1998), and to add a few more.

The Role of Context. Ide and Véronis said the "relative role and importance of information from the different contexts and their inter-relations are not well understood." (p. 18) Although there is still more work to be done in isolating the contribution of different knowledge sources, much is now understood about the role of context, such as the diversity of feature types that can be used as evidence, and the types of features most useful for a few classes of words (see Chap. 8). Perhaps a goal of future WSD research should be to understand how contextual information comes to bear on semantic processing in different applications such as MT and IR and to choose the approach and knowledge sources that best fit the applications.

Sense Division. How to divide senses still remains one of the main open problems of WSD. As discussed in this chapter and throughout the book (see especially Chaps. 2, 3, and 4), semantic granularity is not well understood, and the relation to specific applications is unexplored territory. Given the state of the art, coarse-grained differences could allow for performance closer to an application's needs.

Evaluation. The first Senseval was held at about the time Ide and Véronis (1998) was published. As mentioned above, Senseval's common evaluation framework has focused research, enabled scientific rigor, and generated substantial resources. But, to date, it has worked with only *in vitro* evaluation of generic WSD, separating the task from application. *In vivo* evaluation, or application-specific evaluation, has not yet been approached, but it is precisely this kind of evaluation that could prove the utility of WSD. (See Chapter 4.)

Additional open problems include (following a survey of this book's contributors):

Domain- and Application-Based WSD. We discussed the need for application-specific research above as one major route forward for the field, but this will entail a change in the conception of the task. Knowing the domain of a text can often disambiguate its words, but this assumes a specialized domain lexicon or a general lexicon expanded and tuned with domain-specific information. All-words WSD would be required and *in vivo* evaluation would support the effort. (See Chapters 10 and 11.)

Unsupervised WSD and Cross-Lingual Approaches. Tagging with no, or very little, hand-annotated training data still holds the promise of great riches. Recent work by McCarthy et al. (2004) on tagging with the predominant sense has reinvigorated this direction, and techniques that exploit alignments in parallel or comparable corpora are gaining momentum (Diab 2003; Ng et al. 2003; Bhattacharya et al. 2004; Li and Li 2004; Tufiş et al. 2004). The knowledge acquisition bottleneck is a serious impediment to supervised all-words WSD, but this could be alleviated by advances in robust methods for acquiring large sets of training examples (for all languages) with a minimum of human annotation effort. (See Chapters 6, 9, and 11.)

WSD as an Optimization Problem. Current WSD systems disambiguate texts one word at a time, treating each word in isolation. It is clear though that meanings are interdependent and the disambiguation of a word can affect others in its context. This was clear in earlier systems (e.g., Lesk (1986) and Cowie et al. (1992)). The interdependencies among senses in the context could be modeled and treated as an optimization problem (in contrast to the classification model of WSD).

Applying Deeper Linguistic Knowledge. Significant advances in the performance of current supervised WSD systems could rely on enriched feature representations based on deeper linguistic knowledge, rather than better learning algorithms. We refer, for instance, to sub-categorization frames, syntactic structure, selectional preferences, semantic roles, domain information, and other semantics, which are becoming available in wide-coverage lexical knowledge bases like WordNet, VerbNet (Kipper et al. 2000), and FrameNet (Baker et al. 2003). The recent trend to rediscover semantic interpretation and entailment includes WSD and semantic role labeling as component technologies (Gildea and Jurafsky 2002; Dagan et al. 2005). Coupling these techniques with the currently available resources, we are seeing a shift back to knowledge-based methods, but this time coupled with corpus-based methods.

Sense Discovery. A sense inventory that a priori lists all relevant senses will never be able to cope with borrowed words, new words, new usages, or just rare or spurious usages. In practical terms, this makes it very difficult to move a system into a new domain. Sense discovery was a major component of Schütze's (1998) work (see Chap. 6 (Sect. 6.3)), but little work has been done since, except Véronis (2004). Even identifying which words are being used in a novel (previously unknown) way, either with a completely new meaning or an existing meaning, would be useful in many applications. Senses can also be mined from parallel corpora and the Web (see Chap. 9).

1.8 Overview of This Book

This is the first book that covers the entire topic of word sense disambiguation (WSD) including: all the major algorithms, techniques, performance measures, philosophical issues, applications, and future trends. Leading researchers in the field have contributed chapters that synthesize and overview past and state-of-the-art research in their respective areas of expertise. For researchers, lecturers, students, and developers, we intend the book to answer (or begin answering) questions such as How well does WSD work? What are the main approaches and algorithms? Which technique is best for my application? How do I build it and evaluate it? What performance can I expect? What are the open problems? What is the nature of the relationship between WSD and other language processing components? What *is* a word sense? Is WSD a good topic for my PhD? Where is the field heading?

We hope that the chapters you have in your hands are helpful in this direction.

Chapter 2. WORD SENSES. Adam Kilgarriff explores various conceptions of "word sense", including views from lexicographers to philosophers. He argues that any attempt to pin down an inventory of word senses for WSD will be problematic by considering limiting cases of metaphor, quotation, and reasoning from general knowledge.

Chapter 3. MAKING SENSE ABOUT SENSE. Nancy Ide and Yorick Wilks suggest that the standard fine-grained division of senses by a lexicographer for use by a human reader may not be an appropriate goal for the computational WSD task. Giving an overview of the literature on the psycholinguistic basis of sense in the mental lexicon, they argue that the level of sense-discrimination that NLP needs corresponds roughly to homographs, which are often lexicalized cross-linguistically. Thus, they propose to reorient WSD to what it can actually perform at high accuracy.

Chapter 4. EVALUATION OF WSD SYSTEMS. Martha Palmer, Hwee Tou Ng, and Hoa Trang Dang discuss the methodology for the evaluation of WSD systems, developed through Senseval. They give an overview of previous evaluation exercises and investigate sources of human inter-tagger disagreements. Many errors are at least partially reconciled by a more coarse-grained partition of the senses. Well-defined sense groups can be of value in improving sense tagging consistency for both humans and machines.

Chapter 5. KNOWLEDGE-BASED METHODS FOR WSD. Rada Mihalcea reviews current research on knowledge-intensive methods, including those using overlap of dictionary definitions, similarity measures over semantic networks, selectional preferences for arguments, and several heuristics, such as "one-sense-per-discourse".

Chapter 6. UNSUPERVISED CORPUS-BASED METHODS FOR WSD. Ted Pedersen focuses on knowledge-lean methods that do not rely on external sources of evidence other than the untagged corpus itself. These methods do not assign sense tags to words, but rather discriminate between word uses or induce word-use clusters. The chapter reviews both distributional approaches relying on monolingual corpora and methods based on translational equivalences as found in word-aligned parallel corpora.

Chapter 7. SUPERVISED CORPUS-BASED METHODS FOR WSD. Lluís Màrquez, Gerard Escudero, David Martínez, and German Rigau present methods that automatically induce classification models or rules from manually annotated examples, currently the mainstream approach. This chapter presents a detailed review of the literature, descriptions of five of the key machine learning algorithms including Naïve Bayes and Support Vector Machines, and a discussion of central issues such as learning paradigms, corpora used, sense repositories, and feature representation.

Chapter 8. KNOWLEDGE SOURCES FOR WSD. Eneko Agirre and Mark Stevenson explore the different sources of linguistic knowledge that can be used by WSD systems. An analysis of actual WSD systems reveals that the best results are often obtained by combining knowledge sources and the chapter concludes by analyzing experiments on the effect of different knowledge sources.

Chapter 9. AUTOMATIC ACQUISITION OF LEXICAL INFORMATION AND EXAMPLES. Julio Gonzalo and Felisa Verdejo consider the knowledge acquisition bottleneck faced by supervised corpus-based methods. The chapter reviews current research to remedy the lack of sufficient hand-tagged examples, by using, for example, techniques that mine large corpora for examples of word senses or coupling parallel corpora with knowledge-based methods.

Chapter 10. DOMAIN-SPECIFIC WSD. Paul Buitelaar, Bernardo Magnini, Carlo Strapparava, and Piek Vossen describe approaches to WSD that take the subject, domain, or topic of words into account. They discuss the use of subject codes, the extraction of topic signatures through a combined use of a semantic resource and domain-specific corpora, and domain-specific tuning of semantic resources.

Chapter 11. WSD IN NLP APPLICATIONS. Philip Resnik considers applications of WSD in language technology, looking at established and emerging applications and at more and less traditional conceptions of the task.

1.9 Further Reading

Visit the book website, www.wsdbook.org, for the latest information and updates.

Ide and Véronis's (1998) survey of WSD is an excellent starting point for a thorough analysis and history of WSD. It forms the introduction to the special issue of *Computational Linguistics 24(1)* on WSD. A special issue of *Computer, Speech, and Language 18(4)* (edited by Preiss and Stevenson, 2004) contains more recent contributions.

The article "Disambiguation, lexical" in the *Elsevier Encyclopedia of Language and Linguistics, 2nd ed.* (Edmonds 2005) gives an accessible overview of WSD.

Recent technical surveys are to be found in *Foundations of Statistical Natural Language Processing* (Manning and Schütze 1999), *Speech and Language Processing* (Jurafsky and Martin 2000), and the *Handbook of Natural Language Processing* (Dale et al. 2000). The first introduces WSD in the statistical framework (including the three main approaches) with detailed algorithms of a few selected systems. The second frames the problem in the context of semantic representation and analysis, and includes a discussion of selectional preferences as well as a brief overview of the machine learning focus. The third article, by David Yarowsky, gives a good overview of the characteristics of the WSD problem, and then focuses primarily on machine learning and related solutions. An older survey in Allen's (1995) *Natural Language Understanding* treats WSD as a component in semantic interpretation. Finally, several chapters in *Electric Words* (Wilks et al. 1996) take a lexicographic perspective on WSD and discuss how LDOCE can be used.

A few books focus squarely on WSD. Lexical Ambiguity Resolution (Small et al. 1988) is a collection of papers from a cognitive science perspective. Hirst's (1987) *Semantic Interpretation and the Resolution of Ambiguity* discusses his semantic interpretation system and "Polaroid Words". And Stevenson's (2003) *Word Sense Disambiguation* is based on his PhD dissertation on the benefits of combining knowledge sources.

Evaluation is discussed in two journal special issues: *Computers in the Humanities 34(1–2)* (special issue on Senseval, edited by Kilgarriff and Palmer, 2000) and *Natural Language Engineering 8(4)* (special issue on evaluating word sense disambiguation systems, edited by Edmonds and Kilgarriff, 2002).

The main venues for research papers in WSD are the journals *Computational Linguistics* and *Natural Language Engineering*, and the conference proceedings of the Association for Computational Linguistics (ACL), the International Conference on Computational Linguistics (COLING), and their associated organizations, special interest groups (SIGs), and workshops.

Polysemy is of course discussed frequently in the lexical semantics literature. Cruse's (1986) *Lexical Semantics* gives a solid overview of polysemy, and acts as a good starting point for further reading. Lyons' (1995) *Linguistic Semantics* is worth consulting. Ravin and Leacock's (2000) *Polysemy: Theoretical and Computational Approaches* is a recent summary of activity, with three chapters about computational approaches.

References

Allen, James. 1995. *Natural Language Understanding*. Redwood City, California: Benjamin Cummings.

ALPAC. 1966. *Language and Machine: Computers in Translation and Linguistics*. A report by the Automatic Language Processing Advisory Committee,

Division of Behavioral Sciences, National Research Council. Washington, D.C.: National Academy of Sciences.

Atkins, Sue. 1991. Tools for computer-aided corpus lexicography: The Hector project. *Acta Linguistica Hungarica*, 41: 5–72.

Baker, Collin F., Charles J. Fillmore & Beau Cronin. 2003. The structure of the FrameNet database. *International Journal of Lexicography*, 16(3): 281–296.

Bar-Hillel, Yehoshua. 1960. The present status of automatic translation of languages. *Advances in Computers*, ed. by Franz Alt et al. 91–163. New York: Academic Press.

Bhattacharya, Indrajit, Lise Getoor & Yoshua Bengio. 2004. Unsupervised word sense disambiguation using bilingual probabilistic models. *Proceedings of the 42nd Annual Meeting of the Association for Computational Linguistics (ACL)*, Barcelona, Spain, 288–295.

Black, Ezra. 1988. An experiment in computational discrimination of English word senses. *IBM Journal of Research and Development*, 32(2): 185–194.

Bloehdorn, Stephan & Andreas Hotho. 2004. Text classification by boosting weak learners based on terms and concepts. *Proceedings of the Fourth IEEE International Conference on Data Mining*, 331–334.

Brown, Peter F., Stephen Della Pietra, Vincent J. Della Pietra & Robert L. Mercer. 1991. Word-sense disambiguation using statistical methods. *Proceedings of the 29th Annual Meeting of the Association for Computational Linguistics (ACL)*, Berkeley, California, 264–270.

Carpuat, Marine & Dekai Wu. 2005. Word sense disambiguation vs. statistical machine translation. Proceedings of the *43rd Annual Meeting of the Association for Computational Linguistics (ACL)*, Ann Arbor, Michigan, 387–394.

Chapman, Robert. 1977. *Roget's International Thesaurus (Fourth Edition)*. New York: Harper and Row.

Chlovski, Timothy & Rada Mihalcea. 2002. Building a sense tagged corpus with Open Mind Word Expert. *Proceedings of the Workshop on Word Sense Disambiguation: Recent Successes and Future Directions*, Philadelphia, PA, USA, 116–122.

Clough, Paul & Mark Stevenson. 2004. Cross-language information retrieval using EuroWordNet and word sense disambiguation. *Advances in Information Retrieval, 26th European Conference on IR Research (ECIR)*, Sunderland, UK, 327–337.

Cowie, Jim, Joe A. Guthrie & Louise Guthrie. 1992. Lexical disambiguation using simulated annealing. *Proceedings of the 14th International Conference on Computational Linguistics (COLING)*, Nantes, France, 359–365.

Cruse, D. Alan. 1986. *Lexical Semantics*. Cambridge, UK: Cambridge University Press.

Dagan, Ido, Oren Glickman & Bernardo Magnini. 2005. The PASCAL recognising textual entailment challenge. *Proceedings of the PASCAL Challenges Workshop on Recognising Textual Entailment.*

Dale, Robert, Hermann Moisl & Harold Somers, eds. 2000. *Handbook of Natural Language Processing.* New York: Marcel Dekker.

Diab, Mona. 2003. *Word Sense Disambiguation within a Multilingual Framework.* Ph.D. Thesis, Department of Linguistics, University of Maryland, College Park, Maryland.

Dill, Stephen, Nadav Eiron, David Gibson, Daniel Gruhl, R. Guha, Anant Jhingran, Tapas Kanungo, Sridhar Rajagopalan, Andrew Tomkins, John A. Tomlin & Jason Y. Zien. 2003. SemTag and Seeker: Bootstrapping the Semantic Web via automated semantic annotation. *Proceedings of the Twelfth International Conference on World Wide Web (WWW-2003)*, Budapest, Hungary, 178–186.

Edmonds, Philip & Scott Cotton. 2001. Senseval-2: Overview. *Proceedings of Senseval-2: Second International Workshop on Evaluating Word Sense Disambiguation Systems*, Toulouse, France, 1–5.

Edmonds, Philip & Adam Kilgarriff. 2002. Introduction to the special issue on evaluating word sense disambiguation systems. *Journal of Natural Language Engineering*, 8(4): 279–291.

Edmonds, Philip. 2005. Lexical disambiguation. *The Elsevier Encyclopedia of Language and Linguistics, 2nd Ed.,* ed. by Keith Brown, 607–23. Oxford: Elsevier.

Fellbaum, Christiane, ed. 1998. *WordNet: An Electronic Lexical Database.* MIT Press.

Gale, William, Kenneth Church & David Yarowsky. 1992. Estimating upper and lower bounds on the performance of word-sense disambiguation programs. *Proceedings of the 30th Annual Meeting of the Association for Computational Linguistics (ACL)*, Newark, Delaware, 249–256.

Gildea, Daniel & Daniel Jurafsky. 2002. Automatic labeling of semantic roles. *Computational Linguistics*, 28(3): 245–288.

Guthrie, Joe A., Louise Guthrie, Yorick Wilks & Homa Aidinejad. 1991. Subject dependent co-occurrence and word sense disambiguation. *Proceedings of the 29th Annual Meeting of the Association for Computational Linguistics (ACL)*, Berkeley, California, 146–152.

Hanks, Patrick. 2000. Do word meanings exist? *Computers in the Humanities*, 34(1–2): 205–215.

Hirst, Graeme. 1987. *Semantic Interpretation and the Resolution of Ambiguity.* Cambridge, UK: Cambridge University Press.

Ide, Nancy & Jean Véronis. 1998. Word sense disambiguation: The state of the art. *Computational Linguistics*, 24(1): 1–40.

Jurafsky, Daniel & James H. Martin. 2000. *Speech and Language Processing*. New Jersey, USA: Prentice Hall.

Kaplan, Abraham. 1950. An experimental study of ambiguity and context. Mimeographed, 18pp, November 1950. Published as: Kaplan, Abraham. 1955. An experimental study of ambiguity and context. *Mechanical Translation*, 2(2): 39–46.

Kelly, Edward F. & Philip J. Stone. 1975. *Computer Recognition of English Word Senses*. Amsterdam: North-Holland.

Kilgarriff, Adam. 1997. "I don't believe in word senses". *Computers in the Humanities*, 31(2): 91–113.

Kilgarriff, Adam & Martha Palmer. 2000. Introduction to the special issue on Senseval. *Computers and the Humanities*, 34(1–2): 1–13.

Karin Kipper, Hoa Trang Dang & Martha Palmer. 2000. Class-based construction of a verb lexicon. *Proceedings of the Seventh National Conference on Artificial Intelligence* (AAAI-2000), Austin, Texas.

Lesk, Michael. 1986. Automated sense disambiguation using machine-readable dictionaries: How to tell a pine cone from an ice cream cone. *Proceedings of the 1986 ACM SIGDOC Conference*, Toronto, Canada, 24–26.

Li, Hang & Cong Li. 2004. Word translation disambiguation using bilingual bootstrapping. *Computational Linguistics,* 30(1): 1–22.

Lyons, John. 1995. *Linguistic Semantics: An Introduction*. Cambridge, UK: Cambridge University Press.

Madhu, Swaminathan & Dean W. Lytle. 1965. A figure of merit technique for the resolution of non-grammatical ambiguity. *Mechanical translation*, 8(2): 9–13.

Maedche, Alexander & Steffen Staab. 2001. Ontology learning for the Semantic Web. *IEEE Intelligent Systems,* 16(2): 72–79.

Manning, Christopher D. & Hinrich Schütze. 1999. *Foundations of Statistical Natural Language Processing*. Cambridge, MA: MIT Press.

Masterman, Margaret. 1957. The thesaurus in syntax and semantics. *Mechanical Translation*, 4(1–2): 35–43.

McCarthy, Diana, Rob Koeling, Julie Weeds & John Carroll. 2004. Finding predominant senses in untagged text. *Proceedings of the 42nd Annual Meeting of the Association for Computational Linguistics (ACL)*. Barcelona, Spain, 280–287.

Mihalcea, Rada, Timothy Chlovski & Adam Kilgarriff. 2004. The Senseval-3 English lexical sample task. *Proceedings of Senseval-3: Third International Workshop on the Evaluation of Systems for the Semantic Analysis of Text*, Barcelona, Spain, 25–28.

Mihalcea, Rada & Philip Edmonds, eds. 2004. *Proceedings of Senseval-3: Third International Workshop on the Evaluation of Systems for the Semantic Analysis of Text*, Barcelona, Spain.

Miller, George A., ed. 1990. Special Issue, WordNet: An on-line lexical database. *International Journal of Lexicography*, 3(4).

Ng, Hwee Tou & Hian Beng Lee. 1996. Integrating multiple knowledge sources to disambiguate word sense: An exemplar-based approach. *Proceedings of the 34th Annual Meeting of the Association for Computational Linguistics*, Santa Cruz, California, 40–47.

Ng, Hwee Tou, Bin Wang & Yee Seng Chan. 2003. Exploiting parallel texts for word sense disambiguation: An empirical study. *Proceedings of the 41st Annual Meeting of the Association for Computational Linguistics (ACL)*, Sapporo, Japan, 455–462.

Palmer, Martha, Christiane Fellbaum, Scott Cotton, Lauren Delfs & Hoa Trang Dang. 2001. English tasks: All-words and verb lexical sample. *Proceedings of Senseval-2: Second International Workshop on Evaluating Word Sense Disambiguation Systems*, Toulouse, France, 21–24.

Palmer, Martha, Christiane Fellbaum & Hoa Trang Dang. 2006. Making fine-grained and coarse-grained sense distinctions, both manually and automatically. *Natural Language Engineering*, 12(3).

Preiss, Judita & Mark Stevenson, eds. 2004. *Computer, Speech, and Language*, 18(4). (Special issue on word sense disambiguation)

Procter, Paul, ed. 1978. *Longman Dictionary of Contemporary English*. London: Longman Group.

Quillian, M. Ross. 1968. Semantic memory. *Semantic Information Processing*, ed. by Marvin Minsky, 227–270. Cambridge, MA: MIT Press.

Ravin, Yael & Claudia Leacock. 2000. *Polysemy: Theoretical and Computational Approaches*. Oxford University Press.

Reifler, Edwin. 1955. The mechanical determination of meaning. *Machine Translation of Languages*, ed. William Locke & Donald A. Booth, 136–164. New York: John Wiley & Sons.

Resnik, Philip & David Yarowsky. 1999. Distinguishing systems and distinguishing senses: New evaluation methods for word sense disambiguation. *Natural Language Engineering*, 5(2): 113–133.

Rieger, Chuck & Steven Small. 1979. Word expert parsing. *Proceedings of the 6th International Joint Conference on Artificial Intelligence (IJCAI)*, 723–728.

Ruhl, Charles. 1989. *On Monosemy: A Study in Linguistic Semantics*. Albany: State University of New York Press.

Sanderson, Mark. 1994. Word sense disambiguation and information retrieval. *Proceedings of the 17th Annual International ACM SIGIR Conference on Research and Development in Information Retrieval*, Dublin, Ireland, 142–151.

Schütze, Hinrich. 1998. Automatic word sense discrimination. *Computational Linguistics*, 24(1): 97–123.

Small, Steven, Garrison Cottrell & Michael Tanenhaus, eds. 1988. *Lexical Ambiguity Resolution: Perspectives from Artificial Intelligence, Psychology and Neurolinguistics*. San Mateo: Morgan Kaufman.

Stevenson, Mark & Yorick Wilks. 2001. The interaction of knowledge sources in word sense disambiguation. *Computational Linguistics*, 27(3): 321–349.

Stevenson, Mark. 2003. *Word Sense Disambiguation: The Case for Combination of Knowledge Sources*. Stanford, USA: CSLI Publications.

Tufiş, Dan, Radu Ion & Nancy Ide. Fine-grained word sense disambiguation based on parallel corpora, word alignment, word clustering, and aligned wordnets. *Proceedings of the Twentieth International Conference on Computational Linguistics (COLING)*, Geneva, 1312–1318.

Tuggy, David H. 1993. Ambiguity, polysemy, and vagueness. *Cognitive Linguistics*, 4: 273–90.

Véronis, Jean. 2004. Hyperlex: Lexical cartography for information retrieval. *Computer, Speech and Language*, 18(3): 223–252.

Voorhees, Ellen M. 1993. Using WordNet to disambiguate word senses for text retrieval. *Proceedings of the 16th Annual International ACM SIGIR Conference on Research and Development in Information Retrieval*, Pittsburgh, Pennsylvania, 171–180.

Vossen, Piek, German Rigau, Iñaki Alegria, Eneko Agirre, David Farwell & Manuel Fuentes. 2006. Meaningful results for information retrieval in the MEANING project. *Proceedings of the 3rd Global Wordnet Conference*, Jeju Island, Korea.

Weaver, Warren. 1949. Translation. Mimeographed, 12 pp. Reprinted in William N. Locke & Donald A. Booth, eds. 1955. *Machine Translation of Languages*, 15–23. New York: John Wiley & Sons.

Weiss, Stephen. 1973. Learning to disambiguate. *Information Storage and Retrieval*, 9: 33–41.

Wilks, Yorick. 1975. Preference semantics. *Formal Semantics of Natural Language*, ed. by E. L. Keenan, III, 329–348. Cambridge, UK: Cambridge University Press.

Wilks, Yorick, Dan Fass, Cheng-Ming Guo, James E. MacDonald, Tony Plate & Brian A. Slator. 1990. Providing machine tractable dictionary tools. *Semantics and the Lexicon*, ed. by James Pustejovsky, 341–401. Dordrecht: Kluwer Academic Publishers.

Wilks, Yorick, Louise Guthrie & Brian Slator. 1996. *Electric Words*. Cambridge, MA: MIT Press.

Yarowsky, David. 1992. Word sense disambiguation using statistical models of Roget's categories trained on large corpora. *Proceedings of the 14th International Conference on Computational Linguistics (COLING)*, Nantes, France, 454–460.

Yarowsky, David. 1995. Unsupervised word sense disambiguation rivaling supervised methods. *Proceedings of the 33rd Annual Meeting of the Association for Computational Linguistics (ACL)*, Cambridge, MA, 189–196.

Yarowsky, David. 2000. Word-sense disambiguation. *Handbook of Natural Language Processing*, ed. by Dale et al. 629–654. New York: Marcel Dekker.

Zipf, George Kingsley. 1949. *Human Behaviour and the Principle of Least Effort: An introduction to human ecology*. Cambridge, MA: Addison-Wesley. Reprinted by New York: Hafner, 1972.

2 Word Senses

Adam Kilgarriff

Lexical Computing Ltd. and University of Sussex

The trouble with word sense disambiguation is word senses. There are no decisive ways of identifying where one sense of a word ends and the next begins. This makes the definition of the WSD task problematic. In this chapter we explore the limits of the construct "word sense", gathering evidence from lexicographers and philosophers, by considering cases of metaphor, quotation, and reasoning from general knowledge, which sit at the margins of what a lexicographer might classify as a distinct word sense.

2.1 Introduction

The trouble with word sense disambiguation is word senses. There are no decisive ways of identifying where one sense of a word ends and the next begins. This makes the definition of the WSD task problematic. In this chapter we look at what word senses are.

Word senses are to be found in dictionaries, and modern dictionaries are written on the basis of evidence from language corpora, so we start by describing how lexicographers arrive at the word senses that we find in dictionaries. We show that word senses are abstractions from the data.

For a broader perspective, we then look to the philosophers. A word's senses are its meanings, and meaning has long been a topic of philosophical argument. We consider two contrasting accounts of meaning, the "Fregean" and the "Gricean", and show that only the Gricean, in which a word's meaning is an abstraction from the communicative purposes of the utterances it occurs in, sheds light on word senses.

29

E. Agirre and P. Edmonds (eds.), Word Sense Disambiguation: Algorithms and Applications, 29–46.
© 2007 *Springer.*

A word's meaning can also be thought of as an abstraction from patterns of use; a new meaning arises with a new pattern of use. A speaker will only use a word in a new pattern when they either invent it or acquire it. Section 2.4 looks at the process of adding a new pattern to a speaker's lexicon.

Section 2.5 reports on an experiment in which we sought out new patterns by finding corpus instances of words where the word's use did not straightforwardly fit any of its dictionary senses. The analysis of the "misfits" leads to a number of observations:

- The distinction between lexical and general knowledge is problematic.
- Sheer size: There is a vast quantity of knowledge about words in speakers' heads.
- Quotations: Our knowledge of how other people have used words, in quotations and similar, is a substantial part of our knowledge of how words behave and how we might make use of them.

We finish with a section that points to further reading, in which we indicate the threads of thought that contribute to the lines of argument presented in this chapter, and where the interested reader might find out more.

2.2 Lexicographers

The goal of the lexicographer is to present a full account of the words of a language, in all their meanings and patterns of use. In commercial life, the goal is always compromised by practical considerations such as the market that the dictionary is aimed at, its size, its editorial stance, and the speed with which it must be prepared (which may allow, say, twenty minutes per entry). However, the idealized account remains a valuable point of reference.

For the past twenty years, the use of corpora has been growing in lexicography and it is now widely acknowledged that dictionaries should be based on corpus evidence (see various papers in Corréard (2002)). The basic method for a lexicographer to use a corpus is to call up a KWIC (Key Word In Context) concordance for the word and then to read the corpus lines to identify what different meanings and patterns of use there are. Fig. 2.1 shows a KWIC concordance for the word *sense*.

An idealization of the process provides a working definition of a word sense, as follows. For each word, the lexicographer:

Think, and I use that word in its broadest	*sense,*	I think you should jump on her. At
profoundly different light from common	*sense*	in its materialistic moment; and much
The belief that our sensations are in some	*sense*	to be understood in terms of a set of
Stage' in the development of the infant's	*sense*	of self, has no base in clinical experience
Sure ear for tonal balance and a strong	*sense*	of the orchestra's role as a virtual
Firmly rooted. </p><p> Nor is there any	*sense*	in banning strikes 'temporarily', since
of 'The Hollow Men' is furthered by a	*sense*	of confused identity. Words come to the
strengthening family life and promoting a	*sense*	of individual responsibility. Among
the top of it.) Where are the	*sense*	organs that pick up such external factors
By his fellow students. He has a great	*sense*	of humour and will keep you all well-
transmission, jams the code, prevents	*sense*	being made. The subliminal message of
free and rich, but has also begun to	*sense*	its real power. Today's West Germany

Fig. 2.1. A few lines from a KWIC (Key Word In Context) concordance for the word *sense.*

1. Looks at a KWIC concordance for the word;
2. Divides the corpus lines into clusters, so that, as far as possible, the lines in each cluster have more in common with members of their own cluster than with those of other clusters;
3. For each cluster, works out what it is that makes its members belong together; and
4. Takes these conclusions and codes them in the highly constrained language of a dictionary definition.

This is "the central core of the lexicographer's art, the analysis of the material collected" (Krishnamurthy 1987:75). It focuses on a process of clustering usages, performed by a lexicographer. The lexicographer was probably not explicitly aware of the criteria according to which he or she clustered at the time, and stage 3 is a fallible *post hoc* attempt to make the criteria explicit. Yet it is these criteria that determine the senses that eventually appear in the dictionary. Word senses are a result of this process.

Word senses are a lexicographer's attempt to impose order on a word's role in the language. The task is hard: detailed analysis of most words reveals a web of meanings with shared components, some being developments or specializations of others, some strongly associated with particular collocates or settings or purposes, as we will see in detail in Section 2.5.

2.3 Philosophy

Meaning is hard. The philosophers have been arguing about meaning for two and a half millennia and still the arguments roll on. The article "Meaning" in *The Oxford Companion to the Mind* (Tiles 1987:450–51) puts it as follows:

> The concept of meaning is every bit as problematic as the concept of mind, and for related reasons. For it seems to be the case that it is only for a mind that some things (gestures, sounds, words, or natural phenomena) can mean other things. […] Anyone who conceives of science as objective, and as objectivity as requiring the study of phenomena (objects and the relations between objects), which exist and have their character independently of human thought, will face a problem with the scientific study of meaning.

One philosopher whose work is of particular note here is H. P. Grice. His goal is to specify what it is for a speaker to use a sentence, in a particular context, to *mean* something. The analysis is too complex to present here but is summarized in the article "Meaning" in *The Oxford Companion to Philosophy* (Crane 1995:541–42):

> The meaning of sentences can be reduced to a speaker's intention to induce a belief in the hearer by means of their recognition of that intention.

Grice's account remains current, and while it has been challenged and extended in various ways it retains a central place in the philosophers' understanding of meaning.

2.3.1 Meaning is Something You Do

One point to note about the Gricean account is that meaning is something you do. The base concept requiring definition is the verb *to mean*: what it is for speaker *S* to mean *P* when uttering *U* to hearer *H*. All other types of meaning-event and meaning-phenomenon, such as words or sentences having meanings, will then be explicated in terms that build on the definition of the base meaning-event. If a word has a meaning, it is because there are common patterns to how speakers use it in utterances that they are using to mean (in the base sense) particular things to particular hearers on particular occasions. The word can only be said to have a meaning insofar as there are stable aspects to the role that the word plays in those utterances.

2.3.2 The Fregean Tradition and Reification

One other line of philosophical thinking about meaning is associated with the work of Gottlob Frege, and has played a central role in the development of logic and the foundations of mathematics and computer science.

To reify an abstraction is to treat it "as if it has a concrete or material existence."[1] It is often an effective strategy in science: the reified entity is placed center stage and thereby becomes a proper object of scrutiny. It is only when Newton starts to think of force as an object in its own right, that it becomes appropriate to start asking the questions that lead to Newton's Laws. To take an example from computational linguistics, it is only when we start thinking of parse trees as objects in their own right that we can develop accounts of their geometries and mappings between them.

Frege took the bold step of reifying meaning. He reified the meaning of a sentence as a truth value, and a truth value would be treated as if it were a concrete object.

Once the meanings of sentences are defined as truth values, the path is open for identifying meanings of parts of sentences. The parts are words, phrases, and the grammatical rules that compose words to make larger expressions. The parts should be assigned meanings in such a way that, when the parts are composed to give full sentences, the full sentences receive the appropriate truth values.

The enterprise has been enormously successful, with the modern disciplines of logic and formal semantics building on it. Logic and formal semantics are now central to our everyday lives, underpinning a range of activities from set theory to database access.

2.3.3 Two Incompatible Semantics?

How do the two traditions, the Gricean and the Fregean, relate to each other? The friction has long been apparent. In 1971 the leading Oxford philosopher P. F. Strawson wrote in his essay "Meaning and Truth" (Strawson 1971:271–72):

> What is it for anything to have a meaning at all, in the way, or in the sense, in which words or sentences or signals have meaning? What is it for a particular sentence to have the meaning or meanings it does have? [...]

---

[1] *American Heritage Dictionary of the English Language, Fourth Edition* (Houghton Mifflin Company, 2000).

I am not going to undertake to try to answer these so obviously connected questions [...] I want rather to discuss a certain conflict, or apparent conflict, more or less dimly discernible in current approaches to these questions. For the sake of a label, we might call it the conflict between the theorists of communication-intention and the theorists of formal semantics. [...] A struggle on what seems to be such a central issue in philosophy should have something of a Homeric quality; and a Homeric struggle calls for gods and heroes. I can at least, though tentatively, name some living captains and benevolent shades: on the one side, say, Grice, Austin, and the later Wittgenstein; on the other, Chomsky, Frege, and the earlier Wittgenstein.

Liberman (2003) leads a discussion of the recent history of the field with Strawson's struggle and presents thumbnail sketches of the heroes. He concludes thus:

> The examples of reasoning about layers of intentions and belief found in Grice (and others who have adopted his ideas) are so complicated that many people, while granting the force of the examples, are reluctant to accept his explanations. Attempts to implement such ideas, in fully general form, in computer models of conversation have generally not been impressive. [...] Most linguists believe that linguistic structure is most productively studied in its own terms, with its communicative use(s) considered separately. On the other hand, most linguists believe that Austin, Grice and the later Wittgenstein were right about many aspects of what is commonly called "meaning." There is a difference of opinion about whether a theory of "sentence meaning" as opposed to "speaker meaning," along roughly Fregean lines, is possible or not.

2.3.4 Implications for Word Senses

The WSD community comprises practical people, so should it not simply adopt the highly successful Fregean model and use that as the basis of the account of meaning, and then get on with WSD?

This does not work because it gives no leverage. Truth values are central to the Fregean model, which analyses the differences between meanings of related sentences – for example between *all men are generous* and *some men are generous* – in terms of the different situations in which they are true. When we are distinguishing different meanings of the same word, it is occasionally useful to think in terms of differences of truth value, but more often it is not. Consider *generous* as applied to

1. money (a generous donation),
2. people ("you are most generous"), and
3. portions (a generous helping),

and let us follow dictionary practice in considering these meanings 1, 2, and 3. Can we account for the differences between the three meanings in terms of differences in truth functions for sentences containing them? We might try to do this by saying that *some men are generous-2* might be true but *some men are generous-1* cannot be true (or false) because it is based on a selectional restriction infringement: *generous-1* is applicable to sums of money, not people. (See Chap. 5 for more on the use of selectional restrictions in WSD.)

Already, in this fragment, we have left the Fregean framework behind and have given an analysis of the difference in terms of infringement of selectional restrictions, not difference of truth value. We have lost the clarity of the Fregean framework and replaced it with the unclarity of selectional restrictions, and find ourselves talking about the acceptability of sentences that are, at best, pseudo-English (since *generous-1* is not a word of English).

The Fregean tradition is premised on the reification of meaning. For some areas of language study, this works very well. But for other areas, the assumption that one can abstract away from the communicative process that is the core of what it is to mean something, to manipulable objects that are "the meanings", is not sustainable. We must then fall back to the underlying Gricean account of meaning.

Once the different senses of *generous* are reified, they are to be treated as distinct individuals, and while they might be related as brothers are to sisters or mothers to sons, to talk of a reading being half way between one meaning and another makes no more sense than talking about a person being half way between me and my brother.

Reifying word senses is misleading and unhelpful.

2.4 Lexicalization

Within a Gricean framework, the meaning of a word is an abstraction from the roles it has played in utterances. On the one hand, this makes it unsurprising that different speakers have different understandings of words, since each speaker will have acquired the word, according to their own process of abstraction and according to the utterances they have heard it in. A word-meaning is "in the language" if it is in the lexicon of a large enough proportion of the speakers.[2] It also makes sense of the synchronic and diachronic flexibility of word meanings, since a difference in a word's meaning will follow on from new or different patterns of use. But on the other hand it is not informative about the particular role of a word or phrase as a carrier of meaning. In this section, we focus on the process whereby a word or phrase becomes a carrier of a particular meaning for a speaker. This is the process whereby a new meaning is added to the speaker's lexicon, so we refer to it as *lexicalization*.[3]

We first present and then defend a very broad definition of what it is for a speaker to lexicalize a particular meaning. A meaning is lexicalized for a given speaker if and only if there is some specific knowledge about that meaning in the speaker's long-term memory. By "specific", we mean it must be more than can be inferred from knowledge about other meanings combined with different contexts of utterance and rules.

There are many forms that such specific knowledge may take. Consider a comment by a character in Salman Rushdie's *The Moor's Last Sigh* (1997:5) when the history of India and the spice trade is under review:

> not so much sub-continent as sub-condiment

---

[2] This can be unpacked as follows: 1) Since de Saussure (1916), we are aware that words have two parts: form and meaning. A word is in a language if the form-meaning pairing is in the lexicon of a large enough proportion of the speakers. 2) The situation is essentially the same for word meanings though for the second and subsequent meanings, the form is already in the lexicon, making it a more cumbersome matter to describe. 3) Clearly, given the Gricean account of meaning espoused here, there is no straightforward way in which one speaker's meaning is identical to another's, and to say that you and I both know that word w can mean m is to make a complex claim about correspondences between our uses and interpretations of w.

[3] Lexicalization is the "process of making a word to express a concept" (WordNet 2.0, http://wordnet.princeton.edu/) or "the realization of a meaning in a single word or morpheme rather than in a grammatical construction" (*Merriam-Webster Online Dictionary*, http://www.m-w.com/). Our use of "lexicalization" emphasizes the process of a word (or phrase) being used in a new way, to express a concept that is distinct in some way from the concept(s) the word usually expresses, so emphasizing a different aspect of the process of constructing a new word/meaning pairing over other discussions of lexicalization. Nonetheless, as it is still a process of developing a new word/meaning pairing, we still consider "lexicalization" the appropriate term.

When I first encountered it, all I had to go on to form an interpretation was the standard meaning of the constituent words and the narrative context. To make sense of the utterance – to appreciate the word play – reasoning was required beyond the knowledge I had at that point of what the words might mean. But since that day, whenever I have heard the words *subcontinent* and *condiment*, the Rushdie reference has been available to me to form part of my interpretation. For me, and possibly for you by the time you have read this far, sub-condiments have been lexicalized. There is some new knowledge in my long term memory, and possibly also in yours, about the potential of these words.

Consider also *green lentils*. Is it lexicalized, or is the meaning merely composed from the meanings of its constituents? If we know what green lentils are, that they are called *green lentils*, and for example what they look like, what they taste like or how to cook them, then we have knowledge of *green lentils* over and above our knowledge of *green* and *lentils*.

There are two things to note here. Firstly, much of the interpretation of *green lentils* is clearly composed from the meanings of its constituents but it must nonetheless be lexicalized as long as there is some part that is not.

Secondly, some may find this definition of lexicalization too broad, and may wish to demarcate lexical as opposed to general knowledge. Sadly, there is no basis on which to do so. A lexicographer writing a definition for *turkey* has to decide whether to mention that they are often eaten for Christmas dinner, and to decide whether *roast turkey* is sufficiently salient to merit inclusion. Their decision will be based on the perceived interests of the dictionary's target audience, lexicographic policy, and space; not on a principled distinction between lexical and world knowledge.

We learn languages, words, and word meanings principally through exposure. We hear new words and expressions in contexts. There are two kinds of context: the linguistic, comprising the surrounding words and sentences, and the non-linguistic: what is being observed or done or encouraged or forbidden at the time. For any given word, the salient context may be linguistic, non-linguistic, or both. We make sense of the new word or expression as well as we are able, through identifying what meaning would make sense in that context.

The process is cumulative. When we hear the word or expression again, whatever we have gleaned about it from previous encounters is available as an input for helping us in our interpretation. Our understanding of a word or phrase is the outcome of the situations we have heard it in. An individual's history of hearing a word dictates his or her understanding of the word. A wider range of types of contexts will tend to give an individual a richer understanding of the word. His or her analytic abilities also, naturally, play a role in the understanding that is developed.

In cases of "real world" vocabulary, like *tiger* or *mallet* or *bishop*, once a word is learnt, the nature of the linguistic contexts which helped us learn it may become irrelevant: the word is understood when we know what it denotes. But most words have a less direct connection with the non-linguistic realm: consider *implicit*, *agent*, *thank*, *maintain*. Then a great part of our knowledge of the place of the word in the linguistic system is embedded in the linguistic contexts in which we have encountered it.

The contexts that form the substrate of our knowledge of words and their meanings cannot be dissected into lexical and world knowledge.

In this view, a word is ambiguous if the understanding gleaned from one set of contexts fails to provide all that is needed for interpreting the word in another set of contexts. A homonym provides no useful information for the interpretation of its partner homonym. In the case of polysemy, if one meaning is known to a speaker and a second is not, the contexts for the first sense will provide some useful information for interpreting a first encounter with the second, but further interpretive work will be required for understanding the new sense.

A psycholinguist's metaphor (MacWhinney 1989) may be useful here. We usually travel along well-worn routes. If it is a route thousands of people take every day, there will be a highway. If it has less traffic, maybe across the moors, a footpath. Occasionally, because we want to explore new territory, for curiosity, for fun, we leave the beaten track and make our own way. If it looks interesting, our friends may follow. If they do, all of our footfalls begin to beat a new track, and the seeds are sown for a new path – which could, in time, be a major highway. Our footfalls make for a feedback system. Likewise, innovative word uses may inspire repetition and re-use, and, once they do, lexicalization is under way.

Dictionary senses are a subset of the readings that are lexicalized for many speakers. But which subset? How do lexicographers choose which of the readings that are lexicalized in their own personal lexicon merit dictionary entries?

The lexicographer's response is pragmatic: those that are sufficiently frequent and insufficiently predictable (with respect to the style and target audience of the dictionary in question; the SFIP principle (Kilgarriff 1997)). A reading that is highly predictable (like the 'meat' reading of *warthog*, or the 'picture of x' reading, which is available for any visible object) is not worth using valuable dictionary space on, unless it is particularly frequent: dictionaries will mention the 'meat' sense of *turkey* but not the 'meat' potential of *warthog*. For a reading that is less-than-fully predictable, for example the use of *tangerine* as a color, a lower frequency threshold will be applicable. For homonyms, which are entirely unpredictable, a low baseline frequency (comparable to that required for rare words in general) is all that is required.

2.5 Corpus Evidence

In this section we present some findings and examples from a corpus study on the margins of lexicalization. Kilgarriff (2001) reports the study in full.

As we are interested in the processes whereby new meanings for words come into being, the most interesting cases are the data instances that do not straightforwardly match dictionary definitions. The title of the chapter is "Word senses" so while it might seem that we should be comparing the data instances for one sense with the data instances for another, in practice this gives little purchase on the problem. The sense is lexicalized, the lexicographer has identified it and presents it as a sense, and a certain number of corpus instances match it: it is not clear what more there is to say. The critical process for an understanding of polysemy is the process of lexicalization, and it is most readily visible where a meaning has not yet been institutionalized as a dictionary sense.

The materials were available from the first Senseval project (see Chap. 4). For English Senseval-1, a set of corpus instances were tagged three times in all (by professional lexicographers), and where the taggers disagreed the data was sent to an arbiter. The taggings thereby attained were 95% replicable (Kilgarriff 1999). For a sample of seven word types, all corpus instances that received different tags from different lexicographers were examined by the author. The words were *modest, disability, steering, seize, sack* (noun), *sack* (verb), *onion,* and *rabbit.*

The evidence from the study shows the similarity between the lexicographer's task, when s/he classifies the word's meaning into distinct senses, and the analyst's when s/he classifies instances as standard or non-standard. The lexicographer asks him/herself, "is this pattern of usage sufficiently distinct from other uses, and well-enough embedded in the common knowledge of speakers to count as a distinct sense?" The analyst asks him/herself, "is this instance sufficiently distinct from the listed senses to count as non-standard?" Both face the same confounding factors: metaphors, at word-, phrase-, sentence-, and even discourse-level; uses of words in names and in sublanguage expressions; underspecification and overlap between meanings; and word combinations which mean roughly what one would expect if the meaning of the whole were simply the sum of the meanings of the parts, but that carry some additional connotation.

For many of the non-standard instances, an appropriate model must contain both particular knowledge about some non-standard interpretation, and reasoning to make the non-standard interpretation fit the current context. The "particular knowledge" can be lexical, non-lexical, or indeterminate.

Consider the following example from the Senseval-1 data:

> Alpine France is dominated by new brutalist architecture: stacked rabbit hutches reaching into the sky …

In this case the particular knowledge, shared by most native speakers, is that

- *rabbit hutch* is a collocation,
- rabbit hutches are small boxes, and
- to call a human residence a rabbit hutch is to imply that it is uncomfortably small.

The first time one hears a building, office, flat, or room referred to as a rabbit hutch, some general-purpose interpretation process (which may well be conscious) is needed.[4] But thereafter, the 'building' reading is familiar. Future encounters will make reference to earlier ones. This can be seen as the "general" knowledge that buildings and rooms, when small and cramped, are like rabbits' residences, or as the "lexical" knowledge that *hutch* or *rabbit hutch* can describe buildings and rooms, with a connotation of 'cramped'.

It is the compound *rabbit hutch* rather than *hutch* alone that triggers the non-standard reading. Setting the figurative use aside, *rabbit hutch* is a regular, compositional compound and there is little reason for specifying it in a dictionary. Hutches are, typically, for housing rabbits so, here again, the knowledge about the likely co-occurrence of the words can be seen as general or lexical. (The intonation contour implies it is stored in the mental lexicon.)

---

[4] As ever, there are further complexities. *Hutch* and *warren* are both rabbit-residence words that are also used pejoratively to imply that buildings are cramped. A speaker who is familiar with this use of *warren* but not of *hutch* may well, in their first encounter with this use of *hutch*, interpret by analogy with *warren* rather than interpreting from scratch (whatever that may mean).

That hutches are small boxes is also indeterminate between lexical and general knowledge. It can be seen as the definition of *hutch*, hence lexical, or as based on familiarity with pet rabbit residences, hence general.

To bring all this knowledge to bear in the current context requires an act of visual imagination: to see an alpine resort as a stack of rabbit hutches.

A different sort of non-standard use is seen in the following example:

Santa Claus Ridley pulled another doubtful gift from his sack.

Here, the required knowledge is that Santa Claus has gifts in a sack which he gives out and this is a cause for rejoicing. There is less that is obviously lexical in this case, though gifts and sacks play a role in defining the social construct 'Santa', and it is the co-occurrence of *Santa Claus*, *gifts*, and *sack* that triggers the figurative interpretation.

As with *rabbit hutch*, the figure is not fresh. We have previously encountered ironic attributions of "Santa Claus" or "Father Christmas" to people who are giving things away. Interpretation is eased by this familiarity. In the current context, Ridley is mapped to Santa Claus, and his sack to the package of policies or similar.

These examples have been used to illustrate three themes that apply to almost all of the non-standard uses in this study:

1. Non-standard uses generally build on similar uses, as previously encountered.
2. It is usually a familiar combination of words that triggers the non-standard interpretation.
3. The knowledge of the previously-encountered uses of the words is very often indeterminate between "lexical" and "general".

Any theory which relies on a distinction between general and lexical knowledge will founder.

2.5.1 Lexicon Size

The lexicon is rife with generalization. From generalizations about transitive verbs, to the generalization that *hutch* and *warren* are both rabbit residences, they permeate it, and the facts about a word that cannot usefully be viewed as an instance of a generalization are vastly outnumbered by those that can.

Given an appropriate inheritance framework, once a generalization has been captured, it need only be stated once and inherited: it does not need to to be stated at every word where it applies. So a strategy for capturing generalizations, coupled with inheritance, will tend to make the lexicon smaller: it will take less bytes to express the same set of facts.

But a compact, or smaller, lexicon should not be confused with a small lexicon. The examples from the above study just begin to indicate how much knowledge of previously encountered language a speaker has at his or her disposal. Almost all the non-standard instances in the dataset called on some knowledge that we may not think of as part of the meaning of the word and that the lexicographer did not put in the dictionary used for the exercise, yet that is directly linked to previous occasions on which we have heard the word used. The sample was about 200 citations each per word; had far more data been examined, far more items of knowledge would have been found to be required for the full interpretation of the speaker's meaning.[5] The sample took in just seven word types. There are tens or even hundreds of thousands of words in an adult vocabulary. The quantity of information is immense. A compact lexicon will be smaller than it would otherwise be – but still immense.

2.5.2 Quotations

Speakers recognize large numbers of poems, speeches, songs, jokes, and other quotations. Often, the knowledge required for interpreting a non-standard instance relates to a quotation. One of the words studied in Senseval-1 was *bury*. The *bury* data included three variants of Shakespeare's "I come to bury Caesar, not to praise him" (*Julius Caesar* III.ii), as in:[6]

Graf will not be there to praise the American but to bury her …

We know and recognize vast numbers of quotations. (I suspect most of us could recognize, if not reproduce, snatches from most top ten pop songs from our teenage years.) Without them, many non-standard word uses are not fully interpretable. This may or may not be considered lexical knowledge. Much will and much will not be widely shared in a speaker community: the more narrowly the speaker community is defined, the more will be shared. Many dictionaries, including Samuel Johnson's *Dictionary of*

---

[5] The issue of what should count as an interpretation, or, worse, a 'full' interpretation leads into heady waters (see, for example, Eco (1992)). We hope that a pre-theoretical intuition of what it is for a reader or hearer to grasp what the author or speaker meant will be adequate for current purposes.

[6] For further details on the *Caesar* cases, and a discussion of other related issues in the Senseval data, see Krishnamurthy and Nicholls (2000).

the English Language and the *Oxford English Dictionary*, include quotations, both for their role in the word's history and for their potential to shed light on otherwise incomprehensible uses.

Hanks (1994) talks about word meaning in terms of "norms and exploitations". A word has its normal uses, and much of the time speakers simply proceed according to the norms. The norm for the word is its semantic capital, or meaning potential. But it is always open to language users to exploit the potential, carrying just a strand across to some new setting. As we have seen, an exploitation can then serve as a platform for further exploitations, and there is always the possibility that the exploitation becomes sufficiently established to merit treatment as a norm in its own right.

2.6 Conclusion

There are no decisive ways of identifying where one sense of a word ends and the next begins, and this is at the core of what makes word sense disambiguation hard. The task definition for WSD, in Senseval, includes the inventory of word senses, between which we are to disambiguate (see Chap. 4). But word senses are not easy to inventorize, and any list will incorporate a wide range of choices, both about how to divide up the meaning of an individual word, and, at a "policy" level, about how to address issues including metaphor, systematic polysemy, quotations, proper names, multi-word items and the limits of lexical as opposed to general knowledge. A good dictionary will have been compiled with policies on all of these issues, and will have applied those policies consistently. Still, however good the dictionary, it would be rash to assume that the policies of any particular dictionary are suited to the requirements of any particular application of natural language processing.

In this chapter we have explored what word senses are. The straightforward place to find them is in dictionaries, so we have looked at the process that puts them there. In modern lexicography, they are included in dictionaries on the basis of corpus analysis.

For a broader perspective, we looked to the philosophers. A word's senses are its meanings, and meaning has long been a topic of philosophical argument. We considered two contrasting accounts of meaning, the "Fregean" and the "Gricean", and showed that only the Gricean, in which a word's meaning is an abstraction from the communicative purposes of the utterances it occurs in, sheds light on word senses.

Since a word's meaning is an abstraction from patterns of use, a new meaning arises with a new pattern of use. A speaker will only use a word in a new pattern when they either invent it or acquire it. We looked in some detail at the process of adding a new pattern to a speaker's lexicon, and saw how new patterns come into use through a range of processes that exploit the established uses of the word, calling on general knowledge, quotations, and metaphorical reasoning along the way.

2.7 Further Reading

Two lexicographers who have closely and perceptively described corpus evidence of the behavior of words are Sue Atkins and Patrick Hanks. Atkins and co-authors describe the behavior of a set of verbs of cooking (2002, with particular reference to bilingual lexicography; also Atkins et al. (1986, 1988)) and of sound (Atkins et al. 1997). Fillmore and Atkins (1992) discuss the noun *risk* and in so doing, provide one of the main motivating papers for Fillmore's frame semantics (Fillmore 1982). Hanks (1994, 1996, 1998) addresses in detail nouns including *enthusiasm* and *condescension* and verbs including *check* in the course of developing his theory of norms and exploitations. All of the above references are recommended for readers wishing to find out more, as they present strong primary evidence of the sort of phenomenon that word meaning is, presented by people who, from lifetimes in dictionary-making, speak with experience and expertise on the nature of word meaning. These references are the further reading for Sections 2.4 and 2.5 as well as 2.2, as the discussions explore incipient lexicalizations, and interactions with real-world knowledge and quotations as encountered in corpus evidence. Two studies of the author's are Kilgarriff (1997), which looks particularly at the relation between this view of words senses and WSD, and the one from which the *rabbit* and *sack* examples are drawn, Kilgarriff (2001). Michael Hoey's recent book presents the closely related "lexical priming" theory of language (Hoey 2005).

For philosophy, a key primary text is Wittgenstein's allusive and aphorism-filled *Philosophical Investigations* (Wittgenstein 1953), though readers may be happier with the secondary literature: Honderich (1995) or the online *Dictionary of the Philosophy of Mind* (Eliasmith 2005) are suitable launching-off points. (Grice, in particular, is a very technical writer and readers should not be dismayed if their attempts to read, for example, Grice (1968) bewilder more than they enlighten.)

Acknowledgments

We are most grateful to Oxford University Press for permission to use the Hector database, and to the UK EPSRC for the grant which supported the manual re-tagging of the data, for the experiment described in Section 2.5.

References

Atkins, B. T. Sue. 2002. Then and now: Competence and performance in 35 years of lexicography. *Proceedings of the Tenth EURALEX International Congress on Lexicography (EURALEX 2002)*, Copenhagen, 1–28.

Atkins, B. T. Sue, Judith Kegl, and Beth Levin. 1986. Implicit and explicit information in dictionaries. *Advances in Lexicology: Proceedings of the Second Conference of the UW Centre for the New OED*, Waterloo, Canada, 45–63.

Atkins, B. T. Sue, Judith Kegl, and Beth Levin. 1988. Anatomy of a verb entry: From linguistic theory to lexicographic practice. *International Journal of Lexicography*, 1(2): 84–126.

Atkins, B. T. Sue, Beth Levin, and Grace Song. 1997. Making sense of corpus data: A case study of verbs of sound. *International Journal of Corpus Linguistics*, 2(1): 23–64.

Corréard, Marie-Hélène, ed. 2002. *Lexicography and Natural Language Processing: A Festschrift in Honour of B. T. S. Atkins.* EURALEX.

Crane, Tim. 1995. Meaning. *The Oxford Companion to Philosophy*, ed. by Ted Honderich, 541–42. Oxford University Press.

Eco, Umberto. 1992. *Interpretation and Overinterpretation.* Cambridge University Press.

Eliasmith, Chris, ed. 2005. *Dictionary of the Philosophy of Mind.* (http://philosophy.uwaterloo.ca/MindDict/)

Fillmore, Charles. 1982. Frame semantics. *Linguistics in the Morning Calm.* Seoul, South Korea: Hanshin Publishing Co., 111–137.

Fillmore, Charles and B. T. Sue Atkins. 1992. Towards a frame-based lexicon: The semantics of RISK and its neighbors. *Frames, Fields and Contrasts: New Essays in Semantic and Lexical Organization*, ed. by Adrian Lehrer and Eva Feder Kittay, 75–102. Hillsdale, New Jersey: Lawrence Erlbaum Associates.

Grice, Herbert Paul. 1968. Utterer's meaning, sentence-meaning, and word-meaning. *Foundations of Language* 4: 225–242.

Hanks, Patrick. 1994. Linguistic norms and pragmatic exploitations, or Why lexicographers need prototype theory, and vice versa. *Papers in Computational*

Lexicography: COMPLEX '94, Budapest, ed. by F. Kiefer, G. Kiss, and J. Pajzs, 89–113.

Hanks, Patrick. 1996. Contextual dependency and lexical sets. *International Journal of Corpus Linguistics,* 1(1): 75–98.

Hanks, Patrick. 1998. Enthusiasm and condescension. *Proceedings of the Eighth EURALEX International Congress on Lexicography (EURALEX 1998),* Liège, Belgium, 151–166.

Hanks, Patrick. 2000. Do word meanings exist? *Computers and the Humanities,* 34(1–2): 205–215.

Hoey, Michael. 2005. *Lexical Priming: A New Theory of Words and Language.* London: Routledge.

Honderich, Ted, ed. 1995. *The Oxford Companion to Philosophy.* Oxford University Press.

Kilgarriff, Adam. 1997. "I don't believe in word senses". *Computers and the Humanities,* 31(2): 91–113.

Kilgarriff, Adam. 1999. 95% replicability for manual word sense tagging. *Proceedings of the Ninth Conference of the European Chapter of the Association for Computational Linguistics (EACL), Bergen, Norway,* 277–288.

Kilgarriff, Adam. 2001. Generative lexicon meets corpus data: The case of non-standard word uses. *The Language of Word Meaning,* ed. by Pierrette Bouillon and Federica Busa, 312–330. Cambridge University Press.

Krishnamurthy, Ramesh. 1987. The process of compilation. *Looking up: An Account of the COBUILD Project in Lexical Computing, ed. by* John M. Sinclair. London: Collins ELT.

Krishnamurthy, Ramesh and Diane Nicholls. 2000. Peeling an onion: The lexicographer's experience of manual sense-tagging. *Computers and the Humanities,* 34(1–2): 85–97.

Liberman, Mark. 2003. *Linguistics 001: Introduction to Linguistics,* Course Notes, Univ. of Pennsylvania. (http://www.ling.upenn.edu/courses/Fall_2003/ling001/com_phil.html)

MacWhinney, Brian. 1989. Competition and lexical categorization. *Linguistic Categorization,* ed. by R. Corrigan, F. Eckman, and M. Noonan, 195–242. New York: Benjamins.

Rushdie, Salman. 1997. *The Moor's Last Sigh.* Vintage.

Saussure, Ferdinand de. 1916. *Cours de Linguistique Générale,* trans. by Roy Harris as *Course in General Linguistics,* London: G. Duckworth, 1983.

Strawson, Peter Fredrick. 1971. *Logico-Linguistic Papers.* London: Methuen.

Tiles, J. E. 1987. Meaning. *The Oxford Companion to the Mind,* ed. by Richard L. Gregory, 450–51. Oxford University Press.

Wittgenstein, Ludwig. 1953. *Philosophical Investigations.* Oxford: Blackwell.

3 Making Sense About Sense

Nancy Ide[1] and Yorick Wilks[2]

[1]Vassar College
[2]University of Sheffield

We suggest that the standard fine-grained division of senses and (larger) homographs by a lexicographer for use by a human reader may not be an appropriate goal for the computational WSD task. We argue that the level of sense-discrimination that natural language processing (NLP) needs corresponds roughly to homographs, though we discuss psycholinguistic evidence that there are broad sense divisions with some etymological derivation (i.e., non-homographic) that are as distinct for humans as homographic ones and they may be part of the broad class of sense-divisions we seek to identify here. We link this discussion to the observation that major NLP tasks like machine translation (MT) and information retrieval (IR) seem not to need independent WSD modules of the sort produced in the Research field, even though they are undoubtedly doing WSD by other means. Our conclusion is that WSD should continue to focus on these broad discriminations, at which it can do very well, thereby possibly offering the close-to-100% success that most NLP seemingly requires, with the possible exception of very fine questions of target word choice in MT. This proposal can be seen as reorienting WSD to what it can actually perform at the standard success levels, but we argue that this, rather than some more idealized vision of sense inherited from lexicography, is what humans and machines can reliably discriminate.

3.1 Introduction

In Chapter 2, Kilgarriff identifies the source of the WSD "problem" as the attempt to assign one of several possible senses to a particular occurrence

E. Agirre and P. Edmonds (eds.), Word Sense Disambiguation: Algorithms and Applications, 47–73.
© 2007 *Springer.*

of a word in text – in particular, pre-defined sense lists provided in dictionaries and similar lexical resources. He goes on to suggest that the proper assignment of word senses requires a vast amount of lexical, syntactic, and pragmatic knowledge, together with generative procedures that can be exploited for every occurrence – a position reminiscent of the artificial intelligence (AI) community's objections to statistical natural language processing (NLP) two decades ago. At the same time, Kilgarriff gives a nod to "the important role" of pre-established lists of word senses for WSD, by which we assume he means that the identification of some limited number of broadly defined senses is useful in language processing applications. He seems to be suggesting, at least obliquely, that while lexicographers and linguists seek to represent word meaning in all its depth and complexity, NLP can provide some useful results by relying on far less. This is exactly right, but it begs the question of how much – or, more to the point, how little – information about word meaning is actually required to do something useful in NLP, given our current capabilities.

Interestingly, although this question should be pivotal for those engaged in the WSD activity, within the NLP community very little progress has been made toward answering it directly. Perhaps this results from aiming too high: for example, the organizers of Senseval-2 state that "[Senseval's] underlying mission is to develop our understanding of the lexicon and language in general" (Edmonds and Kilgarriff 2002:289). It is difficult to resist the temptation to answer the hard questions that have been debated by philosophers and linguists for millennia, rather than continue hard practical work within the considerable constraints on our current understanding of lexical semantics. But as Robert Amsler recently pointed out,

> I fear the state of our understanding of theoretical lexical semantics is about where astronomy was 2000 years ago. The theory or even the logical arguments as to what stars in the heavens (or the semantics of words) must be will be debated for years to come without affecting the work of those of us empirically measuring what is observable and predictable (Senseval discussion list,[1] 27 August 2004).

Here we take a practical view of WSD, beginning with a reconsideration of the role of lexicographers in word-sense disambiguation as a computational task, as providers of both legacy material (dictionaries) and special test material for competitions like Senseval. We suggest that the standard fine-grained division of senses and (larger) homographs by a lexicographer for use by a human reader may not be an appropriate goal for the

---

[1] http://listserv.hum.gu.se/mailman/listinfo/senseval-discuss

computational WSD task, and that the level of sense-discrimination that NLP needs corresponds roughly to homographs. We then consider psycho-linguistic evidence that certain etymologically related (i.e., non-homographic) senses that are as distinct for humans as homographic ones may be part of the broad class of sense-divisions required for NLP. We link this discussion to the observation that major NLP tasks like machine translation (MT) and information retrieval (IR) seem not to need independent WSD modules of the sort produced in the research field, even though they are undoubtedly doing WSD by other means. We conclude by recommending that WSD focus on these broad discriminations, thereby reorienting WSD to what it can actually perform at the close-to-100% success rate that most NLP seemingly requires.

3.2 WSD and the Lexicographers

It is a truism of recent NLP that one should use machine learning techniques wherever appropriate, which in turn requires that training material be provided by the relevant experts, who will be translators in the case of MT, and perhaps lexicographers in the case of WSD. This has been roughly the method pursued by the WSD Senseval competition, but there may be reasons for questioning it, by asking whether lexicographers are in fact the experts that NLP needs for WSD training and expert input.

Even raising this question can sound ungracious, in that there have been many fruitful intellectual and personal collaborations between NLPers and lexicographers, of which Church and Hanks (1990) is perhaps the best known. However, there is a serious point behind the question, and one motivated by the peculiar and indefinite nature of word-sense distinctions, right back to early observations that the sense distinctions you wish to make may depend on your purposes at any given moment (Wilks 1972).

That there is no absolutely right number of senses for a word is conceded by the fact that a publisher like Oxford University Press produces its major English dictionary in at least four sizes (Main, Shorter, Concise, Pocket) with a corresponding reduction in the number of senses for most words. But this is made more complex by the fact the senses in a shorter dictionary may not always be a subset of those in a longer one, but a different conceptualization of a word's meanings. Hanks (1994) has noted that lexicographers can be distinguished as "lumpers" and "splitters", where the latter prefer finer sense distinctions and the former prefer larger, more general, senses. And efforts to "map" senses between one dictionary and another, even if coarse-grained senses are mapped to several finer-grained ones that they supposedly subsume, have shown that the correspondences are not always one-to-one (Ide and Véronis 1990).

However, whatever kind of lexicographer one is dealing with, one cannot be sure that their motivation and expertise is what is required for NLP, because their goal is and must be the explanation of meaning to one who does not know it, and it is not obvious that that is what NLP requires in the way of sense distinctions. This is not to question the line of research on the use of machine readable dictionaries in NLP that began at System Development Corporation with Olney et al. (1966) in the Sixties, and which blossomed with the availability of the *Longman Dictionary of Contemporary English* (LDOCE) (Procter 1978) and other learner's dictionaries in the Eighties. It was always a research question whether machine-readable dictionaries (MRDs) would provide large-scale semantics effortlessly in the way optimists hoped. This possibility was questioned as early as (Ide and Véronis 1993) and perhaps it is now fairly clear that, although research with MRDs produced some useful artifacts, such as automatically generated hierarchies (Wilks et al. 1996), and indeed can be said to have started WSD as a subfield and task of NLP, their availability did not produce the revolution that had been hoped for.

None of the above is intended to express skepticism about the expert task of the lexicographer and his intuitions; the issue is whether the product of those intuitions – i.e., a classical dictionary – suits the needs of NLP in semantic analysis. That there has been dissention among lexicographers themselves over their output can be seen from Kilgarriff's published questionings, already touched on above, under titles like "I don't believe in word senses" (1997) as well as Hanks's reported musings that a dictionary could be published consisting entirely of examples of use. Any proponent of such a set of examples of use, as a proto-lexicon in itself, has to explain how it performs either the classic explanatory role of a dictionary for the layman, or the needs of the NLP researcher who is perfectly capable of finding his own corpora, which is all a set of usages could amount to. A set of usages may well guide a foreign learner, directly or by analogy, how to use a word, but they cannot show what it means, in the way that definitions do, whatever their other faults. As to the second need, there may well be additional constraints on a well-balanced corpus for experiments, but there is no reason to imagine the set of usages of a word provided by a lexicographer would constitute a balanced corpus, since such balance was not a consideration in the set's construction. Even if it were, there would be no particular reason to trust a lexicographer to balance a corpus for one, rather than a linguist or a computer algorithm.

These doubts about what lexicographers really have to offer NLP have been exacerbated by the realization that all successful WSD has operated at what, in LDOCE terms, we could call the homograph rather than the sense level. If we look at the results obtained by Yarowsky on small word sets (2000), probably the best known WSD results, they have all been at the *crane*-as-bird-or-machine level – a clear case of an LDOCE homograph. In some of the earliest reported large scale WSD (Cowie et al. 1992) it was clear that much better figures were obtained resolving to the LDOCE homograph, rather than to the sense, level. Moreover, homograph distinctions do not require a lexicographer to locate them, since they are basically those that can be found easily in parallel texts in different languages, a point we shall return to below.

3.3 WSD and Sense Inventories

With few exceptions, contemporary automatic WSD assigns sense labels[2] drawn from a pre-defined sense inventory to words in context. If lexicographers' output (i.e., dictionaries) is not a good source of sense inventories useful in NLP, where do we turn? For nearly a decade, the sense inventory used almost exclusively in WSD is the most recent version of WordNet (currently, version 2.1). In the late Eighties and early Nineties, prior to the availability of WordNet, sense labels were often drawn from the few electronic dictionaries made available for computational linguistics research (LDOCE, *Collins English Dictionary*, etc.). It is interesting to note that both during and before the hey-day of symbolic NLP in the Seventies and early Eighties, word senses were more often represented by groups of features of varying kinds than by pre-defined inventories drawn from lexical resources; dictionaries and thesauri sometimes provided the starting point, but were frequently augmented by adding information from other sources, or by hand (for a more complete history, see Ide and Véronis 1998).

---

[2] We include here not only sense labels derived from sense inventories such as WordNet, traditional dictionaries, and thesauri, but also "concept labels" such as EuroWordNet's inter-lingual index (ILI), "semantic annotations" as used in, say, information extraction systems, as well as codings used in interlingual MT systems.

The problems for WSD arising from the use of the WordNet inventory are well-known. The most common complaints are that unlike traditional dictionaries, WordNet delineates different senses of a word on the basis of synset membership, and that the resulting distinctions are too fine-grained for WSD. At the same time, the community repeatedly acknowledged that for all its imperfections, WordNet has become a *de facto* standard because it is freely available for research. As a result, the European projects Eurowordnet (Vossen 1998) and BalkaNet[3] created parallel wordnets for Western and Balkan languages, and several other wordnets are under development.[4] Whether or not calls for the development of better resources to support it are met, WordNet is likely to remain the benchmark sense inventory for WSD for the near future, at least. But the use of WordNet senses *per se* is not the root of the problem. Although it has been argued that using WordNet senses for WSD produces results worse than using senses from traditional dictionaries (Calzolari et al. 2002), the fact remains that pre-defined, enumerated sense lists from any source have proven to be problematic for WSD.

In recent Senseval exercises (see Chap. 4) and the discussions surrounding them, several fixes to what we can call, a bit unfairly, "the WordNet problem" have been proposed and in some cases implemented. The most often-cited obstacle to correct assignment of pre-defined senses concerns granularity: as early as 1993, Kilgarriff showed that human annotators cannot distinguish well between some of the finer-grained senses delineated in LDOCE (Kilgarriff 1993), and this fact has been re-established in numerous studies since then, at a ceiling of approximately 80% inter-annotator agreement[5] (for English) reported in recent literature (see, e.g., Edmonds and Kilgarriff 2002). Senseval has addressed this problem by adopting a full or partial "coarse-grained" scoring scheme, where

---

[3] http://www.ceid.upatras.gr/Balkanet/publications.htm

[4] http://www.globalwordnet.org/gwa/wordnet_table.htm

[5] A problem we do not address but which must occur to many readers is that, in the case of WSD in particular, claimed and tested success rates in the 90%+ range are strikingly higher than the inter-annotator agreement level of 80%+, and to some this is a paradox. The answer may simply be that the better machine learning systems in fact simulate the better, more sensitive, discriminators and that the low agreement figure reflects the relative difficulty of the task, rather than some inherent level of vagueness in the material. We all know some people are better lexicographers than others, and this is not a "democratic" task like speaking a language. No other explanation seems to fit the experimental data.

sub-senses are collapsed to their highest parent, and partial credit is given for identifying the parent of the correct sense. Collapsing finer-grained distinctions has been suggested repeatedly in the literature (e.g., Dolan 1994, Chen and Chang 1998, Palmer et al. 2006; see also Chap. 4) as a means to avoid the WordNet problem, but this again begs the question of the level at which to stop collapsing, which has so far not been thoroughly addressed by WSD researchers.

More extensive and radical proposals to improve WordNet have also been put forward, suggesting a major over-hauling of the lexicon by adding information such as selectional preferences and frequency information, as well as refining or improving the information it already contains by simplifying hierarchies, making senses mutually exclusive, deleting bad links and esoteric words, and so on (Hanks 2003). While the suggested changes were not necessarily made with the aim of improving the resource for NLP specifically, they would certainly help. However, there seems to be little interest in (or perhaps, funding for) implementing changes to WordNet within the NLP community; despite its widespread use in NLP work, one sees very little in the literature about enhancing or extending WordNet to provide a better basis for automatically determining word senses.

There is of course a tradition that rejects the notion of a pre-defined inventory of senses altogether. One version, usually associated with Wierzbicka (1989) and, later, Pustejovsky (1995), is wholly linguistic; another approaches the problem of determining appropriate sense distinctions by using the kinds of information typically exploited in WSD (context, syntactic role, etc.) to identify groups of word occurrences that should, on these grounds, be regarded as representing a distinct sense (e.g., Schütze 1998; see also Chap. 6).[6] This is a tradition that goes back to Karen Sparck Jones's thesis in the mid-Sixties (1986/1964). While at first glance this approach would seem to be an effort to adapt the answers to the questions rather than the other way around, at the very least it provides some insight into which sense distinctions we can reasonably make given the state of the art. Yet another approach uses cross-lingual correspondences to determine appropriate sense distinctions. Brown et al. (1990) and Dagan and Itai (1994) use translation equivalents as "sense tags" in parallel and

---

[6] The applicability of this approach is not limited to WSD: Hanks (2000) outlines a method by which lexicographers can determine sense distinctions for inclusion in traditional dictionaries by iteratively clustering concordance lines judged to represent the use of a given word in the same sense.

comparable corpora rather than pre-defined senses. More recent work along this line extends to the claim that, for the purposes of NLP, the different senses of a word could be determined by considering only those distinctions that are lexicalized cross-linguistically (Dagan and Itai 1994; Resnik and Yarowsky 1997a, 1997b). Given that many ambiguities are preserved across languages, this approach demands examining translation equivalents in parallel texts from multiple languages, possibly languages spanning the various broad linguistic families to overcome arbitrary effects of joint inheritance. This idea was pursued in a series of studies (Ide 1998; Ide et al. 2001, 2002), where word occurrences in an English text were clustered based on their translation equivalents in parallel texts in seven languages from the Germanic, Romance, Slavic, and Finno-Ugric language families. The results showed that clusters produced automatically and based on translation equivalents agreed with clusters (i.e., groupings of occurrences deemed to be used in the same sense) produced by four human annotators at a level slightly below that of agreement among the annotators themselves (74% vs. 79%), but the clustering algorithm performed well enough to be considered a viable means to delineate senses. Chapter 6, (Sect. 6.4) and Chapter 9 (Sect. 9.3.4) review WSD studies related to cross-lingual issues. Other recent works include Dyvik (1998, 2004), Resnik and Yarowsky (2000), Diab and Resnik (2002), Ng et al. (2003), and Tufiş et al. (2004), which attained similar results to those of Ide.

These "data-driven" approaches to determining word senses are philosophically in the good company of Halliday, Sinclair, Harris, and other major 20th century linguists, but on a practical level they seem unlikely to be used in NLP applications in the near future, if at all. The primary problem is that their implementation to produce a "full" sense inventory would require massive amounts of data, and even continuous re-computation as new data becomes available and languages evolve. Furthermore, it is not even clear that a usable, independent sense "list" could be produced by these means: for example, how would senses in such a list be labeled/distinguished so as to be meaningfully understood and used, without resorting to some sort of definition, such as one would find in a traditional dictionary? If cross-lingual distinctions are used as a basis, do we include any distinction that any language makes, or only the ones most or all languages make? For example, Romanian and Estonian have a special word for *back of the head*, whereas in English the word *head* is generally used without further specification. In the phrase *behind [one's] head*, *head* is translated as *kuklasse* (nominative: *kukal*) in Estonian and *ceafă* in Romanian, whereas in the phrase *above [one's] head*, both Estonian and Romanian use a more general word for *head* (*pea* and *cap*, respectively) that corresponds to the English equivalent. Cross-linguistic data, then, suggests two "senses" to distinguish the concept of the back of the head from the head in general, but it is not clear whether the distinction should be made in sense labeling an English text, or if only the more general concept should be used even if the language being labeled makes the distinction (with language-specific refinements, as in EuroWordNet – see Peters et al. 1998).

Overall, then, no suitable sense inventory for general-purpose WSD has yet been identified or created. However, despite the questions noted above, the use of cross-lingual information to determine an inventory of sense distinctions useful for NLP seems to offer the best potential for developing a meaningful inventory for NLP applications. We return to this point later, in Section 3.5.

3.4 NLP Applications and WSD

In his survey of WSD in NLP applications (Chap. 11), Resnik rightly points out that there is typically no explicit WSD phase in well-established applications such as monolingual IR and MT. MT remains the crucial and original NLP task, not just because of its age but because any NLP theory can almost certainly be expressed and tested in MT terms; moreover MT has undoubted and verifiable evaluation standards, in that it remains a task that can be evaluated outside any theory, simply because many people know what a translation is without any knowledge whatever of NLP or linguistics. That cannot be said of many classic NLP tasks, which require a great deal of skill and experience to evaluate, including WSD. Given that seniority of MT, we also know that tradition asserts firmly that WSD was one of the reasons early MT was not more successful, and this has been used as the justification for WSD since its inception: it would help MT. What we have to discuss and explain here is why the undoubted successes of WSD at the 95% level seem not to have so far materially assisted MT.

Martin Kay wrote somewhere long ago that, even if all the individual problems associated with MT were solved, including WSD and syntactic analysis, that fact alone might not raise the success level of MT substantially. The remark was in a paper that advocated human-aided MT, on the ground that pure MT seemed unlikely to succeed, a prediction that has turned out to be false. However, the remark about MT components now seems prescient. And again, it is worth asking why that is, if it is.

To answer it, we might look at the history of IR, a discipline of about the same maturity as MT. From its beginning, there have been those who argued that IR must need some WSD function to reduce the ambiguity of words in queries. One remembers here Bruce Croft's dictum that, for any IR technique, there is some document collection for which it will improve retrieval. More seriously, Vossen (2001) and Stevenson and Clough (2004) have recently shown that WSD does seem to have a real role in cross-language IR (see also Chap. 10). Nonetheless, the current prevailing view is that explicit WSD must be close to 100% accurate to improve monolingual IR (Krovetz and Croft 1992, Sanderson 1994), and therefore, for the long, standard, queries used in evaluations (as opposed to the short ambiguous queries sent to search engines), separate WSD modules seem to make little difference; it has even been argued that partially erroneous sense assignments from explicit WSD can degrade retrieval results (Voorhees 1999). This is certainly because the operation of an IR system, using as it normally does the overall context defined by the query, seems to perform WSD by indirect methods. So, the 100 terms in a classic query (as in the U.S. TREC competition[7]) will effectively define a domain, and co-occurrence functions used in the retrieval ensure that associations of "inappropriate" senses of words in the query are eliminated in that process.

As for MT, it is a fact that most working MT systems, from Systran[8] onwards to the present, do not have separate and identifiable WSD components, although they undoubtedly do a great deal of WSD somewhere. Does this suggest that some local functions are in fact doing WSD without being so named? Two different examples of systems suggest that this may be the case. Wilks and Stevenson (1998) have shown that, if the lexicon was arranged appropriately, a simple part-of-speech tagger could give 90% WSD. Appropriate lexical organization here meant the sort given in LDOCE where senses are grouped under main homographs and the homograph/sense clusters have all their members with a single part of speech. It is this last fact that allows a POS tagger to do so much sense discrimination at little or no computational cost: for instance if *bark* is tagged as a verb, then we know its sense is that of an animal (possibly human) vocalizing vociferously and need not concern ourselves at all with the ambiguity of that word as a noun.

This result is a serendipitous side effect of LDOCE's particular form of organization, but it does suggest something deeper about the extent to

---

[7] http://trec.nist.gov
[8] http://www.systransoft.com

which sense distinction is not independent of part-of-speech distinction and how the latter can aid the discrimination of the former – i.e., without explicit WSD. Another example, quite different but pointing the same moral, is the generation component of the CANDIDE statistical MT system (Brown et al. 1990) where *prendre* has as its most frequent equivalent in bilingual texts the verb *take*. Yet, when translating *prendre une décision* CANDIDE is able to generate *make a decision* which is more common in U.S. English, even though *take a decision* is not wrong. It does this because of the interaction of trigrams in the target language and bilingual associations. One could say that *prendre* is being disambiguated here but without its English alternatives ever being explicitly considered or compared by the system. The correct output is simply a by-product of the interaction of two very general statistical components.

In general, then, explicit WSD – as implemented in stand-alone systems such as those involved in the Senseval competitions – does not seem to play a role in the most prominent NLP applications.[9] We again have to ask ourselves, why not?

Before answering this question, it is useful to turn it around and ask, why is WSD generally treated as if it is an isolatable language processing step? The reasons would seem to be primarily historical. A "modular" view of language processing was firmly established in the mid-20th century by semioticians and structural linguists, who developed cognitive models that describe language understanding as an aggregative processing of various levels of information (syntax/semantics/pragmatics for the semioticians, morpho-phonological/syntactic/lexico-semantic for the structural linguists). This modular view was taken up by the earliest computational linguists, who treated the process of language understanding as a modular system of sub-systems that could be modeled computationally, and it has remained dominant (abetted by cognitive psychology and neuro-science) to this day. It is apparent in the design of "comprehensive" language processing systems, which invariably include multiple modules devoted to isolatable analytic steps, and it informed the "pipeline" approach to linguistic annotation introduced in the mid-Nineties (Ide and Véronis 1994) that has been implemented in major annotation systems[10] since then. In keeping with the modular approach, it is natural to treat disambiguation in the same way morpho-syntax and syntax were treated in the past: as a step

---

[9] See Chapter 11 for a comprehensive review of the role of WSD in IR and MT.

[10] For example, MULTEXT (Ide and Véronis, 1994), LT XML (McKelvie et al. 1998), GATE (Cunningham 2002), and ATLAS (Bird et al. 2000).

in the language processing pipeline for which independent systems can be developed and tested, and which can then be integrated into more general language processing systems. As a result, for over 40 years considerable research activity has been devoted to the development and evaluation of stand-alone WSD systems, with techniques spanning the use of semantic and neural networks, hand-crafting of complex rules and semantic feature sets, exploitation of knowledge resources such as dictionaries, thesauri, and lexicons like WordNet, as well as the development of sophisticated statistical and machine learning techniques – despite the fact that these systems are rarely used as modules in language processing applications.

The fact that different applications require different *degrees* of disambiguation is rarely considered in discussions of the application needs for WSD. In fact, IR and MT provide what may be the opposite ends of a continuum of WSD needs: IR typically demands "shallow" WSD, while MT may require more disambiguation precision to generate a translation that sounds more or less natural in the target language.[11] In fact, it appears that applications that need deeper linguistic analysis in general, may need finer-grained disambiguation. So, it follows that MT has exploited information gleaned from its more sophisticated linguistic processing to achieve more precise disambiguation, rather than turning to stand-alone WSD. IR, on the other hand, is virtually the only application that has seriously explored the use of stand-alone WSD, since the kind and level of disambiguation needed there is precisely what current WSD systems are good at.

The question is therefore not whether NLP applications such as IR and MT *need* WSD (they do), but rather, what degree of disambiguation they need and whether or not pre-defined sense inventories can provide it. We turn to this question in the next section.

3.5 What Level of Sense Distinctions Do We Need for NLP, If Any?

Dagan and Itai (1994) have long argued that sense distinctions roughly at the homograph level, where *crane* is a bird or a machine for lifting, are the

---

[11] In fact, it is almost certainly the case that the degree of disambiguation required for MT depends on the word in question (more ambiguous words, especially those often used metaphorically such as *hard* and *run*, may demand more analysis to disambiguate) as well as the target language and its similarity to the source language, both etymologically and structurally.

ones actually used for most WSD and therefore those needed, by definition, for NLP. If we look a little more widely in the speculative literature
on word sense, we see that the homograph-as-basic view has more support
than at first appears: Wierzbicka (1989) is sometimes taken as having
argued that there are no word senses, but only a basic sense for each word,
a position held by Ruhl (1989) and, much earlier, by Antal (1965). However, Wierzbicka's position is more complex, in that she accepts homographs – what are often argued to be different words by linguists, and only
masquerading, as it were, as the same word. One can see her in the tradition of those interested in the way a word extends its sense with time,
while retaining a strong semantic link to its origin (which is precisely what
homographic distinctions lack). In the AI/NLP world, this tradition has
manifested itself as those who either want more compacted lexicons (e.g.,
Gazdar's DATR, Pustejovsky) or are interested in rules, or knowledge
functions, by which sense lexicons extend (e.g., Givón, Wilks, Briscoe,
Nirenburg – see Wilks and Catizone (2002) for a comparison of this class
of systems). A similar approach is advocated by some linguist/lexicogra-
phers; for example, Nunberg (1979) argued that distinct senses should not
be represented in the lexicon, but rather that pragmatic principles should
be used to derive related senses from others.[12] This view is also evident in
the psycholinguistics literature: one theory of the mental lexicon holds that
only a "core" meaning of a word is stored in memory, and polysemous
extensions are computed on the fly from contextual features, using pragmatics and plausible reasoning (see, e.g., Anderson and Ortony 1975,
Caramazza and Grober 1976).

The former group, as with Wierzbicka, tend to deny there is an extensive set of senses, whatever there appears to be in many dictionaries, while
the latter group claim that some mechanism could recapitulate the apparent
variety that time and usage have produced. These two variant positions
may not be ultimately distinct, and can be parodied by the example *She sat
on her bicycle and rode away* where, if a bicycle, has, say, 150 distinct
parts one could perhaps argue that *bicycle* in that sentence is 150 ways
ambiguous and needs resolving to *saddle* or *seat*. However, that position is
obviously absurd; it would be far better to say that the word is simply
vague, and that it is AI, knowledge bases, and reasoning that should further
resolve it, if that ever proved necessary, and not NLP or linguistics. To jus-
tify this, one could fall back on some form of Dagan's case: namely that

---

[12] This approach is in contrast to that of other lexicologists such as Zgusta (1971),
who argue for representing each distinguishable sense.

every language will have a word for a bicycle and for each of its parts, but it is hard to imagine a language that would force the specification of a particular part in the example above – though, as we saw, in some specific and limited cases like the Romanian/Estonian *head*, such precision is forced.

In fact, homographs as strictly defined – i.e., etymologically unrelated words which through historical accident have the same "name", like the senses of *bank* and *calf* – are certainly not enough for WSD, since there are many instances where etymologically related senses are as distinct as homographs for most people. Take, for example, the word *paper:* in dictionaries that separate entries by homographs (most notoriously, the *Oxford English Dictionary* (OED)), the senses of *paper* that refer to sheets of material made from wood (as a *sheet of paper*) and a newspaper (as a *daily paper*) appear in the same entry and are therefore etymologically related. Other examples include words like *nail* (a finger nail vs. the metal object one drives with a hammer), *shower* (a rain shower vs. the stall in which one bathes), etc.[13] For such words, certain senses are as distinguishable as homographs, a fact that has been borne out in psycholinguistic experiments. For example, Klein and Murphy (2001) conducted experiments in which subjects were primed with a word in context in one sense and then presented with the same word in another context, reaction time for homographs was no less than reaction time for grossly polysemous words (e.g., *daily paper* vs. *wrapping paper*). This suggests that some senses of an ambiguous word, although not unrelated etymologically, are as distinct in the mind of the hearer as homographs, which in turn suggests that they may be just as relevant for NLP.

Some linguists (e.g., Lakoff 1987, Heine 1992, Malt et al. 1999) have proposed that polysemy develops via a chain of novel extensions to previously known senses, each building on its predecessors. This idea, and computational methods for it surveyed and discussed in Wilks and Catizone (2002), follows nicely on from proposals for the generative lexicon proposed by Pustejovsky (1995) and others, but adds the notion that at some point, senses diverge enough to deserve independent representation in the lexicon (either computational or mental). The problem, of course, is in identifying the point at which two senses become distinct enough to warrant separation for the purposes of NLP (or, for that matter, in dictionaries and the mental lexicon). Klein and Murphy (2002) extended their

---

[13] A list of 175 polysemous words of this type and their most common different senses is given in Durkin and Manning (1989).

earlier study to involve more closely related senses, for instance senses for *paper* in WordNet such as sense 3 ('publication') versus sense 7 ('physical object') in order to address this question. Their results in this second slate of experiments lead them to several conclusions that have ramifications for automatic sense disambiguation. First, their results suggest that some of the different senses of polysemous[14] words are stored independently in memory, supporting the notion that some etymologically related words are as distinguishable as homographs. Second, they experimented with different categorical relations among senses similar to those outlined by Pustejovsky (1995), and determined that different senses of a polysemous word do not seem to correspond to a unified taxonomic, thematic, or *ad hoc* category, but rather that the types of relationships among senses are more or less random and unpredictable. This is bad news for proponents of the generative lexicon, because it means that rule sets for the online derivation of different senses of a given word cannot be determined in any systematic way. Furthermore, Klein and Murphy draw the conclusion that representation of a "core" sense (similar to a homograph) coupled with procedures to generate more refined meanings is inconsistent with their results; rather, they suggest that relational derivation of senses happens historically and/or during language acquisition, and once senses become sufficiently distinct, they are thereafter stored separately in the mental lexicon. This leads them to suggest a processing model for word meaning that they call "radical under-specification", in which a minimal, neutral placeholder is activated when a polysemous word is encountered (e.g., 'something called paper' when "*The paper ...*" is seen) and refined by later context.

Klein and Murphy's work, along with that of other psycholinguists, has ramifications for WSD. First of all, it suggests that there are some etymologically related senses that should be regarded as separate as homographs and could provide insight into which senses belong in this category. Unfortunately, the aim of Klein and Murphy's experiments is to provide evidence for separate representation of etymologically-related senses, rather than to identify which senses of a given word fall into this category and which do not. Therefore, their analysis provides no information concerning which senses might be regarded as the same and therefore collapsed into one, homograph-level sense for the purposes of WSD. This is also the case in other recent psycholinguistic studies concerning word meaning

---

[14] Klein and Murphy's conception of polysemy is defined primarily through examples, and does not seem to rely on a pre-defined sense inventory (although in their 2001 article they mention the use of the OED for determining homographs).

(e.g., Rodd et al. 2002, 2004), which use pre-defined sense inventories as a point of departure without questioning the distinctness among multiple senses of the same homograph. Nonetheless, it is easy to imagine extending the methods and criteria used in psycholinguistic studies of word meaning to determine the distinctness – in terms of the mental lexicon – of senses below the level of the homograph.

On the other hand, it is certainly possible that sufficiently separate senses can be identified using multi-lingual criteria – i.e., by identifying senses of the same homograph that have different translations in some significant number of other languages – as discussed in Section 3.3. For example, the two senses of *paper* cited above are translated in French as *journal* and *papier,* respectively; similarly, the two etymologically-related senses of *nail* (fingernail and the metal object that one hammers) are translated as *ongle* and *clou.* At the same time, there is a danger in relying on cross-lingualism as the basis of sense, since the same historical processes of sense "chaining" (Cruse 1986, Lakoff 1987) can occur in different languages. For example, the English *wing* and its equivalent *ala* in Italian have extended their original sense in the same way, from birds to airplanes, to buildings, and even to soccer positions. The Italian-English cross-corpus correlations of the two words would lead to the conclusion that both have a single sense, when in fact they have wide sense deviations approaching the homographic.

Another source of information concerning relevant sense distinctions is domain, as discussed in Chapter 10. If senses of a given word are distinguished by their use in particular domains, this could offer evidence that they are distinguishable at the homograph-like level. At the same time, senses that are *not* distinguished by domain – take, for example, the sense of *bank* as a financial institution versus its sense as a building that houses a financial institution – might, for all practical purposes, be regarded as a single, homograph-level sense.

The psycholinguistic evidence also suggests that different kinds of evidence are needed to distinguish senses for different words. Experiments with a "multi-engine" WSD system (Stevenson and Wilks 1999) have already showed that the sense-discrimination of particular word-classes – usually part-of-speech classes like nouns or verbs – tended overwhelmingly to be carried out by a particular "engine" using a particular resource: for instance verbs and adjectives, but not nouns, were discriminated to a great degree by the selectional preferences loaded in from LDOCE, while the nouns tended to be discriminated by a combination of LDOCE definitions and thesaurus classes. None of this should be surprising, but it was confirmed strikingly by an overall machine learning algorithm which, in effect, decided for each word, which engine/resource best discriminated it.[15] A further, less trivial, inference to be drawn from this result is that the different semantic resources used in WSD (thesauri, definitions, collocations etc.) are not, as some have suspected, merely different notations for the same semantic facts. Klein and Murphy's assertion that senses of a polysemous word are not unified by a common categorical relation suggests that these processing differences may extend to words of the same part-of-speech category as well, and even further, that the degree and nature of these relations depend not only on the word in question, but often varies for each pair of senses for that word. This notion could be taken to lead to a position similar to Kilgarriff's, that a vast array of knowledge about each word (similar to his "word sketches" in Kilgarriff and Tugwell (2001)) is required for sense disambiguation; but at least for the purposes of NLP, another interpretation is possible.

If we accept that new senses of a given word develop historically through various relations, then we can also assume, based on the psycholinguistic evidence, that at some point a sense becomes distinct enough to be represented separately in the mental lexicon[16] and becomes as distinguishable from other senses of the same word as homographs are from one another. We would argue that these senses are discernable from context to the same degree as homographs, and therefore, WSD systems can achieve the same high degree of success in detecting them as for homographs. It is this level of sense distinction that Amsler referred to as "observable and predictable" in his comments to the Senseval discussion list, and, in our view, this is the only kind of sense distinction that stand-alone WSD should be concerned with. Senses that have not achieved this degree of distinction demand greater knowledge and resources to identify reliably, but in applications like MT that may need finer sense granularity, the results of deeper linguistic processing and knowledge is readily available to assist the disambiguation process.

To summarize, NLP applications, when they need WSD, seem to need homograph-level disambiguation, involving those senses that psycholinguists see as represented separately in the mental lexicon, are lexicalized cross-linguistically, or are domain-dependent. Finer-grained distinctions are rarely needed, and when they are, more robust and different kinds of

---

[15] See Chapter 8 for a more complete survey of knowledge sources for WSD.

[16] Note that there is no psycholinguistic evidence that the links among derived senses are themselves stored.

processing are required. Lexicographers will necessarily continue to be concerned with the latter kind of sense distinction, as they must be; but for the purposes of NLP, work on the problem of WSD should focus on the broader distinctions that can be determined reliably from context.

3.6 What Now for WSD?

At present, WSD work is at a crossroads: systems have hit a reported ceiling of 70% + accuracy (Edmonds and Kilgarriff 2002),[17] the source and kinds of sense inventories that should be used in WSD work is an issue of continued debate, and the usefulness of stand-alone WSD systems for current NLP applications is questionable.

The WSD community has grappled for years with the issue of sense distinctions because of its reliance on pre-defined sense inventories provided in mono-lingual dictionaries and similar reference materials. Such inventories are typically organized according to lexicographical principles, such as grouping senses on the basis of etymology and part of speech. Senses grouped according to these criteria are usually organized, either explicitly or implicitly, by frequency of use, and there is no other indication of the degree of distinguishability among them. Although WordNet is not the best example of a traditional dictionary, its organization is fairly typical; for example, if we stay with the *paper* example, WordNet gives us the following:[18]

paper
1   *paper*: a material made of cellulose pulp derived mainly from wood or rags or certain grasses
2   *composition, paper, report, theme*: an essay (especially one written as an assignment), "he got an A on his composition"
3   *newspaper, paper*: a daily or weekly publication on folded sheets; contains news and articles and advertisements, "he read his newspaper at breakfast"
4   *paper*: a scholarly article describing the results of observations or stating hypotheses, "he has written many scientific papers"

---

[17] Of course, statistics such as these depend on the assumption that the criteria used – in this case, identification of WordNet sense distinctions – are good ones.
[18] Each sense is composed by, first the set of synonyms, followed by a hyphen and the definition, and finally a list of examples in double quotes.

5   *paper*: medium for written communication, "the notion of an office run-
     ning without paper is absurd"
6   *newspaper, paper, newspaper publisher*: a business firm that publishes
     newspapers, "Murdoch owns many newspapers"
7   *newspaper, paper*: a newspaper as a physical object, "when it began to
     rain he covered his head with a newspaper"

Clearly, sense 1 is far more distinguishable from sense 3 than sense 6 is,
but in WSD experiments, senses like these are usually considered to be
distinct. A more intuitive list might collapse senses 1, 5; 2, 4; and 3, 6, 7,
yielding something like:

paper (collapsed)
1   *material*
2   *composition, article*
3   *newspaper, publication, publisher*

This is given as an example and not a scientifically determined set of
senses, based in part on the fact that some other languages lexicalize these
broad distinctions differently (e.g., in French, as *papier, article,* and *journal,* respectively). The WSD community has recently begun discussing
"collapsing" senses that are more related (see Palmer et al. 2006, and also
Chap. 4 (Sect. 4.6)) – or at least, senses that WSD systems have difficulty
distinguishing. This goes in the right direction, but it seems more appropriate to adopt a "top-down" rather than a "bottom-up" approach: that is, the
starting point for WSD should be a bi-polar distinction, between homograph-level distinctions and "everything else". The psycholinguistic evidence
supports this approach, by identifying senses that are, in psychological
terms, represented separately in the mental lexicon; and it is in fact also indicated by the performance of current WSD systems, which show clearly
superior results for disambiguating homographs – and, we would argue,
would do so for all homograph-level distinctions if they were clearly identified.

In fact, there are good reasons to suggest that WSD should focus on a
top-down approach to sense *distinction* rather than sense *determination.*
Klein and Murphy's notion of "radical under-specification" implies such
a model for human processing, by stipulating that disambiguation starts
with only the most general of concepts when an ambiguous word is
encountered, and proceeds by refining meaning as additional context is
provided. For example, when *"the paper…"* is seen or heard, we can imagine that if the remainder of the sentence is *"… was picked up at the corner newsstand"*, the reader will make the homograph-level distinction and

determine that here, *paper* refers to a newspaper. More importantly, only the homograph-level distinction needs to be made: no choice between the newspaper-as-physical-object and information-source senses of *paper* (senses 3 and 7 in the WordNet list above) is necessary – that is, there is no need to choose one of these senses and explicitly eliminate the other. Even if the discourse emphasizes one of the two possibilities, both are likely to exist in the mind as a single encompassing concept that has not (yet) been torn apart. We can hypothesize, then, that sense "disambiguation" is really a process of step-wise sense refinement that progressively distinguishes "sub-senses" as needed for understanding. We argue that there is rarely a need to make distinctions below the homograph-like level for understanding, human or automated; and in the unusual circumstance where it becomes necessary to explicitly throw one of the sub-senses away, we can expect there to be contextual clues that will enable both humans and machines to do so.

Based on all of this, our recommendations for WSD work in the near future are, first, to focus attention on identifying the homograph-level sense distinctions that are necessary for NLP, independent of pre-existing inventories. The obvious sources of this information are cross-lingual and psycholinguistic evidence, together with domain information. Cross-lingual evidence provides inventory-free distinctions based solely on translation equivalents, but will demand further work to acquire sufficient parallel data in order to overcome problems such as parallel sense chaining (as mentioned in the previous section) and mono-lingual synonymy. It will also require determining the number and types (in terms of representatives of different language families, etc.) of languages needed to ensure that all relevant distinctions are captured. At the same time, some threshold must be determined so that fine distinctions made by one or only a few languages, and/or which are highly culture dependent (e.g., different ways to greet a person depending on one's relation to that person, or the time of day), are not included for the general WSD task (although they certainly need to be retained for the purposes of MT).

To gather psycholinguistic evidence, further experimentation will be required, since research in this area has been focused on developing psychological models of language processing and has not directly addressed the problem of identifying senses that are distinct enough to warrant, in psychological terms, a separate representation in the mental lexicon. Also, psycholinguistic experiments currently rely on pre-defined sense inventories from traditional dictionaries, thereby providing sense distinctions *a priori* rather than seeking to determine which distinctions are sufficiently independent. Collaboration between the WSD and psycholinguistic communities could enable experimentation with "inventory-free" distinctions, and provide valuable results for WSD as well as theories of the mental lexicon.

Another source of information about sense distinctions is corpus evidence – that is, differences in patterns of usage for a given word that may signal its use in different senses. For example, the Corpus Pattern Analysis (CPA) project (Hanks and Pustejovsky 2005) is currently compiling a lexicon of verb patterns based on randomly chosen corpus occurrences, consisting of syntactic frame information coupled with semantic types and roles. While the information in such a lexicon may provide a compendium of characteristics that help distinguish different senses of a word, it does not follow that the identified senses are at the level of granularity needed for most NLP applications, or, consequently, that the relatively sophisticated techniques required to automatically detect them is necessary to accomplish adequate WSD. It will, however, be informative to consider correspondences (or lack thereof) between distinctions identified by projects such as CPA and those identified on the basis of domain, cross-lingual evidence, and psycholinguistic experiments.

Our second recommendation is to shift the focus of work on WSD to enhancing stand-alone systems in order to achieve near-100% accuracy for homograph-level distinctions. As we have argued above, disambiguation at the homograph-level is sufficient for IR, MT, and other NLP applications, and robust WSD systems that deliver accurate results at this level are potentially more useful for NLP applications than existing systems have so far proved to be. For example, Sanderson (1994) argued against the use of existing WSD systems for IR based on his observation that inaccurate WSD can negatively impact results. Likely, other NLP applications such as MT could profit from accurate WSD at this level as well.

As a final note, we point out that while concern with sense distinctions at levels finer than the homograph may not be appropriate at this point for WSD research aimed at contributing to NLP applications, it is still a matter of interest for lexicographers and certainly valuable to "develop our understanding of the lexicon and language in general". It may also be relevant for MT systems that seek to generate natural-sounding prose – for example, several alternative translations for *recur* exist in French (*se reproduire, revenir, se retrouver, réapparaître, se représenter*); to generate a natural-sounding translation, additional knowledge and/or reasoning may be applied to determine the nature of the verb's agent (*l'événement se reproduit, l'idée se retrouve, la maladie réapparaît, le problème se représent*) – see, for example, Edmonds and Hirst (2002), who have explored means to choose among near-synonyms in order to produce natural-sounding prose. This type of lexical refinement, however, is primarily the work of lexicography, AI, and knowledge engineering, and should be left to specialized modules outside the scope of mainstream WSD.

3.7 Conclusion

Our conclusions could seem both pessimistic and optimistic for WSD. They are optimistic in that, if something on the order of homograph distinctions are the level of WSD we need for NLP, then we have pretty good techniques for achieving that; the data may be relatively easily obtained from multilingual corpora, and we do not really need the expertise of lexicographers to help us in that task. They may also be considered pessimistic, in that it may be that many NLP systems do not require a separate WSD module at the level of granularity attempted by current systems, and that therefore much of the WSD work of the last decade has been wasted in presenting it as a separate task – however useful it has been as a hothouse of techniques. Given that evaluating WSD, as a free-standing, independent task has been so expensive and time-consuming, this discovery may be a relief all round. But this does not mean that work on stand-alone WSD is finished, by any means. There still remains the considerable task of identifying an "inventory-free" set of homograph-level distinctions that are useful for NLP, since they are not explicitly identified as such in any existing resource. The WSD community therefore has work to do, and should now turn itself to the task.

References

Anderson, Richard C. & Andrew Ortony. 1975. On putting apples into bottles – A problem of polysemy. *Cognitive Psychology*, 7: 167–180.
Antal, László. 1965. *Content, Meaning and Understanding*. The Hague: Mouton.
Bird, Steven, David Day, John Garofolo, John Henderson, Christophe Laprun & Mark Liberman. 2000. ATLAS: A flexible and extensible architecture for linguistic annotation. *Proceedings of the Second International Language Resources and Evaluation Conference (LREC)*, May, 2000, Athens, Greece, 1699–1706.

Brown, Peter F., John Cocke, Stephen A. Della Pietra, Vincent J. Della Pietra, Frederick Jelinek, John Lafferty, Robert Mercer & Paul Roosin. 1990. A statistical approach to machine translation. *Computational Linguistics*, 16(2): 79–85.

Calzolari, Nicoletta, Claudia Soria, Francesca Bertagna, & Francesco Barsotti. 2002. Evaluating lexical resources using Senseval. *Natural Language Engineering*, 8(4): 375–390.

Caramazza, Alfonso & Ellen Grober. 1976. Polysemy and the structure of the subjective lexicon. *Semantics: Theory and application* (27th Georgetown University Round Table on Languages and Linguistics), ed. by Clea Rameh, 181–206. Washington, DC: Georgetown University Press.

Chen, Jen Nan & Jason S. Chang. 1998. Topical clustering of MRD senses based on information retrieval techniques. *Computational Linguistics*, 24(1): 61–95.

Church, Kenneth W. & Patrick Hanks. 1990. Word association norms, mutual information, and lexicography. *Computational Linguistics*, 16(1): 22–29.

Cowie, James, Joe Guthrie & Louise Guthrie. 1992. Lexical disambiguation using simulated annealing. *Proceedings of the 14th International Conference on Computational Linguistics (COLING)*, Nantes, France, 359–365.

Cruse, David. 1986. Lexical semantics. Cambridge: Cambridge University Press.

Cunningham, Hamish. 2002. GATE, A general architecture for text engineering. *Computers and the Humanities*, 36(2): 223–254.

Dagan, Ido & Alon Itai. 1994. Word sense disambiguation using a second language monolingual corpus. *Computational Linguistics*, 20(4): 563–596.

Diab, Mona & Philip Resnik. 2002. An unsupervised method for word sense tagging using parallel corpora. *Proceedings of the 40th Meeting of the Association for Computational Linguistics (ACL)*, Philadelphia, U.S.A., 255–262.

Dolan, William. 1994. Word sense ambiguation: Clustering related senses. *Proceedings of the 14th International Conference on Computational Linguistics* (COLING-94), Kyoto, Japan, 712–716.

Durkin, Kevin & Jocelyn Manning. 1989. Polysemy and the subjective lexicon: Semantic relatedness and the salience of intraword senses. *Journal of Psycholinguistic Research*, 18: 577–612.

Dyvik, Helge. 1998. Translations as semantic mirrors. *Proceedings of the ECAI Workshop on Multilinguality in the Lexicon II*, Brighton, U.K., 24–44.

Dyvik, Helge. 2004. Translations as semantic mirrors: From parallel corpus to Wordnet. *Language and Computers*, 1: 311–326.

Edmonds, Philip & Graeme Hirst. 2002. Near-synonymy and lexical choice. *Computational Linguistics*, 28(2): 105–144.

Edmonds, Philip & Adam Kilgarriff. 2002. Introduction to the special issue on evaluating word sense disambiguation systems. *Journal of Natural Language Engineering*, 8(4): 279–291.

Hanks, Patrick. 1994. personal communication.

Hanks, Patrick. 2000. Do word meanings exist? *Computers and the Humanities*, 34(2): 205–215.

Hanks, Patrick. 2003. WordNet: What is to be done? *Panel presentation at Prague Workshop on Lexico-Semantic Classification and Tagging Linguistic and Knowledge-Based Foundations, Existing Schemes and Taxonomies, and Possible Applications*, Prague, Czech.

Hanks, Patrick & James Pustejovsky. 2005. A pattern dictionary for natural language processing. *Revue Française de Linguistique Appliquée*, 10(2).

Heine, Bernd. 1992. Grammaticalization chains. *Studies in Language*, 16: 335–368.

Ide, Nancy. 1998. Cross-lingual sense determination: Can it work?. *Computers and the Humanities*, 34(1–2): 223–34.

Ide, Nancy, Tomaz Erjavec & Dan Tufiş. 2001. Automatic sense tagging using parallel corpora. *Proceedings of the 6th Natural Language Processing Pacific Rim Symposium*, Tokyo, Japan, 212–219.

Ide, Nancy, Tomaz Erjavec & Dan Tufiş. 2002. Sense discrimination with parallel corpora. *Proceedings of the ACL SIGLEX Workshop on Word Sense Disambiguation: Recent Successes and Future Directions*, Philadelphia, U.S.A., 56–60.

Ide, Nancy & Jean Véronis. 1990. Mapping dictionaries: A spreading activation approach. *Proceedings of the 6th Annual Conference of the Centre for the New Oxford English Dictionary*, Waterloo, Canada, 52–64.

Ide, Nancy & Jean Véronis. 1993. Extracting knowledge bases from machine-readable dictionaries: Have we wasted our time? *Proceedings of the First International Conference on Building and Sharing of Very Large-Scale Knowledge Bases (KB&KS)*, Tokyo, Japan, 257–266.

Ide, Nancy & Jean Véronis. 1994. MULTEXT: Multilingual text tools and corpora. *Proceedings of the 15th International Conference on Computational Linguistics (COLING)*, Kyoto, Japan, 588–592.

Ide, Nancy & Jean Véronis. 1998. Word sense disambiguation: The state of the art. *Computational Linguistics*, 24(1): 1–40.

Kilgarriff, Adam. 1993. Dictionary word sense distinctions: An enquiry into their nature. *Computers and the Humanities*, 26: 356–387

Kilgarriff, Adam. 1997. "I don't believe in word senses". *Computers and the Humanities*, 31(2): 91–113.

Kilgarriff, Adam & David Tugwell. 2001. WASP-Bench: An MT lexicographers' workstation supporting state-of-the-art lexical disambiguation. *Proceedings of 7th Machine Translation Summit*, Santiago de Compostela, Spain, 187–190.

Klein, Devorah & Gregory Murphy. 2001. The representation of polysemous words. *Journal of Memory and Language*, 45: 259–82.

Klein, Devorah & Gregory Murphy. 2002. Paper has been my ruin: Conceptual reations of polysemous senses. *Journal of Memory and Language*, 47: 548–70.

Krovetz, Robert & Bruce Croft. 1992. Lexical ambiguity and information retrieval. *ACM Transactions on Information Systems (TOIS)*, 10(2): 115–141.

Lakoff, George. 1987. *Women, Fire, and Dangerous Things*. Chicago: University of Chicago Press.

Malt, Barbara C., Steven A. Sloman, Silvia Gennari, Meiyi Shi & Yuan Wang. 1999. Knowing vs. naming: Similarity and the linguistic categorization of artifacts. *Journal of Memory and Language*, 40: 230–262.

McKelvie, David, Chris Brew & Henry Thompson. 1998. Using SGML as a basis for data-intensive natural language processing. *Computers and the Humanities*, 31(5): 367–388.

Ng, Hwee Tou, Bin Wang & Yee Seng Chan. 2003. Exploiting parallel texts for word sense disambiguation: An empirical study. *Proceedings of the 41st Annual Meeting of the Association for Computational Linguistics (ACL)*, Sapporo, Japan, 455–462.

Nunberg, Geoffrey. 1979. The non-uniqueness of semantic solutions: Polysemy. *Linguistics and Philosophy*, 3: 143–184.

Olney, John, Carter Revard & Panl Ziff. 1966. *Some Monsters in Noah's Ark*. Research Memorandum, Systems Development Corp., Santa Monica, U.S.A.

Palmer, Martha, Christiane Fellbaum & Hoa Trang Dang. 2006. Making fine-grained and coarse-grained sense distinctions, both manually and automatically. *Natural Language Engineering*, 12(3).

Peters, Wim, Piek Vossen, Pedro Diez-Orzas & Geert Adrians. 1998. Cross-linguistic alignment of wordnets with an inter-lingual index. *Computers and the Humanities*, 32(2–3): 221–51.

Procter, Paul, ed. 1978. *Longman Dictionary of Contemporary English*. Harlow, UK: Longman Group.

Pustejovsky, James. 1995. *The Generative Lexicon*. Cambridge, U.S.A.: MIT Press.

Resnik, Philip & David Yarowsky. 1997a. Distinguishing systems and distinguishing senses: New evaluation methods for word sense disambiguation. *Natural Language Engineering*, 5(2): 113–133.

Resnik, Philip & David Yarowsky. 1997b. A perspective on word sense disambiguation methods and their evaluation. *Proceedings of the ACL SIGLEX*

Workshop on Tagging Text with Lexical Semantics: Why, What, and How?, Washington, U.S.A, 79–86.

Resnik, Philip & David Yarowsky. 2000. Distinguishing systems and distinguishing senses: New evaluation methods for word sense disambiguation". *Natural Language Engineering*, 5(2): 113–133.

Rodd, Jennifer, M. Gareth Gaskell & William Marslen-Wilson. 2002. Making sense of semantic ambiguity: Semantic competition in lexical access. *Journal of Memory and Language*, 46: 245–266.

Rodd, Jennifer, M. Gareth Gaskell & William Marslen-Wilson. 2004. Modelling the effects of semantic ambiguity in word recognition. *Cognitive Science*, 28: 89–104.

Ruhl, Charles. 1989. *On Monosemy: A Study in Linguistic Semantics*. Albany: State University of New York Press.

Sanderson, Mark. 1994. Word sense disambiguation and information retrieval. *Proceedings of the 17th ACM Special Interest Group on Information Retrieval Conference (SIGIR)*, 142–151.

Schütze. Hinrich. 1998. Automatic word sense discrimination. *Computational Linguistics*, 24(1): 97–124.

Sparck Jones, Karen. 1986/1964. *Synonymy and Semantic Classification*. Edinburgh: Edinburgh University Press.

Stevenson, Mark & Paul Clough. 2004. EuroWordNet as a resource for cross-language information retrieval. *Proceedings of the 5th International Conference on Language Resources and Evaluation (LREC)*, Lisbon, Portugal, 777–780.

Stevenson, Mark & Yorick Wilks. 1999. Combining weak knowledge sources for sense disambiguation. *Proceedings of the International Joint Conference for Artificial Intelligence* (IJCAI), Stockholm, Sweden, 884–889.

Tufiş, Dan, Radu Ion & Nancy Ide. 2004. Fine-grained word sense disambiguation based on parallel corpora, word alignment, word clustering, and aligned WordNets. *Proceedings of the 20th International Conference on Computational Linguistics (COLING)*, Geneva, Switzerland, 1312–1318.

Voorhees, Ellen. 1999. Natural language processing and information retrieval. *Information Extraction: Towards Scalable, Adaptable Systems*, ed. by Maria Teresa Pazienza, 32–48. Germany: Springer.

Vossen, Piek. 2001. Extending, trimming and fusing WordNet for technical documents. *Proceedings of the NAACL Workshop on WordNet and Other Lexical Resources Applications, Extensions and Customizations*, Pittsburgh, U.S.A.

Vossen, Piek, ed. 1998. *EuroWordNet: A Multilingual Database With Lexical Semantic Networks*. Amsterdam: Kluwer.

Wierzbicka, Anna. 1989. Semantic primitives and lexical universals. *Quaderni di Semantica*, X(1): 103–121.

Wilks, Yorick. 1972. *Grammar, Meaning and the Machine Analysis of Language*. London and Boston: Routledge.

Wilks, Yorick & Roberta Catizone. 2002. What is lexical tuning?. *Journal of Semantics*, 19(2): 167–190.

Wilks, Yorick & Mark Stevenson. 1998. The grammar of sense: Using part-of-speech tags as a first step in semantic disambiguation. *Natural Language Engineering*, 4(2): 74–87.

Wilks, Yorick, Brian Slator & Louise Guthrie. 1996. *Electric Words: Dictionaries, Computers and Meanings*. Cambridge, U.S.A.: MIT Press.

Yarowsky, David. 2000. Hierarchical decision lists for word sense disambiguation. *Computers and the Humanities*, 34(2): 179–186.

Zgusta, Ladislav. 1971. *Manual of Lexicography*. The Hague: Mouton.

4 Evaluation of WSD Systems

Martha Palmer,[1] Hwee Tou Ng,[2] Hoa Trang Dang[3]

[1]University of Colorado
[2]National University of Singapore
[3]National Institute of Standards and Technology

In this chapter we discuss the evaluation of automatic word sense disambiguation (WSD) systems. Some issues, such as evaluation metrics and the basic methodology for hand-tagging evaluation data, are well agreed upon by the WSD community. However, other important issues remain to be resolved, including the question of which sense distinctions are important and relevant to the sense-tagging task, and how to evaluate WSD systems in real NLP applications. We give an overview of previous evaluation exercises and investigate sources of human inter-annotator disagreements. The errors are at least partially reconciled by a more coarse-grained view of the senses, and we present the groupings that were used for quantitative coarse-grained evaluation. Well-defined sense groups can be of value in improving sense tagging consistency for both humans and machines.

4.1 Introduction

Highly ambiguous words pose continuing problems for natural language processing (NLP) applications. They can lead to irrelevant document retrieval in information retrieval systems, and inaccurate translations in machine translation systems (Palmer et al. 2000a). To tackle the word sense disambiguation (WSD) task, many different approaches have been implemented (see Chaps. 5–7 and 10). The question naturally arises as to which approach is the best. People producing WSD systems have always needed to evaluate them. However, each system or developer historically used a different evaluation scheme, making it difficult, if not impossible,

E. Agirre and P. Edmonds (eds.), Word Sense Disambiguation: Algorithms and Applications, 75–106.
© 2007 *Springer.*

to compare the relative merits of different implementations and approaches to WSD.

In recent years, a corpus-based approach to NLP has gained popularity. This data-oriented approach is robust and able to achieve high accuracy on many tasks ranging from part-of-speech tagging to syntactic parsing. Empirical evaluation on real-world, unrestricted text is a crucial part of this approach. By evaluating on common benchmark data sets, we can measure the performance of competing approaches and calibrate the progress made over time. The requirement for empirical evaluation naturally applies also to the task of word sense disambiguation.

4.1.1 Terminology

The following is an overview of some key terms and issues in evaluation of automatic WSD systems.

Sense Inventory. Probably the most important decision in designing an evaluation exercise for WSD is the choice of the sense inventory, which is a computational lexicon or machine-readable dictionary that partitions the meaning of each word into senses. An ideal sense inventory should make clear and consistent sense distinctions for each word. Unfortunately, sense inventories for a language can be discouragingly diverse, with significant differences with respect to entries for polysemous words. The granularity of the sense distinctions also plays a major factor in the suitability of a sense inventory for a particular application and in the quality of the sense-tagged data used to evaluate WSD systems.

Task Definition. There are two possible types of evaluation for WSD systems (Ide and Véronis 1998). The first is *in vitro* evaluation, where the WSD task is defined independently of any particular application, and systems are tested using specially constructed benchmarks. Alternatively, *in vivo* evaluation scores a WSD component in terms of its contribution to the overall performance of a particular NLP application. Since the importance of automatic WSD is primarily in its utility in real NLP applications, there is much that can be said in favor of the latter approach (see Chap. 11). However, almost no attempts have been made to evaluate embedded WSD components. Rather, evaluation has concentrated on WSD as a standalone classification task, much like part-of-speech tagging, primarily because this evaluation framework is easier to define and implement.

Standalone WSD can be framed as either a lexical sample task or an all-words task. In the *all-words* task, systems are required to tag all words (or all content words) in a running text or discourse. While superficially similar to part-of-speech tagging, the all-words task is significantly different in that a different set of sense tags is required for each word lemma. This severely limits the choice of possible sense inventories, because it requires access to a publicly available wide-coverage dictionary that is preferably also low-cost. In the *lexical sample* task, a sample of words is carefully selected from the lexicon, along with a number of corpus instances of each word; systems are required to tag these instances of the sample words in short extracts of text. Unlike the all-words task, dictionary entries are required only for these select words, so there is more flexibility in dictionary choice.

The methodology for manual annotation depends on which variant of the WSD task is being examined. Words can be annotated more quickly and consistently if all instances of a word (type) are tagged at once (targeted tagging), instead of tagging all words sequentially as they appear in text. The advantages of targeted tagging make the lexical sample task easier to implement than the all-words task, so most efforts at WSD evaluation have focused on lexical sample tasks. If one had to choose between the two tasks, the lexical sample task is preferable in that more systems would be able to be evaluated against it, because systems designed to compete in the all-words task would also be able to compete in the lexical sample task, but not vice versa. However, the all-words task may more closely mimic the requirements of real NLP applications such as machine translation, where all content words in a sentence may need to be disambiguated for correct lexical choice.

Corpus. The data for the lexical sample task is typically a large number of naturally occurring sentences containing a given target word, each of which has been tagged with a pointer to a sense entry from the sense inventory. A section of the tagged data may be set aside as training data for supervised machine learning systems (see Chap. 7), while another section is reserved for testing purposes. Rule-based and unsupervised systems (see Chaps. 5 and 6) can also be evaluated against the same test data, which is considered to be a "gold" standard. Several factors contribute to selecting the number or proportion of words that one might want to set aside as training data. Because performance generally increases with the amount of training data, typical evaluation of machine learning techniques would set aside a relatively large proportion of the data for training, on the order of 10:1 or 5:1, to estimate the best performance possible with the current amount of data. In light of the relatively small number of manually sense-tagged instances that are generally available for each word, however, providing less training data (using a ratio of 2:1) may provide a more realistic indication of a system's performance. At the extreme, no training data may be provided, testing a system's ability to address the sense-tagging task by leveraging from other resources. This is necessarily the case for the all-words task, because in practice it is infeasible to provide training data for every content word in any corpus of nontrivial size.

Scoring. The simplest way of scoring a system on a particular test item uses the exact-match criterion; the system receives a score of 1 if the sense tag that it assigns exactly matches the correct sense tag, and 0 otherwise. If a system chooses to assign multiple tags to a single test instance w, with associated probabilities for each tag, the system's score can be computed simply as the probability that it assigns to the correct sense tag c given w and its context:[1]

$$Score = \Pr(c \mid w, context(w)) \qquad (4.1)$$

If a test item has more than one correct sense tag, the system's score is the sum of all probabilities that it assigns to any of the correct sense tags:

$$Score = \sum_{t=1}^{C} \Pr(c_t \mid w, context(w)) \qquad (4.2)$$

where t ranges over the C correct tags. That is, the multiple tags are interpreted disjunctively.

When the sense inventory is hierarchically organized, three granularity levels can be defined for scoring: fine-grained, coarse-grained, and mixed-grained. At the fine-grained level, only identical sense tags count as a match. At the coarse-grained level, all sense tags given in the gold standard and system guesses are mapped to the top-level sense tag, and the system receives a score of 1 if its guess has the same top-level sense as the correct tag.

Mixed-grain scoring is applicable when the sense inventory is hierarchical and systems are allowed to guess (and humans are allowed to assign) any one of the senses in the hierarchy (Melamed and Resnik 2000). Each tree-structured tag set is interpreted as an IS-A hierarchy, and guessing a tag that is a descendant of the correct tag produces a score of 1. Guessing a tag that is an ancestor of the correct tag is computed by assuming that a parent's probability is divided uniformly among its children; the score of

---

[1] Resnik and Yarowsky (1999) propose additional methods for computing the system's score using cross-entropy or related measures such as perplexity and Kullback-Leibler divergence.

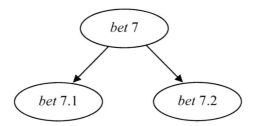

Fig. 4.1. Hierarchically structured tag set for *bet*.

the (guessed) ancestor tag is simply the probability of the (correct) descendant tag, given the ancestor. For example, suppose that the correct sense tag for a test item is sense 7 from the hierarchically-structured tag set for *bet* in Fig. 4.1. A system would receive a score of 1 if it guesses either sense 7, or sense 7.1, or sense 7.2. If the correct sense tag were sense 7.1, a system would receive a score of 1 for guessing sense 7.1, 0.5 for guessing sense 7, and 0 for guessing sense 7.2. For systems that guess multiple sense tags with some probability, the scores are the sum of scores for each guess, weighted by the probability that the system assigns to each guess.

A system that is presented with the set of all word instances to tag may choose to attempt to tag all the words or just a subset. The *coverage* of a system is the percentage of items in the evaluation set for which the system guesses some sense tag. The *precision* of a system is computed by summing the scores over all test items that the system guesses on, and dividing by the number of guessed-on items. *Recall* is computed by summing the system's scores over all items (counting unguessed-on items as zero score), and dividing by the total number of items in the evaluation set. For the sense-tagging task, *accuracy* is reported as recall.

Lower bound. As with any evaluation, system performance must be interpreted in comparison with one or more baselines, which show the performance of simple algorithms on the same benchmark data. The simplest baseline is choosing the most frequent sense (Gale et al. 1992), though other simple standard algorithms may also be appropriate such as the Lesk algorithm (see Sect. 4.4.1 below). Baselines present an expected lower bound on the performance of automatic systems and indicate whether a more complicated system is worth the additional implementation effort.

Upper bound. A notional upper bound for automatic system performance is human inter-annotator agreement (ITA) on the same or comparable data (Gale et al. 1992)), since the consistency of the systems cannot be expected to surpass that of humans. Inter-annotator agreement is computed by looking at how two or more people who have been given the same tagging guidelines annotate the same data; when multiple tags are allowed, agreement may be measured as exact match or as overlap. Agreement may be reported as the percentage of times that the annotators assigned the same sense tag to each instance. Alternatively, Cohen's (1960) kappa coefficient measures the agreement between annotators after factoring out the agreement that may be due to chance (Bruce and Wiebe 1999, Ng et al. 1999), though kappa is not well defined when multiple tags are allowed.

An alternative measure of upper bound on performance is replicability (Kilgarriff and Rosenzweig 2000). This replicates the entire process of arriving at the original gold standard (double-blind annotation followed by adjudication) and compares the agreement between the two sets of gold standards. However, replicability is extremely expensive to compute, so inter-annotator agreement is the usual measure of upper bound.

Many factors affect inter-annotator agreement, including the choice of words, the quality of the sense inventory and examples, and how well the inventory matches the corpus to be tagged. High human inter-annotator agreement provides reassurance of the quality of the tagged data. This is, in turn, facilitated by a high-quality sense inventory with clear sense distinctions. Examining inter-annotator disagreements can provide feedback for modifying the sense inventory to make the sense distinctions and definitions more clear.

Early work by Gale et al. (1992) dealt mainly with two-way ambiguities and estimated lower and upper bound WSD performance of 75% and 96.8%, respectively. While these figures turn out to be relatively optimistic, their proposal to use the most frequent sense as the lower bound and human inter-annotator agreement as the upper bound remains applicable.

4.1.2 Overview

In this chapter, we examine the issues involved in trying to evaluate different WSD systems. We review initial, individual attempts to create corpora annotated with sense tags to enable the training and evaluation of supervised WSD systems. We then describe the first community-wide evaluation exercises for WSD, as represented by Senseval-1 and Senseval-2, and discuss the impact that the choice of sense inventory had on them. We discuss general criteria for sense distinctions and present sources of inter-annotator disagreement. We then present some semantic groupings of related WordNet senses and show their effect on human inter-annotator agreement. Automatic WSD systems should not be expected to make sense distinctions that humans cannot make, and the groupings address the question: Which senses *can* be distinguished? There is a separate but related question that is equally important: Which senses *need* to be distinguished? The answer to this, however, depends on the domain and the application (see Chaps. 2, 3, 10, and 11). Evaluation exercises have concentrated on WSD as a standalone classification task, with one fixed sense inventory that is considered general enough to be useful across domains. However, only some of these sense distinctions need to be made by various NLP applications. We will end with a review of Senseval-3, the most recent evaluation activity, and a discussion of future directions.

4.2 Background

4.2.1 WordNet and Semcor

For WSD, the list of senses of a word is assumed to be fixed in advance according to some dictionary, so one prerequisite for evaluating a WSD program is the existence of a sense inventory for the words in a language. Up until the early 1990s, most dictionaries for English existed only in paper form. A few were available in electronic form but only to a limited group of researchers. This hampered the progress of the field.

At this point WordNet entered the scene, a public-domain electronic dictionary and thesaurus for English freely available for research purposes since about 1993. Created by George Miller and his team at Princeton University, WordNet (Miller 1990, Miller and Fellbaum 1991, Fellbaum 1998) is a large electronic database organized as a semantic network built on paradigmatic relations including synonymy, hyponymy, antonymy, and entailment. WordNet has become the most widely used lexical database today for NLP research, and its approach has now been ported to several other languages, such as the European languages in EuroWordNet (Vossen 1998) and in BalkaNet (Tufiş et al. 2004).

WordNet lists the different senses (called synonym sets, or synsets) for each English open-class word (nouns, verbs, adjectives, and adverbs). It groups 155,327 words into 117,597 synsets. So, from the viewpoint of WSD, since WordNet has an extensive coverage of the English language and is freely available for research purposes, it is a practical choice as the sense inventory required for large scale WSD evaluation. WordNet has undergone regular updates since its first release. The latest release version is WordNet 2.1, although most published WSD research uses earlier versions, in particular, WordNet 1.6 and 1.7. Wordnets for other languages are also used in WSD research, of course.

The creators of WordNet also annotated part of the Brown Corpus (Francis and Kučera 1982) with WordNet 1.6 senses. This sense-tagged portion of the Brown Corpus is known as Semcor (semantic concordance) (Miller et al. 1993). Of the 500 files that constitute the Brown Corpus, 186 files have all occurrences of their nouns, verbs, adjectives, and adverbs sense-tagged. An additional set of 166 Brown Corpus files has all verb occurrences sense-tagged. In all, more than 234,000 word occurrences have been tagged with senses from WordNet 1.6. Semcor could thus serve as an evaluation corpus for WSD research.

Unfortunately, Semcor by itself is too small for building robust corpus-based WSD programs. To date, the success of the corpus-based approach to NLP has relied on large annotated corpora so that supervised machine learning algorithms can learn the underlying linguistic regularity from the annotated corpora. Rapid progress in part-of-speech tagging and syntactic parsing was achieved due in part to the availability of large, manually annotated corpora such as the Penn Treebank (Marcus et al. 1993). Models learned from annotated corpora by supervised learning algorithms are able to achieve good performance on many NLP tasks, and compare favorably to performance obtained by the laboriously handcrafted rules of linguists (Manning and Schütze 1999).

Extrapolating to the task of WSD, a corpus-based approach would similarly require a large, manually sense-tagged corpus. Compared to part-of-speech tagging and syntactic parsing, WSD presents additional difficulties. Since each word is associated with its unique set of senses, supervised learning algorithms would require a substantial number of sense-tagged examples for each word of English. Specifically, while there are only 45 Penn Treebank part-of-speech tags for all of English, there are more than 75,000 polysemous WordNet sense tags for all English nouns, verbs, adjectives, and adverbs.

Since Semcor annotates running text, there are insufficient sense-tagged examples for each word of English. This "knowledge acquisition bottleneck" of insufficient training examples remains a critical impediment to further progress in WSD today (Ng 1997a) (see also Chap. 7 (Sects. 7.2.1 and 7.4.3)).

4.2.2 The Line and Interest Corpora

Initial research on the supervised learning approach to WSD performed evaluation on isolated words. Two notable early corpora are the *line-hard-serve* (Leacock et al. 1993, Mooney 1996) and *interest* (Bruce and Wiebe 1994) corpora.

The *line-hard-serve* corpus consists of about 4,000 sense-tagged examples of each of the words *line* (noun), *hard* (adjective), and *serve* (verb) with subsets of their WordNet 1.5 senses. Examples are drawn from the *Wall Street Journal*, the *American Printing House for the Blind*, and the *San Jose Mercury*. For instance, instances of *line* are given one of the following six senses:

line

1   A product: "a new line of workstations"
2   A formation of people or things: "stand in line"
3   Spoken or written text: "a line from Shakespeare"
4   A thin, flexible object; cord: "a nylon line"
5   An abstract division: "a line between good and evil"
6   A telephone connection: "the line went dead"

When trained on 1,200 training examples and tested on 894 test examples, accuracy above 70% was achieved using the Naïve Bayes and Perceptron algorithms (see Chap. 7 for details of the Naïve Bayes algorithm). For this corpus, since the six senses are evenly distributed in the training and test examples, the baseline accuracy (picking the most frequent sense) can be estimated as 17%.

The *interest* corpus consists of 2,369 sense-tagged examples of the noun *interest* in the following six senses:

interest

1   Readiness to give attention
2   Quality of causing attention to be given
3   Activity, subject, etc., which one gives time and attention to
4   Advantage, advancement, or favor
5   A share (in a company, business, etc.)
6   Money paid for the use of money

When trained on 1,769 training examples and tested on 600 test examples, accuracy of 78% was achieved by (Bruce and Wiebe 1994). For this corpus, picking the most frequent sense (which is sense 6) gives a baseline accuracy of 53%.

4.2.3 The DSO Corpus

Up until 1996, evaluation of WSD was still done on only a few or at most a dozen words, where each word only had two or perhaps a few senses. To test the scalability of the corpus-based approach to WSD, Ng and Lee (1996) collected a large sense-tagged corpus. This corpus included 192,800 occurrences of the most frequent nouns and verbs of English which had been manually sense-tagged with senses from WordNet. This corpus, known as the DSO corpus and subsequently available through the Linguistic Data Consortium, was almost two orders of magnitude larger in size than the above *line-hard-serve* or *interest* data sets. Manual tagging was done by university undergraduates majoring in linguistics, and approximately one man-year of effort was expended in tagging this corpus. These occurrences consisted of 121 nouns and 70 verbs that were the most frequently occurring and ambiguous words of English.

The 121 nouns were:

action activity age air area art board body book business car case center century change child church city class college community company condition cost country course day death development difference door effect effort end example experience face fact family field figure foot force form girl government ground head history home hour house information interest job land law level life light line man material matter member mind moment money month name nation need number order part party picture place plan point policy position power pressure problem process program public purpose question reason result right room school section sense service side society stage state step student study surface system table term thing time town type use value voice water way word work world

The 70 verbs were:

add appear ask become believe bring build call carry change come consider continue determine develop draw expect fall give go grow happen help hold indicate involve keep know lead leave lie like live look lose mean meet move need open pay raise read receive remember require return rise run see seem send set show sit speak stand start stop strike take talk tell think turn wait walk want work write

For this set of nouns and verbs, the average number of WordNet 1.5 senses per noun (verb) was 7.8 (12.0). The sentences containing these occurrences were drawn from the combined corpus of the 1 million words Brown Corpus and a 2.5 million words *Wall Street Journal* (WSJ) corpus. For every word type, up to 1,500 sentences (each sentence containing an

Table 4.1. Evaluation on DSO corpus.

Test set	Number of test examples	Baseline accuracy	WSD accuracy
BC50	7,119	47.1%	58.7%
WSJ6	14,139	63.7%	75.2%

occurrence of the word) were extracted from the combined corpus. In all, there were about 113,000 noun occurrences and about 79,800 verb occurrences. It was estimated that about 20% of all noun and verb occurrences in any unrestricted English text were one of these 191 words.

Two subsets were set aside for testing. The first, named BC50, consisted of occurrences of the 191 content words in 50 text files of the Brown Corpus, while the second test set, named WSJ6, consisted of occurrences of the 191 content words in 6 text files of the WSJ corpus. Empirical results reported by Ng and Lee (1996) and Ng (1997b) achieved by an exemplar-based learning algorithm are given in Table 4.1, as well as the baseline accuracy obtained by always picking the most frequent sense in the training set.

In contrast to Semcor, which assigned sense tags to all words in a running text and thus resulted in an insufficient number of training examples per word for a supervised learning approach, the DSO corpus focused on tagging the senses of a targeted set of words that occurred most frequently in an English text. The experiments carried out with the DSO corpus prompted the subsequent evaluation efforts of Senseval.

More sources of sense-tagged data are listed in Edmonds and Kilgarriff (2002).

4.2.4 Open Mind Word Expert

The Open Mind Word Expert project (OMWE) (Chklovski and Mihalcea 2002) is gathering a sense-tagged corpus by enticing regular Web users to participate in a "game" to disambiguate words in context. The effort has so far resulted in a fair amount of data being produced (70,000 examples of 230 words annotated with WordNet 1.7 senses (Edmonds and Kilgariff 2002)), however quality control is an issue since Web users are novices at the task compared to the linguistically trained annotators of previous tagging efforts (Semcor, DSO, and Senseval). The inter-annotator agreement is somewhat lower than that attained by more traditional methods, but was computed somewhat differently: 67% (Mihalcea et al. 2004) versus 85.5% in Senseval-2 (Kilgarriff 2001). Part of the OMWE corpus was used in

Senseval-3 (see Sect. 4.7 below). Chapter 9 (Sect. 9.3.5) discusses OMWE further.

4.3 Evaluation Using Pseudo-Words

Before there was enough sense-tagged data for evaluation, researchers nevertheless needed a way to evaluate their WSD systems. Yarowsky (1993) reported on a method to automatically evaluate WSD systems that used *pseudo-words*, artificial sense ambiguities introduced into a corpus by taking two words with the same part of speech (e.g., *guerilla* and *reptile*) and replacing each of their occurrences in the corpus with an ambiguous word (*guerilla/reptile*). A WSD system can either be trained on the modified corpus, or have its disambiguation rules modified to reflect the new lexicon. Evaluation is obviously trivial. Although the method has been used by others (e.g., Schütze (1998)), it has been criticized because it creates a simulated test bed that does not reflect real sense ambiguity. For instance, Sanderson (1994) remarks that the various senses of a pseudo-word are not related in the same way that real senses are related, especially for polysemous words. Thus, pseudo-words might be effective only for homograph-level distinctions.

4.4 Senseval Evaluation Exercises

The Senseval enterprise[2] is the first open, community-based evaluation exercise for word sense disambiguation. Started in 1997 following a workshop, *Tagging Text with Lexical Semantics: Why, What, and How?* (Palmer and Light 1999), it is run by a small elected committee under the auspices of ACL-SIGLEX (the Association for Computational Linguistics' Special Interest Group on the Lexicon). It uses a DARPA-style evaluation format where the participants are provided with hand-annotated training data and test data and a pre-defined metric for evaluation. Unlike true DARPA evaluations, Senseval is a more grassroots exercise, self-initiated by the WSD researchers. More than just a bake-off of automatic WSD systems, its underlying goal is to further the understanding of lexical semantics and polysemy.

---

[2] http://www.senseval.org

Senseval has now had three competitions. We discuss Senseval-1 and Senseval-2 below, and leave Senseval-3 to Section 4.7 after we have discussed some of the theoretical implications that such evaluations have brought to light (e.g., the difficulty of sense-tagging and sense granularity).

4.4.1 Senseval-1

Senseval-1 (Kilgarriff 1998, Kilgarriff and Palmer 2000), the first evaluation exercise in automatic WSD for English, took place in 1998.[3] The lexical inventory was the Hector lexicon (Atkins 1993), developed jointly by DEC and Oxford University Press using a corpus-based approach and traditional hierarchical dictionary entries (Kilgarriff and Rosenzweig 2000), such as the following entry:

> **bother** *intransitive verb* **1** (make an effort), after negation, usually with to infinitive; (of a person) to take the trouble or effort needed (to do something). Ex. *About 70 percent of the shareholders did not bother to vote at all.* **1.1** (can't be bothered), idiomatic, be unwilling to make the effort needed (to do something). Ex. *The calculations needed are so tedious that theorists cannot be bothered to do them.*

Thirty-four words were selected using a stratified random sample taken from the lexicon, with sub-samples for part of speech (noun, verb, and adjective), frequency, and number of senses:

> *accident amaze band behavior bet bitter bother brilliant bury calculate consume deaf derive disability excess float/floating generous giant hurdle invade knee modest onion promise rabbit sack sanction scrap seize shake shirt slight steering wooden*

After selecting the target lexical items, professional lexicographers tagged sentences containing those items that had been extracted from the Hector corpus (a pilot for the British National Corpus). By allowing for discussion and revision of confusing lexical entries before the final test data was tagged, inter-annotator agreement of over 80% was eventually achieved; replicability for four words (*generous, onion, sack, shake*) was

---

[3] Romanseval, an evaluation for French and Italian, was run in parallel (Segond 2000; Calzolari and Corazzari 2000). The French and Italian sense inventories (*Petit Larousse* and *Dizionario Garzanti di Italiano*, respectively) were traditional dictionaries that were more encyclopedic than corpus-based.

95.5%. Twenty-four systems participated in the exercise, including both supervised and unsupervised systems.

Evaluation and Scoring

The evaluation scheme followed Melamed and Resnik's (2000) proposal, which provides a scoring method for exact matches to fine-grained senses as well as one for partial matches at a more coarse-grained level. Several simple baseline algorithms were run, including RANDOM, COMMONEST, LESK, LESK-DEFINITION, and LESK-CORPUS (Kilgarriff and Rosenzweig 2000). RANDOM gave equal weight to all sense tags for the word. COMMONEST always selected the most frequent sense appearing in the training data for the word. LESK used a simplification of Lesk's (1986) strategy of choosing the sense whose dictionary definition and example sentences had the most words in common with the word to be disambiguated (see Chap. 5 (Sect. 5.2)). LESK-DEFINITION and LESK-CORPUS were like LESK, but only considered the words in the sense definition or in the training instances with that sense, respectively.

In the end, the choice of evaluation metric made little difference in the relative rankings of the systems. The best scoring system achieved a fine-grained accuracy of 77.1% and a coarse-grained accuracy of 81.4%. In general, the lower the system performance, the larger the gap between the fine-grained and coarse-grained scores. The highest fine-grained score on just the verbs, which had an average polysemy of 7.79, was 70.5%. In the graph of the results, the best system's performance was indistinguishable from that of the best baseline (LESK-CORPUS) (Kilgarriff and Rosenzweig 2000).

4.4.2 Senseval-2

The Senseval-1 workshop provided convincing evidence that automatic systems can perform WSD satisfactorily, given clear, consistent sense distinctions and suitable training data. However, the Hector lexicon was very small and under proprietary constraints, and the question remained whether it was possible to have a publicly available, broad-coverage lexical resource for English and other languages, with the requisite clear, consistent sense distinctions.

Subsequently, the Senseval-2 (Edmonds and Cotton 2001) exercise was run, which included WSD tasks for 10 languages.[4] A concerted effort was made to use existing WordNets as sense inventories because of their widespread popularity and availability. Some languages included only the lexical sample task, some had only the all-words task, and some included both. Notably, the Japanese task included a lexical sample task in which the sense inventory was defined by translations of Japanese into English, so that only those sense distinctions which surfaced as different translations would be made. Most languages had either just the lexical sample task or just the all-words task, but English included both. We present the English tasks as illustrative of the evaluation exercises.

English All-Words Task

The English all-words task involved 5,000 words of running text consisting of three Penn Treebank II articles (Palmer et al. 2001) representing different genres. Annotators preparing the data were allowed to indicate at most one multi-word construction for each content word to be tagged, but could give multiple senses for the construction. The annotation was done under a double-blind scheme by two linguistics students, and was then adjudicated and corrected by a different person. Task participants were given only the test data, so participating systems were either unsupervised rule-based systems or supervised systems trained on a different annotated corpus (e.g., Semcor, and example sentences in the dictionary definition). A baseline strategy that simply tagged each headword with the first WordNet sense for the corresponding Treebank part-of-speech tag had a score of 57%, as compared to the best system score of 69% (from Southern Methodist University). An upper bound based on inter-annotator agreement was estimated to be 80%.

English Lexical Sample Task

The English lexical sample task for Senseval-2 was the result of a collaboration between the University of Pennsylvania, which provided training/test data for the verbs, and the University of Brighton, which provided the training/test data for the nouns and adjectives (Kilgarriff 2001, Palmer

---

[4] The originally planned languages were Basque, Chinese, Czech, Danish, Dutch, English, Estonian, Italian, Japanese, Korean, Spanish, and Swedish. However, the Chinese and Danish tasks were not prepared in time for the competition, and Dutch had no participants.

et al. 2001). A total of 73 nouns, adjectives, and verbs were chosen from WordNet 1.7, and between 75 and 300 instances of each were hand-tagged, depending on the number of senses. The data came primarily from the Penn Treebank II *Wall Street Journal* corpus, but was supplemented with data from the British National Corpus whenever there was an insufficient number of Treebank instances. The instances for each verb were partitioned into training/test data using a ratio of 2:1; as mentioned above, this low ratio of training/test data was intended to give a more realistic indication of a system's performance (since more varied contexts per word would be tested) and to level the playing field between supervised and unsupervised systems.

The most polysemous words are typically verbs, so they will remain the focus for the rest of the chapter. Twenty-nine of the most polysemous verbs (an average polysemy of 16.28 senses using the pre-release version of WordNet 1.7) from the all-words task were chosen for the lexical sample task. Double-blind annotation by two linguistically trained annotators was performed on corpus instances, with a third linguist adjudicating between inter-annotator differences to create the gold standard. Most of the revisions of sense definitions in WordNet 1.7 were done by the adjudicator prior to the bulk of the tagging, although there was much less discussion among the taggers of how senses were to be applied than there had been with the Senseval-1 taggers. The average inter-annotator agreement rate achieved with these verb senses was 71%,[5] which is lower than in Senseval-1 but similar to the 73% agreement for all words for Semcor, which had a much lower average polysemy. (Note that nouns and adjectives had an inter-annotator agreement of 85.5%).

WordNet does not offer the same type of hierarchical entry that Hector does, so the verbs were also grouped by two or more people, with differences being reconciled, and the sense groups were used for coarse-grained scoring of the systems. These groups and their utility for addressing common sources of inter-annotator disagreement will be discussed in Section

---

[5] We do not include Cohen's kappa coefficient because the standard formulation of kappa doesn't address our situation where multiple tags are allowed for each instance. Although there were relatively few multiply tagged instances in the gold standard (84 out of over 5,000 instances), in the raw human annotator data there are substantially more. We also find that inter-annotator agreement is sufficient for the comparisons that we wish to make between system and human performance, and between Senseval-1 and Senseval-2.

4.6. Using the grouped senses the inter-annotator agreement figures rose to 82%.

For system comparisons the same simple baseline algorithms that were used for Senseval-1, described above, were applied in Senseval-2. In contrast to Senseval-1, in which none of the competing systems performed significantly better than the highest baseline, this time most of the systems performed well against the highest baseline (LESK-CORPUS, at 45.5%), with approximately half performing better, and the top system achieving 57.6% (Palmer et al. 2001) for the verbs lexical sample task (see Table 1.2 in Chap. 1 for the Senseval-2 results). For the entire lexical sample task, the highest system scores (from Johns Hopkins University) were 64.2% (fine-grained) and 71.3% (coarse-grained). In general the nouns and adjectives had lower polysemy and higher inter-annotator agreement and system scores (polysemy 4.9; 85.5% inter-annotator agreement; 64% fine-grained system score; see Yarowsky et al. (2001)). For the most part the lexical sample tasks in other languages were similar, with the results somewhere in the 60s or low 70s. It is very difficult, however, to do any true cross-language comparison without first doing a detailed comparison of the sense inventories. Are the distinctions fine-grained or coarse-grained? Do the criteria for distinguishing senses tend to be syntactic or semantic, and how clearly are they spelled out?

4.4.3 Comparison of Tagging Exercises

Since the first two Senseval evaluation exercises used different sense inventories, they provide an opportunity to study the impact of different sense inventories on system performance and inter-annotator agreement. Prior to the Senseval-2 exercise, there were concerns expressed about whether or not WordNet had the requisite clear and consistent sense distinctions. Both inter-annotator agreement and system performance in Senseval-2 were lower than in Senseval-1, which seemingly substantiates these concerns. However, one must bear in mind the highly polysemous nature of the verbs, which are on average twice as polysemous as the Senseval-1 verbs, an average polysemy of 16.28 compared to 7.79.[6] High polysemy has a detrimental effect on both manual and automatic tagging, although it does not correlate inversely with system performance as closely

---

[6] Overall polysemy for Senseval-1 is 10.7.

as high entropy[7] does (Palmer et al. 2001). There were also generally less training data made available to the systems; ignoring outliers, there were on average half as many training samples for each verb in Senseval-2 as there were in Senseval-1. A comparison of system performance on words of similar polysemy in Senseval-1 and Senseval-2 showed very little difference in accuracy (Palmer et al. 2006). When controlling for polysemy, even with different amounts of training instances, Senseval-2 data gives rise to very similar system performance as Senseval-1 data. Hence, we conclude that the lower system performance overall on Senseval-2 is due to the higher average polysemy and entropy of the verbs in the task. We can assume that, in spite of the lower inter-annotator agreement figures for Senseval-2, the double-blind annotation and adjudication provided a reliable enough filter to ensure consistently tagged data with WordNet senses, and the smaller set of training examples was not a major factor.

In the next section, we will first examine the nature of sense distinctions, and the sources of sense tagging disagreements. We then present the criteria for creating sense groups, and discuss the impact these groups have on the inter-annotator disagreements for the highly polysemous Senseval-2 verbs.

4.5 Sources of Inter-Annotator Disagreement

The difficulty of achieving accurate sense-tagged data has been thoroughly attested to in the literature (Kilgarriff 1997; Hanks 2000). A mapping between Hector and WordNet 1.6 that was made available for Senseval-1 provides striking evidence of the different choices lexicographers can make in determining sense distinctions. It is immediately apparent that Hector and WordNet often have different numbers of senses for the same lemma. Closer examination of individual words such as *shake* reveals even

---

[7] Entropy is the measure of disorder in a system. In terms of information theory, it gives us the average amount of information in bits in some attribute of an instance. This can be captured as $-\log_2(p)$, the amount of information in bits associated with an event of probability p. If there are several possible events (several possible sense tags), the number of bits for each outcome is multiplied by its p and summed over all of the outcomes. A word that has almost all of its instances tagged with its most frequent sense (so, for example, p for that sense is 0.8 or higher, whereas the p for the other senses is very low) has a very low entropy, that is, it is considered to be an orderly, predictable system.

more fundamental mismatches. They each have the same number of main senses (8). However, there is variation in the verb-particle constructions they have chosen to include. For instance, Hector includes verb and noun senses for *shake down* and *shake out*, while WordNet only has the noun senses. The result is that Hector has 27 total senses while WordNet has only 15. They also make different decisions as to which criteria to use to differentiate between senses. These distinctions can all be seen as valid choices, but they carve the available space up in very different ways.

In this section we examine more closely the rates of inter-annotator agreement (ITA) on manual sense-tagging. We focus on verbs, which tend to have the lowest ITA scores. In Senseval-2, the ITA ranged from the low scores of 28.8% (*train*) and 44.3% (*find*) to high scores of 90.8% (*serve*) and 86.5% (*dress*). For each of several of the verbs, including *develop*, a subset of 50 sentences distributed as evenly as possible among the different possible senses (in the gold standard) was chosen and tagged again by two annotators, and the disagreements were carefully examined. There are at least four different clear sources of annotator errors: sense subsumption, missing or insufficient dictionary entries, vague usages, and world knowledge (Fellbaum et al. 2001).

Sense Subsumption. There were several disagreements on *develop* which stemmed from the choice between a more general or a more specific entry, well-known among lexicographers as "lumping" versus "splitting" (Fellbaum et al. 2005). Two easily confused *develop* senses involve the creation of new entities, characterized as either "products, or mental or artistic creations" (Sense 1, physical creation) or "a new theory of evolution" (Sense 2, created by mental act). Three of the *develop* disagreements (25%) involved determining which of these two senses should be applied to phrases like *develop a better way to introduce crystallography techniques*. Either definition could fit; it's merely a question of determining among the annotators ahead of time whether *ways* should be treated as things or theories. Since Sense 1 specifically mentions *mental creations* in addition to other types of creations, it can be seen as a more general definition which could *subsume* Sense 2. These more general senses, when present, provide the requisite flexibility for encompassing new usages, another sense-tagging challenge.

Missing or Insufficient Dictionary Entries. Other disagreements are introduced because the sense inventory against which an annotator is annotating may have gaps or redundancies. The glosses may also have ambiguous wordings or contradictory examples. Even if the annotator is working with an extremely clear, extensive entry, it may not cover novel or unusual usages, or domain-specific ones. For instance, WordNet 1.7 did not have a domain-specific sense of *develop* to handle the real-estate sense of *developing land*. The annotators agreed on the meaning of these verb tokens when they appeared, but used different strategies to stretch the pre-existing sense inventory to fit this usage, hesitating between two senses. Sometimes, in fact, one annotator would double-tag a particular instance while the second annotator chose a single sense that matched one of the two selected by the first annotator. Two of the *develop* disagreements (16.7%) involved deciding whether or not *understanding* (as in *develop a much better understanding of ...*) constituted an attribute (Sense 3) or a physical characteristic (Sense 4). In this case neither of the pre-existing senses is general enough to subsume the other.

Vague Contexts. There are sentences where an author intentionally invokes a rich representation of a word that includes two or more related senses. Puns are classic examples of this, but there are more subtle uses of multiple meanings. For instance, *onion* (Senseval-1) typically has a food sense and a plant sense, and in a phrase such as *planting, harvesting and marketing onions* both are invoked (Krishnamurthy and Nicholls 2000). In an instance of *play* (Senseval-2), *he played superbly*, it was clear from the context that music was being played, but did the author intend to praise the playing of the instrument (Sense 3) or the melody (Sense 6) or both?

World Knowledge. Perhaps the most intractable tagging issues arise when the meaning of a word in a particular context depends not only on its syntactic use or the semantics of its arguments, but on world knowledge. For instance, the final seven of the *develop* disagreements (58%) all pertained to a single group. Three of the sentences involved the development of *cancer tumors*. Do cancer tumors originate spontaneously, as would a religious movement (Sense 5), or are they more like a flower, a product of natural growth and evolution (Sense 10)? This choice involves a depth of medical knowledge which few doctors would claim, and in such a case tagging with a more coarse-grained sense that subsumes both senses offers a wiser choice.

The twelve *develop* errors that could be categorized into these four types were also reconciled by the Senseval-2 groups (see Table 4.3, in Sect. 4.6 below). Measured against the gold standard, the fine-grained score on *develop* was 66% (33 correct tags) while the coarse-grained score rose to 90%. In general the ITA scores rose between 10% and 20% when measured against the grouped senses, resulting in an average ITA of 82% for coarse-grained senses versus 71.3% for fine-grained senses. The improvement in ITA using the groupings did not come simply from the lower number of tag choices for each verb, because when the senses for each verb were randomly distributed into the same number of groups, ITA rose to only 74%.

Differences in annotator choices often involve subtle semantic distinctions between senses where one sense might be slightly more specific or more applicable (in the case of a gap) than the other. Extremely high ITA with highly polysemous words is an unrealistic goal, given the inherent difficulty in attaining a consensus on word meaning and the changeable nature of language. Since a semantic grouping of senses with similar meanings puts the most easily confused senses in the same group, the annotator disagreements can often be reconciled by evaluating with the groups instead of the more fine-grained senses. Equally valuable is the opportunity to treat the group as a more underspecified sense in itself, for new usages that do not exactly fit a pre-existing sense. These benefits however, could be outweighed by the drawback of losing important distinctions, no matter how subtle they are.

4.6 Granularity of Sense: Groupings for WordNet

We begin by introducing the criteria for creating the Senseval-2 verb groups, which led to significant revisions of pre-existing WordNet groups, and discuss the factors behind their success. There are situations where, rather than trying to force an exact match with a fine-grained sense, it may be more prudent to equivocate by choosing a less-specific cluster of senses. Coarser-grained sense distinctions can sometimes alleviate the difficulties involved in mapping between sense inventories, as well as reconcile inter-annotator disagreements (Palmer et al. 2000b).

One of the main differences between WordNet and a standard dictionary is the lack of a hierarchical organization for the distinct senses of an entry. They are all simply listed sequentially. WordNet supplies a wealth of inheritance information via hypernyms and synonym sets. However, these do not lend themselves readily to forming natural sense hierarchies, and have not been especially beneficial for evaluating automatic WSD systems at a coarse-grained level (Lin 1998; Mihalcea and Moldovan 2001). The variation in hypernyms that occur in most of the Senseval-2 groups provides evidence for why automatic grouping by hypernyms has not been more successful. For example, group 4 of *play* involves three WordNet senses which all involve producing music from musical instruments, as shown in Table 4.2. In spite of the semantic similarity of these senses each one has a different WordNet hypernym, highlighting subtle distinctions in emphasis.

Table 4.2. Senseval-2 group 4 for WordNet 1.7 *play*.

Sense	WordNet gloss	Hypernym
3	Play (music) on an instrument	*perform*
6	Play a melody	*recreate*
7	Perform music (on a musical instrument)	*sound*

WordNet also has a distinct entry for each syntactic use of a verb, so the two variants involved in a standard causative/inchoative alternation such as *John broke the window/The window broke* will each have different senses.

4.6.1 Criteria for WordNet Sense Grouping

WordNet 1.6 had groupings that were limited to linking together certain pairs of syntactic frames, such as the causative/inchoative alternations mentioned above. These existing WordNet 1.6 groupings were substantially revised and augmented for WordNet 1.7. This was done after the tagging had already been completed, so the annotators did not annotate with the groups. The groups were simply used as a scoring device. Coarse-grained sense distinctions are only slightly easier to define than fine-grained ones, and there are often cases where a sense appropriately belongs to more than one group. However, the simplest possible style of grouping was chosen, allowing for no overlaps between groups. The groupings were made without reference to any corpus instances and by annotators who had not annotated that particular word. The confusion matrices for the ITA were not used, so the grouping was done without any reference to annotator discrepancies. The senses for each lemma were grouped independently by two separate annotators, following specific syntactic and semantic criteria. Discrepancies in the groupings were discussed and then adjudicated by a third annotator (Fellbaum et al. 2001). In contrast to hierarchical dictionary entries, this approach has a distinctly bottom-up, self-organizing flavor, and varies quite a bit from verb to verb.

Syntactic criteria. Syntactic structure performed two distinct functions in the groupings. Syntax is often considered a mirror of the underlying semantics, and major differences in subcategorization frames for the same verb can reflect correspondingly major differences in meaning (e.g., *John left the room* vs. *Mary left her daughter-in-law her pearls in her will*). When this is the case, the two senses belong to different groups, and applying a coarse syntactic filter to a verb's usages can be the simplest way to quickly capture the underlying sense distinction. On the other hand, recognizable alternations

with similar corresponding predicate-argument structureswere often a factor in choosing to group senses together, as in the Levin (1993) classes,
where the changes in meaning can be very slight. The groupings that were
determined by this criterion had the most overlap with the previous groupings from WordNet 1.6. The pre-existing WordNet 1.6 groups only affected
3.5% of the senses of the Senseval-2 verbs, and had no impact on system
performance or reconciliation of inter-annotator agreements.

Semantic criteria. Clear semantic criteria for groupings are even more
variable. Senses were grouped together if they were more specialized versions of a general sense. The criteria for putting senses into separate
groups included differences in semantic classes of arguments (abstract versus concrete, animal versus human, animacy versus inanimacy, different
instrument types, and so on), differences in the number and type of arguments (often reflected in the subcategorization frame as discussed above),
differences in entailments (whether an argument refers to a created entity
or a resultant state), differences in the type of event (abstract, concrete,
mental, emotional, and so on), whether there is a specialized subject domain,
and so on. Table 4.3 illustrates the four primary groups for *develop*, leaving
out three more domain-specific groups having to do with chess, film, and
mathematics.

4.6.2 Analysis of Sense Grouping

Senseval-2 inter-annotator agreement on WordNet 1.7 verb sense tags
improved significantly when evaluated against the groups, from 71.3% to
82%, as mentioned above. Since the data had already been tagged, this
evaluation simply involved a change in scoring. If the annotators had chosen two different senses that were in the same group, they were evaluated
as matching. If they were in two different groups, they did not match. As a
baseline, to ensure that the improvement in inter-annotator agreement using
the groups did not come simply from the lower number of tag choices for
each verb, random groupings were created in which each verb had the
same number of groups, but with the senses distributed randomly. These
random groups provided almost no benefit to the inter-annotator agreement
figures (74% instead of 71%), confirming the greater coherence of the
manual groupings. The original WordNet 1.6 groups reduced the polysemy
of the same verbs from 14 to 13.5, and had even less effect on performance. In subsequent studies annotators have been given the grouped senses

Table 4.3. The four primary Senseval-2 groups for WordNet 1.7 *develop.*

Group	Sense	WordNet gloss	Hypernym
1 – New (abstract)	1	Products, or mental creations	*Create*
	2	Mental creations: "new theory"	*Create*
2 – New (property)	3	Personal attribute: "a passion for …"	*Change*
	4	Physical characteristic: "a beard"	*Change*
3 – New (self)	5	Originate: "new religious movement"	*Become*
	9	Gradually unfold: "the plot …"	*Occur*
	10	Grow: "a flower developed …"	*Grow*
	14	Mature: "The child developed …"	*Change*
	20	Happen: "report the news as it …"	*Occur*
4 – Improve item	6	Resources: "natural resources"	*Improve*
	7	Ideas: "ideas in your thesis"	*Theorize*
	8	Train animate beings: "violinists"	*Teach*
	11	Civilize: "developing countries"	*Change*
	12	Make, grow: "develop the grain"	*Change*
	13	Business: "develop the market"	*Generate*
	19	Music: "develop the melody"	*Complicate*

for tagging, and the ITA goes up to 89%, and the tagging speed is almost quadrupled (Weischedel and Palmer 2004). The groupings have an intuitive appeal; a reader can readily appreciate the semantic coherence of the senses. However, if too much information is being lost by failing to make the more fine-grained distinctions, the groups will avail us little. It remains to be seen whether or not the groupings can be effective in NLP applications.

4.7 Senseval-3

The most recent Senseval, Senseval-3 (Mihalcea and Edmonds 2004), was held in Barcelona, Spain in conjunction with ACL-2004. The scope of the evaluation expanded yet again, this time including 14 different tasks and 55 participating teams with 160 systems. The English all-words and lexical sample tasks had over 47 and 26 submissions each, respectively (Mihalcea et al. 2004; Snyder and Palmer 2004). The traditional sense-tagging tasks followed the established Senseval-2 protocols; the new semantic annotation tasks involved semantic role labeling based on FrameNet (Baker et al. 2003) and for logical form annotation; there was also a task for disambiguating

WordNet glosses. The results are shown in Table 1.3 (Chap. 1). One major difference was that the English lexical sample task tried to avoid the expensive overhead of using linguistically trained annotators by making use of the OMWE project (Chklovski and Mihalcea 2002), as mentioned in Section 4.2.4 above. A portion of the OMWE data comprising about 12,000 tagged examples of 59 words was used. The inter-annotator agreement on this portion was somewhat lower than that attained by more traditional methods: 67% (Mihalcea et al. 2004) versus 85.5% in Senseval-2 (Kilgarriff 2001). The lower ITA may be accounted for by the fact that the tagging was done by novice Web users and not linguistically trained annotators. However, that does not explain the surprisingly high system performance of up to 72%. Chapter 9 (Sect. 9.3.5) discusses OMWE further.

Many new WSD techniques were described at the workshop; supervised machine learning approaches that aggregate a range of features, such as Support Vector Machines (SVMs), achieved the best performance. However, on the whole, system performance is still tied to inter-annotator agreement, which is in turn tied to the quality of the sense inventory; when this is low, system performance follows suit.

Much interest was generated by two panel discussions, one on planning for future Sensevals and another focusing on potential uses of WSD in natural-language applications. There was a general consensus that the traditional *in vitro* task had reached a plateau, and was not likely to lead to fundamentally new research, but many still liked the task because of its clear definition. Applications promise to play a larger role in Senseval-4: possibilities discussed included WSD as lexical selection in machine translation, and WSD as sense equivalence in an IR or paraphrasing framework (see Chap. 11 for more information on applications of WSD).

4.8 Discussion

This chapter has discussed the data preparation for the evaluation of automatic WSD systems. The successful Senseval program has developed common evaluation metrics and hand-tagging annotation methodologies, which are now widely accepted as being appropriate for *in vitro* word sense disambiguation evaluation. Explicit WSD to a fixed sense inventory is a robust task: The three evaluation exercises run by Senseval show that over a variety of word types, frequencies, and sense distributions, systems are achieving consistent and respectable accuracy levels that are approaching human performance on the task.

However, there are still several open issues. One of the most important factors in evaluation has been the choice of sense inventory, which affects the consistency with which sense distinctions can be made by humans (and hence automatic systems), and which can be largely dependent on the final application of the WSD subtask. Although there are questions about whether or not it provides an appropriate level of granularity, WordNet has emerged as the most likely candidate for any large-scale evaluation, primarily because it has a broad coverage, it is in the public domain, and much effort has gone into linking it to WordNets of other languages.

This highlights the relevance of achieving a more coarse-grained view of WordNet verb senses through manual groupings of these senses. In examining the instances that proved troublesome to the human annotators, we have discussed in this chapter several categories of errors that were tied to subtle sense distinctions which were reconciled by backing off to the more coarse-grained sense groups. These categories include different perspectives on sense subsumption, insufficient sense entries, vague contexts, or inadequate world knowledge.

Lexicographers have long recognized that many natural occurrences of polysemous words are embedded in underspecified contexts and could correspond to more than one specific sense. There will also always be gaps in inventories and available world knowledge. In such cases both manual and automatic tagging discrepancies are inevitable. Annotators and automatic systems need the option of selecting, as an alternative to an explicit sense, either a group of specific senses or a single, broader sense, where specific meaning nuances are subsumed (Palmer 1990; Pustejovsky 1991). Although present to some degree in the hierarchical entries of traditional dictionaries, these have previously played only a small role in WordNet. The verb groupings presented here represent a step in the direction of making WordNet more effective in computational applications.

Another open question remains as to whether or not significantly more training instances would benefit high polysemy verbs. Although additional data has proven useful for Chinese sense tagging (Dang et al. 2002), enlarging the Senseval-2 training set by 30–40% for the English verbs by using a 9:1 partition instead of 2:1, and using 10-fold cross-validation, improved system scores by only 1.9%. Also, the *interest* and *line* corpora had an order of magnitude greater number of examples, but did not give rise to significantly higher performance. Further experimentation is needed to determine the impact of additional training data. Yarowsky and Florian (2002) found a significant drop in performance with smaller training sets. Ng (1997a) found that increasing the size of the training data set improves

WSD accuracy on the DSO corpus (see also Chap. 7 (Sect. 7.3.2 and Table 7.3)).

Another area for exploration is measuring the impact of WSD on the performance of applications. Up to this point in time, evaluation of WSD has focused on *in vitro* evaluation, determining the correct sense of a word in context when the sense is chosen from a fixed list according to some dictionary. As such, WSD is treated as a separate subtask divorced from any application, much like part-of-speech tagging and syntactic parsing. While such an evaluation has the advantage that we are focused on the performance of the WSD subtask, it is subject to the criticism that the utility of WSD is not measured directly, in terms of improvements brought about by WSD to the performance of an application in which WSD is embedded.

To address this concern, Senseval would do well to include an *in vivo* application-oriented evaluation task, in addition to the current lexical sample task and the all-words task, in future evaluations. One possible application is machine translation (MT), where applying WSD would correspond to improved lexical choice, i.e., selecting better words in the target language as translations of words in the source language. As MT appears to be an NLP application that would directly benefit from improved WSD, it would be good to quantify such improvements, making it clear that WSD can make a difference. Preliminary versions of such tasks were run at Senseval-2 (Japanese) and Senseval-3 (Hindi). A multilingual lexical sample task where the "correct" tags are determined by different translations in a second language is also a potential application-oriented task. The training data in such a task could be obtained by automatic alignment of parallel texts, as was done by Ng et al. (2003) in using Chinese-English parallel texts to obtain training data for word sense disambiguation. Chapter 9 (Sect. 9.3.4) elaborates on this approach.

In summary, much progress has been made on the task of regularizing the evaluation of word sense disambiguation systems, but much work remains to be done. There are still issues around the choice of the sense inventory being used for evaluation, especially for English. An equally important future goal is a clear demonstration of the positive impact of WSD on the performance of NLP applications, and plans are underway to include that in Senseval-4.

References

Atkins, Sue. 1993. Tools for computer-aided corpus lexicography: The Hector project. *Acta Linguistica Hungarica*, 41: 5–72.

Baker, Collin F., Charles J. Fillmore & Beau Cronin. 2003. The structure of the FrameNet database. *International Journal of Lexicography*, 16(3): 281–296.

Bruce, Rebecca & Janyce Wiebe. 1994. Word-sense disambiguation using decomposable models. *Proceedings of the 32nd Annual Meeting of the Association for Computational Linguistics*, Las Cruces, New Mexico, 139–145.

Bruce, Rebecca & Janyce Wiebe. 1999. Recognizing subjectivity: A case study in manual tagging. *Natural Language Engineering*, 5(2): 187–205.

Calzolari, Nicoletta & Ornella Corazzari. 2000. Senseval/Romanseval: The framework for Italian. *Computers and the Humanities*, 34(1-2): 61–78.

Chklovski, Timothy & Rada Mihalcea. 2002. Building a sense tagged corpus with Open Mind Word Expert. *Proceedings of the workshop on word sense disambiguation: Recent successes and future directions*, Philadelphia, PA, USA, 116–122.

Cohen, J. 1960. A coefficient of agreement for nominal scales. *Educational and Psychological Measurement*, 20: 37–46.

Dang, Hoa Trang, Ching-yi Chia, Fu-Dong Chiou & Martha Palmer. 2002. Simple features for Chinese word sense disambiguation. *Proceedings of the 19th International Conference on Computational Linguistics (COLING-2002)*, Taipei, Taiwan.

Edmonds, Philip & Scott Cotton. 2001. Senseval-2: Overview. *Proceedings of Senseval-2: Second International Workshop on Evaluating Word Sense Disambiguation Systems*, Toulouse, France, 1–5.

Edmonds, Philip & Adam Kilgarriff. 2002. Introduction to the special issue on evaluating word sense disambiguation systems. *Natural Language Engineering*, 8(4): 279–291.

Fellbaum, Christiane, ed. 1998. *WordNet: An Electronic Lexical Database*. Cambridge, MA: MIT Press.

Fellbaum, Christiane, Martha Palmer, Hoa Trang Dang, Lauren Delfs & Susanne Wolf. 2001. Manual and automatic semantic annotation with WordNet. *Proceedings of the Workshop on WordNet and Other Lexical Resources*, Pittsburgh, PA.

Fellbaum, Christiane, Lauren Delfs, Susanne Wolf & Martha Palmer. 2005. Word meaning in dictionaries, corpora, and the speaker's mind. *Meaningful Texts: The Extraction of Semantic Information from Monolingual and Multilingual Corpora* ed. by Geoff Barnbrook, Pernilla Danielsson & Michaela Mahlberg. London: Continuum.

Francis, W. Nelson & Henry Kučera. 1982. *Frequency Analysis of English Usage: Lexicon and Grammar.* Boston, MA: Houghton Mifflin.

Gale, William, Kenneth Ward Church & David Yarowsky. 1992. Estimating upper and lower bounds on the performance of word-sense disambiguation programs. *Proceedings of the 30th Annual Meeting of the Association for Computational Linguistics*, 249–256.

Hanks, Patrick. 2000. Do word meanings exist? *Computers and the Humanities*, 34(1–2): 205–215.

Ide, Nancy & Jean Véronis. 1998. Introduction to the special issue on word sense disambiguation. *Computational Linguistics*, 24(1): 1–40.

Kilgarriff, Adam. 1997. "I don't believe in word senses". *Computers and the Humanities*, 31(2): 91–113.

Kilgarriff, Adam. 1998. Senseval: An exercise in evaluating word sense disambiguation programs. *Proceedings of the European Conference on Lexicography (EURALEX)*, 176–174, Liège, Belgium. Also in *Proceedings of the 1st Conference on Language Resources and Evaluation (LREC)*, Granada, Spain, 581–588.

Kilgarriff, Adam & Martha Palmer. 2000. Introduction to the special issue on Senseval. *Computers and the Humanities*, 34(1–2): 1–13.

Kilgarriff, Adam & Joseph Rosenzweig. 2000. Framework and results for English SENSEVAL. *Computers and the Humanities*, 34(1–2): 15–48.

Kilgarriff, Adam. 2001. English lexical sample task description. *Proceedings of Senseval-2: Second International Workshop on Evaluating Word Sense Disambiguation Systems*, Toulouse, France, 17–20.

Krishnamurthy, Ramesh & Diane Nicholls. 2000. Peeling an onion: The lexicographer's experience of manual sense-tagging. *Computers and the Humanities*, 34(1–2): 85–97.

Leacock, Claudia, Geoffrey Towell & Ellen Voorhees. 1993. Corpus-based statistical sense resolution. *Proceedings of the ARPA Human Language Technology Workshop*, 260–265.

Lesk, Michael. 1986. Automatic sense disambiguation: How to tell a pine cone from an ice cream cone. *Proceedings of SIGDOC-86: 5th International Conference on Systems Documentation*, Toronto, Canada, 24–26.

Levin, Beth. 1993. *English Verb Classes and Alternations: A Preliminary Investigation.* Chicago: University of Chicago Press.

Lin, Dekang. 1998. Automatic retrieval and clustering of similar words. *Proceedings of the 17th International Conference on Computational Linguistics (COLING-ACL-98). Montreal, Canada,* 768–774.

Manning, Christopher D. & Hinrich Schütze. 1999. *Foundations of Statistical Natural Language Processing.* Cambridge, MA: MIT Press.

Marcus, Mitchell P., Beatrice Santorini & Mary Ann Marcinkiewicz. 1993. Building a large annotated corpus of English: The Penn Treebank. *Computational Linguistics*, 19(2): 313–330.

Melamed, I. Dan & Philip Resnik. 2000. Tagger evaluation given hierarchical tag sets. *Computers and the Humanities*, 34(1–2): 79–84.

Mihalcea, Rada & Dan Moldovan. 2001. Automatic generation of a coarse grained wordnet. *Proceedings of NAACL-2001 Workshop on WordNet and Other Lexical Resources*, Pittsburgh, PA, 35–41.

Mihalcea, Rada & Philip Edmonds, eds. 2004. *Proceedings of Senseval-3: Third International Workshop on the Evaluation of Systems for the Semantic Analysis of Text*, Barcelona, Spain. (http://www.senseval.org/)

Mihalcea, Rada, Timothy Chlovski & Adam Kilgarriff. 2004. The Senseval-3 English lexical sample task. *Proceedings of Senseval-3: Third International Workshop on the Evaluation of Systems for the Semantic Analysis of Text*, Barcelona, Spain, 25–28.

Miller, George A., ed. 1990. Special Issue, WordNet: An on-line lexical database. *International Journal of Lexicography*, 3(4).

Miller, George A. & Christiane Fellbaum. 1991. Semantic networks of English. *Cognition*, 41(1–3): 197–229.

Miller, George A., Claudia Leacock, Randee Tengi, and R. T. Bunker. 1993. A semantic concordance. *Proceedings of the ARPA Workshop on Human Language Technology*, San Francisco, 303–308.

Mooney, Raymond J. 1996. Comparative experiments on disambiguating word senses: An illustration of the role of bias in machine learning. *Proceedings of the Conference on Empirical Methods in Natural Language Processing (EMNLP)*, 82–91.

Ng, Hwee Tou & Hian Beng Lee. 1996. Integrating multiple knowledge sources to disambiguate word sense: An exemplar-based approach. *Proceedings of the 34th Annual Meeting of the Association for Computational Linguistics*, Santa Cruz, California, 40–47.

Ng, Hwee Tou. 1997a. Getting serious about word sense disambiguation. *Proceedings of the ACL SIGLEX Workshop on Tagging Text with Lexical Semantics: Why, What, and How?* Washington D.C., USA, 1–7.

Ng, Hwee Tou. 1997b. Exemplar-based word sense disambiguation: Some recent improvements. *Proceedings of the Second Conference on Empirical Methods in Natural Language Processing (EMNLP)*, Providence, Rhode Island, USA, 208–213.

Ng, Hwee Tou, Chung Yong Lim & Shou King Foo. 1999. A case study on inter-annotator agreement for word sense disambiguation. *Proceedings of the ACL*

SIGLEX Workshop on Standardizing Lexical Resources, College Park, Maryland, USA, 9–13.

Ng, Hwee Tou, Bin Wang & Yee Seng Chan. 2003. Exploiting parallel texts for word sense disambiguation: An empirical study. *Proceedings of the 41st Annual Meeting of the Association for Computational Linguistics*, Sapporo, Japan, 455–462.

Palmer, Martha. 1990. Customizing verb definitions for specific semantic domains. *Machine Translation*, 5: 5–30.

Palmer, Martha & Marc Light. 1999. Introduction to the special issue on semantic tagging. *Natural Language Engineering*, 5(2): i–iv.

Palmer, Martha, Chunghye Han, Fei Xia, Dania Egedi & Joseph Rosenzweig. 2000a. Constraining lexical selection across languages using TAGs. *Tree Adjoining Grammars: Formal, Computational and Linguistic Aspects,* ed. by Anne Abeille & Owen Rambow., Palo Alto, CA: CSLI.

Palmer, Martha, Hoa Trang Dang, Joseph Rosenzweig. 2000b. Sense tagging the Penn Treebank. *Proceedings of the Second International Conference Language Resources and Evaluation Conference (LREC 2000)*, Athens, Greece.

Palmer, Martha, Christiane Fellbaum, Scott Cotton, Lauren Delfs & Hoa Trang Dang. 2001. English tasks: All-words and verb lexical sample. *Proceedings of Senseval-2: Second International Workshop on Evaluating Word Sense Disambiguation Systems*, Toulouse, France, 21–24.

Palmer, Martha, Christiane Fellbaum & Hoa Trang Dang. 2006. Making fine-grained and coarse-grained sense distinctions, both manually and automatically. *Natural Language Engineering*, 12(3).

Pustejovsky, James. 1991. The generative lexicon. *Computational Linguistics*, 17(4): 409–411.

Resnik, Philip & David Yarowsky. 1999. Distinguishing systems and distinguishing senses: New evaluation methods for word sense disambiguation. *Natural Language Engineering*, 5(2): 113–133.

Sanderson, Mark. 1994. Word sense disambiguation and information retrieval. *Proceedings of the 17th Annual International ACM SIGIR Conference on Re-search and Development in Information Retrieval*, Dublin, Ireland, 142–151.

Schütze, Hinrich. 1998. Automatic word sense discrimination. *Computational Linguistics*, 24(1): 97–123.

Segond, Frédérique. 2000. Framework and results for French. *Computers and the Humanities*, 34(1–2): 49–60.

Snyder, Ben & Martha Palmer. 2004. The English all-words task. *Proceedings of Senseval-3: Third International Workshop on the Evaluation of Systems for the Semantic Analysis of Text*, Barcelona, Spain, 41–43.

Tufiş, Dan, Dan Cristea & Sofia Stamou. 2004. BalkaNet: Aims, methods, results, and perspectives. A general overview. *Romanian Journal of Information Science and Technology*, 7(1–2): 9–43.

Vossen, Piek, ed. 1998. *EuroWordNet: A Multilingual Database with Lexical Semantic Networks*. Dordrecht: Kluwer Academic Publishers.

Weischedel, Ralph & Martha Palmer. 2004. An OntoBank pilot study: Annotating word sense and co-reference. DARPA TIDES PI Meeting, Philadelphia, PA, July 13–15.

Yarowsky, David. 1993. One sense per collocation. *Proceedings of ARPA Human Language Technology Workshop*, Princeton, NJ, 266–271.

Yarowsky, David, Radu Florian, Siviu Cucerzan & Charles Schafer. 2001. The Johns Hopkins Senseval-2 system description. *Proceedings of Senseval-2: Second International Workshop on Evaluating Word Sense Disambiguation Systems*, Toulouse, France, 163–166.

Yarowsky, David & Radu Florian. 2002. Evaluating sense disambiguation performance across diverse parameter spaces. *Natural Language Engineering*, 8(4): 293–310.

5 Knowledge-Based Methods for WSD

Rada Mihalcea

University of North Texas

This chapter provides an overview of research to date in knowledge-based word sense disambiguation. It outlines the main knowledge-intensive methods devised so far for automatic sense tagging: 1) methods using contextual overlap with respect to dictionary definitions, 2) methods based on similarity measures computed on semantic networks, 3) selectional preferences as a means of constraining the possible meanings of words in a given context, and 4) heuristic-based methods that rely on properties of human language including the most frequent sense, one sense per discourse, and one sense per collocation.

5.1 Introduction

Knowledge-based methods represent a distinct category in word sense disambiguation (WSD). Along with corpus-based methods, accounted for in detail in Chapters 6 and 7, they represent one of the main categories of algorithms developed for automatic sense tagging. The performance of such knowledge intensive methods is usually exceeded by their corpus-based alternatives, but they have the advantage of a larger coverage. Knowledge-based methods for WSD are usually applicable to *all words* in unrestricted text, as opposed to corpus-based techniques, which are applicable only to those words for which annotated corpora are available.

This chapter overviews the main approaches for knowledge-intensive sense tagging as currently used. The introduction to this book (Chap. 1) reviews some other historical knowledge-based systems. While the techniques be presented in this chapter are generally applicable in conjunction with any lexical knowledge base that defines word senses (and relations

E. Agirre and P. Edmonds (eds.), Word Sense Disambiguation: Algorithms and Applications, 107–131.
© 2007 Springer.

among them), WordNet (Miller 1995) is used most often. Four main types of knowledge-based methods are presented:

1. The Lesk algorithm, in which the most likely meanings for the words in a given context are identified based on a measure of contextual overlap among dictionary definitions pertaining to the various senses of the ambiguous words.
2. Measures of semantic similarity computed over semantic networks. This category includes methods for finding the semantic density/ distance between concepts. Depending on the size of the context they span, these measures are in turn divided into two main categories:
   - Methods applicable to a *local context*, where semantic measures are used to disambiguate words connected by a) syntactic relations; or b) their locality.
   - Methods applicable to a *global context*, where lexical chains are derived based on measures of semantic similarity (a lexical chain is a thread of meaning drawn throughout an entire text).
3. Automatically or semi-automatically acquired selectional preferences, as a means of constraining the possible meanings of a word, based on the relation it has with other words in context.
4. Heuristic methods, consisting of simple rules that can reliably assign a sense to certain word categories, including:
   - Most frequent sense
   - One sense per collocation
   - One sense per discourse

These four types of methods are explored in detail in the following sections. Two other knowledge-based methods: 5) methods relying on semantic knowledge induced across aligned parallel texts, and 6) methods based on information derived from semantic domains are covered in Chapters 9 and 10, respectively.

5.2 Lesk Algorithm

The Lesk algorithm (Lesk 1986) is one of the first algorithms developed for the semantic disambiguation of all words in unrestricted text. The only resource required by the algorithm is a set of dictionary entries, one for each possible word sense, and knowledge about the immediate context where the sense disambiguation is performed.

---

(1) for each sense i of W_1
(2)　for each sense j of W_2
(3)　　compute *Overlap(i,j)*, the number of words in common
　　　　between the definitions of sense i and sense j
(4) find i and j for which *Overlap(i,j)* is maximized
(5) assign sense i to W_1 and sense j to W_2

Fig. 5.1. Dictionary-based Lesk algorithm.

Although traditionally considered a *dictionary-based* method, the idea behind the Lesk algorithm represents the starting seed for today's corpus-based algorithms. Almost every supervised WSD system relies one way or another on some form of contextual overlap (see Chap. 7), with the overlap being typically measured between the context of an ambiguous word and contexts specific to various meanings of that word, as learned from previously annotated data.

The main idea behind the original definition of the algorithm is to disambiguate words by finding the overlap among their sense definitions. Namely, given two words, W_1 and W_2, each with N_{W1} and N_{W2} senses defined in a dictionary, for each possible sense pair W_1^i and W_2^j, $i = 1..N_{W1}$, $j = 1..N_{W2}$, we first determine the overlap of the corresponding definitions by counting the number of words they have in common. Next, the sense pair with the highest overlap is selected, and therefore a sense is assigned to each word in the initial word pair. Fig. 5.1 illustrates the main steps of the algorithm.

As an example, consider the task of disambiguating the words *pine* and *cone* in the word pair *pine cone*.[1] The *Oxford Advanced Learner's Dictionary* defines four senses for *pine* and three senses for *cone*:

pine
1*　seven kinds of evergreen tree with needle-shaped leaves
2　pine
3　waste away through sorrow or illness
4　pine for something, pine to do something

cone
1　solid body which narrows to a point
2　something of this shape, whether solid or hollow
3*　fruit of certain evergreen trees (fir, pine)

---

[1] The example and corresponding dictionary definitions are from Lesk (1986).

The first definition for *pine* and the third definition for *cone* have the largest overlap among all possible sense combinations, with three words in common: *evergreen*, *tree*, and *pine*, and therefore these are the meanings selected by the Lesk algorithm for the given pair *pine cone*.

The Lesk algorithm was evaluated on a sample of ambiguous word pairs manually annotated with respect to the *Oxford Advanced Learner's Dictionary*; a precision of 50–70% was observed (Lesk 1986).

5.2.1 Variations of the Lesk Algorithm

Since the original definition of the Lesk algorithm in 1986, several variations of the algorithm have been proposed, including: i) versions of the algorithm that attempt to solve the combinatorial explosion of possible word sense combinations when more than two words are considered, ii) algorithm variations where each word in a given context is disambiguated individually, by measuring the overlap between its corresponding dictionary definitions and the current sentential context, and iii) alternatives where the semantic space of a word meaning is augmented with definitions of semantically related words.

Simulated Annealing

One notorious problem with the original Lesk algorithm is the fact that it leads to a combinatorial explosion when applied to the disambiguation of more than two words. Consider for instance the text *I saw a man who is 98 years old and can still walk and tell jokes*, with nine open class words, each with several possible senses:[2] *see(26), man(11), year(4), old(8), can(5), still(4), walk(10), tell(8), joke(3)*. A total of 43,929,600 sense combinations are possible for this text, and thus trying to figure out the optimal combination using definition overlaps is not a tractable approach.

A possible solution to this problem is to use simulated annealing, as proposed by Cowie et al. (1992). They define a function E that reflects the combination of word senses in a given text, and whose minimum should correspond to the correct choice of word senses. For a given combination of senses, all corresponding definitions from a dictionary are collected, and each word appearing at least once in these definitions receives a score equal to its number of occurrences. Adding all these scores together gives the *redundancy* of the text. The E function is then defined as the inverse of

---

[2] Numbers of senses (indicated in parentheses) are determined based on WordNet.

(1) for each sense *i* of *W*
(2)   determine *Overlap(i)*, the number of words in common
       between the definition of sense *i* and current sentential context
(3) find sense *i* for which *Overlap(i)* is maximized
(4) assign sense *i* to *W*

Fig. 5.2. Simplified Lesk algorithm.

redundancy, and the goal is to find a combination of senses that minimizes this function. To this end, an initial combination of senses is determined (e.g., pick the most frequent sense for each word), and then several iterations are performed, where the sense of a random word in the text is replaced with a different sense, and the new selection is considered as correct only if it reduces the value of the *E* function. The iterations stop when there is no change in the configuration of senses. Tests performed on 50 example sentences using this optimized Lesk algorithm led to 47% disambiguation precision at sense level, and 72% at homograph level. The method was also evaluated by Stevenson and Wilks (2001), who reimplemented the simulated annealing algorithm as part of their larger WSD system. A similar average precision was observed during their experiments (65.24%) on a corpus annotated with senses from the *Longman Dictionary of Contemporary English* (LDOCE).

Simplified Lesk Algorithm

Another version of the Lesk algorithm, which also attempts to solve the combinatorial explosion of word sense combinations, is a simplified variation that runs a separate disambiguation process for each ambiguous word in the input text. In this simplified algorithm, the correct meaning of each word in a text is determined individually by finding the sense that leads to the highest overlap between its dictionary definition and the current context. Rather than seeking to simultaneously determine the meanings of all words in a given text, this approach tackles each word individually, regardless of the meaning of the other words occurring in the same context. Fig. 5.2 illustrates the main steps of this algorithm.

A comparative evaluation performed by Vasilescu et al. (2004) has shown that the simplified Lesk algorithm can significantly outperform the original definition of the algorithm, both in terms of precision and efficiency. By evaluating the disambiguation algorithms on the Senseval-2

```
(1)   for each sense i of W
(2)        set Weight(i) to 0
(3)   for each [unique] word w in surrounding context of W
(4)        if w appears in the training examples or
           dictionary definition of sense i
(5)             add Weight(w) to Weight(i)
(6)   choose sense i with highest Weight(i)
```

Fig. 5.3. Corpus-based Lesk algorithm.

English all words data, they measured a 58% precision using the simplified Lesk algorithm compared to only 42% under the original algorithm.[3]

A similar variation of the Lesk algorithm is frequently used to solve the semantic ambiguity of a target word, using manually annotated corpora (see Chaps. 4 and 7 for details). This corpus-based variation has the capability to augment the sense-centered context of a word with additional tagged examples. Subsequently, the most likely sense for a new occurrence of the ambiguous target word is identified as the one with the highest overlap between the sense-centered contexts and the new context.

Fig. 5.3 illustrates the corpus-based Lesk algorithm used to disambiguate one target word provided that a set of annotated training examples is available. The weight of a word is defined using a measure borrowed from the information retrieval community: $Weight(w)$ is the inverse "document" frequency (IDF) of the word w over the examples and dictionary definitions. The IDF of a word is $-\log(p(w))$, where $p(w)$ is estimated as the fraction of examples and definitions including the word w.

Incidentally, the corpus-based variation of Lesk algorithm is one of the best performing baselines in comparative evaluations of supervised WSD learning systems. Among all baselines evaluated during the Senseval-1 exercise (Kilgarriff and Rosenzweig 2000), the Lesk algorithm relying on corpus and phrase filtering achieves 69.1% precision for fine-grained filtering, as compared to 56.6% achieved using the most-frequent-sense heuristic, and a low precision of 16.2% achieved by a random sense selection.

---

[3] Note that their implementation considers a back-off strategy for words not covered by the algorithm, consisting of the most frequent sense defined in WordNet. This means that words for which all their possible meanings lead to zero overlap with current context or with other word definitions are by default assigned sense number one in WordNet (see Sect. 5.5.1 for details on the most frequent sense heuristic).

The algorithm was ranked the seventh among eleven different supervised and unsupervised systems, with the best performing system achieving 78.1% precision. In Senseval-2 (Kilgarriff 2001), the Lesk baseline led to similar results: 51.2% precision, compared to the performance of 64.2% achieved by the best supervised system (see Chap. 4 for additional information on Senseval).

Augmented Semantic Spaces

Another variation of the Lesk algorithm, called the *adapted Lesk algorithm*, was introduced by Banerjee and Pedersen (2002), in which definitions of related words are used in addition to the definitions of the word itself to determine the most likely sense for a word in a given context. Banerjee and Pedersen employ a function similar to the one defined by Cowie et al. (1992) to determine a score for each possible combination of senses in a text, and attempt to identify the sense configuration that leads to the highest score.

The novelty of their approach consists of the type of information used for a given word sense. While the original Lesk algorithm considers strictly the definition of a word meaning as a source of contextual information for a given sense, Banerjee and Pedersen extend this algorithm to related concepts and their definitions. Based on the WordNet hierarchy, the adapted Lesk algorithm takes into account hypernyms, hyponyms, holonyms, meronyms, troponyms, attribute relations, and their associated definitions to build an enlarged context for a given word meaning. Hence, they attempt to enlarge the dictionary-context of a word sense by taking into account definitions of semantically related concepts. In comparative evaluations performed on the Senseval-2 English noun data set, they show that the adapted Lesk algorithm on a set of 4,320 ambiguous instances doubles the precision (to 32%).

Summary

Overall, the Lesk algorithm is an appealing solution for identifying word senses when the only resource available is a set of dictionary definitions. Among all variations of this algorithm, the simplified Lesk method is the one that improves most over the original algorithm both in terms of efficiency (it overcomes the combinational sense explosion problem) and precision (comparative evaluations have shown that this alternative leads to better disambiguation results). Moreover, enriched semantic spaces, which consider definitions of semantically related words in addition to the definition of the ambiguous words themselves, were found to almost double the disambiguation precision. Finally, if a sense-annotated corpus is available, information learned from the annotated data can be naturally integrated into the Lesk algorithm, leading to improved results in the disambiguation process.

5.3 Semantic Similarity

Words in a discourse must be related in meaning for the discourse to be coherent (Halliday and Hasan 1976). This is a natural property of human language and at the same time one of the most powerful constraints used in automatic word sense disambiguation. Words that share a common context are usually closely related in meaning, and therefore the appropriate senses can be selected by choosing those meanings found within the smallest semantic distance (Rada et al. 1989).

While this kind of semantic constraint is often able to provide unity to an entire discourse, its scope has been usually limited to a small number of words found in the immediate vicinity of a target word, or to words connected by syntactic dependencies with the target word. These methods target the *local context* of a given word, and do not take into account additional contextual information found outside a certain window size.

There are however other methods that rely on a *global context* and attempt to build threads of meaning throughout an entire text, with their scope extended beyond a small window centered on target words. Lexical chains are an example of such semantic relations drawn across several words in a text.

Similar to the Lesk algorithm, these similarity methods become extremely computationally-intensive when more than two words are involved. However, solutions designed to increase the efficiency of the Lesk algorithm are equally applicable here, as for instance the algorithm proposed in Agirre and Rigau (1996) in which each ambiguous word in disambiguated individually, using a method similar in spirit with to the simplified Lesk algorithm.

5.3.1 Measures of Semantic Similarity

There are a number of similarity measures that were developed to quantify the degree to which two words are semantically related. Most such measures rely on semantic networks and follow the original methodology proposed by

Rada et al. (1989) for computing metrics on semantic nets. A comprehensive survey of semantic similarity measures is reported by Budanitsky and Hirst (2001), and a software tool that computes similarity metrics on WordNet is made available by Patwardhan et al. (2003).[4]

We present below several similarity measures proved to work well on the WordNet hierarchy. Most of these measures assume as input a pair of concepts and return a value indicating their semantic relatedness.

1. Leacock et al. (1998) determine the minimum length of a connecting path between synsets including the input words. This value is normalized by the depth of the taxonomy. In Eq. 5.1 $Path(C_1,C_2)$ represents the length of the path connecting the two concepts (i.e., the number of arcs in the semantic network that are traversed going from C_1 to C_2), and D is the overall depth of the taxonomy.

$$Similarity\,(C_1,C_2) = -\log\!\left(\frac{Path(C_1,C_2)}{2D}\right) \qquad (5.1)$$

2. Hirst and St-Onge (1998) integrate into their similarity measure the direction of the links that form the connecting path. In addition to the length, the path should not "change direction too often." In Eq. 5.2, C and k are constants, $Path$ is defined similarly as above, and d represents the number of changes of direction.

$$Similarity\,(C_1,C_2) = C - Path(C_1,C_2) - kd \qquad (5.2)$$

3. Resnik (1995) defines the notion of information content, which is a measure of the specificity of a given concept, and is defined based on its probability of occurrence in a large corpus (Eq. 5.3).

$$IC(C) = -\log(P(C)) \qquad (5.3)$$

Given a textual corpus, $P(C)$ is the probability of encountering an instance of type C. The value for $P(C)$ is therefore larger for concepts listed higher in the semantic hierarchy, and reaches its maximum value for the topmost concept (if the hierarchy has only one top, then the P value for this concept is 1). Starting with this concept of information content, Resnik defines a measure of semantic relatedness between words (Eq. 5.4) by quantifying the information content of the lowest common subsumer (LCS) of two concepts (that is, the first common

---

[4] The Perl module "WordNet::Similarity" implements various measures of semantic similarity and relatedness (http://search.cpan.org/dist/WordNet-Similarity).

node in the semantic network encountered by traveling from the two given concepts toward the root).

$$Similarity(C_1, C_2) = IC(LCS(C_1, C_2)) \tag{5.4}$$

Jiang and Conrath's (1997) alternative to Resnik's definition (Eq. 5.5) uses the difference in the information content of the two concepts to indicate their similarity (Eq. 5.5).

$$\begin{aligned} Similarity\,(C_1, C_2) = 2 \times IC(LCS\,(C_1, C_2)) \\ - (IC(C_1) + IC(C_2)) \end{aligned} \tag{5.5}$$

Lin (1998) gives another formulation that combines the information content of the lowest common subsumer with the information content of the concepts involved (Eq. 5.6)

$$Similarity\,(C_1, C_2) = \frac{2 \times IC(LCS\,(C_1, C_2))}{IC(C_1) + IC(C_2)} \tag{5.6}$$

4. Mihalcea and Moldovan (1999) introduce a formula to measure the semantic similarity between independent hierarchies, including hierarchies for different parts of speech. All previously mentioned measures are applicable only to concepts that are explicitly connected through arcs in the semantic network. Mihalcea and Moldovan create virtual paths between different hierarchies through the gloss definitions found in WordNet. In Eq. 5.7 $|CD_{12}|$ is the number of common words to the definitions in the hierarchy of C_1 and C_2, descendants(C_2) is the number of concepts in the hierarchy of C_2, and W_k is a weight associated with each concept and is determined as the depth of the concept within the semantic hierarchy.

$$Similarity(C_1, C_2) = \frac{\sum_{k=1}^{|CD_{12}|} W_k}{\log(descendants(C_2))} \tag{5.7}$$

This measure was found to work well for the disambiguation of nouns and verbs connected by a syntactic relation (e.g., verb-object, noun-modifier, and others).

5. Agirre and Rigau (1996) introduce the notion of conceptual density, defined as the overlap between the semantic hierarchy rooted by a given concept C, and the words in the context of C. In Eq. 5.8, m is the total number of word meanings in the context of C found in the hierarchy rooted by C, and descendants(C) represents the total number of concepts in the hierarchy rooted by C. W_k is a weight associated with each concept in the hierarchy (*nhyp* is the number of

hyponyms for the given node in the hierarchy, and the optimal value for α was empirically determined to be 0.20).

$$CD(C) = \frac{\sum_{k=0}^{m} W_k}{descendants(C)}, \text{ where } W_k = nhyp^{k^\alpha} \qquad (5.8)$$

To identify the sense of a target word in a given context, the conceptual density formula is applied to all possible meanings of the target word, and ultimately the sense leading to the highest conceptual density score is selected. The conceptual density formula may be regarded as a variation of Lesk algorithm. While the original Lesk measure considers definitions for the various senses of a target word to compute the contextual overlap, the conceptual density measure takes into consideration entire sub-hierarchies rooted by different word senses. Similarly, it then computes the number of common words between these sub-hierarchies and the current context, and subsequently the correct sense is the one leading to the highest overlap. Experiments performed with this measure on the disambiguation of nouns in Semcor (Miller et al. 1994) led to an overall precision of 66.4%, including monosemous words, and coverage of 88.6%, figures that are promising given the difficulty of the task and the wide coverage of the method.

5.3.2 Using Semantic Similarity Within a Local Context

The application of measures of semantic similarity to the disambiguation of words in unrestricted text is not always a straightforward process. A text usually involves more than two ambiguous words, and therefore we typically deal with *sets* of ambiguous words in which the distance of a word to all the other words in the context influences its meaning in the given text.

Work in this area has considered the use of local context as an additional constraint to limit the number of words in the set of ambiguous words. Patwardhan et al. (2003) applied the first five similarity measures above to decide upon the correct sense of 1,723 instances of ambiguous nouns from the Senseval-2 English lexical sample data. They computed a cumulative score by adding the semantic distances from the target word to the words in its immediate vicinity (i.e., one word to the left and one word to the right). The sense that is selected is the one with the highest cumulative score. They found that, among the five different measures of similarity, Jiang and

Conrath (1997) leads to the best overall performance, and Hirst and St-Onge (1998) provides the most consistent behavior across various words.

Syntactic dependencies are another possible constraint that can be applied to words involved in a similarity relation. Stetina et al. (1998) devised a method that relies on syntactic dependencies among words, and on a very simple similarity measure that defines two words as similar if they belong to the same WordNet synset. Experiments using syntactic dependencies learned from about 100 Semcor texts led to an overall disambiguation precision of 80.3% measured on 15 Semcor test files. On the same test set, they obtained 75.2% using a simple baseline that chooses the most frequent sense.

5.3.3 Using Semantic Similarity Within a Global Context

Lexical chains are some of the most widely known structures of meaning. A lexical chain is a sequence of semantically related words, which creates a context and contributes to the continuity of meaning and the coherence of a discourse (Halliday and Hasan 1976). They are considered useful for various tasks in natural language processing, including text summarization, text categorization, and word sense disambiguation. Lexical chains are drawn independently of the grammatical structure of the text, and may span long distances in the text.

A generic chaining algorithm consists of three main steps:

1. Select the candidate words from the text. These are words for which we can compute semantic relatedness measures and therefore most of the time they have the same part of speech.[5]
2. For each such candidate word, and for each meaning for this word, find a chain to receive the candidate word sense, based on a semantic relatedness measure between the concepts that are already in the chain and the candidate word meaning.
3. If such a chain is found, insert the word into the chain; otherwise, create a new chain.

All chains that exceed a certain threshold are selected.

Galley and McKeown (2003) evaluated a lexical chaining algorithm on the nouns from a subset of Semcor, reporting 62.1% disambiguation

---

[5] With almost no exception, previous work in lexical chaining has considered only the nouns in the text as candidate chain elements.

precision, which represented an improvement over previous lexical chain implementations.

Okumura and Honda (1994) report a closely related evaluation in which lexical chains are derived based on a Japanese thesaurus, and give an overall precision of 63.4% computed on five different test texts.

A procedure similar to lexical chaining was proposed by Mihalcea and Moldovan (2000), where chains of meaning are derived starting with *anchor* points in the text (an *anchor* point is a word that can be reliably annotated with its corresponding meaning, e.g., monosemous words or various named entities). These anchors are then starting points for lexical chains. Mihalcea and Moldovan (2000) report a high overall precision of over 90% at a recall of 60%, measured on a subset of the Semcor corpus.

More recently, Mihalcea (2005) proposed a graph-based algorithm for sequence data labeling, using random walks on graphs encoding word sense dependencies. The graphs are constructed automatically using definition similarities, and then used to automatically select the most likely sense for each word using a graph-based ranking algorithm such as PageRank (Brin and Page 1998). Her algorithm is completely unsupervised, as it ignores all supervised sources of information, including the sense order available in WordNet. In an evaluation conducted on the Senseval-2 English all-words data, the algorithm led to a precision of 55.2%, which compared favorably with the simplified Lesk algorithm on the same data set (48.7%). Erkan and Radev (2004) have a similar approach.

5.4 Selectional Preferences

Some of the earliest algorithms for word sense disambiguation rely on selectional preferences as a way of constraining the possible meanings of a word in a given context.

Selectional preferences capture information about the possible relations between word categories, and represent commonsense knowledge about classes of concepts. EAT-FOOD, DRINK-LIQUID, are examples of such semantic constraints, which can be used to rule out incorrect word meanings and select only those senses that are in harmony with commonsense rules. For instance, given the sentence *Mary drank burgundy*, the 'color' sense of *burgundy* does not fit in context since the verb *to drink* requires a liquid as a direct object.

While selectional preferences are intuitive, and occur to us in a natural way, it is difficult to put them into practice to solve the problem of WSD.

The main reason seems to be the circular relation between selectional preferences and WSD: learning accurate semantic constraints requires knowledge of the word senses involved in a candidate relation, and, vice versa, WSD can improve if large collections of selectional preferences are available.

Here we give an account of the most frequently used approaches that try to overcome this circularity and automatically learn selectional preferences based on frequency counts, information-theory measures, or class-to-class relations acquired from manually-crafted taxonomies. Brockmann and Lapata (2003) give a detailed analysis of these approaches and comparative evaluations against human judgments.

5.4.1 Preliminaries: Learning Word-to-Word Relations

Frequency counts of word-to-word relations are useful measures to account for the *semantic fit* between words. Given two words W_1 and W_2, and the syntactic relation R that connects them, the semantic fit between these words can be quantified by counting in a large corpus the number of times that the two words occur in the relation R, which we formalize here as $Count(W_1, W_2, R)$.

An alternative method is to use conditional probabilities to estimate the semantic fit of a given relation. Under the same assumption that selectional preferences are learned for two words W_1 and W_2 connected by a relation R, the conditional probability is determined as in Eq. 5.9, where the word W_2 imposes the selectional preferences on W_1. The constraint can be expressed in the other direction as well, with conditional probabilities where the roles of the two words are reversed.

$$P(W_1 \mid W_2, R) = \frac{Count(W_1, W_2, R)}{Count(W_2, R)} \qquad (5.9)$$

5.4.2 Learning Selectional Preferences

Several approaches have been proposed to determine the selectional preference between two concepts, between a concept and an entire semantic class, or between two semantic classes. A comparative evaluation of these various approaches in a WSD task is reported in Agirre and Martínez (2001) (see Sect. 5.4.3 below).

Resnik (1993) suggests selectional *associations* as a measure of the semantic fit between a word and a semantic class (in particular, Resnik's work deals with verbs and the semantic class of their noun arguments). In selectional associations, the contribution of a semantic class in a given relation is quantified using the contribution of all the concepts subsumed by that class. Given a word W and a semantic class C connected by the relation R, the selectional association is estimated as in Eq. 5.10, based on Eqs. 5.11 and 5.12.

$$A(W, C, R) = \frac{P(C\,|\,W, R)\log(P(C\,|\,W, R)/P(C))}{\sum_C P(C\,|\,W, R)\log(P(C\,|\,W, R)/P(C))} \qquad (5.10)$$

$$P(C\,|\,W, R) = \frac{Count(W, C, R)}{Count(W, R)} \qquad (5.11)$$

$$Count(W, C, R) = \sum_{W' \in C} \frac{Count(W, W', R)}{Count(W')} \qquad (5.12)$$

Since the meaning of the words is unknown, Resnik assumes an equal sense distribution, and thus a word with N senses will have its corpus frequency equally distributed among its possible meanings.

Agirre and Martínez (2001) propose a method to determine class-to-class selectional preferences, which are more general than the previously proposed models of word-to-word or word-to-class selectional constraints. Their model requires a sense-tagged corpus to make the class estimates. Eq. 5.13 is used to seek the sense of the word W_2 that leads to the maximum probability of co-occurrence of its semantic class with the class of the word it relates to.

$$P(W_1^i\,|\,W_2, R) \qquad (5.13)$$

$$= \max_{W_2^j\, senses} \sum_{W_1^i \subseteq W_i} \sum_{W_2^j \subseteq W_2} P(W_1^i\,|\,W_1)P(W_2^j\,|\,W_2)P(W_1\,|\,W_2)$$

$$= \max_{W_2^j\, senses} \sum_{W_1^i \subseteq W_i} \sum_{W_2^j \subseteq W_2} \frac{Cnt(W_1^i, W_1)}{Cnt(W_1)} \frac{Cnt(W_2^j, W_2)}{Cnt(W_2)} \frac{Cnt(W_1, W_w, R)}{Cnt(W_2)}$$

In Eq. 5.13, W_1^i and W_2^j represent the possible senses of W_1 and W_2. Since they assume the availability of a sense-tagged corpus, the frequency counts (abbreviated to *Cnt* for space) $Cnt(W_1^i, W_1)$ and $Cnt(W_2^j, W_2)$ can be easily derived, and do not have to rely on the assumption of equal sense distributions, as proposed by Resnik (1997).

In addition to these two methods, there are several other approaches that were proposed to derive selectional preferences, including the Bayesian networks approach proposed by Ciaramita and Johnson (2000) and the tree cut model of Li and Abe (1998).

5.4.3 Using Selectional Preferences

The application of word-to-word, word-to-class, and class-to-class selectional preferences to WSD was evaluated by Agirre and Martínez (2001). While the results they obtain on a subset of Semcor nouns do not exceed the most-frequent-sense baseline, they observed, however, that class-to-class models lead to significantly better disambiguation results compared to word-to-word or word-to-class selectional preferences. For instance, on a set of 8 nouns, the most-frequent-sense baseline leads to 69% precision and 100% coverage, the word-to-word selectional preferences give 95.9% precision and 26% coverage, word-to-class preferences decrease the precision to 66.9% and increase the coverage to 86.7%, and finally the class- to-class preferences have a precision of 66.6% and a coverage of 97.3%.

Selectional preferences were also evaluated by Stevenson and Wilks (2001), who implemented them as features in their larger WSD system. In their work, selectional preferences are derived using 1) the LDOCE semantic codes, 2) a custom-built hierarchy over these codes that indicates for instance that Solid, Liquid, and Gas are all a kind of Inanimate, and 3) grammatical relations such as subject-verb, verb-object, and noun-modifier identified using a shallow syntactic analyzer. They evaluated the individual contribution of each knowledge source in their WSD system, and found that selectional preferences alone could lead to a disambiguation precision of 44.8% on a corpus annotated with LDOCE senses (see also Chap. 8, Sect. 8.5.6).

The use of selectional preferences for WSD is an appealing method, in particular when these preferences can be learned without making use of sense-tagged data. For example, McCarthy and Carroll (2003) automatically acquired selectional preferences for use in an unsupervised WSD system. They achieved 52.3% precision at a recall of only 20% on the Senseval-2 all-words corpus (58.5% precision on the nouns only), which, incidentally, reveals, the sparse applicability of selectional preferences. The performance of WSD methods based on selectional preferences is however usually exceeded by the simple most-frequent-sense baseline (e.g., the all-words baseline in Senseval-2 was 57%), suggesting that more work needs to be done for learning accurate selectional preferences (Ciaramita and Johnson 2000).

5.4 Heuristics for Word Sense Disambiguation

An easy and yet fairly precise way to predict word meanings is to rely on heuristics drawn from linguistic properties observed on large texts. One such heuristic, which is often used as a baseline in the evaluation of many WSD systems is the most-frequent-sense heuristic. The other two heuristics that we address in this section refer to the tendency of a word to exhibit the same meaning in all its occurrences in a given discourse (one-sense-per-discourse), in the same collocation (one-sense-per-collocation), or in the same domain (see Chap. 10 on domains).

5.5.1 Most Frequent Sense

Among all possible meanings that a word may have, it is generally true that one meaning occurs more often than the other meanings. It is interesting to notice that word meanings exhibit a Zipfian distribution: one sense has a dominant frequency of occurrence, followed by a significant decrease in frequency for the remaining word senses (Zipf 1949). Therefore, assuming the availability of word frequency data, a very simple disambiguation method can be designed that assigns to each word its most frequent meaning, according to this a priori sense distribution.

This very simple method is often used as a baseline for WSD, and according to Gale et al. (1992a) "most reasonable systems should outperform this baseline."

Even though conceptually very simple, and almost trivial to implement, there is an important drawback associated with this method: sense distributions may not always be available, and therefore the most-frequent-sense heuristic is applicable only to those few languages for which significantly large sense-tagged corpora are available.[6] Moreover, a change in domain or genre can significantly affect the sense distributions, considerably decreasing the performance of this simple heuristic (see Chap. 10 and also Martínez and Agirre (2000)).

---

[6] Currently only English. See Chapters 4 and 9.

There is also an alternative method for finding the most frequent sense, which does not assume the availability of sense-tagged data. McCarthy et al. (2004) show how a measure of similarity between various meanings of a word and distributionally similar words can be used to determine the predominant sense in a given domain. Additional details on this method are provided in Chapter 6 (Sect. 6.1.2).

5.5.2 One Sense Per Discourse

This heuristic was introduced by Gale et al. (1992b). It states that a word tends to preserve its meaning across all its occurrences in a given discourse. This is a rather strong rule since it allows for the automatic disambiguation of all instances of a certain word, given that its meaning is identified in at least one such occurrence.

Initially, the one-sense-per-discourse hypothesis was tested on nine words with 2-way ambiguity in an experiment performed with five subjects. The subjects were given 82 pairs of concordance lines, and asked to determine if they correspond to the same sense or not. Overall, they found that with a probability of 98%, two word occurrences in the same discourse would have the same sense (Gale et al. 1992b).

While this hypothesis is extremely likely to hold for words with coarse-grained sense distinctions, Krovetz (1998) experimented with words that have more than two possible senses and/or finer sense distinctions, and found that such words tend to have more than one sense per discourse. He based his evaluation on Semcor and the DSO corpus. About 33% of the words in these texts were found to have multiple senses per discourse, and therefore the overall disambiguation precision achieved in this case is less than 70%.

Yarowsky (1995) used both one-sense-per-discourse (and one-sense-per-collocation) in his iterative bootstrapping algorithm, which improved performance from 90.6% to 96.5% (see Chap. 7 (Sect. 7.2.4) for a description of the algorithm.)

5.5.3 One Sense Per Collocation

The one-sense-per-collocation heuristic is similar in spirit to the one-sense-per-discourse hypothesis, but it has a different scope. It was introduced by Yarowsky (1993), and it states that a word tends to preserve its meaning when used in the same collocation. In other words, nearby words provide strong and consistent clues to the sense of a target word. It was also observed that this effect is stronger for adjacent collocations, and becomes weaker as the distance between words increases.

Initial experiments with this hypothesis considered again coarse-grained sense distinctions, mostly words with 2-way ambiguity. An overall precision of 97% was observed across a large set of hand-annotated examples.

As with the one-sense-per-discourse assumption, further experiments performed with different types of corpora and finer levels of ambiguity showed that the strength of the hypothesis diminishes significantly when fine-grained sense distinctions are employed. Martínez and Agirre (2000) tested the one-sense-per-collocation hypothesis under a different experimental setting, in which the annotated corpora involve genre and topic variations – Semcor and DSO – and word meanings are defined with respect to the fine-grained sense entries from WordNet. Similar to Krovetz's findings in the case of the one-sense-per-discourse hypothesis, Martínez and Agirre found that the precision of the one-sense-per-collocation heuristic drops significantly to about 70% or even less when words with higher degrees of ambiguity are considered.

An interesting aspect observed by Martínez and Agirre relates to the consistency of this heuristic across different corpora. Specifically, experiments performed on texts with genre and topic variations led to the conclusion that one-sense-per-collocation holds across corpora. However, as they noticed, the number of collocations found in common between independent corpora is usually very low, which causes the low cross-corpora performance.

5.6 Knowledge-Based Methods at Senseval-2

Several of the systems that participated in Senseval-2 (see Chap. 4) relied on various flavors of knowledge-based algorithms.

The simplified Lesk algorithm (Sect. 5.2.1), together with several other heuristics (e.g., collocational patterns, topic area), was used in Litkowski's (2001) system in the Senseval-2 English all-words task, achieving a precision and recall of 45%.

A form of lexical chains (Sect. 5.3.3) – called structural semantic interconnections–was used by Navigli and Velardi (2004) in a system designed to find the meaning of the words in the WordNet glosses (a Senseval-3 task), by identifying paths along concepts in WordNet, for an overall precision and recall of 68.5%.

A method based on metrics of semantic similarity (Sect. 5.3.1) was used in Tat et al. (2001) for the disambiguation of all the words in a text. Specifically, they use a conceptual density method that identifies the relatedness between two concepts based on a dictionary (LDOCE), for a precision and recall of 36.0% obtained during the Senseval-2 English all-words task.

Automatically acquired selectional preferences (Sect. 5.4.2) were used by McCarthy et al. (McCarthy et al. 2001; McCarthy and Carroll 2003) to disambiguate the nouns and verbs in the texts provided during the Senseval-2 English all-words task. They report a precision in the range 54.5–59.8%, for a recall of 14–16.9%.

Finally, among the methods described in this chapter, the most-frequent-sense heuristic (Sect. 5.5.1) is playing a special role in these evaluations, as a baseline for most of the Senseval tasks.

5.7 Conclusions

This chapter has addressed the main knowledge-based methods proposed so far in word WSD. Four types of methods were presented: 1) Lesk-type algorithms, relying on measures of contextual overlap among dictionary definitions or among definitions and current sentential context, 2) measures of semantic similarity in a local or global context, 3) selectional restrictions as means of imposing semantic constraints on the possible meanings of words participating in a given relation, and 4) methods based on properties of human language, including the most-frequent-sense heuristic, and the one-sense-per-discourse and one-sense-per-collocation hypotheses.

Lesk algorithms provide reasonable disambiguation precision when the only resource available is a set of dictionary definitions. In particular, variations of this algorithm, addressing each word individually or using richer sense representations based on information drawn from semantic networks have been found to significantly improve Lesk's original algorithm in precision and efficiency.

If additional resources are available (e.g., a set of semantic relations from a semantic network or a minimal set of annotated data) other knowledge-based methods can be applied. For instance, the most-frequent-sense heuristic was found to lead to good disambiguation results if a sense-annotated corpus is available to derive the required sense frequency information. Selectional preferences or measures of semantic similarity are also appealing methods for word sense disambiguation if relations between word senses are available. Finally, once a subset of the words in a text is disambiguated with reasonable precision, the one-sense-per-discourse and one-sense-per-collocation heuristics can be used to propagate these meanings to the other occurrences in the text.

The knowledge-based methods overviewed in this chapter have an important advantage over corpus-based methods: Although they sometimes lead to smaller disambiguation precision,[7] knowledge-intensive algorithms are not restricted to the few target words for which large sense-tagged data are available, but rather can be applied to *all words* in unrestricted text. Another important advantage is the fact that they are not tight to the availability of sense-annotated corpora, and thus they can be easily ported to other languages or domains for which a sense inventory is available.

References

Agirre, Eneko & German Rigau. 1996. Word sense disambiguation using conceptual density. *Proceedings of the International Conference on Computational Linguistics (COLING),* Copenhagen, Denmark, 16–22.

Agirre, Eneko & David Martínez. 2001. Learning class-to-class selectional preferences. *Proceedings of the Conference on Natural Language Learning,* Toulouse, France, 15–22.

Banerjee, Sid & Ted Pedersen, 2002. An adapted Lesk algorithm for word sense disambiguation using WordNet. *Proceedings of the Conference on Computational Linguistics and Intelligent Text Processing (CICLING),* Mexico City, Mexico, 136–145.

Brin, Sergei & Larry Page. 1998. The anatomy of a large-scale hypertextual Web search engine *Computer Networks and ISDN Systems*, 30(1–7): 107–117.

Brockmann, Carsten & Mirella Lapata. 2003. Evaluating and combining approaches to selectional preference acquisition. *Proceedings of the European Association for Computational Linguistics (EACL),* Budapest, Hungary, 27–34.

Budanitsky, Alex & Graeme Hirst, 2001. Semantic distance in WordNet: An experimental, application-oriented evaluation of five measures. *Proceedings of the NAACL Workshop on WordNet and Other Lexical Resources,* Pittsburgh, U.S.A., 29–34.

Ciaramita, Massimiliano & Mark Johnson. 2000. Explaining away ambiguity: Learning verb selectional preference with Bayesian networks. *Proceedings of*

---

[7] See the comparative evaluations of supervised and unsupervised systems participating in Senseval in Chapter 8 (Sect. 8.5.1).

the International Conference on Computational Linguistics (COLING), Saarbrucken, Germany, 187–193.

Cowie, Jim, Joe A. Guthrie & Louise Guthrie. 1992. Lexical disambiguation using simulated annealing. *Proceedings of the International Conference on Computational Linguistics (COLING)*, Nantes, France, 157–161.

Diab, Mona & Philip Resnik. 2002. An unsupervised method for word sense tagging using parallel corpora. *Proceedings of the Annual Meeting of the Association for Computational Linguistics (ACL)*, Philadelphia, U.S.A., 255–262.

Edmonds, Philip. 2005. Lexical disambiguation. *The Elsevier Encyclopedia of Language and Linguistics, 2nd Ed.*, ed. by Keith Brown, 607–23. Oxford: Elsevier.

Erkan, Güneş & Dragomir R. Radev. 2004. Lexrank: Graph-based centrality as salience in text summarization. *Journal of Artificial Intelligence Research*, 22: 457–479.

Fernandez-Amoros, David, Julio Gonzalo & Felisa Verdejo. 2001. The UNED system at Senseval-2. *Proceedings of Senseval-2: Second International Workshop on Evaluating Word Sense Disambiguation Systems*, Toulouse, France, 75–78.

Galley, Michel & Kathy McKeown. 2003. Improving word sense disambiguation in lexical chaining. *Proceedings of the International Joint Conference in Artificial Intelligence (IJCAI)*, Acapulco, Mexico, 1486–1488.

Gale, William, Ken Church & David Yarowsky. 1992a. Estimating upper and lower bounds on the performance of word-sense disambiguation programs. *Proceedings of the Annual Meeting of the Association for Computational Linguistics (ACL)*, Newark, U.S.A., 249–256.

Gale, William, Ken Church & David Yarowsky. 1992b. One sense per discourse. *Proceedings of the DARPA Speech and Natural Language Workshop*, New York, U.S.A, 233–237.

Halliday, Michael & Ruqaiya Hasan. 1976. *Cohesion in English*. London: Longman.

Hirst, Graeme & David St-Onge. 1998. Lexical chains as representations of context in the detection and correction of malapropisms. In *WordNet: An electronic lexical database*, ed. by Christiane Fellbaum, 305–332. Massachusetts, U.S.A.: MIT Press.

Jiang, Jian & David Conrath. 1997. Semantic similarity based on corpus statistics and lexical taxonomy. *Proceedings of the International Conference on Research in Computational Linguistics*, Taipei, Taiwan.

Kilgarriff, Adam & Joseph Rosenzweig. 2000. English SENSEVAL: Report and results. *Proceedings of the International Conference on Language Resources and Evaluations (LREC)*, Athens, Greece, 1239–1244.

Kilgarriff, Adam. 2001. English lexical sample task description. *Proceedings of Senseval-2: Second International Workshop on Evaluating Word Sense Disambiguation Systems*, Toulouse, France, 17–20.

Krovetz, Robert. 1998. More than one sense per discourse. *Proceedings of the Workshop on Evaluating Word Sense Disambiguation Systems (SENSEVAL-1)*, Sussex, England.

Leacock, Claudia, Martin Chodorow & George A. Miller. 1998. Using corpus statistics and WordNet relations for sense identification. *Computational Linguistics,* 24(1): 147–165.

Lesk, Michael. 1986. Automatic sense disambiguation using machine readable dictionaries: How to tell a pine cone from an ice cream cone. *Proceedings of the ACM-SIGDOC Conference*, Toronto, Canada, 24–26.

Li, Hang & Naoki Abe. 1998. Generalizing case frames using a thesaurus and the MDL principle. *Computational Linguistics*, 24(2): 217–244.

Lin, Dekang. 1998. An information theoretic definition of similarity. *Proceedings of the International Conference on Machine Learning*, Madison, U.S.A., 296–304.

Litkowski, Ken. 2001. Use of machine readable dictionaries for word sense disambiguation in Senseval-2. *Proceedings of Senseval-2: Second International Workshop on Evaluating Word Sense Disambiguation Systems*, Toulouse, France, 107–110.

Magnini, Bernardo, Carlo Strapparava, Giovanni Pezzulo & Alfio Gliozzo. 2001. Using domain information for word sense disambiguation. *Proceedings of Senseval-2: Second International Workshop on Evaluating Word Sense Disambiguation Systems*, Toulouse, France, 111–114.

Martínez, David & Eneko Agirre. 2000. One sense per collocation and genre/topic variations. *Proceedings of the Conference on Empirical Methods in Natural Language Processing (EMNLP),* Hong Kong, 207–215.

McCarthy, Diana, John Carroll & Judita Preiss. 2001. Disambiguating noun and verb senses using automatically acquired selectional preferences. *Proceedings of Senseval-2: Second International Workshop on Evaluating Word Sense Disambiguation Systems*, Toulouse, France, 119–122.

McCarthy, Diana, and John Carroll. 2003. Disambiguating nouns, verbs and adjectives using automatically acquired selectional preferences. *Computational Linguistics,* 29(4): 639-654.

McCarthy, Diana, Robert Koeling, Julie Weeds & John Carroll. 2004. Finding predominant senses in untagged text. *Proceedings of the Annual Meeting of the Association for Computational Linguistics (ACL),* Barcelona, Spain, 280–287.

Mihalcea, Rada & Dan Moldovan. 1999. A method for word sense disambiguation of unrestricted text. *Proceedings of the Annual Meeting of the Association for Computational Linguistics (ACL),* Maryland, U.S.A., 152–158.

Mihalcea, Rada & Dan Moldovan. 2000. An iterative approach to word sense disambiguation. *Proceedings of Florida Artificial Intelligence Research Society,* Orlando, U.S.A., 219–223.

Mihalcea, Rada. 2005. Large vocabulary unsupervised word sense disambiguation with graph-based algorithms for sequence data labeling. *Proceedings of the Joint Human Language Technology and Empirical Methods in Natural Language Processing Conference (HLT/EMNLP),* Vancouver, Canada, 411–418.

Miller, George, Martin Chodorow, Shari Landes, Claudia Leacock & Robert Thomas. 1994. Using a semantic concordance for sense identification. *Proceedings of the Fourth ARPA Human Language Technology Workshop,* 303–308.

Miller, George. 1995. Wordnet: A lexical database. *Communications of the ACM,* 38(11): 39–41.

Navigli, Roberto & Paola Velardi. 2004. Structural semantic interconnection: A knowledge-based approach to word sense disambiguation. *Proceedings of Senseval-3: Third International Workshop on the Evaluation of Systems for the Semantic Analysis of Text,* Barcelona, Spain, 179–182.

Okumura, Manabu & Takeo Honda. 1994. Word sense disambiguation and text segmentation based on lexical cohesion. *Proceedings of the International Conference on Computational Linguistics (COLING),* Kyoto, Japan, 755–761.

Patwardhan, Sid, Satanjeev Banerjee & Ted Pedersen. 2003. Using measures of semantic relatedness for word sense disambiguation. *Proceedings of the Conference on Computational Linguistics and Intelligent Text Processing (CICLING),* Mexico City, Mexico, 241–257.

Rada, Roy, Hafedh Mili, Ellen Bicknell & Maria Blettner. 1989. Development and application of a metric on semantic nets. *IEEE Transactions on Systems, Man, and Cybernetics,* 19(1): 17–30.

Resnik, Philip. 1993. *Selection and information: A class-based approach to lexical relationships.* Ph.D. Thesis, University of Pennsylvania.

Resnik, Philip. 1995. Using information content to evaluate semantic similarity. *Proceedings of the International Joint Conference on Artificial Intelligence (IJCAI),* Montreal, Canada, 448–453.

Resnik, Philip. 1997. Selectional preference and sense disambiguation. *Proceedings of ACL Workshop on Tagging Text with Lexical Semantics, Why, What and How?* Washington, U.S.A., 52–57.

Resnik, Philip & David Yarowsky. 1999. Distinguishing systems and distinguishing senses: New evaluation methods for word sense disambiguation. *Natural Language Engineering* 5(2): 113–133.

Stetina, Jiri, Sadao Kurohashi & Makoto Nagao. 1998. General word sense disambiguation method based on a full sentential context. *Proceedings of the workshop on Usage of WordNet in Natural Language Processing*, Montreal, Canada, 1–8.

Stevenson, Mark & Yorick Wilks. 2001. The interaction of knowledge sources in word sense disambiguation. *Computational Linguistics,* 27(3): 321–349.

Tat, Lim B., Zaharin Yusoff, Tang E. Kong & Guo C. Ming. 2001. Primitive-based word sense disambiguation for Senseval-2. *Proceedings of Senseval-2: Second International Workshop on Evaluating Word Sense Disambiguation Systems*, Toulouse, France, 103–106.

Vasilescu, Florentina, Philippe Langlais & Guy Lapalme. 2004. Evaluating variants of the Lesk approach for disambiguating words. *Proceedings of the Conference on Language Resources and Evaluation (LREC),* Lisbon, Portugal, 633–636.

Yarowsky, David. 1993. One sense per collocation. *Proceedings of the ARPA Human Language Technology Workshop*, Plainsboro, U.S.A., 265–271.

Yarowsky, David. 1995. Unsupervised word sense disambiguation rivaling supervised methods. *Proceedings of the 33rd Annual Meeting of the Association for Computational Linguistics (ACL),* Cambridge, U.S.A., 189–196.

6 Unsupervised Corpus-Based Methods for WSD

Ted Pedersen

University of Minnesota, Duluth

This chapter focuses on unsupervised corpus-based methods of word sense discrimination that are knowledge-lean, and do not rely on external knowledge sources such as machine readable dictionaries, concept hierarchies, or sense-tagged text. They do not assign sense tags to words; rather, they discriminate among word meanings based on information found in unannotated corpora. This chapter reviews distributional approaches that rely on monolingual corpora and methods based on translational equivalence as found in word-aligned parallel corpora. These techniques are organized into type- and token-based approaches. The former identify sets of related words, while the latter distinguish among the senses of a word used in multiple contexts.

6.1 Introduction

Research in word sense disambiguation (WSD) has resulted in the development of algorithms that rely on a variety of resources. These include knowledge-rich techniques that employ dictionaries, thesauri, or concept hierarchies (Chap. 5), and corpus-based approaches that take advantage of sense-tagged text (Chap. 7). Unfortunately, the resources required for such approaches must be hand-built by humans and are therefore expensive to acquire and maintain. This inevitably leads to knowledge acquisition bottlenecks when attempting to handle larger amounts of text, new domains, or new languages.

There are two alternative avenues that eliminate this dependence on manually created resources. The first are *distributional* approaches that make distinctions in word meanings based on the assumption that words

E. Agirre and P. Edmonds (eds.), Word Sense Disambiguation: Algorithms and Applications, 133–166.
© 2007 *Springer.*

that occur in similar contexts will have similar meanings (see, e.g., Harris (1968), Miller and Charles (1991)). The second are *translational-equivalence* approaches based on parallel corpora, which identify translations of a word to a target language that are dependent on the sense of the word in the source language. These different sense-dependent translations of a word can then be used as a kind of sense inventory for that word in the source language. Both distributional and translational-equivalence methods can be considered *knowledge-lean*, since they require no resources beyond unannotated monolingual corpora or word-aligned parallel text.

A key characteristic of distributional approaches is that they do not categorize words based on a pre-existing sense inventory, but rather cluster words based on their contexts as observed in corpora. This is an appealing alternative to knowledge-intensive methods, since sense inventories are usually hand-crafted, and approaches that depend on them will necessarily be constrained to those words where a human expert has enumerated the possible meanings. Even if a sense inventory already exists, it is unlikely to be generally useful, since the nature and degree of sense distinctions that will be of interest will vary across a range of applications (see Chaps. 2, 3, and 11).

Distributional approaches do not assign meanings to words, but rather allow us to *discriminate* among the meanings of a word by identifying clusters of similar contexts, where each cluster shows that word being used in a particular meaning. This is quite distinct from the traditional task of word sense disambiguation, which classifies words relative to existing senses.

Methods based on translational equivalence rely on the fact that the different senses of a word in a source language may translate to completely different words in a target language. These approaches have two attractive properties. First, they automatically derive a sense inventory that makes distinctions that are relevant to the problem of machine translation. Second, a sense-tagged corpus based on these distinctions can be automatically created and used as training data for traditional methods of supervised learning.

6.1.1 Scope

This chapter is about knowledge-lean methods that rely on monolingual or parallel corpora. These methods are distinct in that they do not assign meanings relative to a pre-existing sense inventory, but rather make distinctions in meaning based on distributional similarity or translational equivalence. They are highly portable, robust, and do not require dictionaries, concept hierarchies, or any other hand-crafted knowledge source. As such, they are unsupervised in a strict sense, since they are not guided by manually created examples or knowledge resources. However, "unsupervised" has become a polysemous term in the word sense disambiguation literature, and can be a source of some confusion.

One common sense of "unsupervised" literally means "not supervised", and includes any method that does not use supervised learning from sense-tagged text. This definition leads to approaches that rely on manually created resources such as WordNet being referred to as unsupervised (e.g., Rigau et al. (1997), Resnik (1997), and Buitelaar, et al. (2001)). In fact, this is the definition of unsupervised that has been used in the Senseval-2 and Senseval-3 WSD evaluation exercises (see Chap. 4). However, we exclude such methods from this chapter since they are based on knowledge-rich resources and are not knowledge-lean even though they don't use sense-tagged text. Instead, these methods are discussed in Chapter 5.

"Unsupervised" can also be used to describe methods that are minimally supervised. These are approaches that bootstrap from a small number of sense-tagged training examples, and use those to build a simple model or classifier that then tags a few more contexts. The newly tagged contexts are added to the training data and the process is repeated until a large amount of data has been sense-tagged. While these methods use a smaller amount of sense-tagged text, there is still some manual intervention required, and often times the goal is to classify words based on a pre-existing sense inventory.

Yarowsky's (1995) algorithm is the most prominent example of such an approach. It is initialized with a set of seed collocations that are selected by a human. These seeds include the target word and are strongly indicative of a particular sense, as in *manufacturing plant* versus *flowering plant*. While this method does not require the use of a sense inventory, the fact that a human selects the seed collocations leads to it not being considered knowledge-lean. Instead, it is discussed in Chapter 7 (Sect 7.2.4).

Thus, polysemy is a fact of life even in scientific literature, and we would have it no other way. While the different senses of "unsupervised" may result in some confusion, each of them represents a reasonable and distinct type of solution to the problem of semantic ambiguity. This chapter defines "unsupervised" to mean knowledge-lean approaches that do not require sense-tagged text and do not utilize other manually-crafted knowledge as found in dictionaries or concept hierarchies. These methods are data-driven and language-independent, and rely on the distributional characteristics of unannotated corpora, and translational equivalences in word aligned parallel text.

6.1.2 Motivation

Given the very tight constraints placed on knowledge-lean approaches, it seems reasonable to ask why even attempt such an apparently unpromising and difficult task. Why not take advantage of rich lexical resources that already exist such as the *Longman Dictionary of Contemporary English* (LDOCE) or WordNet? Why not undertake a systematic and long-term effort to create sense-tagged text, or make do with existing sense-tagged corpora?

The motivation for knowledge-lean approaches follows quite naturally from arguments against the very idea of word senses, particularly as expressed in the form of a fixed sense inventory (see Kilgarriff (1997) and Chaps. 2 and 3). The principal objection is that all dictionaries impose their own unique interpretation and organization on the meanings of a word, and that this is at best an imperfect and approximate representation of what might really exist in language. Each dictionary draws the boundaries between different senses of a word at disparate points along the spectrum of meaning.

Thus, any approach to WSD that is dependent on a particular sense inventory is permanently locked into a fixed view of word meanings that will not be able to evolve or adapt as circumstances warrant. Sense-tagged text is the most obvious example, since the tags are normally associated with senses from a selected dictionary. But the same limitations apply to approaches based on the structure or content of resources such as WordNet or LDOCE, since typically their sense inventories are inherited along with this other information. Thus, such methods not only depend on a particular sense inventory, their disambiguation algorithm may be based on a certain organization or structure that is unique to that resource.

For example, numerous disambiguation algorithms rely on the noun *is-a* hierarchies of WordNet, the subject codes in LDOCE, or the semantic categories in *Roget's International Thesaurus* (Chaps. 5 and 10). However, the very formulation of such disambiguation algorithms may be specific to these underlying knowledge-rich resources and not able to generalize to other similar or related resources. This has the long-term effect of locking the algorithm to a particular sense inventory and making it impossible to adapt or extend the algorithm beyond the boundaries imposed by a particular resource and its sense inventory.

A second danger of developing methods that are tightly coupled with knowledge-rich resources is that this frequently introduces a high degree of language dependence, and makes it difficult to apply them to a variety of languages. Thus, if one rejects the use of pre-existing sense inventories and rich knowledge resources on the grounds of maintaining portability and adaptability across resources and languages, then unsupervised knowledge-lean approaches are appealing. They are based on the belief that sense inventories are not absolute arbiters of word meanings, and that disambiguation algorithms should not be limited to a particular sense inventory or knowledge-rich resource, and that they should port readily to new languages.

Distributional Methods

Distributional methods identify words that appear in similar contexts without regard to any particular underlying sense inventory. Schütze (1998), for example, decomposes word sense disambiguation into a two step process. The first is to discriminate among the different meanings of a given target word by dividing the contexts in which it occurs into clusters that share distributional characteristics. The second is to label each cluster with a gloss that describes the underlying meaning of the target word in those contexts. This is quite distinct from the usual view of word sense disambiguation, where the labels (i.e., sense-tags) are assumed to exist prior to discrimination.

This "discriminate and label" view of disambiguation corresponds to a somewhat idealized view of a lexicographer's technique for defining a word. A lexicographer collects multiple contexts of a target word from a large corpus that is representative of the audience for whom the dictionary is being created. For example, when compiling a children's dictionary the corpus should consist of text written for children, whereas when creating a dictionary of technical terminology the corpus should be from the particular specialty that is to be the focus of the dictionary. The lexicographer studies the resulting concordance lines, which show the target word in many contexts, and begins to divide the occurrences of that word into various piles or clusters, gradually discriminating among the various meanings of the word without any preconceived ideas about how many clusters should be created (see Chap. 2 (Sect. 2.2), Chap. 3 (Sect. 3.2), and Hanks (2000)). Thus, distributional approaches can be seen as an effort to automate the discrimination portion of the two step approach to word sense disambiguation.

The result of the discrimination step is some number of clusters that capture the different meanings of the word, as observed in the particular corpus used to create the concordance. Then, the lexicographer must study each cluster and compose a definition that acts as a sense tag or a label. This establishes the sense of the word that will appear in the dictionary that the lexicographer is crafting. In effect this labeling is a form of summarization, which briefly describes all of the contexts of the target word that make up the cluster. Given the limited space available in dictionaries, this is by necessity brief and abstracts away many details. Composing a definition that describes a cluster made up of multiple examples of a word in context is a challenging problem even for a human expert, and it no doubt requires that they draw upon real-world knowledge in addition to the content of the concordance.

Despite the apparent difficulty, automatic labeling of clusters of contexts of a target word with definitions of that word is an important problem to pursue. One possible solution is to identify sets of words that are related to the contents of each cluster using *type-based* methods of discrimination as will be discussed in this chapter. In brief, rather than crafting a traditional definition, a set of word types that are associated with a cluster could be used as an approximation of a sense-tag. For example, a cluster of contexts of the target word *line* might contain a set of related words such as *phone, telephone, call,* and *busy*. While this is not as rich or informative as a carefully drawn definition, it is certainly indicative of the underlying meaning of the cluster.

Knowledge-lean approaches can address the discrimination and/or labeling phase of the two-step view of word sense disambiguation. If such methods are successfully developed, the result will be an automatic language-independent process of word sense disambiguation that will not fall victim to knowledge acquisition bottlenecks.

However, until such methods are available, a reasonable alternative may be to label the clusters of contexts found by distributional methods with information from existing knowledge-rich resources. McCarthy et al. (2004) present one particularly promising approach. Given a corpus that includes multiple occurrences of a particular target noun, they use Lin's (1998) distributional method to identify a set of word types that are contextually and syntactically related to that target word. They find the k nearest neighbors to this word to characterize the domain in which the target word occurs. They use the Jiang and Conrath (1997) and Banerjee and Pedersen (2003) measures to determine the degree of semantic similarity or relatedness between the word and its neighbors. (See Chap. 5 for other related measures).

The sense of the target word judged most similar (semantically) to the set of word types representing the domain is considered to be the predominant sense in that domain. Then, the target word is assigned that sense in all of the contexts in which it occurs in the given corpus. McCarthy et al. show that this method attains accuracy of 64% on the nouns of the Senseval-2 English all-words task, where the most-frequent-sense baseline is 69%. This is an impressive result as all but two of the participating systems in the Senseval-2 all-words task achieved accuracy lower than the baseline.

Since McCarthy et al.'s method uses WordNet; it is not an unsupervised knowledge-lean approach. However, it is related to such methods since it could be used to augment clusters of contexts discovered via distributional methods with sense tags from WordNet. For example, McCarthy et al. show that the nearest distributional neighbors of *pipe* as found in contexts from the British National Corpus (BNC) include the following: *tube, cable, wire, tank, hole, cylinder, fitting, tap, cistern, plate*. This set of words proves to be most related to the sense of *pipe* that means "a tube made of metal or plastic used to carry water, oil, or gas etc." Their experiment did not attempt to discriminate among the different meanings of *pipe* that may be present in the BNC (and as such found a dominant sense, which was their goal). However, suppose that the contexts in which *pipe* occurs were first clustered via some distributional method – we could then apply McCarthy et al.'s method to each resulting cluster, and thereby assign a sense of *pipe* to each of the clusters.

Translational Equivalence

As introduced above, translational-equivalence methods have the potential to make distinctions in meaning that are relevant to machine translation, which has long been suggested as an application that would benefit from WSD (see Chap. 11 (Sect. 11.3)). It is often difficult to determine if a sense inventory is appropriate for a particular domain or application, and there seems to be general agreement that there is no single inventory that will always be the best choice. For example, the senses relevant to an information retrieval task are not likely the same ones that matter to machine translation. The nature of the sense distinctions to be made must reflect both the domain of the text and the underlying application for which disambiguation is being employed (see Chap. 3 (Sect 3.4)). Resnik and Yarowsky (1997) note that methods based on translational equivalence have the potential to address both problems since the sense distinctions observed in parallel corpora represent the actual distinctions that will be useful for machine translation. This is a critical point, since the utility of sense inventories as provided in a dictionary or other lexical resource is sometimes dubious with respect to specific applications. For example, the distinctions in WordNet are in many cases more fine grained than may be needed, and there is no hierarchy of senses that allows for easy generalization from fine- to coarse-grained senses of a word. Methods based on translational equivalence can also be used to derive bilingual dictionaries automatically from parallel corpora, which may allow them to be more specific to a given domain.

6.1.3 Approaches

Distributional approaches function at two levels of granularity. *Type-based* methods identify sets (or clusters) of words that are deemed to be related by virtue of their use in similar contexts. These methods often rely on measuring similarity between word co-occurrence vectors, and produce sets of word types such as *(line, cord, tie, cable)* and *(line, telephone, busy)*. Note that the resulting clusters do not include any information regarding the individual occurrences of each word, which is why they are known as type-based methods.

Token-based methods cluster all of the contexts in which a given target word (or words) occur based on the similarity of those contexts. In the following example, *line* and *queue* are the target words. The contexts in which they occur have been assigned to two different clusters:

Cluster 1:   *The line was occupied.*
            The operator came onto the line abruptly.

Cluster 2:   *The line was really long and it took forever to be served.*
            I stood in the queue for about 10 minutes.

Cluster 1 refers to the telephone sense of *line*, while Cluster 2 refers to the formation in which people wait for service. This illustrates the overall goal of such methods, which is to assign each context in which a target word occurs to a cluster that contains contexts that use the target word in the same sense. This is referred to as token-based discrimination, since each context in which the target word occurs is preserved in a cluster.

The input to a token-based method is a corpus of text where a particular target word (or words) has been specified. It attempts to differentiate among the multiple contexts that contain the target word(s) based on their similarity. For example, suppose there are 100 contexts, each of which contains the word *line*. The output is some number of clusters, each of which is made up of the contexts that are judged to be more similar to each other than they are to any of the contexts in the other clusters. Thus, such an approach might recognize that *line* has been used in three distinct senses. However, these methods do not label the resulting clusters, and it would be necessary for a human to examine the three clusters and determine, for example, that one contained contexts associated with the telephone, one with queues, and another with a line of text.

Note that type- and token-based methods of discrimination are related in that some degree of token-based discrimination may need to occur before a set of related types can be discovered. In the example above, it would be reasonable to extend the results of the token-based clusters to conclude that the types *line* and *queue* form a set of related words, since both occur in contexts that are assigned to the same cluster.

Methods of translational equivalence also have type and token-based interpretations. A token-based method labels each occurrence of a target word with its appropriate translation, which is a type in the source language that is assumed to represent a distinct sense. For example, given a parallel corpus of English and Spanish, all the occurrences of *bill* that mean 'invoice' will be tagged as *cuenta,* while those that mean 'bird jaw' will be tagged as *pico.* The end result will be a corpus of "sense-tagged" text, where the tags are the translational equivalences of the target words in that context. The tags of the tokens in one language are in fact the types of the translational equivalences in the other. While this may often result in an unambiguous sense distinction, there is some possibility that the resulting tags may be polysemous since the translational equivalences may have ambiguities in the target language. These methods can be used to derive sense-tagged text (which is a token-based level of discrimination) or to create bilingual dictionaries (which is a type-based resource). For each word in the target language, a bilingual dictionary provides a set of related words in the source language.

6.2 Type-Based Discrimination

Type-based approaches create a representation of the different words in a corpus that attempts to capture their contextual similarity, often in a high-dimensional feature space. These representations are usually based on counts of word co-occurrences or measures of association between words. Given such information about a word, it is possible to identify other words that have a similar profile and are thereby presumed to have occurred in related contexts and have similar meanings. Some of these methods explicitly account for the polysemy of words and represent each possible meaning of a word, while others do not and simply arrive at an averaged or predominant sense.

Upon first consideration, the conflation of the multiple possible meanings of a word into a single representation, or simply the identification of the predominant sense, may not seem terribly useful. However, it is widely agreed that the most-frequent-sense baseline is often a very successful method of word sense disambiguation. So, coupled with the one-sense-per-discourse hypothesis (when true), typed-based methods can potentially perform WSD in a particular domain (see Chap. 5 on the baseline and hypothesis).

In addition, type-based methods that account for polysemy will allow the same word type to appear in multiple sets of related words, where each set essentially disambiguates itself. For example, (*line, cable, tie, cord*) clearly refers to the rope-like sense, while (*line, telephone, call*) is related to communication. While *line* occurs in both sets, its meaning in each is disambiguated by the other words in each set.

6.2.1 Representation of Context

Type-based techniques often rely on high-dimensional spaces defined by word co-occurrences. As a generic example, if there are N word types in a corpus, then a symmetric $N \times N$ co-occurrence matrix can be constructed, where each word type is represented by a particular row (or column). Each cell in such a matrix contains a count of the number of times the words of words represented by the row and column co-occur within some window of context. These may indicate pairs of co-occurring words without regard to order, or they may be ordered co-occurrences, which we will refer to as "bigrams". When order doesn't matter, then *oil rig* and *rig oil* have the same frequency count; when order does matter then the counts will likely be different.

If the matrix contains unordered co-occurrence counts, then it will be symmetric and square. However, if it contains bigram counts, then it will be rectangular and asymmetric. Fig. 6.1 is an example of a bigram matrix made up of count values. It shows that *oil rig* occurs 20 times, *oil trap* 3 times, *grease rig* 5 times, and *grease trap* 10 times. Note that if we allow some number of intervening words between the words of interest, it is not explicitly indicated in such a matrix. After building this matrix, each word has a row and column vector that defines the contexts in which it occurs.

	rig	trap
oil	20	3
grease	5	10

Fig. 6.1. Bigram matrix.

	trap	¬trap	Total
grease	$n_{11} = 10$	$n_{12} = 5$	$n_{1p} = 15$
¬grease	$n_{21} = 15$	$n_{22} = 970$	$n_{2p} = 985$
Total	$n_{p1} = 25$	$n_{p2} = 975$	$n_{pp} = 1{,}000$

Fig. 6.2. 2 × 2 contingency table of bigram counts.

There are many variations possible in these matrices beyond ordered bigrams versus unordered co-occurrences. Rather than counts, the cells in the matrix could contain scores of measures of association such as the log-likelihood ratio (G^2) or pointwise mutual information (PMI). These measures indicate the degree to which two words occur together more often than would be expected by chance. The co-occurrence counts are normally represented in a 2 × 2 contingency table. For example, Fig. 6.2 gives a more detailed view of the counts associated with the bigram *grease trap*. This shows that *grease trap* occurs 10 times (n_{11}), that *grease* is the first word in a bigram with words other than *trap* 5 times (n_{12}), that *grease* occurs as the first word of a bigram 15 times (n_{1p}), and so forth. The column and row totals are referred to as marginal counts, and are indicated by values that have a "p" in their subscripts. Finally, this table shows that there are 1,000 bigrams in the corpus (n_{pp}).

The log-likelihood ratio compares the divergence of these observed frequencies with the counts that would be expected if the two words were truly independent (and only occurring together by chance), as shown in Eq. 6.1.

$$G^2 = 2 \times \sum_{i,j=1}^{2} n_{ij} \log \frac{n_{ij}}{m_{ij}} \tag{6.1}$$

The expected value m_{ij} is calculated by multiplying the frequency of the two marginal totals, and dividing by the number of bigrams in the sample. For example, in the *grease trap* example $m_{11} = (15 \times 25)/1000 = 0.375$. The expected values are calculated for each cell in the 2 × 2 table and then compared to the observed values in order to see how much the observed and expected values diverge. If the expected and observed values are comparable, the overall score will be close to 0, which indicates that the two

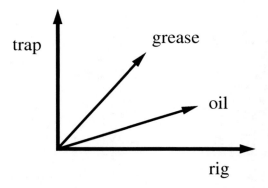

Fig. 6.3. Context vectors created from the bigram matrix.

words have occurred together by chance and are not significantly associated. Values greater than 0 show that the observed values diverge greatly from those expected if the words in the bigram were independent, which is interpreted as evidence that the words in the bigram are associated, and that the bigram is a collocation. For the given example of *grease trap* the log-likelihood ratio is 59.41, which shows considerable deviation between the observed and expected values, and suggests (strongly) that the observed values do not support the hypothesis that the two words are independent. Thus, we would conclude that *grease trap* is a significant bigram.

After the co-occurrence matrix is created, a word type can be represented in a multi-dimensional space by treating its corresponding row as a vector in an *N*-dimensional space, where the vector begins at the origin. For example, Fig. 6.3 shows vectors for *oil* and *grease* based on the co-occurrence data found in Fig. 6.1.

The contextual similarity between word types can be measured by the cosine between their corresponding vectors. In general, the cosine is defined as in Eq. 6.2, where $\vec{x}$ and $\vec{y}$ are the word vectors being compared. Their dot products are scaled by the product of their vector lengths. This value measures the distance between the different contexts in which the words being compared occur.

$$\cos(\vec{x}, \vec{y}) = \frac{\vec{x} \cdot \vec{y}}{|\vec{x}||\vec{y}|} \tag{6.2}$$

6.2.2 Algorithms

Three different type-based algorithms are discussed in this section. They include Latent Semantic Analysis (LSA)[1] (Deerwester et al. 1991, Landauer and Dumais 1997, Landauer et al. 1998), the Hyperspace Analogue to Language (HAL) (Burgess and Lund 1997, 2000), and Clustering by Committee (CBC)[2] (Lin and Pantel 2002).

HAL and LSA represent a corpus by populating a multi-dimensional space with vectors, where each vector represents the context in which a word type occurs. Note that each word type is only represented by a single vector, so it is not possible to directly represent the polysemy of individual words. Rather, HAL and LSA will measure the similarity between word types observed in a given corpus. For example, they might conclude that *rock, boulder*, and *stone* are all related.

HAL relies on word-by-word co-occurrence matrices to represent context, while LSA is based on word-by-context representations. HAL measures Euclidean distance between the endpoints of vectors, while LSA measures the cosine between two vectors. Note that LSA can be extended to measure the similarity between a pair of sentences or contexts by averaging the vectors associated with words that make up each context being compared. In fact, when we consider token-based methods we will see that this technique is at the center of several methods of word sense discrimination.

CBC discovers clusters of word types associated with the underlying senses of a target word, using word-by-context co-occurences. For example, given *rock* as the target, CBC might identify two clusters, one associated with music that consists of *meringue, calypso*, and *reggae,* and another associated with geology that is made up of *marble, sandstone*, and *granite*. Thus, CBC identifies synonyms associated with the different senses of a word, while HAL and LSA represent each word type with a single sense.

All three rely on multi-dimensional representations of co-occurrence data. In LSA the contexts are short articles or paragraphs, whereas in CBC the contexts are syntactic. As a result, CBC is not knowledge-lean in the same sense as HAL or LSA, but it remains a viable approach since it uses no knowledge beyond syntactic parses and is able to make sense distinctions for a single word type, which is something neither HAL nor LSA is capable of in their standard formulations.

---

[1] LSA: http://lsa.colorado.edu/

[2] CBC: http://www.isi.edu/~pantel/Content/Demos/LexSem/cbc.htm

Latent Semantic Analysis (LSA)

LSA traces its origins to a technique in information retrieval known as Latent Semantic Indexing (LSI) (Furnas et al. 1988, Deerwester et al. 1990). The objective of LSI is to improve the retrieval of documents by reducing a large term-by-document matrix into a much smaller space using Singular Value Decomposition (SVD). LSA uses much the same methodology, except that it employs a word-by-context representation.

LSA represents a corpus of text as an $M \times N$ co-occurrence matrix, where the M rows correspond to word types, and the N columns provide a unit of context such as a phrase, sentence, or paragraph. Each cell in this matrix contains a count of the number of times that a word given in the row occurs in the context provided by the column.

LSI and LSA differ primarily in regards to their definition of context. For LSI it is a document, while for LSA it is more flexible, although it is often a paragraph of text. If the unit of context in LSA is a document, then LSA and LSI become essentially the same technique.

After the co-occurrence cell counts are collected and possibly smoothed or transformed in some way, the $M \times N$ matrix is decomposed via Singular Value Decomposition (SVD), which is a form of factor or principal components analysis. SVD reduces the dimensionality of the original matrix so that similar contexts are collapsed into each other. SVD is based on the fact that any rectangular matrix can be decomposed into the product of three other matrices. This decomposition can be achieved without any loss of information if no more factors than the minimum of N and M are used. In such cases the original matrix may be perfectly reconstructed.

However, as it is normally used, LSA reduces matrices of tens of thousands of dimensions down to a few hundred, and is therefore unable to perfectly reconstruct the original matrix. While this might sound undesirable, in fact this is exactly the goal of LSA. The effect of this is analogous to smoothing, where columns (contexts) that are only marginally different from each other are brought together, thus allowing for similarity judgments to be made. The hope is that the information that is lost because of the imperfect reconstruction is noise, and therefore the dimensionality reduction causes the similarity among words and contexts to become more apparent.

Landauer et al. (1997) presents an evaluation of the ability of LSA to discriminate among synonyms via a vocabulary test from the Test of English as a Foreign Language (TOEFL). The test taker is given a word and then asked to choose the most similar word from among four others. For example, if *levied* is the word in question, then the choice of the most similar word must be made from among *imposed, believed, requested,* or *correlated. Grolier's Encyclopedia* served as the corpus, where the first paragraph from each article served as a context and was represented as a column, and the word types therein were represented in the rows. This resulted in a matrix of 60,000 rows (words) and 30,473 columns (article paragraphs, on average 73 tokens long).

This matrix was decomposed to approximately 300 dimensions by SVD, and then reconstructed from this reduced representation. Then the test was taken simply by finding the cosine between the given word and each of the four alternatives. LSA chose the word with the smallest cosine to the given word as its answer. This proved to be correct 65% of the time, which is comparable to that of human test takers. When these cosine measures were computed using the original 30,000 × 60,000 matrix, the accuracy fell to 37%, suggesting that the decomposition is removing noise and achieving a better representation of synonymy.

This experiment was repeated by Turney (2001), who attained accuracy of 74% on the TOEFL test. Rather than using LSA or another high-dimensional representation, he calculated Pointwise Mutual Information values for the given word and each of the possible selections based on frequency counts obtained from the Alta Vista search engine. These two approaches both rely on evidence found in large corpora, however for LSA the corpora is represented by an SVD reduced co-occurrence matrix, while in the Turney work the World Wide Web acts as the corpus.

Hyperspace Analogue to Language (HAL)

HAL is based on word-by-word co-occurrence statistics (Burgess and Lund 1997, 2000). Unlike LSA it does not include larger units of context, but instead captures co-occurrence data for words that occur within a window of 10 positions of each other. The co-occurrences are order dependent, so in some respects the results can be thought of as a bigram matrix (although not exactly as described previously). This matrix allows the number of intervening positions between the two words to be up to 10. This is selected as the window size in order to capture some long distance dependencies among words, but yet still localized enough to avoid overwhelming frequency counts.

The bigram counts are scaled inversely proportional to the number of positions between the two words. Adjacent words receive a score of 10, while word pairs separated by nine intervening words receive a score of 1. The bigram matrix is not symmetric. Each word is represented by a row and a column, where the values in the row reflect the count of the number of times that word follows each word represented in the columns. Likewise, each column represents the number of times the word represented in the column precedes the words represented in the rows. Thus there are two context vectors created for each word. The word is finally represented by a single vector that is a concatenation of its row and column vector, which represent the co-occurrence behavior of the word as the first and second member of a bigram.

This matrix forms a high-dimensional space that is converted into a much smaller distance-based representation via Multidimensional Scaling (MDS). Normally MDS reduces a very large multidimensional space down to two or three dimensions, so that similar or related concepts can be clearly seen graphically by a human observer. This reduction also allows for the computation of Euclidean distance measures between word types, which are interpreted as representing semantic distances. MDS can be seen as a very extreme form of SVD. Since it reduces to so few dimensions, MDS is able to provide visual representations of synonymy which are easily interpreted by a human.

Burgess and Lund (1997) describe several experiments, all of which are based on a 300 million word corpus of Usenet newsgroup postings. This resulted in a co-occurrence matrix for the 70,000 most frequent words in the corpus that was then reduced using MDS. Once situated in 2-dimensional space, similarities between words can be measured as distances between these points.

Their first experiment assessed the degree to which HAL was able to distinguish among categories. They restricted their analysis to word types whose meanings conflated to one of four categories: animals, body parts, cities, and geographic locations. They extracted the vectors associated with types belonging to these categories and then applied MDS to convert the co-occurrence data into distances. Visual inspection of the resulting distances between types shows that clear distinctions are drawn among them. A second experiment restricts the analysis to parts of speech, and shows that selected nouns, prepositions, and determiners are clearly distinguished in the resulting distance space.

Clustering By Committee (CBC)

CBC takes a word type as input, and finds clusters of words that represent each sense of the word (Lin and Pantel 2002). The clusters will be made up of synonyms or words that are otherwise related to the discovered senses. For example, if *conference* is input, CBC produces two sets: the first including *summit*, *meeting*, *council*, and *session*, while the second includes

Big East, Big Ten, and *ACC* (which are university athletic conferences in the USA).

CBC is distinct from HAL and LSA in that it finds synonyms of different senses of a word and does not conflate all the meanings of a word into a single representation. It is also unique (and technically not knowledge-lean according to our standards) in that it requires a parsed corpus. This is not a difficult constraint for languages such as English which have suitable tools available, but it could pose challenges for languages with less developed resources.

CBC is a three stage algorithm. In the first stage a co-occurrence matrix is constructed, such that each cell in the matrix contains the Pointwise Mutual Information between a word and a particular context as found in the given corpus of text. Contexts are not simply co-occurring words but rather syntactic contexts in which a word has occurred in the parsed corpus. In particular, these contexts are dependency triples (Lin 1998) which consist of two words and the syntactic relation between them. For example, "threaten with X" is a context of *handgun*. The top k elements (words) associated with the target word are found by sorting these values. Lin and Pantel recommend values for k between 10 and 20.

These k most similar elements become the input to the second stage of CBC. For each of these elements, CBC finds its most similar elements from the same co-occurrence matrix as used in the first stage, and then clusters them using average link clustering. Each discovered cluster is assigned a similarity score, and the elements in the most similar cluster form a committee. Thus, each of the k most similar elements to the target word will have their own k most similar elements. For each of the latter elements, a committee will be formed that consists of the elements that prove (via clustering) to be most similar to each other. This continues recursively until a final set of committees is identified, where each committee represents a list of word types that characterize a sense of the target word.

Lin and Pantel (2002) evaluate CBC by comparing the lists of words assigned to each cluster with the contents of WordNet synsets. This suggests that the best case for the algorithm would be to find lists of synonyms associated with senses of words. They make this comparison by measuring the number of transformations (similar to edit distance) that would be required to convert one of their discovered senses into a WordNet synset. This results in a measure of cluster quality or purity, meaning that if no transformations were required then the discovered cluster exactly corresponds to the existing standard. They found that CBC achieved 60%

and 65% cluster quality on two randomly selected test sets, which was better than any of the other clustering algorithms they considered.

6.2.3 Discussion

Type-based methods are particularly useful in domains where a single sense for a word may be dominant. As shown by McCarthy et al. (2004), a method of disambiguation that relies on identifying the most frequent sense of a word for a particular domain can perform nearly as well as systems that are based on manually sense-tagged examples, and better than unsupervised systems that are based on un-annotated corpora or knowledge-rich resources.

Thus, type-based methods can provide an important first step towards carrying out disambiguation in more flexible and adaptable ways since the sets of related words that they identify depend entirely on the nature of the corpora from which they are extracted. A simple but effective method of disambiguation can follow in which a set of related words is associated with a single sense, and all the occurrences of the words in the set that occur in a particular corpus could be assigned that same sense.

In addition, type-based methods may be suitable for assigning labels to clusters that are discovered by token-based discrimination. In this case, a set of words related to the content of the clusters could be generated, and that set would be used as a label to describe or define the cluster. If successful, this could fully automate word sense disambiguation and make it possible to avoid the use of pre-existing sense inventories.

6.3 Token-Based Discrimination

The goal of token-based discrimination is to cluster the contexts in which a given target word occurs, such that the resulting clusters will be made up of contexts that use the target word in the same sense. Each context in which the target word occurs is a member of one of the resulting clusters. This is the basis of referring to these methods as *token-based*, since each occurrence of the target word (i.e., each token) is preserved.

The methods described in this section are based on the use of first- and second-order features. First-order features occur directly in a context being clustered, while second-order features are those that occur with a first order feature, but may not occur in the context being clustered.

We discuss two examples of token-based approaches. First, we describe Schütze's (1998) adaptations of LSI/LSA to token-based discrimination using second-order co-occurrence features. Then work by Pedersen and Bruce (1997, 1998) is presented, in which a small number of localized syntactic and co-occurrence features are employed in a first order representation. Finally, we briefly review a comparative study by Purandare and Pedersen (2004) of first- and second-order methods.

6.3.1 Representation of Context

The input to token-based discrimination is multiple contexts that contain a specified word type (i.e., the target word). This is similar to the input to supervised learning algorithms, with the very notable exception that there are no sense tags included in the data. When sense-tagged training examples are available, a supervised learning algorithm can determine which features are indicative of particular senses, and thereby build a model that takes advantage of this information. However, knowledge-lean approaches group contexts together based on their similarity, and it is presumed that a target word that occurs in similar contexts will have similar meanings.

6.3.2 Algorithms

This discussion focuses on two early approaches to word sense discrimination: Schütze's (1998) context group discrimination, and Pedersen and Bruce's (1997, 1998) work with a form of average link clustering known as McQuitty's Similarity Analysis. Both rely on different sets of features than those of the type-based approaches described in Section 6.2. Schütze adapts LSI/LSA so that it represents entire contexts rather than single word types using second-order co-occurrences of lexical features. Pedersen and Bruce rely on a small numbers of first-order features to create matrices that show the pairwise (dis)similarity between contexts. These features are localized around the target word and include word co-occurrences and part-of-speech tags.

The clusters that are created by all of these approaches are made up of contexts that represent a similar or related sense. However, it is challenging to evaluate such clusters without manually inspecting them or comparing them to a previously created gold standard that indicates a desired clustering. Schütze overcomes this difficulty by carrying out disambiguation of pseudo-words and performing a manual analysis, while Pedersen and Bruce as well as Purandare and Pedersen compare the discovered sense clusters with those previously determined by human judges while creating sense-tagged text.

Context Group Discrimination

Context group discrimination clusters together the contexts in which a given word type occurs. Like LSA, it uses SVD to reduce the dimensionality of a co-occurrence matrix. However, it goes one step beyond LSA and averages together word vectors to create a representation of a context that is then based on second-order co-occurrences.

In general, a word has a second-order co-occurrence with another if the words do not occur with each other, but both occur with a third word frequently. In effect, these are words that are joined by a "friend of a friend" relation. As a simple example, in *traffic cop* and *traffic accident, cop* is a second-order co-occurrence of *accident*, because both are first-order co-occurrences with *traffic*. Schütze argues for the use of second-order co-occurrences because they are less sparse and more likely to capture semantic content.

Context group discrimination represents the senses of a word by building a series of three vector spaces. The first is known as a "Word Space" and is a co-occurrence matrix where each word is represented by a vector of co-occurrence data, much as is done in LSA and HAL. There are two methods by which the words that make up the dimensions of the co-occurrence matrix are determined. In global selection, features are selected based on their frequency in a large corpus of text and without regard to whether they occur anywhere near the target word. Schütze uses the 20,000 most frequent words as features and creates a co-occurrence matrix with the 2,000 most frequent words, based on counts obtained from 60 million words of *New York Times* articles. Local selection does not consider this entire corpus but rather only the contexts in which the target word occurs. It performs a Chi-squared test of association between the target word and any word that occurs within 25 positions. Those surrounding words that prove to be strongly associated with the target are indicative of one of the senses of the target word and are therefore included as features. In Schütze's experiments, local selection finds 1,000 features, which leads to a 1,000 × 1,000 Word Space.

The dimensionality of the Word Space may be reduced by Singular Value Decomposition, although this is not required. This has the effect of smoothing out zero counts, and conflating words that appear in nearly the same contexts. However, Schütze finds that the discrimination results don't tend to vary much regardless of whether or not SVD was performed.

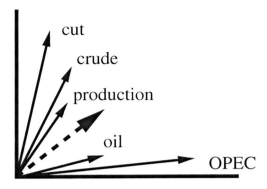

Fig. 6.4. Context vector (dashed) as average of word vectors (solid).

Both local and global selection result in a vector associated with each word type, and in fact one can find sets of related word types by measuring the cosines between these vectors. However, context group discrimination goes on to create *context vectors* from the Word Space that represent the contexts in which each target word occurs. A context vector is the centroid (or average) of the vectors in the Word Space associated with the words that occur in that particular context and are included in the Word Space.

A context vector is created for each context in which a given target word occurs. For example, Fig. 6.4 shows a hypothetical context vector for the sentence *OPEC has cut production of crude oil*. Note that stop words are eliminated, so there is a vector associated with each of the following words: *OPEC, cut, production, crude*, and *oil*. The context vector is the average of these word vectors, and ultimately represents the context.

Second-order co-occurrences of the target word come about indirectly via this representation. The Word Space represents first-order co-occurrences by creating a vector for each word which shows the words with which it occurs (within a given number of positions) in a large corpus of text. These first-order vectors are then used to create a second-order representation of each context in which a target word occurs, by averaging together all the vectors of all the words that occur in a given vector. This results in a context vector, which represents the target word in that context based on the first-order co-occurrences of the words in its surrounding context, which are therefore the second-order co-occurrences of the target word.

Once all of the context vectors for a word type have been created, *sense vectors* are discovered by identifying clusters of similar context vectors. This is done with the Buckshot clustering algorithm (Cutting et al. 1992), which uses the results of an agglomerative clustering algorithm as seeds for the EM algorithm (Dempster et al. 1977). The sense vectors that are discovered represent the different senses of the target word.

Context group discrimination is evaluated by dividing a corpus into training and test portions. The local and global selection of co-occurrence features and subsequent creation of the Word Space are carried out relative to the training data, as is the derivation of the context and sense vectors. Each context in the test data is assigned to the sense vector whose centroid is closest to the context vector that represents that test context.

In Schütze's experiments, the training and test data was taken from the *New York Times*. There were approximately 60 million word tokens in the training data and 5.4 million words in the test data. These two sets of data were taken from different time periods in order to guarantee that there are differences in vocabulary which will introduce some noise into the context vectors and lead to a more stringent and realistic evaluation.

Schütze presents results with ten pseudo-words and ten naturally occurring words. The pseudo-words were created by conflating two word types into one. For example, all occurrences of *banana* and *door* are conflated to *banana-door*. This is a convenient means of creating data for evaluation since the correct sense of each occurrence of a pseudo-word is simply its original form (Yarowsky 1993) (see also Chap 4. (Sect. 4.3)). While pseudo-words could be used to create multiple-way ambiguities, in these experiments they were always two-way. In order to also use naturally occurring ambiguous words in his experiments, Schütze sense-tagged test data for these words. He reports accuracies for the pseudo-words and the naturally occurring words separately. For the 10 pseudo-words, the local features attain average accuracy (when identifying two clusters) of 89.9%. When using the global features the accuracy is 98.6%. The most-frequent-sense baseline for the pseudo-words is approximately 60%. For the 10 naturally occurring words, the local features result in accuracy of 76%, and 80.8% for the global features. The most frequent sense for the naturally occurring words is approximately 65%. The greater level of success for the pseudo-words is not surprising, given that the distinctions made were quite coarse and artificial. For example, one of the pseudo words was the conflation of *pete rose* and *nuclear power*, which will usually occur in very different contexts.

McQuitty's Similarity Analysis

Pedersen and Bruce (1997, 1998) cluster the contexts in which a target word occurs based on the use of a small set of localized features. This approach is distinct from the others in this chapter in that it does not employ large co-occurrence vectors to represent words or contexts. Each context in which a target word appears is converted into a relatively small feature vector that includes simple morphological features, the part of speech of surrounding words, and a small number of co-occurrence features. A first-order feature vector is created to represent each context, and that vector indicates which features occur in a particular context.

Pedersen and Bruce consider nouns, verbs, and adjectives as possible target words in the discrimination task, and explore the use of several different combinations of features. They identify their features from the contexts that are to be clustered, which is in contrast to Schütze's approach of finding co-occurrence features in the training data while holding out the test contexts that are to be clustered. However, Pedersen and Bruce use at most a few thousand contexts for each word being discriminated, and this may not provide a sufficient quantity of data to have a separate set of data for feature identification. The feature sets are formed from the following types of features:

- **Morphology (Mo):** The morphological form of the target word. For nouns it is either plural or singular, and for verbs one of seven possible tenses are encoded. It is not used for adjectives.
- **Part of speech (PL_i, PR_i):** The part of speech of the word i positions to the left (L) and right (R) of the target word. Four such features were used, 1 and 2 positions to the left and right. There are only five part of speech distinctions made: noun, verb, adjective, adverb, and "other".
- **Co-occurrences (C_i):** Binary features that are set if any of the three most frequent content words observed with the target word occur in this particular context.
- **Unrestricted collocations (UL_i UR_i):** Features with 20 possible values that indicate if one of the top 19 most frequent words occurs in position i to the left (UL_i) or right (UR_i) of the target word.
- **Content collocations (CL_i CR_i):** Identical to the unrestricted collocations, except they exclude function words and only represent content words.

There are three feature sets formed from various combinations of these features, which are described below as F1, F2, and F3. The number of possible feature value combinations is shown in parentheses, which indicates how small these features spaces are when compared to the approaches discussed previously.

F1: Mo, PL_2, PL_1, PR_1, PR_2, C_1, C_2, C_3 (5,000–35,000)
F2: Mo, UL_2, UL_1, UR_1, UR_2 (194,481–1,361,367)
F3: Mo, PL_2, PL_1, PR_1, PR_2, CL_1, CR_1 (275,625–1,929,375)

Each of the N contexts of the target word is represented by a vector that includes M features. This $N \times M$ representation is then converted into an $N \times N$ dissimilarity matrix, where each cell in the matrix represents the number of features that are different between the two contexts corresponding to the row and column values. Thus, if two contexts are identical then the value of the associated cell would be 0, while if they had no features in common the value would be M.

McQuitty's (1966) method is a form of average link clustering, and as such is an agglomerative clustering algorithm. Like all such approaches it begins by assuming that each context of a target words forms its own cluster (and therefore represents a unique sense). Then, it merges the two contexts that have the lowest average dissimilarity between them (and are therefore most alike). It continues until some specified number of clusters is found or until there are no clusters with a dissimilarity value less than a specified cutoff.

Pedersen and Bruce conduct an experimental evaluation relative to the 12-word sense-tagged corpus of Bruce and Wiebe (1994) as well as with the *line* corpus (Leacock et al. 1993). The sense-tagged data was filtered such that 2 or 3 senses remained, and the clustering algorithm was set to find the number of clusters that existed in the sense-tagged data. Each word was treated separately, so discrimination for a word was carried out using only those contexts that included the target word. As a result, the sizes of the corpora are quite small. The largest are the *line* data, which has approximately 4,000 paragraph sized contexts, and the *interest* data, which is one of the 12 Bruce and Wiebe words and has approximately 2,500 sentence-long contexts. Other words had from several hundred to a thousand contexts. While the text had already been manually sense-tagged, this information was not used during any stage of feature identification or clustering, but was only employed as a point of comparison for evaluation.

The clusters that are discovered do not have sense labels attached to them. Thus, evaluation is carried out by determining an optimal assignment of actual sense tags to the discovered clusters. This is possible because they discriminated text for which the "correct" sense tags were already known, and could thereby use that as a gold standard. The evaluation methodology is modeled after the idea that a human might examine clusters and manually select the sense for which most of the contexts seem to apply. The objective of the evaluation is to determine which assignment of senses to clusters would result in optimal accuracy.

Pedersen and Bruce found that McQuitty's similarity analysis performed more accurately than did Ward's (1963) method of minimum variance and the EM algorithm (Dempster et al. 1977). They found that feature set F2 performs best for nouns, and F3 for adjectives and verbs. They found that feature set F1 did not fare terribly well with any part of speech, suggesting that local part-of-speech information and three binary collocation features simply don't provide enough information to make distinctions in senses. Feature set F2 is based on co-occurrences near the target word, and the fact that it performs well with nouns is consistent with findings in supervised learning, suggesting that collocations involving the target word are significant sources of disambiguation information (cf. Yarowsky (1995)). Interestingly, no method or feature set resulted in greater accuracy than the most frequent sense for the verbs and adjectives, however, those sense distributions were rather skewed, with most verbs and adjectives having a majority sense between 70% and 90%. The nouns had a more balanced distribution of senses and the results of McQuitty's method in combination with feature set F2 improved upon the most frequent sense by at least 10%.

6.3.3 Discussion

Purandare and Pedersen (2004) developed first- and second-order approaches to clustering contexts that incorporate ideas from both of the preceding works.[3] Rather than using localized first-order features, they use lexical features such as unigrams, bigrams, and co-occurrences that occur near the target word. They also developed a method similar to Schütze's that relies on second order co-occurrences. They carried out a comparative evaluation of these various methods using the Senseval-2 English lexical sample data, as well as the *line, hard,* and *serve* sense-tagged corpora (Leacock et al. 1993).

The Senseval-2 corpus generally has at most one or two hundred training examples per word, while the *line, hard,* and *serve* corpora have four to five thousand for each word.

In their experiments they identified features in the training corpus (following Schütze) and then used those in clustering a held out test set. They found that first-order features performed more effectively when given larger amounts of training data (as with *line, hard,* and *serve)* and that the second-order features fared better with the smaller Senseval-2 corpus. This

---

[3] These experiments were performed with the SenseClusters package (http://senseclusters.sourceforge.net).

suggests that when a sufficient volume of data is available, directly identifying features in training data provides adequate information for representing the contexts of an ambiguous word, while with smaller amounts of data the indirect relationships captured by second order features are necessary.

There are still considerable obstacles to be overcome in developing these methods. In particular, evaluation is difficult since the sense distinctions made are not relative to any existing inventory. It is unclear how to evaluate discovered senses (especially those that are domain specific) since the main objective behind such approaches is to create and make distinctions that are not currently documented in existing resources. In this case it may be that evaluation relative to applications like machine translation and Web search is the most effective means of measuring progress in these   areas (see Chap. 11 (Sect 11.4.2)).

6.4 Translational Equivalence

One of the characteristics of knowledge-lean unsupervised methods is that a mapping between similar contexts as found in a cluster and a known word sense in an existing resource may not be entirely clear. In fact, this is inevitable when the only knowledge source employed is an unannotated corpus of text, and there is no reference made to any underlying dictionary or sense inventory. In the end, this is a desirable property of these methods in that it offers a means of discovering new senses of words, and makes it possible to organize contexts in ways that existing resources would be unable to support.

Parallel corpora offer an alternative to unsupervised discrimination in that the translations between a source and target language will be indicative of sense distinctions in either language. Consider the following example from Brown et al. (1991), where the French verb *prendre* can be translated as *take* or *make*. In *Je vais prendre ma propre décision, prendre* should be translated as *make*, meaning *I will make my own decision*. However, in *Je vais prendre ma propre voiture*, it is translated as *take,* as in *I will take my own car*. Thus, a corpus of parallel French-English text could reveal that when *prendre* is used with *décision* it means one thing, and another with *voiture*. Early approaches to take advantage of this characteristic were Brown et al. (1991), Dagan et al. (1991), and Gale et al. (1992a, 1992b).

6.4.1 Representation of Context

Methods that take advantage of translational equivalences normally require that the parallel corpus be word-aligned. That is, each word or phrase in the source language should be connected to its corresponding translation in the target language. This connection is usually made via automatic means, as it is difficult and time consuming to manually align translated text. Prior to word alignment, it is usually assumed that the corpus has been sentence-aligned. While there are reliable techniques for sentence alignment available, word alignment remains an open problem. However, there are sufficiently good results to allow for the creation of word-aligned parallel corpora for finding translational equivalences in a wide range of languages. This has been demonstrated in comparative evaluations of word alignment systems for English-French and Romanian-English parallel corpora (Mihalcea and Pedersen 2003) and then again for Romanian-English, English-Hindi, and English-Inuktitut (Martin et al. 2005).

Once a parallel corpus is word-aligned, then typically lexical or syntactic features that are local to the potential target word and its translational equivalences are employed to create a training context. In the previous example, *décision* and *voiture* are features that could indicate if *prendre* should be translated as *make* or *take*. In the following section we present two early approaches, those of Brown et al. (1991) and Gale et al. (1992a, 1992b).

6.4.2 Algorithms

Brown et al. (1991) describe a method that chooses between two possible translations of a given source word in a target language. The candidates for translation are identified after word alignment is carried out on a large corpus of parallel text. The method is based on identifying a single key lexical feature near the word to be translated that will be indicative of the appropriate sense/translational-equivalence. It goes through a procedure very much like decision list learning to determine the most discriminating features for each potential translation. The method is described for French and English text, but is not dependent on any particular language pair.

The features employed for a French word to be translated into English include the word to the left, the word to the right, the first noun to the left, the first noun to the right, the first verb to the left, the first verb to the right, and the tense of the target word (if a verb) or the first verb to the left of the word (if a verb is not being translated). Given a corpus of parallel text, the mutual information of each feature is calculated with respect to each of the possible English translations, and the most informative feature is selected. Then the particular values of that feature are divided via an iterative process into two groups, one associated with the first sense of the word and the other with the second. Then a French word can be assigned an English sense by determining which of the feature values occurred in a particular context.

This is a very early example of a WSD method that was integrated into an application and evaluated. They incorporated this algorithm into their statistical machine translation system and reported a 13% reduction in the error rate. However, much more recently Carpuat and Wu (2005) found that inclusion of WSD into a statistical MT system does not improve results. As such it remains unclear whether WSD will have a significant impact on MT (but see Chap. 11 (Sect. 11.3.4) for further discussion).

Gale et al. (1992a, 1992b) demonstrate that parallel text can be used to create training data that can then be used to train a supervised learning algorithm for WSD. First they align the Canadian Hansards, an English-French parallel corpus, sentence by sentence. Then they identify the French sentences that contain words that are associated with a sense of a given polysemous English word. For example, one of the words they study is *duty*, which means an obligation (*He has a duty to report to work*) or a tax (*You must pay duty on those purchases you made in Mexico*). In French, these two senses are translated as *devoir* and *droit*. They identify the French sentences that contain these words, and then tag the corresponding occurrences of *duty* in English with one of two sense tags. They use the resulting sense-tagged text to train a Naïve Bayes classifier to perform supervised WSD (see Chap 7 (Sect. 7.3.1)). As features they use are a simple bag of words of the surrounding 100 words. For each English word, they train on 60 examples for each sense, and then evaluate this on 90 held out contexts. They report that training data collected in this way results in more than 90% accuracy for six polysemous English words (*duty, drug, land, language, position,* and *sentence)* that exhibit coarse-grained distinctions.

6.4.3 Discussion

The efficacy of using translations of words as found in parallel corpora as the basis of sense distinctions rather than those made in a dictionary is well established. Ng et al. (2003) show that using Chinese translations as sense tags for English words results in disambiguation accuracy on nouns that is comparable to those systems that participated in the Senseval-2 exercise. Likewise, the Senseval-3 English-Hindi multilingual lexical sample task (Chklovski et al. 2004) showed that systems trained with Hindi translations of English word senses could achieve disambiguation accuracy of approximately 65%, which is comparable to that attained using training examples that were manually annotated with sense distinctions. This exercise used Hindi translations of a set of 41 target words as the sense tags for English words that appeared in context. These tags were then assigned to the English text by bilingual speakers of English and Hindi, and used as training data for a range of supervised learning techniques.

However, challenges remain for deploying these techniques on a large scale. While great progress has been made in word alignment, it is still a challenging problem, especially when dealing with less studied languages. In addition, it is still difficult to obtain large quantities of parallel text for many language pairs, again especially for those languages that are less studied and associated with regions or cultures that have less of an online presence.

Chapters 9 (Sect. 9.3.4) and 11 (Sect. 11.4.3) discuss more recent approaches in using translational equivalence.

6.5 Conclusions and the Way Forward

Knowledge-lean approaches to WSD discriminate among the meanings of words based on the similarity exhibited among the contexts in which words occur in unannotated corpora. They avoid dependence on preexisting sense inventories. This is based on the distributional hypothesis, which holds that words that occur in similar contexts will have similar meanings. Supervised and knowledge-rich approaches to WSD are generally tied to a particular sense inventory, which limits their portability and flexibility in the face of new domains, changing applications, or different languages.

While there is great diversity in the work discussed in this chapter, a few dominant themes emerge. First, counts or measures of association between co-occurring words are an extremely useful information source for these methods. They are easy to derive from large corpora, and they result in a flexible representation that allows one to distinguish among different contexts in any language. Second, there is very little linguistic knowledge employed. Feature sets tend to be made up of lexical features, part-of-speech tags, and possibly syntactic dependencies like verb-object relations. The lack of such information may seem to impoverish these methods, but on the other hand it makes them portable to a wide variety of languages without any difficulty. However, clearly the use of more extensive syntactic information is one direction in which these approaches could evolve, especially for languages with relatively well-developed tools such as parsers, chunkers, and part-of-speech taggers.

There is tremendous potential in developing word sense disambiguation approaches that follow Schütze's two step model, where discrimination is performed first, and then followed by methods that label the resulting clusters. This would break open the knowledge acquisition bottleneck that afflicts supervised and knowledge-rich approaches, and make word sense disambiguation highly portable and robust.

However, even without labeling, clusters discovered via discrimination techniques are useful. For example, Schütze (1998) shows that unlabeled clusters of occurrences of a word representing the same sense result in improved information retrieval, and Landauer et al. (1998) demonstrated that type-based distinctions can provide useful information about semantic similarity.

Acknowledgments

Phil Edmonds and Eneko Agirre have been wise and patient editors. I am most appreciative of their support and hard work in making this book possible. I would also like to thank Satanjeev Banerjee, Saif Mohammad, Amruta Purandare, and Anagha Kulkarni for their comments on drafts of this chapter, and many interesting discussions on related issues. Finally, I am grateful to the National Science Foundation (USA) for the support they have provided Satanjeev Banerjee, Amruta Purandare, Anagha Kulkarni, and myself via a Faculty Early Career Development (CAREER) Award (#0092784).

References

Banerjee, Satanjeev & Ted Pedersen. 2003. Extended gloss overlaps as a measure of semantic relatedness. *Proceedings of the 18th International Joint Conference on Artificial Intelligence (IJCAI),* Acapulco, Mexico, 805–810.
Brown, Peter F., Stephen A. Della Pietra, Vincent J. Della Pietra & Robert L. Mercer. 1991. Word-sense disambiguation using statistical methods

proceedings of the 29th Meeting of the Association for Computational Linguistics (ACL), Berkeley, U.S.A., 264–270.

Bruce, Rebecca & Janyce Wiebe. 1994. Word sense disambiguation using decomposable models. *Proceedings of the 32nd Meeting of the Association for Computational Linguistics,* Las Cruces, U.S.A., 139–146.

Buitelaar, Paul, Jan Alexandersson, Tilman Jaeger, Stephan Lesch, Norbert Pfleger, Diana Raileanu, Tanja von den Berg, Kerstin Klöckner, Holger Neis & Hubert Schlarb. 2001. An unsupervised semantic tagger applied to German. *Proceedings of the Conference on Recent Advances in Natural Language Processing,* Tzigov Chark, Bulgaria, 52–57.

Burgess, Curt & Kevin Lund. 1997. Modeling parsing constraints with high-dimensional context space. *Language and Cognitive Processes,* 12(2–3): 177–210.

Burgess, Curt & Kevin Lund. 2000. The dynamics of meaning in memory. *Cognitive Dynamics: Conceptual Representational Change in Humans and Machines,* ed. by Eric Dietrich and Arthur Markman, 117–156. Mahmah, U.S.A.: Lawrence Erlbaum Associates.

Carpuat, Marine & Dekai Wu. 2005. Word sense disambiguation vs. statistical machine translation. *Proceedings of the 43rd Annual Meeting of the Association for Computational Linguistics,* Ann Arbor, U.S.A., 387–394.

Chklovski, Tim, Rada Mihalcea, Ted Pedersen & Amruta Purandare. 2004. The Senseval-3 multilingual English-Hindi lexical sample task. *Proceedings of Senseval-3: Third International Workshop on the Evaluation of Systems for the Semantic Analysis of Text,* Barcelona, Spain, 5–8.

Cutting, Douglas, Jan Pedersen, David Karger & John Tukey. 1992. Scatter/Gather: A cluster-based approach to browsing large document collections. *Proceedings of the 15th Annual International ACM Conference on Research and Development in Information Retrieval (SIGIR),* Copenhagen, Denmark, 318–329.

Dagan, Ido, Alon Itai & Ulrike Schwall. 1991. Two languages are more informative than one. *Proceedings of the 29th Meeting of the Association for Computational Linguistics,* Berkeley, U.S.A, 130–137.

Deerwester, Scott, Susan T. Dumais, George W. Furnas, Thomas K. Landauer & Richard Harshman. 1990. Indexing by Latent Semantic Analysis. *Journal of the American Society for Information Science,* 41(6): 391–407.

Dempster, Arthur P., Nam M. Laird & Donald B. Rubin. 1977. Maximum likelihood from incomplete data via the EM algorithm. *Journal of the Royal Statistical Society B,* 39: 1–38.

Furnas, George W., Scott Deerwester, Susan T. Dumais, Thomas K. Landauer, Richard Harshman, L. A. Streeter & K. E. Lochbaum. 1988. Information retrieval using a Singular Value Decomposition model of latent semantic structure. *Proceedings of the 11th Annual International ACM Conference on Research and Development in Information Retrieval (SIGIR),* Grenoble, France, 465–480.

Gale, William, Kenneth W. Church & David Yarowsky. 1992a. Using bilingual materials to develop word sense disambiguation methods. *Proceedings of the 4th International Conference on Theoretical and Methodological Issues in Machine Translation,* Montreal, Canada, 101–112.

Gale, William, Kenneth W. Church & David Yarowsky. 1992b. A method for disambiguating word senses in a large corpus. *Computers and the Humanities,* 26(5): 415–439.

Hanks, Patrick. 2000. Do word meanings exist? *Computers and the Humanities.* 34(1–2): 205–215.

Harris, Zellig. 1968. *Mathematical structures of language.* New York: Interscience Publishers.

Jiang, Jay & David Conrath. 1997. Semantic similarity based on corpus statistics and lexical taxonomy. *International Conference on Research in Computational Linguistics,* Taipei, Taiwan, 19–33.

Kilgarriff, Adam. 1997. "I don't believe in word senses". *Computers and the Humanities,* 31(2): 91–113.

Landauer, Thomas K. & Susan T. Dumais. 1997. A solution to Plato's problem: The Latent Semantic Analysis theory of acquisition, induction and representation of knowledge. *Psychological Review,* 104: 211–240.

Landauer, Thomas K., Peter W. Foltz & Darrell Laham. 1998. An introduction to Latent Semantic Analysis. *Discourse Processes,* 25: 259–284.

Leacock, Claudia, Geoff Towell & Ellen Voorhees. 1993. Corpus based statistical sense resolution. *Proceedings of the ARPA Workshop on Human Language Technology,* Plainsboro, U.S.A., 260–265.

Lin, Dekang. 1998. Automatic retrieval and clustering of similar words. *Proceedings of the 17th International Joint Conference on Computational Linguistics and the 36th Annual Meeting of the Association for Computational Linguistics (IJCAI/ACL),* Montreal, Canada, 768–774.

Lin, Dekang & Patrick Pantel. 2002. Concept discovery from text. *Proceedings of the 19th International Conference on Computational Linguistics (COLING),* Taipei, Taiwan, 577–583.

Martin, Joel, Rada Mihalcea & Ted Pedersen. 2005. Word alignment for languages with scarce resources. *Proceedings of the ACL Workshop on Building and Using Parallel Texts,* Ann Arbor, U.S.A., 65–74.

McCarthy, Diana, Rob Koeling, Julie Weeds & John Carroll. 2004. Finding predominant senses in untagged text. *Proceedings of the 42nd Annual Meeting of the Association for Computational Linguistics*, Barclona, Spain, 577–583.

McQuitty, Louis. 1966. Similarity analysis by reciprocal pairs for discrete and continuous data. *Educational and Psychological Measurement*, 26: 825–831.

Mihalcea, Rada & Ted Pedersen. 2003. An evaluation exercise for word alignment. *Proceedings of the HLT/NAACL Workshop on Building and Using Parallel Texts: Data Driven Machine Translation and Beyond,* Edmonton, Canada, 1–10.

Miller, George & Walter Charles. 1991. Contextual correlates of semantic similarity. *Language and Cognitive Processes*, 6(1): 1–28.

Ng, Hwee Tou, Bin Wang & Yee Seng Chan. 2003. Exploiting parallel texts for word sense disambiguation: An empirical study. *Proceedings of the 41st Annual Meeting of the Association for Computational Linguistics*, Sapporo, Japan, 455–462.

Pedersen, Ted & Rebecca Bruce. 1997. Distinguishing word senses in untagged text. *Proceedings of the Second Conference on Empirical Methods in Natural Language Processing,* Providence, U.S.A., 197–207.

Pedersen, Ted & Rebecca Bruce. 1998. Knowledge lean word sense disambiguation. *Proceedings of the 15th National Conference on Artificial Intelligence,* Madison, U.S.A., 800–805.

Purandare, Amruta & Ted Pedersen. 2004. Word sense discrimination by clustering contexts in vector and similarity spaces. *Proceedings of the Conference on Computational Natural Language Learning*, Boston, U.S.A., 41–48.

Resnik, Philip. 1997. Selectional preference and sense disambiguation. *Proceedings of the ACL SIGLEX Workshop on Tagging Text with Lexical Semantics: Why, What, and How?,* Washington, U.S.A., 52–57.

Resnik, Philip & David Yarowsky. 1997. A perspective on word sense disambiguation methods and their evaluation. *ACL SIGLEX Workshop on Tagging Text with Lexical Semantics: Why, What, and How?,* Washington, U.S.A., 79–86.

Rigau, German, Jordi Atserias & Eneko Agirre. 1997. Combining unsupervised lexical knowledge methods for word sense disambiguation. *Proceedings of the 35th Annual Meeting of the Association for Computational Linguistics (ACL),* Madrid, Spain, 48–55.

Schütze, Hinrich. 1998. Automatic word sense discrimination. *Computational Linguistics,* 24(1): 97–123.

Turney, Peter. 2001. Mining the Web for synonyms: PMI-IR versus LSA on TOEFL. *Proceedings of the 12th European Conference on Machine Learning*, Freiburg, Germany, 491–502.

Ward, J. 1963. Hierarchical grouping to optimize an objective function. *Journal of the American Statistical Association*, 58: 236–244.

Yarowsky, David. 1993. One sense per collocation. *Proceedings of the ARPA Workshop Human Language Technology*, Plainsboro, U.S.A., 265–271.

Yarowsky, David. 1995. Unsupervised word sense disambiguation rivaling supervised methods. *Proceedings of the 33rd Annual Meeting of the Association for Computational Linguistics (ACL)*, Cambridge, U.S.A., 189–196.

7 Supervised Corpus-Based Methods for WSD

Lluís Màrquez,[1] Gerard Escudero,[1] David Martínez,[2] German Rigau[3]

[1]Universitat Politècnica de Catalunya
[2]University of Sheffield
[3]University of the Basque Country

In this chapter, the supervised approach to word sense disambiguation is presented, which consists of automatically inducing classification models or rules from annotated examples. We start by introducing the machine learning framework for classification and some important related concepts. Then, a review of the main approaches in the literature is presented, focusing on the following issues: learning paradigms, corpora used, sense repositories, and feature representation. We also include a more detailed description of five statistical and machine learning algorithms, which are experimentally evaluated and compared on the DSO corpus. In the final part of the chapter, the current challenges of the supervised learning approach to WSD are briefly discussed.

7.1 Introduction to Supervised WSD

In the last fifteen years, empirical and statistical approaches have significantly increased their impact on natural language processing (NLP). Among them, the algorithms and techniques coming from the machine learning (ML) community have been applied to a large variety of NLP tasks with remarkable success and they are becoming the focus of increasing interest. The reader can find excellent introductions to ML in Mitchell (1997), and its relation to NLP in Manning and Schütze (1999) and Cardie and Mooney (1999).

The type of NLP problems initially addressed by statistical and machine learning techniques are those of language ambiguity resolution, in which

E. Agirre and P. Edmonds (eds.), Word Sense Disambiguation: Algorithms and Applications, 167–216.
© 2007 *Springer.*

the correct interpretation should be selected, among a set of alternatives, in a particular context (e.g., word choice selection in speech recognition or machine translation, part-of-speech tagging, word sense disambiguation, co-reference resolution, etc.). They are particularly appropriate for ML because they can be seen as *classification* problems, which have been studied extensively in the ML community.

More recently, ML techniques have also been applied to NLP problems that do not reduce to a simple classification scheme. We place in this category sequence tagging (e.g., with part-of-speech, named entities, etc.), and assignment of hierarchical structures (e.g., parse trees, complex concepts in information extraction, etc.). These approaches typically proceed by decomposition of complex problems into simple decision schemes or by generalizing the classification setting in order to work directly with complex representations and outputs.

Regarding automatic word sense disambiguation (WSD), one of the most successful approaches in the last ten years is *supervised learning* from examples, in which statistical or ML classification models are induced from semantically annotated corpora. Generally, supervised systems have obtained better results than the unsupervised ones, as shown by experimental work and international evaluation exercises such as Senseval (see Chap. 4). However, the knowledge acquisition bottleneck is still an open problem that poses serious challenges to the supervised learning approach for WSD.

The overall organization of this chapter is as follows. The next subsection introduces the machine learning framework for classification. Section 7.2 contains a survey on the state of the art in supervised WSD, concentrating on topics such as learning approaches, sources of information, and feature codification. Section 7.3 describes five learning algorithms which are experimentally compared on the DSO corpus. The main challenges posed by the supervised approach to WSD are discussed in Section 7.4. Finally, Section 7.5 concludes and devotes some words to the possible future trends.

7.1.1 Machine Learning for Classification

The goal in supervised learning for classification consists of inducing from a training set S, an approximation (or hypothesis) h of an unknown function f that maps from an input space X to a discrete unordered output space $Y = \{1, \ldots, K\}$.

The training set contains m training examples, $S = \{(\mathbf{x}^1, y^1),...,(\mathbf{x}^m, y^m)\}$, which are each pairs $(\mathbf{x}, y)$ where $\mathbf{x}$ belongs to X and $y = f(\mathbf{x})$. The $\mathbf{x}$ component of each example is typically a vector $\mathbf{x} = (x_1,..., x_n)$, whose components, called *features* (or attributes), are discrete- or real-valued and describe the relevant information/properties about the example. The values of the output space Y associated with each training example are called *classes* (or categories). Therefore, each training example is completely described by a set of attribute-value pairs and a class label.

In the field of statistical learning theory (Vapnik 1998), the function f is viewed as a probability distribution $P(X,Y)$ and not as a deterministic mapping, and the training examples are considered as a sample (independent and identically distributed) from this distribution. Additionally, X is usually identified as $\mathfrak{R}^n$, and each example $\mathbf{x}$ as a point in $\mathfrak{R}^n$ with one real-valued feature for each dimension. In this chapter we will try to maintain the descriptions and notation compatible with both approaches.

Given a training set S, a learning algorithm induces a classifier, denoted h, which is a hypothesis about the true function f. In doing so, the learning algorithm can choose among a set of possible functions H, which is referred to as the *space of hypotheses*. Learning algorithms differ in which space of hypotheses they take into account (e.g., linear functions, domain partitioning by axis parallel hyperplanes, radial basis functions, etc.) in the representation language used (e.g., decision trees, sets of conditional probabilities, neural networks, etc.), and in the *bias* they use for choosing the best hypothesis among several that can be compatible with the training set (e.g., simplicity, maximal margin, etc.).

Given new $\mathbf{x}$ vectors, h is used to predict the corresponding y values, that is, to classify the new examples, and it is expected to be coincident with f in the majority of the cases, or, equivalently, to perform a small number of errors. The measure of the error rate on unseen examples is called *generalization* (or true) *error*. It is obvious that the generalization error cannot be directly minimized by the learning algorithm since the true function f, or the distribution $P(X,Y)$, is unknown. Therefore, an inductive principle is needed. The most common way to proceed is to directly minimize the *training* (or empirical) *error*, that is, the number of errors on the training set. This principle is known as "empirical risk minimization", and gives a good estimation of the generalization error in the presence of sufficient training examples. However, in domains with few training examples, forcing a zero training error can lead to overfit the training data and to generalize badly. The risk of overfitting is increased in the presence of outliers and noise (i.e., very exceptional and wrongly classified training examples, respectively). A notion of complexity of the hypothesis function *h*, defined in terms of the expressiveness of the functions in *H*, is also directly related to the risk of overfitting. This complexity measure is usually computed using the Vapnik-Chervonenkis (VC) dimension (see Vapnik (1998) for details). The trade-off between training error and complexity of the induced classifier is something that has to be faced in any experimental setting in order to guarantee a low generalization error.

An Example on WSD

Consider the problem of disambiguating the verb *to know* in a sentence. The senses of the word *know* are the classes of the classification problem (defining the output space *Y*), and each occurrence of the word in a corpus will be codified into a training example ($\mathbf{x}^i$), annotated with the correct sense. In our example the verb *to know* has 8 senses according to WordNet 1.6. Senses 1 and 4 are shown here:

> **to know**
> Sense 1: *know, cognize* (be cognizant or aware of a fact or a specific piece of information), "I *know* that the President lied to the people", "I want to *know* who is winning the game!", "I *know* it's time".
> Sense 4: *know* (be familiar or acquainted with a person or an object), "She doesn't *know* this composer", "Do you *know* my sister?", "We *know* this movie".

The representation of examples usually includes information about the *context* in which the ambiguous word occurs. Thus, the features describing an example may codify the bigrams and trigrams of words and part-of-speech (POS) tags next to the target word and all the words appearing in the sentence (a "bag-of-words" representation). Section 7.2.3, below, expands on example representation.

A decision list is a simple learning algorithm that can be applied in this domain. It acquires a list of ordered classification rules of the form:

> *if* (**feature** = **value**) *then* **class**

When classifying a new example **x**, the list of rules is checked in order and the first rule that matches the example is applied. Supposing that such a list of classification rules has been acquired from training examples, Table 7.1 contains the set of rules that match the example sentence: *There is nothing in the whole range of human experience more widely **known** and universally felt than spirit*. They are ordered by decreasing values of a log-

Table 7.1. Classification example of the word *know* using decision lists.

Feature	Value	Sense	Log-likelihood
±3-word-window	*"widely"*	4	2.99
word-bigram	*"known widely"*	4	2.99
word-bigram	*"known and"*	4	1.09
sentence-window	*"whole"*	1	0.91
sentence-window	*"widely"*	4	0.69
sentence-window	*"known"*	4	0.43

likelihood measure indicating the confidence of the rule. We can see that only features related to the first and fourth senses of *know* receive positive values of its 8 WordNet senses. Classifying the example by the first two tied rules (which are activated because the word *widely* appears immediately to the left of the word *know*), sense 4 will be assigned to the example.

Finally, we would like to briefly comment on a terminological issue that can be rather confusing in the WSD literature. Recall that, in machine learning, the term "supervised learning" refers to the fact that the training examples are annotated with the class labels, which are taken from a pre-specified set. "Unsupervised learning" refers to the problem of learning from examples when there is no set of pre-specified class labels. That is, the learning consists of acquiring the similarities between examples to form clusters that can be later interpreted as classes (this is why it is usually referred to as clustering). In the WSD literature, "unsupervised learning" is sometimes used with another meaning, which is the acquisition of disambiguation models or rules from non-annotated examples and external sources of information (e.g., lexical databases, aligned corpora, etc.). Note that in this case the set of class labels (which are the senses of the words) are also specified in advance. See Chapter 6 (especially Sect. 6.1.1) for more discussion on this issue.

7.2 A Survey of Supervised WSD

In this section we overview the supervised approach to WSD. To begin, the first three subsections introduce important issues related to the supervised paradigm: corpora, sense inventories, and feature design, respectively. (More thorough discussion can be found on corpora in Chapter 4 and feature codification and knowledge sources in Chapter 8).

7.2.1 Main Corpora Used

As we have seen in the previous section, supervised machine learning algorithms use semantically annotated corpora to induce classification models for deciding the appropriate word sense for each particular context. The compilation of corpora for training and testing such systems requires a large human effort since all the words in these annotated corpora have to be manually tagged by lexicographers with semantic classes taken from a particular lexical semantic resource – most commonly WordNet (Miller 1990, Fellbaum 1998).

Despite the good results obtained, supervised methods suffer from the lack of widely available semantically tagged corpora, from which to construct broad-coverage systems. This is known as the *knowledge acquisition bottleneck*. And the lack of annotated corpora is even worse for languages other than English. The extremely high overhead for supervision (all words, all languages) explains why supervised methods have been seriously questioned.

Due to this obstacle, the first attempts to use statistical techniques for WSD tried to avoid the manual annotation of a training corpus. This was achieved by using pseudo-words (Yarowsky 1993), aligned bilingual corpora (Gale et al. 1993), or by working with the related problem of form (e.g., accent) restoration (Yarowsky 1994).

Pseudo-words are artificial ambiguities introduced into untagged corpora. Given a set of related words, for instance {*match, party*}, a pseudo-word corpus can be created by replacing all the instances of the words with a new word (in this case, *match/party*) maintaining as labels the original words (which act as senses). (Chapter 4 (Sect. 4.3) further discusses pseudo-words).

Methods that use bilingual corpora rely on the fact that the different senses of a word in a given language are translated using different words in another language. For example, the Spanish word *partido* translates to *match* in English in the sports sense and to *party* in the political sense. Therefore, if a corpus is available with a word-to-word alignment, when a translation of a word like *partido* is made, its English sense can be automatically determined as *match* or *party*. Word-aligned parallel corpora have only recently become available. Section 7.4.3 below continues this discussion.

Several manually annotated corpora do exist, and have been used extensively in research into supervised methods:

- Semcor (Miller et al. 1993) is a portion of the Brown Corpus (Francis and Kučera 1982) annotated with WordNet 1.6 senses. All words in some 186 files, and verbs in a further 166 files, are annotated totalling 234,000 sense-annotated words.
- The DSO corpus (Ng and Lee 1996) contains sentences from the *Wall Street Journal* corpus (WSJ) and the Brown Corpus. 192,800 words (121 frequent nouns and 70 frequent verbs) are annotated with WordNet 1.5 senses.
- Senseval produced several corpora in different languages. The main English corpora for the lexical sample task comprise about 8,000 instances of 41 words (Senseval-1), 12,000 instances of 73 words (Senseval-2), and 12,000 instances of 59 words (Senseval-3), all annotated with WordNet senses. See Section 7.2.5 below.
- The Open Mind Word Expert project (OMWE) (Chklovski and Mihalcea 2002) has volunteers on the Web manually annotate examples. The examples are extracted from three sources: Penn Treebank corpus, *Los Angeles Times* collection (provided for the TREC conferences), and Open Mind Common Sense. While the two first sources are well known, the Open Mind Common Sense corpus provides sentences that are not usually found in current corpora. They consist mainly in explanations and assertions similar to glosses of a dictionary, but phrased in less formal language, and with many examples per sense. Chklovski and Mihalcea suggest that these sentences could be a good source of keywords to be used for disambiguation. The examples obtained from this project were used in the English lexical-sample task in Senseval-3.

These resources are discussed in greater detail in Chapter 4 (Sect. 4.2), and OMWE in Chapter 9 (Sect. 9.3.4).

7.2.2 Main Sense Repositories

Initially, machine readable dictionaries (MRDs) were used as the main repositories of word sense distinctions to annotate word examples with senses. For instance, LDOCE, the *Longman Dictionary of Contemporary English* (Procter 1978) was frequently used as a research lexicon (Wilks et al. 1993) and for tagging word sense usages (Bruce and Wiebe 1994).

At Senseval-1, the English lexical sample task used the Hector lexicon to label each sense instance. This lexicon was produced jointly by Oxford University Press and DEC dictionary research project. However, WordNet (Miller 1991, Fellbaum 1998) and EuroWordNet (Vossen 1998) are nowadays becoming the most common knowledge sources for sense distinctions.

Many corpora have been annotated using various versions of WordNet and EuroWordNet (e.g., Semcor, the DSO corpus, the Senseval corpora, and OMWE). Although using different WordNet versions can be seen as a problem for the standardization of these valuable lexical resources, successful algorithms have been proposed for providing compatibility across the European wordnets and the different versions of the Princeton WordNet (Daudé et al. 1999, 2000, 2001).

7.2.3 Representation of Examples by Means of Features

Before applying any ML algorithm, all the examples of a particular word have to be codified in a way that the learning algorithm can handle them. As explained in Section 7.1.1, the most usual way of codifying training examples is as feature vectors. In this way, they can be seen as points in an n-dimensional feature space, where n is the total number of features used.

Features try to capture information and knowledge about the context of the target words to be disambiguated. Computational requirements of learning algorithms and the availability of the information impose some limitations on the features that can be considered, thus they necessarily codify only a simplification (or generalization) of the word sense instances (see Chap. 8 for more details on features codified).

Usually, a complex pre-processing step is performed to build a feature vector for each context example. This step often considers the use of a windowing scheme or a sentence-splitter for the selection of the appropriate context (to select a fixed number of content words or sentences around the target word), a POS tagger to establish POS patterns around the target word, ad hoc routines for detecting multi-words or capturing n-grams, or parsing tools for detecting dependencies between lexical units.

Although this pre-processing step could be seen as independent from the ML algorithm to be used, there are strong dependencies between the kind and codification of the features and the appropriateness for each learning algorithm (e.g., exemplar-based learning is very sensitive to irrelevant features, decision tree induction does not properly handle attributes with many values, etc.). Escudero et al. (2000b) discuss how the feature representation affects both the efficiency and accuracy of two learning systems for WSD. See also Agirre and Martínez (2001) for a survey on the types of knowledge sources that could be relevant for codifying training examples.

The feature sets most commonly used in the supervised WSD literature can be grouped as follows:

1. **Local features:** The local context features comprise n-grams of POS tags, lemmas, word forms and their positions with respect to the target word. Sometimes, local features include a bag-of-words or lemmas in a small window around the target word (the position of these words is not taken into account). These features are able to capture knowledge about collocations, argument-head relations and limited syntactic cues.
2. **Topical features:** Such featues represent more general contexts (wide windows of words, other sentences, paragraphs, documents), usually in a bag-of-words representation. These features aim at capturing the semantic domain of the text fragment or document.
3. **Syntactic dependencies:** At a sentence level, dependencies have also been used to try to better model syntactic cues and argument-head relations.

7.2.4 Main Approaches to Supervised WSD

We will categorize the supervised methods according to the induction principle they use for acquiring their classification models. Our categorization does not aim to be exhaustive, but we have attempted to be thorough, nonetheless. The combination of many paradigms is another possibility, which is covered in Section 7.4.6. Note that for the algorithms that are included in the experiments of Section 7.3, we will keep the description in this section to an minimum and expand on it in Section 7.3.1.

Probabilistic Methods

Statistical methods usually estimate a set of probabilistic parameters that express the conditional or joint probability distributions of categories and contexts (described by features). These parameters can be then used to assign to each new example the particular category that maximizes the conditional probability of a category given the observed context features.

The Naïve Bayes algorithm (Duda et al. 2001) is the simplest algorithm of this type, which uses the Bayes inversion rule and assumes the conditional independence of features given the class label (see Sect. 7.3.1 below). It has been applied to many investigations into WSD (Gale et al. 1992, Leacock et al. 1993, Pedersen and Bruce 1997, Escudero et al. 2000b) and, despite its simplicity, Naïve Bayes is claimed to obtain state-of-the-art accuracy in many papers (Mooney 1996, Ng 1997a, Leacock et al. 1998).

A potential problem of Naïve Bayes is the independence assumption. Bruce and Wiebe (1994) present a more complex model known as the "decomposable model", which considers different characteristics dependent on each other. The main drawback of their approach is the enormous number of parameters to be estimated, proportional to the number of different combinations of the interdependent characteristics. As a consequence, this technique requires a great quantity of training examples. In order to solve this problem, Pedersen and Bruce (1997) propose an automatic method for identifying the optimal model by means of the iterative modification of the complexity level of the model.

The Maximum Entropy approach (Berger et al. 1996) provides a flexible way to combine statistical evidence from many sources. The estimation of probabilities assumes no prior knowledge of data and it has proven to be very robust. It has been applied to many NLP problems and it also appears as a promising alternative in WSD (Suárez and Palomar 2002).

Methods Based on the Similarity of the Examples

The methods in this family perform disambiguation by taking into account a similarity metric. This can be done by comparing new examples to a set of learned vector prototypes (one for each word sense) and assigning the sense of the most similar prototype, or by searching in a stored base of annotated examples for the most similar examples and assigning the most frequent sense among them.

There are many ways to calculate the similarity between two examples. Assuming the Vector Space Model (VSM), one of the simplest similarity measures is to consider the angle that both example vectors form (i.e., the cosine measure). Leacock et al. (1993) compared VSM, Neural Networks, and Naïve Bayes methods, and drew the conclusion that the two first methods slightly surpass the last one in WSD. Yarowsky et al. (2001) included a VSM model in their system that combined the results of up to six different supervised classifiers, and obtained very good results in Senseval-2. For training the VSM component, they applied a rich set of features (including syntactic information), and weighting of feature types.

The most widely used representative of this family of algorithms is the k-Nearest Neighbor (kNN) algorithm, which we also describe and test in section 7.3. In this algorithm the classification of a new example is performed by searching the set of the k most similar examples (or *nearest neighbors*) among a pre-stored set of labeled examples, and performing an "average" of their senses in order to make the prediction. In the simplest case, the training step reduces to storing all of the examples in memory (this is why this technique is called memory-based, exemplar-based, instance-based, or case-based learning) and the generalization is postponed until each new example is classified (this is why it is sometimes also called Lazy learning). A very important issue in this technique is the definition of an appropriate similarity (or distance) metric for the task, which should take into account the relative importance of each attribute and be efficiently computable. The combination scheme for deciding the resulting sense among the k nearest neighbors also leads to several alternative algorithms. kNN-based learning is said to be the best option for WSD by Ng (1997a). Other authors (Daelemans et al. 1999) argue that exemplar-based methods tend to be superior in NLP problems because they do not apply any kind of generalization on data and, therefore, they do not forget exceptions.

Ng and Lee (1996) did the first work on kNN for WSD. Ng (1997a) automatically identified the optimal value of k for each word improving the previously obtained results. Escudero et al. (2000b) focused on certain contradictory results in the literature regarding the comparison of Naïve Bayes and kNN methods for WSD. The kNN approach seemed to be very sensitive to the attribute representation and to the presence of irrelevant features. For that reason alternative representations were developed, which were more efficient and effective. The experiments demonstrated that kNN was clearly superior to Naïve Bayes when applied with an adequate feature representation and with feature and example weighting, and sophisticated similarity metrics. Stevenson and Wilks (2001) also applied kNN in order to integrate different knowledge sources, reporting high precision figures for LDOCE senses (see Sect. 7.4.6).

Regarding Senseval evaluations, Hoste et al. (2001, 2002a) used, among others, a kNN system in the English all-words task of Senseval-2, with good performance. At Senseval-3, a new system was presented by Decadt et al. (2004) winning the all-words task. However, they submitted a similar system to the lexical sample task, which scored lower than kernel-based methods.

Methods Based on Discriminating Rules

Decision lists and decision trees use selective rules associated with each word sense. Given an example to classify, the system selects one or more rules that are satisfied by the example features and assign a sense based on their predictions.

A decision list (DL), introduced in the example of Section 7.1.1 above, is an ordered list of rules of the form (*condition, class, weight*). According to Rivest (1987), decision lists can be considered as weighted if-then-else rules where the exceptional conditions appear at the beginning of the list (high weights), the general conditions appear at the bottom (low weights), and the last condition of the list is a "default" accepting all remaining cases. Weights are calculated with a scoring function describing the association between the condition and the particular class, and they are estimated from the training corpus. When classifying a new example, each rule in the list is tested sequentially and the class of the first rule whose condition matches the example is assigned as the result. Decision lists are tested in Section 7.3.

Yarowsky (1994) used decision lists to solve a particular type of lexical ambiguity: Spanish and French accent restoration. In subsequent work, Yarowsky (1995a) applied decision lists to WSD. In this work, each condition corresponds to a feature, the values are the word senses and the weights are calculated by a log-likelihood measure indicating the plausibility of the sense given the feature value.

Some more recent experiments suggest that decision lists could also be very productive for high precision feature selection for bootstrapping (Martínez et al. 2002).

A decision tree (DT) is a way to represent classification rules underlying data by an *n*-ary branching tree structure that recursively partitions the training set. Each branch of a decision tree represents a rule that tests a conjunction of basic features (internal nodes) and makes a prediction of the class label in the terminal node. Although decision trees have been used for years in many classification problems in artificial intelligence they have not been applied to WSD very frequently. Mooney (1996) used the C4.5 algorithm (Quinlan 1993) in a comparative experiment with many ML algorithms for WSD. He concluded that decision trees are not among the top performing methods. Some factors that make decision trees inappropriate for WSD are: i) the data fragmentation performed by the induction algorithm in the presence of features with many values, ii) the computational cost is high in very large feature spaces, and iii) terminal nodes corresponding to rules that cover very few training examples do not produce reliable estimates of the class label. Part of these problems can be partially mitigated by using simpler related methods such as decision lists. Another way of effectively using DTs is considering the weighted combination of many decision trees in an ensemble of classifiers (see below).

Methods Based on Rule Combination

The combination of many heterogeneous learning modules for developing a complex and robust WSD system is currently a common practice, which is explained in Section 7.4.6. In the current section, "combination" refers to a set of homogeneous classification rules that are learned and combined by a single learning algorithm. The AdaBoost learning algorithm is one of the most successful approaches.

The main idea of the AdaBoost algorithm is to linearly combine many simple and not necessarily very accurate classification rules (called weak rules or weak hypotheses) into a strong classifier with an arbitrarily low error rate on the training set. Weak rules are trained sequentially by maintaining a distribution of weights over training examples and by updating it so as to concentrate weak classifiers on the examples that were most difficult to classify by the ensemble of the preceding weak rules (see Sect. 7.3.1 for details). AdaBoost has been successfully applied to many practical problems, including several NLP tasks (Schapire 2003) and it is especially appropriate when dealing with unstable learning algorithms (e.g., decision tree induction) as the weak learner.

Several experiments on the DSO corpus (Escudero et al. 2000a, 2000c, 2001), including the one reported in Section 7.3.2 below, concluded that the boosting approach surpasses many other ML algorithms on the WSD task. We can mention, among others, Naïve Bayes, exemplar-based learning and decision lists. In those experiments, simple decision stumps (extremely shallow decision trees that make a test on a single binary feature) were used as weak rules, and a more efficient implementation of the algorithm, called LazyBoosting, was used to deal with the large feature set induced.

Linear Classifiers and Kernel-Based Approaches

Linear classifiers have been very popular in the field of information retrieval (IR), since they have been used successfully as simple and efficient models for text categorization. A linear (binary) classifier is a hyperplane in an n-dimensional feature space that can be represented with a weight vector $\mathbf{w}$ and a bias b indicating the distance of the hyperplane to the origin. The weight vector has a component for each feature, expressing the importance of this feature in the classification rule (see Eq. 7.6, below). There are many on-line learning algorithms for training such linear classifiers (e.g., Perceptron, Widrow-Hoff, Winnow, Exponentiated-Gradient,

Sleeping Experts, etc.) that have been applied to text categorization (see, for instance, Dagan et al. (1997)).

Despite their success in IR, the use of linear classifiers in the late 1990s for WSD had few papers. Mooney (1996) used the Perceptron algorithm and Escudero et al. (2000c) used the SNoW architecture (based on Winnow). In both cases, the results obtained with the linear classifiers were very low.

The expressivity of this type of classifier can be improved by allowing the learning of non-linear functions by introducing a non-linear mapping of the input features to a higher-dimensional feature space, in which new features can be expressed as combinations of many basic features and standard linear learning is performed. If example vectors appear only inside dot product operations in the learning algorithm and the classification rule, then the non-linear learning can be performed efficiently (i.e., without making explicit non-linear mappings of the input vectors), via the use of *kernel functions*. The advantage of using kernel-methods is that they offer a flexible and efficient way of defining application-specific kernels for exploiting the singularities of the data and introducing background knowledge. Currently, there exist several kernel implementations for dealing with general structured data. Regarding WSD, we find some recent contributions in Senseval-3 (Strapparava et al. 2004, Popescu 2004).

Support Vector Machines (SVM), introduced by Boser et al. (1992), is the most popular kernel-method. The learning bias consists of choosing the hyperplane that separates the positive examples from the negatives with maximum margin; see Cristianini and Shawe-Taylor (2000) and also Section 7.3.1 for details. This learning bias has proven to be very powerful and has lead to very good results in many pattern recognition, text, and NLP problems. The first applications of SVMs to WSD are those of Murata et al. (2001) and Lee and Ng (2002).

More recently, an explosion of systems using SVMs was observed in the Senseval-3 evaluation (most of them among the best performing systems). Among others, we highlight Strapparava et al. (2004), Lee et al. (2004), Agirre and Martínez (2004a), Cabezas et al. (2004), and Escudero et al. (2004).

Other kernel-methods for WSD presented at Senseval-3 and recent conferences include: Kernel Principal Component Analysis (KPCA) (Carpuat et al. 2004, Wu et al. 2004), Regularized Least Squares (Popescu 2004), and Averaged Multiclass Perceptron (Ciaramita and Johnson 2004). We think that kernel-methods are the most popular learning paradigm in NLP because they offer a remarkable performance in most of the desirable properties: accuracy, efficiency, ability to work with large and complex feature sets, and robustness in the presence of noise and exceptions. Moreover, some robust and efficient implementations are currently available.

Artificial Neural Networks, characterized by a multi-layer architecture of interconnected linear units, are an alternative for learning non-linear functions. Such connectionist methods were broadly used in the late eighties and early nineties to represent semantic models in the form of networks. More recently, Towell et al. (1998) presented a standard supervised feed-forward neural network model for disambiguating highly ambiguous words in a framework including the combined use of labeled and unlabeled examples.

Discourse Properties: The Yarowsky Bootstrapping Algorithm

The Yarowsky algorithm (Yarowsky 1995a) was, probably, one of the first and more successful applications of the bootstrapping approach to NLP tasks. It can be considered a semi-supervised method, and, thus, it is not directly comparable to the rest of the approaches described in this section. However, we will devote this entire subsection to explain the algorithm given its importance and impact on the subsequent work on bootstrapping for WSD. See, for instance, Abney (2004) and Section 7.4.4, below.

The Yarowsky algorithm is a simple iterative and incremental algorithm. It assumes a small *seed* set of labeled examples, which are representatives of each of the senses, a large set of examples to classify, and a supervised base learning algorithm (decision lists, in this particular case). Initially, the base learning algorithm is trained on the seed set and used to classify the entire set of (un-annotated) examples. Only those examples that are classified with a confidence above a certain threshold are kept as additional training examples for the next iteration. The algorithm repeats this re-training and re-labeling procedure until convergence (i.e., when no changes are observed from the previous iteration).

Regarding the initial seed set, Yarowsky (1995a) discusses several alternatives to find them, ranging from fully automatic to manually supervised procedures. This initial labeling may have very low coverage (and, thus, low recall) but it is intended to have extremely high precision. As iterations proceed, the set of training examples tends to increase, while the pool of unlabeled examples shrinks. In terms of performance, recall improves with iterations, while precision tends to decrease slightly. Ideally, at convergence, most of the examples will be labeled with high confidence.

Some well-known discourse properties are at the core of the learning process and allow the algorithm to generalize to label new examples with confidence. We refer to: one-sense-per-collocation, language redundancy, and one-sense-per-discourse (heuristic WSD methods based on these discourse properties have been covered in Chap. 5 (Sect. 5.4)). First, the one-sense-per-collocation heuristic gives a good justification for using a decision list as the base learner, since a DL uses a single rule, based on a single contextual feature, to classify each new example. Actually, Yarowsky refers to contextual features and collocations indistinctly.

Second, we know that language is very redundant. This means that the sense of a concrete example is overdetermined by a set of multiple relevant contextual features (or collocations). Some of these collocations are shared among other examples of the same sense. These intersections allow the algorithm to learn to classify new examples, and, by transitivity, to increase recall with each iteration. This is the key point in the algorithm for achieving generalization. For instance, borrowing Yarowsky's (1995a) original examples, a seed rule may establish that all the examples of the word *plant* in the collocation *plant life* should be labeled with the vegetal sense of *plant* (as opposed to its industrial sense). If we run a DL on the set of seed examples determined by this collocation, we may obtain many other relevant collocations for the same sense in the list of rules, for instance, "presence of the word *animal* in a ±10-word window". This rule would allow the classification of some new examples at the second iteration that were left unlabeled by the seed rule, for instance, the example *contains a varied plant and animal life.*

Third, Yarowsky also applied the one-sense-per-discourse heuristic as a post-process at each iteration to uniformly label all the examples in the same discourse with the majority sense. This has a double effect. On the one hand, it allows the algorithm to extend the number of labeled examples, which, in turn, will provide new "bridge" collocations that cannot be captured directly from intersections among currently labeled examples. On the other hand, it allows the algorithm to correct some misclassified examples in a particular discourse.

Yarowsky's (1995a) evaluation showed that, with a minimum set of annotated seed examples, this algorithm obtained comparable results to a fully supervised system (again, using DLs). The evaluation framework consisted of a small set of words limited to binary homographic sense distinctions.

Apart from simplicity, we would like to highlight another good property of the Yarowsky algorithm, which is the ability of recovering from initial misclassifications. The fact that at each iteration all the examples are relabeled makes it possible that an initial wrong prediction for a concrete example may lower its strength in subsequent iterations (due to the more informative training sets) until the confidence for that collocation falls below the threshold. In other words, we might say that language redundancy makes the Yarowsky algorithm self-correcting.

As a drawback, this bootstrapping approach has been theoretically poorly understood since its appearance in 1995. Recently, Abney (2004) performed some advances in this direction by analyzing a number of variants of the Yarowsky algorithm, showing that they optimize natural objective functions. Another criticism refers to real applicability, since Martínez and Agirre (2000) observed a far less predictive power of the one-sense-per-discourse and one-sense-per-collocation heuristics when tested in a real domain with highly polysemous words.

7.2.5 Supervised Systems in the Senseval Evaluations

Senseval (see Chap. 4), in the style of international competitions sponsored by the American government (e.g., MUC and TREC), was designed to compare and evaluate within a controlled framework the performance of the different approaches and systems for WSD (see Chap. 4). In an all-words task, the evaluation consists of assigning the correct sense to all content words of a text. In a lexical sample task, the evaluation consists of assigning the correct sense to all the occurrences of a few words. Other tasks included, for instance, a translation task. Basically, Senseval classifies systems into two different types: supervised and unsupervised systems, but some systems are difficult to classify. In principle, knowledge-based systems (mostly unsupervised) could compete in all tasks, whereas corpus-based systems (mostly supervised) could normally only participate in the lexical sample task and other tasks with sufficient training data. However, many supervised systems trained on external data can actually participate in the all-words task.

Senseval-1 (Kilgarriff and Rosenszweig 2000) had lexical sample tasks for English, French, and Italian, with 25 participating systems, 17 in English. The best performing systems achieved 75–80% accuracy.

Senseval-2 (Edmonds and Cotton 2001) included tasks for 12 languages. About 26 systems took part in the English lexical sample task, and the best were in the 60–65% range of accuracy, but the task was more difficult (see Chap. 4 (Sect 4.3.3)).

In Senseval-3 (Mihalcea and Edmonds 2004) the English lexical sample task had 37 systems considered to be supervised, and only 9 unsupervised. The best system (72.9% accuracy) (Grozea 2004) was way ahead of the most-frequent-sense baseline (55.2%), a significant improvement over Senseval-2.[1] The results of the top systems had little difference in performance. This suggests that a plateau had been reached for the lexical sample task with these kinds of ML approaches. The top performing systems were predominantly kernel-based methods (e.g., SVM; see Sect. 7.3.1). Other approaches, used by several systems, were the combination of algorithms by voting, and the usage of complex features such as syntactic dependencies and domain tags.

Regarding the English all-words task at Senseval-3, 20 systems competed, the best achieving an accuracy of 65.1% compared to the WordNet-first-sense baseline of 60.9% or 62.4% (depending on the treatment of multi-words and hyphenated words). The top nine systems were supervised. Unlike the English lexical sample task, a plateau was not observed, since significantly different approaches with significant differences in performance were present among the top systems. The supervised methods relied mostly on Semcor to get manually-tagged examples, but several groups incorporated other resources like the DSO corpus, WordNet definitions and glosses, previous Senseval corpora, and even the *line-hard-serve* corpus. Most of the participant systems included rich features in their models, especially syntactic dependencies and domain information.

An interesting issue is that the teams with good results in the English lexical sample and those in the all-words do not overlap. The reason could be the different behavior of the algorithms with respect the different settings of each task: the number of training examples per word, number of words to deal with, and so on.

A more detailed analysis of the knowledge sources used by the Senseval systems is given in Chapter 8.

7.3 An Empirical Study of Supervised Algorithms for WSD

Outside of the Senseval framework, one can find many other papers in the recent literature presenting empirical comparisons among several machine learning algorithms for WSD, from different perspectives (e.g., Escudero et al. (2000c), Pedersen (2001), Lee and Ng (2002), and Florian et al.

---

[1] Factors explaining the better results of Senseval-3 reside in the corpus characteristics: it contained more examples per word, the different senses were more regularly populated, and the corpus contained no multi-words, proper nouns, or phrasal verbs, which were difficult to detect and process in Senseval-2.

(2002)). This section presents an experimental comparison, in the framework of the DSO corpus, among five significant machine learning algorithms for WSD. The comparison is presented from the fundamental point of view of the accuracy and agreement achieved by all competing classifiers. Other important aspects, such as knowledge sources, efficiency, and tuning, have been deliberately left out for brevity.

7.3.1 Five Learning Algorithms Under Study

In this section, the five algorithms that will be compared in Section 7.3.2 are presented. Due to space limitations the description cannot be very detailed. We try to provide the main principles that the algorithms rely on, and the main design decisions affecting the specific implementations tested. Some references to more complete descriptions are also provided.

Naïve Bayes (NB)

Naïve Bayes is the simplest representative of probabilistic learning methods (Duda et al. 2001). In this model, an example is assumed to be "generated" first by stochastically selecting the sense s of the example and then each of the features independently according to their individual distributions $P(x_i|s)$. The classification rule of a new example $\mathbf{x} = (x_1,...,x_m)$ consists of assigning the sense s that maximizes the conditional probability of the sense given the observed sequence of features, as shown in Eq. 7.1.

$$\underset{s}{\arg\max}\, P(s\,|\,x_1,...,x_m) = \underset{s}{\arg\max}\, \frac{P(x_1,...,x_m\,|\,s)P(s)}{P(x_1,...,x_m)} \qquad (7.1)$$

$$= \underset{s}{\arg\max}\ P(s)\prod_{i=1}^{m} P(x_i\,|\,s)$$

The first equality in Eq. 7.1 is the Bayesian inversion, while the factorization comes from the independence assumption: $P(x_i\,|\,s,x_{j\neq i})=P(x_i\,|\,s)$. Since we are calculating an maximum over s there is no need to keep the denominator, which is independent of s, in the objective function. $P(s)$ and $P(x_i|s)$ are the probabilistic parameters of the model and they can be estimated from the training set using relative frequency counts (i.e., maximum likelihood estimation, MLE). For instance, the a priori probability of sense s, $P(s)$, is estimated as the ratio between the number of examples of sense s and the total number of examples in the training set. $P(x_i|s)$ is the probability of observing the feature x_i given that the observed sense is s. The MLE estimation in this case is the number of sense-s examples that have the feature x_i active divided by the total number of examples of sense s.

In order to avoid the effects of zero counts when estimating the conditional probabilities of the model, a very simple smoothing technique, proposed by Ng (1997a), has been used in this experiment. It consists in replacing zero counts of $P(x_i|s)$ with $P(s)/n$ where n is the number of training examples.

Exemplar-Based Learning (kNN)

We will use a k-Nearest-Neighbor (kNN) algorithm as a representative of exemplar-based learning. As described in Section 7.2.4, all examples are stored in memory during training and the classification of a new example is based on the senses of the k most similar stored examples. In order to obtain the set of nearest neighbors, the example to be classified, $\mathbf{x}=(x_1,\ldots,x_m)$, is compared to each stored example $\mathbf{x}^i=(x^i_1,\ldots,x^i_m)$, and the distance between them is calculated. The most basic distance metric for cases with symbolic features is the overlap metric (also called Hamming distance), defined in Eq. 7.2, where w_j is the weight of the j-th feature and $\delta(x_j, x^i_j)$ is the distance between two values, which is 0 if $x_j = x^i_j$ and 1 otherwise.

$$\Delta(\mathbf{x}, \mathbf{x}^i) = \sum_{j=1}^{m} w_j \delta(x_j, x^i_j) \qquad (7.2)$$

In the implementation tested in these experiments, we used Hamming distance to measure closeness and the Gain Ratio measure (Quinlan 1993) to estimate feature weights. For k values greater than 1, the resulting sense is the weighted majority sense of the k nearest neighbors – where each example votes its sense with a strength proportional to its closeness to the test example. There exist more complex metrics for calculating graded distances between symbolic feature values, for example, the modified value difference metric (MVDM) (Cost and Salzberg 1993) that could lead to better results. We do not use MVDM here for reasons of simplicity. Working with MVDM has a significant computational overhead and its advantage in performance is reduced to a minimum when using feature and example weighting to complement the simple Hamming distance (Escudero et al. 2000b), as we do in this experimental setting.

The kNN algorithm is run several times using a different number of nearest neighbors: 1, 3, 5, 7, 10, 15, 20, and 25. The results corresponding to the best choice for each word are reported.

Decision Lists (DL)

As we saw in Section 7.2.4, a decision list consists of a set of ordered rules of the form (*condition, sense, weight*). In this setting, the algorithm works as follows. The training data is used to estimate the importance of individual features, which are weighted with a log-likelihood measure (Yarowsky 1995a, 2000) indicating the likelihood of a particular sense given a particular feature value. The list of all rules is sorted by decreasing values of this weight. When testing new examples, the decision list is checked, and the feature with highest weight that matches the test example selects the winning word sense.

The original formula in Yarowsky (1995a) can be adapted in order to handle classification problems with more than two classes. In this case, the weight of sense s_k when feature i occurs in the context is computed as the logarithm of the probability of sense s_k given feature f_i divided by the sum of the probabilities of the other senses given f_i (see Eq. 7.3).

$$\text{weight}(s_k, f_i) = \log\left(\frac{P(s_k \mid f_i)}{\sum_{j \neq k} P(s_j \mid f_i)}\right) \tag{7.3}$$

These probabilities can be calculated using the maximum likelihood estimate, and some kind of smoothing so as to avoid the problem of zero counts. There are many approaches for smoothing probabilities (we already used a simple method applied to NB above). A complete survey of different smoothing techniques can be found in Chen (1996). For our experiments, we adopted a very simple solution, replacing the denominator by 0.1 when the frequency is zero.

AdaBoost (AB)

As seen in Section 7.2.4, AdaBoost is a general method for obtaining a highly accurate classification rule by combining many weak classifiers, each of which need only be moderately accurate. A generalized version of the AdaBoost algorithm, which combines weak classifiers with confidence-rated predictions (Schapire and Singer 1999) has been used in these experiments. This particular boosting algorithm has been successfully applied to a number of practical problems.

The weak hypotheses are learned sequentially, one at a time, and, conceptually, at each iteration the weak hypothesis is biased to classify the examples which were most difficult to classify by the ensemble of preceding weak hypotheses. AdaBoost maintains a vector of weights as a distribution

D_t over examples. At round t, the goal of the weak learner algorithm is to find a weak hypothesis, $h_t : X \rightarrow \Re$, with moderately low error with respect to the weight distribution D_t. In this setting, weak hypotheses $h_t(\mathbf{x})$ make real-valued confidence-rated predictions. Initially, the distribution D_1 is uniform, but after each iteration, the boosting algorithm exponentially increases (or decreases) the weights $D_t(i)$ for which $h_t(\mathbf{x}^i)$ makes a bad (or good) prediction, with a variation proportional to the confidence $|h_t(\mathbf{x}^i)|$. The final combined hypothesis, $h_t : X \rightarrow \Re$, computes its predictions using a weighted vote of the weak hypotheses:

$$f(\mathbf{x}) = \sum_{t=1}^{T} \alpha_t \cdot h_t(\mathbf{x}) \qquad (7.4)$$

For each example $\mathbf{x}$, the sign of $f(\mathbf{x})$ is interpreted as the predicted class (the basic AdaBoost works only with binary outputs, -1 or $+1$), and the magnitude $|f(\mathbf{x})|$ is interpreted as a measure of confidence in the prediction. Such a function can be used either for classifying new unseen examples or for ranking them according to the confidence degree.

In this work we have used decision stumps as weak hypotheses. They are rules that test the value of a single binary (or Boolean) feature and make a real-valued prediction based on that value. Features describing the examples are predicates of the form: "the word X appears immediately to the left of the *target word* to be disambiguated." Formally, based on a given predicate p, weak hypotheses h are considered that make predictions of the form:

$$h(\mathbf{x}) = \begin{cases} c_0 & \text{if } p \text{ holds in } \mathbf{x} \\ c_1 & \text{otherwise} \end{cases} \qquad (7.5)$$

where c_0 and c_1 are real numbers. See Schapire and Singer (1999) for the details about how to select the best predicate p at each iteration, the c_i values associated with p, and the weight α_i corresponding to the resulting weak rule.

Regarding the particular implementation used in these experiments, two final details should be mentioned. First, WSD defines multi-class classification problems, not binary. We have used the AdaBoost.MH algorithm that generalizes AdaBoost to multi-class multi-label classification (Schapire and Singer 2000). Second, a simple modification of the AdaBoost algorithm, which consists of dynamically selecting a much reduced feature set at each iteration, has been used to significantly increase the efficiency of the learning process with no loss in accuracy. This variant is called Lazy-Boosting and it is described in Escudero et al. (2000a).

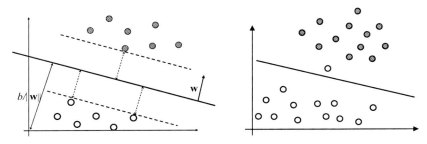

Fig. 7.1. Geometrical interpretation of Support Vector Machines.

Support Vector Machines (SVM)

SVMs are based on the principle of Structural Risk Minimization from the Statistical Learning Theory (Vapnik 1998) and, in their basic form, they learn a linear discriminant that separates a set of positive examples from a set of negative examples with maximum margin (the margin is defined by the distance of the hyperplane to the nearest of the positive and negative examples). This learning bias has proved to have good properties in terms of generalization bounds for the induced classifiers. The left plot in Fig. 7.1 shows the geometrical intuition about the maximal margin hyperplane in a two-dimensional space. The linear classifier is defined by two elements: a weight vector $\mathbf{w}$ (with one component for each feature), and a bias b which stands for the distance of the hyperplane to the origin. The classification rule assigns $+1$ or -1 to a new example $\mathbf{x}$ as follows:

$$h(\mathbf{x}) = \begin{cases} +1 & \text{if } (\mathbf{w} \cdot \mathbf{x}) + b \geq 0 \\ -1 & \text{otherwise} \end{cases} \qquad (7.6)$$

The positive and negative examples closest to the $(\mathbf{w}, b)$ hyperplane (on the dashed lines) are called *support vectors*.

Learning the maximal margin hyperplane $(\mathbf{w}, b)$ can be simply stated as a convex quadratic optimization problem with a unique solution, consisting of (primal form): minimize $\|\mathbf{w}\|$ subject to the constraints (one for each training example) $y_i\,[(\mathbf{w} \cdot \mathbf{x}_i) + b] \geq 1$, indicating that all training examples are classified with a margin equal or greater than 1.

Sometimes, training examples are not linearly separable or, simply, it is not desirable to obtain a perfect hyperplane. In these cases it is preferable to allow some errors in the training set so as to maintain a better solution hyperplane (see the right plot of Fig. 7.1). This is achieved by a variant of the optimization problem, referred to as *soft margin*, in which the contribution to the objective function of the margin maximization and the training errors can be balanced through the use of a parameter called *C*.

As discussed in Section 7.2.4, SVMs can be used in conjunction with kernel functions to produce non-linear classifiers. Thus, the selection of an appropriate kernel to the dataset is another important element when using SVMs. In the experiments presented below we used the SVM^{light} software,[2] a freely available implementation. We present only the results with linear kernels, performing a tuning of the *C* parameter directly on the DSO corpus. No significant improvements were achieved by using polynomial kernels.

7.3.2 Empirical Evaluation on the DSO Corpus

We tested the algorithms on the DSO corpus. Of the 191 words tagged in the DSO corpus, a group of 21 words that frequently appear in the WSD literature was selected to perform the comparative experiment. We chose 13 nouns (*age, art, body, car, child, cost, head, interest, line, point, state, thing, work*) and 8 verbs (*become, fall, grow, lose, set, speak, strike, tell*) and we treated them as independent classification problems. The number of examples per word ranged from 202 to 1,482 with an average of 801.1 examples per word (840.6 for nouns and 737.0 for verbs). The level of ambiguity is quite high in this corpus. The number of senses per word is between 3 and 25, with an average of 10.1 senses per word (8.9 for nouns and 12.1 for verbs).

Two kinds of information are used to perform disambiguation: *local* and *topical* context. Let $[w_{-3}, w_{-2}, w_{-1}, w, w_{+1}, w_{+2}, w_{+3}]$ be the context of consecutive words around the word *w* to be disambiguated, and p_i, $-3 \leq i \leq 3$, be the POS tag of word w_i. Fifteen feature patterns referring to local context are considered: $p_{-3}, p_{-2}, p_{-1}, p_{+1}, p_{+2}, p_{+3}, w_{-1}, w_{+1}, (w_{-2}, w_{-1}), (w_{-1}, w_{+1}), (w_{+1}, w_{+2}), (w_{-3}, w_{-2}, w_{-1}), (w_{-2}, w_{-1}, w_{+1}), (w_{-1}, w_{+1}, w_{+2})$, and (w_{+1}, w_{+2}, w_{+3}). The last seven correspond to collocations of two and three consecutive words. The topical context is formed by the bag of words $\{c_1,...,c_m\}$, which is an unordered set of *m* open class words appearing in the sentence. The feature set includes those used by Ng (1996) with the exception of the morphology of the target word and the verb-object syntactic relation (see Chap. 8).

The methods evaluated in this section codify the features in different ways. AB and SVM algorithms require binary features. Therefore, local

---

[2] http://svmlight.joachims.org

Table 7.2. Percentage accuracy and standard deviation of all learning methods.

	MFC	NB	kNN	DL	AB	SVM
Nouns	46.59 ±1.08	62.29 ±1.25	63.17 ±0.84	61.79 ±0.95	66.00 ±1.47	**66.80** ±1.18
Verbs	46.49 ±1.37	60.18 ±1.64	64.37 ±1.63	60.52 ±1.96	66.91 ±2.25	**67.54** ±1.75
ALL	46.55 ±0.71	61.55 ±1.04	63.59 ±0.80	61.34 ±0.93	66.32 ±1.34	**67.06** ±0.65

context attributes have to be binarized in a pre-process, while the topical context attributes remain as binary tests about the presence or absence of a concrete word in the sentence. As a result of this binarization, the number of features is expanded to several thousands (from 1,764 to 9,900 depending on the particular word). DL has been applied also with the same example representation as AB and SVM.

The binary representation of features is not appropriate for NB and kNN algorithms. Therefore, the 15 local-context attributes are considered as is. Regarding the binary topical-context attributes, the variants described by Escudero et al. (2000b) are considered. For kNN, the topical information is codified as a single set-valued attribute (containing all words appearing in the sentence) and the calculation of closeness is modified so as to handle this type of attribute. For NB, the topical context is conserved as binary features, but when classifying new examples only the information of words appearing in the example (positive information) is taken into account.

Experiments

We performed a 10-fold cross-validation experiment in order to estimate the performance of the systems. The accuracy figures reported below are micro-averaged over the results of the 10 folds and over the results on each of the 21 words. We have applied a paired Student's t-test of significance with a confidence value of $t_{9,0.995}=3.250$ (see Dietterich (1998) for information about statistical tests for comparing ML classification systems). When classifying test examples, all methods are forced to output a unique sense, resolving potential ties among senses by choosing the most frequent sense among all those tied.

Table 7.2 presents the results (accuracy and standard deviation) of all methods in the reference corpus. MFC stands for a most-frequent-sense classifier, that is, a naïve classifier that learns the most frequent sense of the training set and uses it to classify all the examples of the test set. Averaged results are presented for nouns, verbs, and overall and the best results are printed in boldface.

All methods clearly outperform the MFC baseline, obtaining accuracy gains between 15 and 20.5 points. The best performing methods are SVM and AB (SVM achieves a slightly better accuracy but this difference is not statistically significant). On the other extreme, NB and DL are methods with the lowest accuracy with no significant differences between them. The kNN method is in the middle of the previous two groups. That is, according to the paired t-test, the partial order between methods is:

$$SVM \approx AB > kNN > NB \approx DL > MFC$$

where "A $\approx$ B" means that the accuracies of A and B are not significantly different, and "A > B" means that the accuracy of A is significantly better than B.

The low performance of DL seems to contradict some previous research, in which very good results were reported with this method. One possible reason for this failure is the simple smoothing method applied. Yarowsky (1995b) showed that smoothing techniques can help to obtain good estimates for different feature types, which is crucial for methods like DL. These techniques were also applied to different learning methods in (Agirre and Martínez 2004b), showing a significant improvement over the simple smoothing. Another reason for the low performance is that when DL is forced to make decisions with few data points it does not make reliable predictions. Rather than trying to force 100% coverage, the DL paradigm seems to be more appropriate for obtaining high precision estimates. In Martínez et al. (2002) decision lists are shown to have a very high precision for low coverage, achieving 94.90% accuracy at 9.66% coverage, and 92.79% accuracy at 20.44% coverage. These experiments were performed on the Senseval-2 datasets.

In this corpus subset, the average accuracy values achieved for nouns and verbs are very close; the baseline MFC results are almost identical (46.59% for nouns and 46.49% for verbs). This is quite different from the results reported in many papers taking into account the whole set of 191 words of the DSO corpus. For instance, differences of between 3 and 4 points can be observed in favor of nouns in Escudero et al. (2000b). This is due to the particular subset of 13 nouns studied here, which are more difficult words. In the whole DSO corpus, the MFC for nouns (56.4%) is higher than in this subset (46.6%) and an AdaBoost-based system is able to achieve 70.8% on nouns (Escudero et al. 2000b) compared to the 66.0% on this subset. Also, the average number of senses per noun is higher than in the entire corpus. Despite this fact, a difference between two groups of methods can be observed regarding the accuracy on nouns and verbs. On the one hand, the worst performing methods (NB and DL) do better on

Table 7.3. Overall percentage accuracy of AB and SVM classifiers by groups of words of increasing average number of examples per sense.

	≤35	35–60	60–120	120–200	>200
AB	60.19	57.40	**70.21**	**65.23**	**73.93**
SVM	**63.59**	**60.18**	70.15	64.93	72.90

nouns than on verbs. On the other hand, the best performing methods (*k*NN, AB, and SVM) are able to better learn the behavior of verb examples, achieving an accuracy value around 1 point higher than for nouns.

Some researchers, Schapire (2003) for instance, argue that the AdaBoost algorithm may perform poorly when training from small samples. In order to verify this statement, we calculated the accuracy obtained by AB in several groups of words sorted by increasing size of the training set, that is, the average number of examples per sense. Table 7.3 shows the results obtained, including a comparison with the SVM method. As expected, the accuracy of SVM is significantly higher than that of AB for small training sets (up to 60 examples per sense). However, AB outperforms SVM in the larger training sets (over 120 examples per sense). Recall that the overall accuracy is comparable in both classifiers (Table 7.2).

In absolute terms, the overall results of all methods can be considered quite low (61–67%). We do not claim that these results cannot be improved by using richer feature representations, by a more accurate tuning of the systems, or by the addition of more training examples. Additionally, it is known that the DSO words included in this study are among the most polysemous English words and that WordNet is a very fine-grained sense repository. Supposing that we had enough training examples for every ambiguous word in the language, it seems reasonable to think that a much more accurate all-words system could be constructed based on the current supervised technology. However, this requirement is not met at present, and the best current supervised systems for English all-words disambiguation achieve accuracy figures around 65% (see Senseval-3 results). Our opinion is that state-of-the art supervised systems still have to be *qualitatively* improved in order to be really practical.

Apart from accuracy figures, the observation of the predictions made by the classifiers provides interesting information about the comparison between methods. Table 7.4 presents the percentage of agreement and the Kappa statistic between all pairs of systems on the test sets. "DSO" stands for the annotation of the DSO corpus, which is taken as the correct annotation. Therefore, the agreement rates with respect to DSO contain the accuracy results previously reported. The kappa coefficient (Cohen 1960) is a

Table 7.4. Kappa coefficient (below diagonal) and percentage of agreement (above diagonal) between all pairs of systems on the DSO corpus.

	DSO	MFC	NB	kNN	DL	AB	SVM
DSO	–	46.6	61.5	63.6	61.3	66.3	67.1
MFC	–0.19	–	73.9	58.9	64.9	54.9	57.3
NB	0.24	–0.09	–	75.2	76.7	71.4	76.7
kNN	0.39	–0.15	0.43	–	70.2	72.3	78.0
DL	0.31	–0.13	0.39	0.40	–	69.9	72.5
AB	0.44	–0.17	0.37	0.50	0.42	–	80.3
SVM	0.44	–0.16	0.49	0.61	0.45	0.65	–

measure of inter-annotator agreement, which reduces the effect of chance agreement, and which has been used for measuring inter-annotator agreement during the construction of some semantically annotated corpora (Véronis 1998, Ng et al. 1999b; see Chap. 4). A kappa value of 1 indicates perfect agreement, values around 0.8 are considered to indicate very good agreement (Carletta 1996), and negative values are interpreted as systematic disagreement on non-frequent cases.

NB obtains the most similar results to MFC in agreement rate and kappa value. The 73.9% of agreement means that almost 3 out of 4 times it predicts the most frequent sense (which is correct in less than half of the cases). SVM and AB obtain the most similar results with regard to DSO in agreement rate and kappa values, and they have the least similar kappa and agreement values to MFC. This indicates that SVM and AB are the methods that best learn the behavior of the DSO examples. It is also interesting to note that the three highest values of kappa (0.65, 0.61, and 0.50) are between the top performing methods (SVM, AB, and kNN), and that despite that NB and DL achieve a very similar accuracy on the corpus, their predictions are quite different, since the kappa value between them is one of the lowest (0.39).

The kappa values between the methods and the DSO annotation are very low. But as Véronis (1998) suggests, evaluation measures should be computed relative to the agreement between the human annotators of the corpus and not to a theoretical 100%. It seems pointless to expect more agreement between the system and the reference corpus than between the annotators themselves. Besides that, although hand-tagging initiatives that proceed through discussion and arbitration report fairly high agreement rates (Kilgarriff and Rosenszweig 2000), this is not the case when independent groups hand-tag the same corpus separately. For instance, Ng et al. (1999b) report an accuracy rate of 56.7% and a kappa value of 0.317

when comparing the annotation of a subset of the DSO corpus performed by two independent research groups. Similarly, Véronis (1998) reports values of Kappa near to zero when annotating some special words for the Romanseval corpus (see Chap. 4).

From this point of view, the kappa values of 0.44 achieved by SVM and AB could be considered high results. Unfortunately, the subset of the DSO corpus treated in this work does not coincide with Ng et al. (1999b) and, therefore, a direct comparison is not possible.

7.4 Current Challenges of the Supervised Approach

Supervised methods for WSD based on machine learning techniques are undeniably effective and they have obtained the best results to date. However, there exists a set of practical questions that should be resolved before stating that the supervised approach is a realistic way to construct accurate systems for wide-coverage WSD on open text. In this section, we will discuss some of the problems and current efforts at overcoming them.

7.4.1 Right-Sized Training Sets

One question that arises concerning supervised WSD methods is the quantity of data needed to train the systems. Ng (1997b) estimates that to obtain a high accuracy domain-independent system, about 1,000 occurrences of each of at least 3,200 words should be tagged. The necessary effort for constructing such a training corpus is estimated to be 16 person-years, according to the experience of Ng and Lee (1996). However, Ng (1997b) suggests that active learning methods, described afterwards in this section, could reduce the required effort significantly.

Unfortunately, many people think that Ng's estimate might fall short, as the annotated corpus produced in this way is not guaranteed to enable high accuracy WSD. In fact, recent studies using DSO have shown that: 1) the performance for state-of-the-art supervised WSD systems continues to be 60–70% for this corpus (Escudero et al. 2001), and 2) some highly polysemous words get very low performance (20–40% accuracy).

There has been some work exploring the learning curves of each different word to investigate the amount of training data required. Ng (1997b) trained the exemplar-based-learning LEXAS system for a set of 137 words with at least 500 examples each, and for a set of 43 words with at least 1,300 examples each. In both situations, the accuracy of the system was still rising with the whole training data. In independent work, Agirre and Martínez (2000) studied the learning curves of two small sets of words (containing nouns, verbs, adjectives, and adverbs) using different corpora (Semcor and DSO). Words of different types were selected, taking into account their characteristics: high/low polysemy, high/low frequency, and high/low skew of the most frequent sense in Semcor. Using decision lists as the learning algorithm, they observed that Semcor is not big enough to get stable results. However, on the DSO corpus, results seemed to stabilize for nouns and verbs before using all the training material. The word set tested in DSO had on average 927 examples per noun, and 1,370 examples per verb.

The importance of having enough examples is also highlighted in our experiment above (Sect. 7.3.2), where the best performance is clearly achieved on the words with the most examples (more than 200 per sense).

7.4.2 Porting Across Corpora

The porting of corpora to new genre/domains also presents important challenges. Some studies show that the assumptions for supervised learning do not hold when using different corpora, and that there is a dramatic degradation of performance (cf. domain-specific WSD, Chap. 10).

Escudero et al. (2000c) studied the performance of some ML algorithms (Naïve Bayes, exemplar-based learning, decision lists, AdaBoost, etc.) when tested on a different corpus (target corpus) than the one they were trained on (source corpus), and explored their ability to adapt to new domains. They carried out three experiments to test the portability of the algorithms. For the first and second experiments, they collected two equal-sized sets of sentence examples from the WSJ and Brown Corpus portions of the DSO corpus. The results obtained when training and testing across corpora were disappointing for all ML algorithms tested, since significant decreases in performance were observed in all cases. In some of them the cross-corpus accuracy was even lower than the most-frequent-sense baseline. A tuning technique was applied that added an increasing percentage of supervised training examples from the target corpus; however, this did not significantly improve the accuracy of the systems. Moreover, the results achieved in this mixed training situation were only slightly better than training on the small supervised part of the target corpus, thus making no use at all of the set of examples from the source corpus.

The third experiment showed that WSJ and Brown have very different sense distributions and that relevant features acquired by the ML algorithms are not portable across corpora, since they were indicating different senses in many cases.

Martínez and Agirre (2000) also attribute the low performance in cross-corpora tagging to the change in domain and genre. Again, they used the DSO corpus and a disjoint selection of the sentences from the WSJ and Brown parts. In Brown, texts are classified according to predefined genres (*reportage*, *religion*, *science-fiction*, etc.); this allowed them to perform tests on the effect of the domain and genre on cross-corpus tagging.

Their experiments, trained on WSJ and tested on Brown and vice versa, show that the performance drops significantly from the performance on each corpus separately. This happened mainly because there were few common collocations, but also because some collocations received systematically different tags in each corpus – a similar observation to that of Escudero et al. (2000c). Subsequent experiments were conducted taking into account the genre of the documents in Brown, showing that results were better when two independent corpora shared genre/topic than when using the same corpus with different genre/topic. The main conclusion is that the one-sense-per-collocation constraint does hold across corpora, but that collocations vary from one corpus to other, following genre and topic variations. They argued that a system trained on a specific genre/topic would have difficulties to adapt to new genres/topics. Besides, methods that try to extend automatically the set of examples for training should also take into account these phenomena.

7.4.3 The Knowledge Acquisition Bottleneck

As we mentioned in the introduction, an important issue for supervised WSD systems is the knowledge acquisition bottleneck. In most of the tagged corpora available it is difficult to find at least the required minimum number of occurrences per each sense of a word. In order to overcome this problem, a number of lines of research are currently being pursued, including:

1. automatic acquisition of training examples,
2. active learning,
3. combining training examples from different words,
4. exploiting parallel corpora, and
5. learning from labeled and unlabeled examples.

We will focus on the former four in this section, and devote the next section to the latter.

Automatic Acquisition of Training Examples

In automatic acquisition of training examples, an external lexical source, for instance WordNet, or a sense-tagged corpus is used to obtain new examples from a very large untagged corpus (e.g., the Internet).

Leacock et al. (1998) used a pioneering knowledge-based technique to automatically find training examples from a very large corpus. WordNet was used to obtain monosemous words semantically related to those word senses to be disambiguated (monosemous relatives).

Similarly, Mihalcea and Moldovan (1999) used information in WordNet (e.g., monosemous synonyms and glosses) to construct queries, which later fed the Altavista Web search engine. Four procedures were used sequentially, in a decreasing order of precision, but with increasing levels of retrieved examples. Results were evaluated by hand: over 91% of the examples were correctly retrieved among a set of 1,080 instances of 120 word senses. However, the number of examples acquired did not correlate with the frequency of senses, and the resulting corpus was not used for training a real WSD system. The above two algorithms are elaborated in Chapter 9 (Sect. 9.3.1).

Mihalcea (2002a) generated a sense-tagged corpus (GenCor) by using a set of seeds consisting of sense-tagged examples from four sources: Semcor, WordNet, examples created using the method above, and manually-tagged examples from other sources (e.g., the Senseval-2 corpus). The method, fully described in Chap. 9 (Sect 9.3.2), boosted her system to first place in the Senseval-2 all-words task.

This approach was also taken by Agirre and Martinez (2004c), where they rely on monosemous relatives of the target word to query the Internet and gather sense-tagged examples. In this case, they analyze the effect of the bias of the word senses in the performance of the system. They propose to integrate the work from McCarthy et al. (2004) on automatically determining the predominant sense in an unlabeled corpus (see Chap. 6 (Sect. 6.1.2)). Combining this method with their automatically sense-tagged corpus, Agirre and Martinez (2004c) improve over the performance of the best unsupervised systems in the Senseval-2 English lexical sample.

Following also similar ideas, Cuadros et al. (2004) present ExRetriever, a software tool for automatically acquiring large sets of sense-tagged examples from large collections of text or the Web. This tool has been used to directly compare on Semcor different types of query construction strategies. Using the powerful and flexible declarative language of ExRetriever, new strategies can be easily designed, executed and evaluated.

Active Learning

Active learning is a technique used to choose informative examples for manual-tagging in order to reduce the acquisition cost. Argamon-Engelson and Dagan (1999) describe two main types of active learning: membership queries and selective sampling. In the first approach, the learner constructs examples and asks a teacher to label them. This approach would be difficult to apply to WSD. Instead, in selective sampling the learner selects the most informative examples from unlabeled data. The informativeness of the examples can be measured using the amount of uncertainty in their classification, given the current training data. Lewis and Gale (1994) use a single learning model and select those examples for which the classifier is most uncertain (uncertainty sampling). Argamon-Engelson and Dagan (1999) propose another method, called committee-based sampling, which randomly derives several classification models from the training set, and the degree of disagreement among them is used to measure the informativeness of the examples. Regarding WSD, Fujii et al. (1998) applied selective sampling to the acquisition of examples for disambiguating verb senses, in an iterative process with human taggers. The disambiguation method was based on nearest neighbor classification, and the selection of examples via the notion of "training utility". Utility is determined based on two criteria: number of neighbors in unsupervised data (i.e., examples with many neighbors will be more informative in next iterations), and similarity of the example with other supervised examples (the less similar, the more interesting). A comparison of their method with uncertainty and committee-based sampling showed a significantly better learning curve for the training utility approach.

In the OMWE data (Chklovski and Mihalcea 2002) (see Sect. 7.2.1 above), examples are selected for tagging by selective sampling. Two different classifiers are independently applied on untagged data. The classifiers have low inter-annotator agreement, but high accuracy when they agree (and low accuracy when they disagree). This makes the disagreement cases the hardest to annotate, therefore they are presented to the user.

Combining Training Examples from Different Words

Another recent trend to alleviate the knowledge acquisition bottleneck is the combination of training data from different words. Kohomban and Lee (2005) build semantic classifiers by merging the training data from words in the same semantic class. Once the system selects the class, simple heuristics are applied to obtain the fine-grained sense. The classifier follows the memory-based learning paradigm, and the examples are weighted according to their semantic similarity to the target word (computed using WordNet similarity; see Chap. 5 (Sect. 5.3.1)). Their final system improved over the best system of the Senseval-3 all-words competition. Another approach that uses training data from different words is presented by Niu et al. (2005). They build a word-independent model to compute the similarity between two contexts. A Maximum Entropy algorithm is trained with the all-words Semcor corpus, and the model is used for clustering the instances of a given target word. Evaluation is a problem in clustering approaches (see Chap. 6 (Sect. 6.3.2)), and in this case they map the clusters to the Senseval-3 lexical sample data by looking at 10% of the examples in the training data. Their final system obtained the best results for unsupervised systems on the English Senseval-3 lexical sample task.

Parallel Corpora

Methods that use bilingual corpora rely on the fact that the different senses of a word in a given language are translated using different words in another language. For example, the Spanish word *partido* translates to *match* in English in the sports sense and to *party* in the political sense. Therefore, if a corpus is available with a word-to-word alignment, when a translation of a word like *partido* is made, its English sense can be automatically determined as *match* or *party*. Gale et al. (1993) used an aligned French-English corpus and achieved 92% accuracy. Working with aligned corpora has the obvious limitation that the learned models are able to distinguish only those senses that are translated into different words in the other language.

Another potential source for automatically obtaining WSD training data is parallel corpora. This approach was already suggested a few years ago by Resnik and Yarowsky (1997) but only recently has been applied to real WSD. The key point is that by using the alignment tools from the statistical machine translation community one can align at word level all the sentence pairs in both languages using unsupervised techniques. By using the alignments in the two directions and some knowledge sources (e.g., WordNet) to test consistency and eliminate noisy alignments, one can extract all possible translations for each given word in the source language, which, in turn, can be considered as the relevant senses to disambiguate. Two recent papers present very promising evidence for the validity of this approach (Tufiş et al. 2004, Chan and Ng 2005). The latter validates the approach by evaluating on the Senseval-2 all-words task (restricted to nouns) by mapping the coarse-grained "senses" of translation pairs to the fine-grained sense inventory of WordNet. They conclude that using a 680 megabyte Chinese-English parallel corpus is enough to achieve the accuracy of the best Senseval-2 system at competition time. (Chapters 6 (Sect. 6.4), 9 (Sect. 9.3.4), and 11 (Sect. 11.4.3) discuss translational equivalence and WSD.)

7.4.4 Bootstrapping

As a way to partly overcome the knowledge acquisition bottleneck, some methods have been devised for building sense classifiers when only a few annotated examples are available together with a high quantity of unannotated data. These methods are often referred to as *bootstrapping* methods (Abney 2002, 2004). Among them, we can highlight *co-training* (Blum and Mitchell 1998), their derivatives (Collins and Singer 1999; Abney 2002, 2004), and *self-training* (Nigam and Ghani 2000).

Briefly, co-training algorithms work by learning two complementary classifiers for the classification task trained on a small starting set of labeled examples, which are then used to annotate new unlabeled examples. From these new examples only the most confident predictions are added to the set of labeled examples, and the process starts again with the re-training of classifiers and re-labeling of examples. This process may continue for several iterations until convergence, alternating at each iteration from one classifier to the other. The two complementary classifiers are constructed by considering two different *views* of the data (i.e., two different feature codifications), which must be conditionally independent given the class label. In several NLP tasks, co-training has provided moderate improvements with respect to not using additional unlabeled examples.

One important aspect of co-training consist on the use of different views to train different classifiers during the iterative process. While Blum and Mitchell (1998) stated the conditional independence of the views as a requirement, Abney (2002) shows that this requirement can be relaxed. Moreover, Clark et al. (2003) show that simply re-training on all the newly labeled data can, in some cases, yield comparable results to agreement-based co-training, with only a fraction of the computational cost.

Self-training starts with a set of labeled data, and builds a unique classifier (there are no different views of the data), which is then used on the unlabeled data. Only those examples with a confidence score over a certain threshold are included in the new labeled set. The classifier is then re-trained on the new set. This process continues for several iterations. Notice that only a single classifier is derived. The Yarowsky bootstrapping algorithm (Yarowsky 1995a) (see Sect. 7.2.4 above) is the best known representative of this family of algorithms.

Mihalcea (2004) introduced a new bootstrapping scheme that combines co-training with majority voting, with the effect of smoothing the bootstrapping learning curves and improving the average performance. However, this approach assumes a comparable distribution of classes between both labeled and unlabeled data (see Sect. 7.4.2). At each iteration, the class distribution in the labeled data is maintained by keeping a constant ratio across classes between already labeled examples and newly added examples. This requires one to know a priori the distribution of sense classes in the unlabeled corpus, which seems unrealistic.

Pham et al. (2005) also experimented with a number of co-training variants on the Senseval-2 lexical sample and all-words tasks, including the ones in Mihalcea (2004). Although the original co-training algorithm did not provide any advantage over using only labeled examples, all the sophisticated co-training variants obtained significant improvements (taking Naïve Bayes as the base learning method). The best reported method was Spectral Graph Transduction Co-training.

7.4.5 Feature Selection and Parameter Optimization

Another current trend in WSD is the automatic selection of features. Some recent work has focused on defining separate feature sets for each word, claiming that different features help to disambiguate different words. The exemplar-based learning algorithm is very sensitive to irrelevant features, so in order to overcome this problem Mihalcea (2002b) used a forward-selection iterative process to select the optimal features for each word. She ran cross-validation on the training set, adding the best feature to the optimal set at each iteration, until no improvement was observed. The final system achieved good results in the Senseval-2 competition.

Very interesting research has been conducted connecting parameter optimization and feature selection. Hoste et al. (2002b) observed that although there have been many comparisons among ML algorithms trying to determine the method with the best bias for WSD, there are large variations on performance depending on three factors: algorithm parameters, input representation (i.e., features), and interaction between both. They claim that changing any of these factors produces large fluctuations in accuracy, and that exhaustive optimization of parameters is required in order to obtain reliable results. They argue that there is little understanding of the interaction among the three influential factors, and while no fundamental data-independent explanation is found, data-dependent cross-validation can provide useful clues for WSD. In their experiments, they show that memory-based WSD benefits from optimizing architecture, information sources, and algorithmic parameters. The optimization is carried out using cross-validation on the learning data for each word. In order to do it, one promising direction is the use of genetic algorithms (Daelemans and Hoste 2002), which lead to very good results in the Senseval-3 English all-words task (Decadt et al. 2004) – though the results were less satisfactory in the English lexical sample task.

Martínez et al. (2002) made use of feature selection for high precision disambiguation at the cost of coverage. By using cross validation on the training corpus, a set of individual features with a discriminative power above a certain threshold was extracted for each word. The threshold parameter allows one to adjust the desired precision of the final system. This method was used to train decision lists, obtaining 86% precision for 26% coverage, or 95% precision for 8% coverage on the Senseval-2 data. In principle, such a high precision system could be used to acquire almost error-free new examples in a bootstrapping framework.

Another approach to feature engineering consists of using smoothing methods to optimize the parameters of the models. Agirre and Martinez (2004c) integrate different smoothing techniques from the literature with four well-known ML methods. The smoothing techniques focus on the different feature types and provide better probability estimations for dealing with sparse data. They claim that the systems are more robust when integrating smoothing techniques. By combining the individual methods, the best ensemble of algorithms improves the best results in the English Senseval-2 lexical sample task.

7.4.6 Combination of Algorithms and Knowledge Sources

The combination paradigm, known as *ensembles of classifiers*, is a very well-known approach in the machine learning community. It helps to reduce variance and to provide more robust predictions for unstable base classifiers. The key for improving classification results is that the different classifiers combined commit non-correlated errors. For an in-depth analysis on classifier combination one may consult Dietterich (1997). The AdaBoost algorithm already explained in Sections 7.2.4 and 7.3.1, above, can be seen as a method of constructing an ensemble of classification rules. When the different classifiers are heterogeneous (e.g., coming from different learning algorithms), an important issue is to define an appropriate combination scheme to decide an output class from individual predictions. The most common combination schemes are based on a weighted voting strategy with a winner-take-all rule. Sometimes, an additional learning problem can be set in order to learn how to combine the available classifiers. In this case we talk about meta-learning.

The integration of heterogeneous ML methods and knowledge sources in combined systems has been one of the most popular approaches in recent supervised WSD systems, including many of the best performing systems at the Senseval-2 and Senseval-3. For instance, the JHU-English system (Yarowsky et al. 2001, Florian et al. 2002), which used a voting scheme, obtained the best performance at the English lexical sample task in Senseval-2. Based on this architecture, Yarowsky and Florian (2002) carried out a large set of experiments evaluating different parameter settings. The main conclusions of their study are that the feature space has significantly greater impact than the algorithm choice, and that the combination of different algorithms helps to construct significantly more robust WSD systems.

In Agirre et al. (2005) we find an example of recent work on dealing with the sparseness of data by means of combining classifiers with different feature spaces. Three possible improvements of the system are tested: i) applying Singular Value Decomposition (SVD) to find correlations in the feature space, ii) using unlabeled data from a related corpus for background knowledge, and iii) partitioning the feature space and training different voting classifiers. They found that each of the parameters improves the results of their kNN learner, and overall they obtained the best published results on the English Senseval-3 lexical sample task.

The use of ensembles helps to improve results in almost all learning scenarios and it constitutes a very helpful and powerful tool for system engineering. However, the improvement obtained by the majority of combined WSD systems is only marginal. Thus, our impression is that combination itself is not enough and other issues such as the knowledge taken into account must be addressed for overcoming the limitations of the current supervised systems.

Another approach is the combination of different linguistic knowledge sources to disambiguate all the words in the context, as in Stevenson and Wilks (2001). In this work, they integrate the answers of three partial taggers based on different knowledge sources in a feature-vector representation for each sense. The vector is completed with information about the sense (including rank in the lexicon), and simple collocations extracted from the context. The TiMBL memory-based learning algorithm is then applied to classify the new examples. The partial taggers apply the following knowledge: i) dictionary definition overlap, optimized for all-words by means of simulated annealing, ii) selectional preferences based on syntactic dependencies and LDOCE codes, and iii) subject codes from LDOCE using the Yarowsky (1992) algorithm (see Chap. 10). They obtained very good results, with accuracies over 90% in this experimental setting under the LDOCE sense inventory.

Montoyo et al. (2005) present a different approach to combination. Their work explores three different schemes of collaboration between knowledge-based and corpus-based WSD methods. Two complementary methods are presented: Specification Marks and Maximum Entropy. The results show that the combination of both methods outperforms each of them individually, demonstrating that both approaches can collaborate to obtain an enhanced WSD system.

7.5 Conclusions and Future Trends

This chapter has presented the state of the art of the supervised approach to WSD, which consists of automatically inducing classification (or disambiguation) models from examples. We started by introducing the machine learning framework for classification, including an in-depth review of the main ML approaches present in the WSD-related literature. We focused on the following issues: learning paradigms, corpora used, sense repositories, and feature representation. We included a description of five machine learning algorithms, which we experimentally evaluated and compared in a controlled framework. Finally, we briefly described some of the current challenges of the supervised learning approach.

The supervised approach to WSD makes use of semantically annotated corpora to train machine learning algorithms in order to decide which word sense to choose in which contexts. The words in these annotated corpora are manually tagged with semantic classes taken from a particular lexical-semantic resource. Many standard ML techniques have been investigated on the literature, including: probabilistic models, exemplar-based learning, decision lists, and, more recently, learning methods based on rule combination (like AdaBoost), and kernel functions and margin maximization (like Support Vector Machines).

Despite the work devoted to the task, it can be said that no large-scale broad-coverage accurate WSD system has been built up to date (Snyder and Palmer 2004). Although performance figures reported greatly vary from work to work (depending on the sense inventory used, the experimental setting, the knowledge sources used, etc.) it seems clear that the performance of current state-of-the-art systems is still below the operational threshold, making it difficult to empirically test the advantages of using WSD components in a broader NLP system that addresses a real task (see Chap. 11 for WSD in applications). Therefore, we still consider WSD as an important open problem in NLP.

As we have seen in Senseval, machine learning classifiers are undeniably effective, but, due to the knowledge acquisition bottleneck, they will not be feasible until reliable methods for acquiring large sets of training examples with a minimum human annotation effort are available. Furthermore, automatic methods for helping in the collection of examples should be robust to noisy data and changes in sense frequency distributions and corpus domain (or genre). The WSD classifiers should be also noise-tolerant (both in class-label and feature values), easy to adapt to new domains, robust to overfitting, and efficient for learning thousands of classifiers using large training sets and high-dimensional feature spaces.

The interrelated use of the individually learned classifiers in order to obtain a full text disambiguation (e.g., in an all-words scenario) is an issue that still has to be faced. A solution to this problem might have important implications in the way in which individual classifiers are learned.

In order to make significant advances in the performance of current supervised WSD systems, we also think that the feature representation must be enriched with a set of features with linguistic knowledge that is not currently available in wide-coverage lexical knowledge bases. We refer, for instance, to sub-categorization frames, syntactic structure, selectional preferences, semantic roles and domain information. Moreover, future WSD systems will need to automatically detect and group spurious sense distinctions, as well as to discover, probably in an on-line learning setting, occurrences of new senses in running text.

Acknowledgments

The research presented in this work has been partially funded by the Spanish Research Department (HERMES project, TIC2000-0335-C03-02) and by the European Commission (MEANING project, IST-2001-34460). David Martínez was supported by a Basque Government research grant: AE-BFI:01.245. The authors want to thank the reviewer of the first draft of the chapter for her/his useful comments and suggestions.

References

Abney, Steven. 2002. Bootstrapping. *Proceedings of the 40th Annual Meeting of the Association for Computational Linguistics (ACL)*, Philadelphia, U.S.A., 360–367.

Abney, Steven. 2004. Understanding the Yarowsky algorithm. *Computational Linguistics*, 30(3): 365–395.

Agirre, Eneko & David Martínez. 2000. Exploring automatic word sense disambiguation with decision lists and the Web. *Proceedings of the Semantic Annotation and Intelligent Annotation Workshop*, organized by COLING. Luxembourg, 11–19.

Agirre, Eneko & David Martínez. 2001. Knowledge sources for WSD. *Proceedings of the Fourth International Text Speech and Dialogue Conference (TSD)*, Plzen , Czech Republic, 1–10.

Agirre, Eneko & David Martínez. 2004a. The Basque Country University system: English and Basque tasks. *Proceedings of Senseval-3: Third International Workshop on the Evaluation of Systems for the Semantic Analysis of Text*, Barcelona, Spain, 44–48.

Agirre, Eneko & David Martínez. 2004b. Smoothing and word sense disambiguation. *Proceedings of España for Natural Language Processing (EsTAL)*, Alicante, Spain, 360–371.

Agirre, Eneko & David Martínez. 2004c. Unsupervised WSD based on automatically retrieved examples: the importance of bias. *Proceedings of the 10th Conference on Empirical Methods in Natural Language Processing (EMNLP)*, Barcelona, Spain, 25–32.

Agirre Eneko, Oier Lopez de Lacalle, & David Martínez. 2005. Exploring feature spaces with SVD and unlabeled data for word sense disambiguation. *Proceedings of the 5th Conference on Recent Advances on Natural Language Processing (RANLP)*, Borovets, Bulgary, 32–38.

Argamon-Engelson, Shlomo & Ido Dagan. 1999. Committee-based sample selection for probabilistic classifiers. *Journal of Artificial Intelligence Research*, 11: 335–460.

Berger, Adam, Steven Della Pietra & Vincent Della Pietra. 1996. A maximum entropy approach to natural language processing. *Computational Linguistics*, 22(1): 39–72.

Boser, Bernhard E., Isabelle M. Guyon & Vladimir N. Vapnik. 1992. A training algorithm for optimal margin classifiers. *Proceedings of the 5th Annual Workshop on Computational Learning Theory (CoLT)*, Pittsburgh, U.S.A., 144–152.

Blum, Avrim & Thomas Mitchell. 1998. Combining labeled and unlabeled data with co-training. *Proceedings of the 11th Annual Conference on Computational Learning Theory (CoLT)*, 92–100.

Bruce, Rebecca & Janice Wiebe. 1994. Word-sense disambiguation using decomposable models. *Proceedings of the 32nd Annual Meeting of the Association for Computational Linguistics (ACL)*, Las Cruces, U.S.A., 139–146.

Cabezas, Clara, Indrajit Bhattacharya & Philip Resnik. 2004. The University of Maryland Senseval-3 system descriptions. *Proceedings of Senseval-3: Third International Workshop on the Evaluation of Systems for the Semantic Analysis of Text*, Barcelona, Spain, 83–87.

Cardie, Claire & Raymond Mooney. 1999. Guest editors' introduction: Machine learning and natural language. *Machine Learning*, 34: 5–9.

Carletta, Jean C. 1996. Assessing agreement of classification tasks: The Kappa statistic. *Computational Linguistics*, 22(2): 249–254.

Carpuat, Marine, Weifeng Su & Dekai Wu. 2004. Augmenting ensemble classification for word sense disambiguation with a kernel PCA model. *Proceedings of Senseval-3: Third International Workshop on the Evaluation of Systems for the Semantic Analysis of Text*, Barcelona, Spain, 88–92.

Chen, Stanley F. 1996. *Building Probabilistic Models for Natural Language*. Ph.D. thesis, Technical Report TR-02-96, Center for Research in Computing Technology, Harvard University.

Ciaramita, Massimiliano & Mark Johnson. 2004. Multi-component word sense disambiguation. *Proceedings of Senseval-3: Third International Workshop on the Evaluation of Systems for the Semantic Analysis of Text*, Barcelona, Spain, 97–100.

Chan, Yee S. & Hwee T. Ng. 2005. Scaling up word sense disambiguation via parallel texts. *Proceedings of the 20th National Conference on Artificial Intelligence (AAAI)*, Pittsburgh, U.S.A., 1037–1042.

Chklovski, Timothy & Rada Mihalcea. 2002. Building a sense tagged corpus with Open Mind Word Expert. *Proceedings of the ACL Workshop on Word Sense Disambiguation: Recent Successes and Future Directions*, Philadelphia, U.S.A., 116–122.

Clark, Stephen, James Curran & Miles Osborne. 2003. Bootstrapping POS taggers using unlabelled data. *Proceedings of 7th Conference of Natural Language Learning (CoNLL)*, Edmonton, Canada, 164–167.

Cohen, Jacob. 1960. A coefficient of agreement for nominal scales. *Journal of Educational and Psychological Measurement*, 20: 37–46.

Collins, Michael & Yoram Singer. 1999. Unsupervised models for named entity classification. *Proceedings of the Joint SIGDAT Conference on Empirical*

Methods in Natural Language Processing and Very Large Corpora (EMNLP/VLC), College Park, U.S.A., 100–110.

Cost, Scott & Steven. Salzberg. 1993. A weighted nearest neighbor algorithm for learning with symbolic features. *Machine Learning*, 10(1): 57–78.

Cristianini, Nello & John Shawe-Taylor. 2000. *An Introduction to Support Vector Machines*. Cambridge, U.K.: Cambridge University Press.

Cuadros, Montse, Jordi Atserias, Mauro Castillo & German Rigau. 2004. Automatic acquisition of sense examples using exretriever. *Proceedings of the Iberamia Workshop on Lexical Resources and The Web for Word Sense Dismabiguation*, Puebla, México, 97–104.

Dagan, Ido, Yael Karov & Dan Roth. 1997. Mistake-driven learning in text categorization. *Proceedings of the 2nd Conference on Empirical Methods in Natural Language Processing (EMNLP)*, Providence, U.S.A., 55–63.

Daudé Jordi, Lluís Padró & German Rigau. 1999. Mapping multilingual hierarchies using relaxation labelling. *Proceedings of Joint SIGDAT Conference on Empirical Methods in Natural Language Processing and Very Large Corpora (EMNLP/VLC)*, College Park, U.S.A., 12–19.

Daudé Jordi, Lluís Padró & German Rigau. 2000. Mapping WordNets using structural information. *Proceedings of the 38th Annual Meeting of the Association for Computational Linguistics (ACL)*, Hong Kong, China, 504–511.

Daudé Jordi, Lluís Padró & German Rigau. 2001. A complete WN1.5 to WN1.6 mapping. *Proceedings of NAACL Workshop on WordNet and Other Lexical Resources: Applications, Extensions and Customizations*, Pittsburg, U.S.A., 83–88.

Daelemans, Walter, Antal Van den Bosch & Jakub Zavrel. 1999. Forgetting exceptions is harmful in language learning. *Machine Learning*, 34: 11–41.

Daelemans, Walter & Véronique Hoste. 2002. Evaluation of machine learning methods for natural language processing tasks. *Proceedings of the 3rd International Conference on Language Resources and Evaluation (LREC)*, Las Palmas, Spain, 755–760.

Decadt Bart, Véronique Hoste, Walter Daelemans & Antal van den Bosch. 2004. GAMBL, genetic algorithm optimization of memory-based WSD. *Proceedings of Senseval-3: Third International Workshop on the Evaluation of Systems for the Semantic Analysis of Text*, Barcelona, Spain, 108–112.

Dietterich, Thomas G. 1997. Machine learning research: four current directions. *Artificial Intelligence Magazine*, 18(4): 97–136.

Dietterich, Thomas G. 1998. Approximate statistical tests for comparing supervised classification learning algorithms. *Neural Computation*, 10(7): 1895–1923.

Duda, Richard O., Peter E. Hart & David G. Stork. 2001. *Pattern classification, 2nd Edition.* New York: John Wiley & Sons.

Edmonds, Philip & Scott Cotton. 2001. Senseval-2: Overview. *Proceedings of Senseval-2: Second International Workshop on Evaluating Word Sense Disambiguation Systems,* Toulouse, France, 1–6.

Escudero, Gerard, Lluís Màrquez & German Rigau. 2000a. Boosting applied to word sense disambiguation. *Proceedings of the 12th European Conference on Machine Learning (ECML),* Barcelona, Spain, 129–141.

Escudero, Gerard, Lluís Màrquez & German Rigau. 2000b. Naive bayes and exemplar-based approaches to word sense disambiguation revisited. *Proceedings of the 14th European Conference on Artificial Intelligence (ECAI),* Berlin, Germany, 421–425.

Escudero, Gerard, Lluís Màrquez & German Rigau. 2000c. On the portability and tuning of supervised word sense disambiguation systems. *Proceedings of the joint SIGDAT Conference on Empirical Methods in Natural Language Processing and Very Large Corpora (EMNLP/VLC),* Hong Kong, China, 172–180.

Escudero, Gerard, Lluís Màrquez & German Rigau. 2001. Using LazyBoosting for word sense disambiguation. *Proceedings of Senseval-2: Second International Workshop on Evaluating Word Sense Disambiguation Systems,* Toulouse, France.

Escudero, Gerard, Lluís Màrquez & German Rigau. 2004. TALP system for the English lexical sample task. *Proceedings of Senseval-3: Third International Workshop on the Evaluation of Systems for the Semantic Analysis of Text,* 113–116, Barcelona, Spain.

Fellbaum, Christiane, ed. 1998. *WordNet: An Electronic Lexical Database.* Cambridge, U.S.A.: The MIT Press.

Florian, Radu, Silviu Cucerzan, C. Schafer & David Yarowsky. 2002. Combining classifiers for word sense disambiguation. *Natural Language Engineering,* 8(4): 327–341.

Francis, W. Nelson & Henry Kučera. 1982. *Frequency analysis of English usage: Lexicon and grammar.* Boston: Houghton Mifflin Company.

Fujii, Atsushi, Kentaro Inui, Takenobu Tokunaga & Hozumi Tanaka. 1998. Selective sampling for example-based word sense disambiguation. *Computational Linguistics,* 24(4): 573–598.

Gale, William, Kenneth Church & David Yarowsky. 1992. One sense per discourse. *Proceedings of the DARPA Speech and Natural Language Workshop,* 233–237.

Gale, William, Kenneth Church & David Yarowsky. 1993. A method for disambiguating word senses in a large corpus. *Computers and the Humanities,* 26: 415–439.

Grozea, Cristian. 2004. Finding optimal parameter settings for high performance word sense disambiguation. *Proceedings of Senseval-3: Third International Workshop on the Evaluation of Systems for the Semantic Analysis of Text*, Barcelona, Spain, 125–128.

Hoste, Véronique, Anne Kool & Walter Daelemans. 2001. Classifier optimization and combination in the English all words task. *Proceedings of Senseval-2: Second International Workshop on Evaluating Word Sense Disambiguation Systems*, Toulouse, France, 83–86.

Hoste, Véronique, Walter Daelemans, Iris Hendrickx & Antal van den Bosch. 2002a. Evaluating the results of a memory-based word-expert approach to unrestricted word sense disambiguation. *Proceedings of the Workshop on Word Sense Disambiguation: Recent Successes and Future Directions*, Philadelphia, U.S.A., 95–101.

Hoste, Véronique, Iris Hendrickx, Walter Daelemans & Antal van den Bosch. 2002b. Parameter optimization for machine-learning of word sense disambiguation. *Natural Language Engineering*, 8(4): 311–325.

Kilgarriff, Adam. 1998. Senseval: An exercise in evaluating word sense disambiguation programs. *Proceedings of the European Conference on Lexicography (EURALEX)*, 176–174, Liege, Belgium. Also in *Proceedings of the 1st Conference on Language Resources and Evaluation (LREC)*, Granada, Spain, 581–588.

Kilgarriff, Adam & Joseph Rosenzweig. 2000. English Senseval: Report and results. *Proceedings of the 2nd Conference on Language Resources and Evaluation (*LREC), Athens, Greece, 1239–1244.

Kohomban, Upali S. & Wee S. Lee. 2005. Learning semantic classes for word sense disambiguation. *Proceedings of the 43rd Annual Meeting of the Association for Computational Linguistics (ACL)*, Ann Harbor, U.S.A., 34–41.

Leacock, Claudia, Geoffrey Towell & Ellen Voorhees. 1993. Towards building contextual representations of word senses using statistical models. *Proceedings of the ACL SIGLEX Workshop on Acquisition of Lexical Knowledge from Text*, 10–20.

Leacock, Claudia, Martin Chodorow & George A. Miller. 1998. Using corpus statistics and WordNet relations for sense identication. *Computational Linguistics*, 24(1): 147–165.

Lee, Yoong K. & Hwee T. Ng. 2002. An empirical evaluation of knowledge sources and learning algorithms for word sense disambiguation. *Proceedings of the 7th Conference on Empirical Methods in Natural Language Processing (EMNLP)*, Philadelphia, U.S.A., 41–48.

Lee, Yoong K., Hwee T. Ng & Tee K. Chia. 2004. Supervised word sense disambiguation with support vector machines and multiple knowledge sources.

Proceedings of Senseval-3: Third International Workshop on the Evaluation of Systems for the Semantic Analysis of Text, Barcelona, Spain, 137–140.

Lewis, David & William Gale. 1994. Training text classifiers by uncertainty sampling. *Proceedings of the International ACM Conference on Research and Development in Information Retrieval*, 3–12.

Manning, Christopher & Hinrich Schütze. 1999. *Foundations of Statistical Natural Language Processing*, Cambridge, U.S.A.: The MIT Press.

Martínez, David, Eneko Agirre & Lluís Màrquez. 2002. Syntactic features for high precision word sense disambiguation. *Proceedings of the 19th International Conference on Computational Linguistics (COLING)*, Taipei, Taiwan, 1–7.

Martínez David & Eneko Agirre. 2000. One sense per collocation and genre/topic variations. *Proceedings of the Joint SIGDAT Conference on Empirical Methods in Natural Language Processing and Very Large Corpora (EMNLP/VLC)*, Hong Kong, China, 207–215.

McCarthy, Diana, Rob Koeling, Julie Weeds & John Carroll. 2004. Finding predominant senses in untagged text. *Proceedings of the 42nd Annual Meeting of the Association for Computational Linguistics (ACL)*. Barcelona, Spain, 151–154.

Mihalcea, Rada. 2002a. Bootstrapping large sense tagged corpora. *Proceedings of the 3rd International Conference on Languages Resources and Evaluation (LREC)*, Las Palmas, Spain.

Mihalcea, Rada. 2002b. Instance based learning with automatic feature selection applied to word sense disambiguation. *Proceedings of the 19th International Conference on Computational Linguistics (COLING)*, Taipei, Taiwan.

Mihalcea Rada. 2004. Co-training and self-training for word sense disambiguation. *Proceedings of the Conference on Natural Language Learning (CoNLL)*. Boston, U.S.A., 33–40.

Mihalcea, Rada & Philip Edmonds, eds. 2004. *Proceedings of Senseval-3: Third International Workshop on the Evaluation of Systems for the Semantic Analysis of Text*, Barcelona, Spain. (http://www.senseval.org/)

Mihalcea, Rada & Dan Moldovan. 1999. An automatic method for generating sense tagged corpora. *Proceedings of the 16th National Conference on Artificial Intelligence (AAAI)*, Orlando, U.S.A., 461–466.

Miller, George. 1990. WordNet: An on-line lexical database. *International Journal of Lexicography*, 3(4): 235–312.

Miller, George A., Claudia Leacock, Randee Tengi & Ross T. Bunker. 1993. A semantic concordance. *Proceedings of the ARPA Workshop on Human Language Technology*, Princeton, U.S.A., 303–308.

Mitchell, Tom. 1997. *Machine Learning*. McGraw Hill.

Montoyo Andrés, Armando Suárez, German Rigau & Manuel Palomar. 2005. Combining knowledge- and corpus-based word-sense-disambiguation methods. *Journal of Artificial Intelligence Research*, 23: 299–330.

Mooney, Raymond J. 1996. Comparative experiments on disambiguating word senses: an illustration of the role of bias in machine learning. *Proceedings of the 1st Conference on Empirical Methods in Natural Language Processing (EMNLP)*, Philadelphia, U.S.A., 82–91.

Murata, Masaki, Masao Utiyama, Kiyotaka Uchimoto, Qing Ma, & Hitoshi Isahara. 2001. Japanese word sense disambiguation using the simple Bayes and support vector machine methods. *Proceedings of Senseval-2: Second International Workshop on Evaluating Word Sense Disambiguation Systems*, Toulouse, France, 135–138.

Ng, Hwee T. & Hian B. Lee. 1996. Integrating multiple knowledge sources to disambiguate word senses: An exemplar-based approach. *Proceedings of the 34th Annual Meeting of the Association for Computational Linguistics (ACL)*, Santa Cruz, U.S.A., 40–47.

Ng, Hwee T. 1997a. Exemplar-based word sense disambiguation: Some recent improvements. *Proceedings of the 2nd Conference on Empirical Methods in Natural Language Processing (EMNLP)*, Providence, U.S.A., 208–213.

Ng, Hwee T. 1997b. Getting serious about word sense disambiguation. *Proceedings of the ACL SIGLEX Workshop on Tagging Text with Lexical Semantics: Why, What, and How?*, Washington, U.S.A., 1–7.

Ng, Hwee T., C. Y. Lim & Foo, S. K. 1999. A case study on inter-annotator agreement for word sense disambiguation. *Proceedings of the ACL SIGLEX Workshop on Standarizing Lexical Resources*, College Park, U.S.A., 9–13.

Nigam, Kamal & Rayid Ghani. 2000. Analyzing the effectiveness and applicability of co-training. *Proceedings of the 9th International Conference on Information and Knowledge Management (CIKM)*, McLean, U.S.A., 86–93.

Niu, Chen, Wei Li, Rohini K. Srihari, & Huifeng Li. 2005. Word independent context pair classification model for word sense disambiguation. *Proceedings of the Ninth Conference on Computational Natural Language Learning (CoNLL)*, Ann Arbor, U.S.A., 33–39.

Pedersen, Ted & Rebecca Bruce. 1997. A new supervised learning algorithm for word sense disambiguation. *Proceedings of the 14th National Conference on Artificial Intelligence (AAAI)*, Providence, U.S.A., 604–609.

Pedersen, Ted. 2001. A decision tree of bigrams is an accurate predictor of word senses. *Proceedings of the 2nd Meeting of the North American Chapter of the Association for Computational Linguistics (NAACL)*, Pittsburgh, U.S.A., 79–86.

Pham, Thanh P., Hwee T. Ng, & Wee S. Lee. 2005. Word sense disambiguation with semi-supervised learning. *Proceedings of the 20th National Conference on Artificial Intelligence (AAAI)*, Pittsburgh, U.S.A., 1093–1098.

Popescu, Marius. 2004. Regularized least-squares classification for word sense disambiguation. *Proceedings of Senseval-3: Third International Workshop on the Evaluation of Systems for the Semantic Analysis of Text*, Barcelona, Spain, 209–212.

Procter, Paul, ed. 1978. *Longman Dictionary of Contemporary English.* London: Longman Group.

Quinlan, John R. 1993. *C4.5: Programs for Machine Learning.* San Mateo, U.S.A.: Morgan Kaufmann.

Resnik, Philip & David Yarowsky. 1997. A perspective on word sense disambiguation methods and their evaluation. *Proceedings of the ACL SIGLEX Workshop on Tagging Text with Lexical Semantics: Why, What, and How?*, Washington, U.S.A., 79–86.

Rivest, Ronald. 1987. Learning decision lists. *Machine Learning*, 2(3): 229–246.

Schapire, Robert E. & Yoram Singer. 1999. Improved boosting algorithms using confidence-rated predictions. *Machine Learning*, 37(3): 297–336.

Schapire, Robert E. & Yoram Singer. 2000. Boostexter: A boosting-based system for text categorization. *Machine Learning*, 39(2/3)135–168.

Schapire, Robert E. 2003. The boosting approach to machine learning: An overview. *Nonlinear Estimation and Classification*, ed. by D. D. Denison, M. H. Hansen, C. C. Holmes, B. Mallick, & B. Yu. New York, U.S.A.: Springer.

Snyder, Benjamin & Martha Palmer. 2004. The English all-words task. *Proceedings of Senseval-3: Third International Workshop on the Evaluation of Systems for the Semantic Analysis of Text*, Barcelona, Spain, 41–43.

Stevenson, Mark & Yorick Wilks. 2001. The interaction of knowledge sources in word sense disambiguation. *Computational Linguistics*, 27(3): 321–349.

Strapparava, Carlo, Alfio Gliozzo & Claudio Giuliano. 2004. Pattern abstraction and term similarity for word sense disambiguation: IRST at Senseval-3. *Proceedings of Senseval-3: Third International Workshop on the Evaluation of Systems for the Semantic Analysis of Text*, Barcelona, Spain, 229–234.

Suárez, Armando & Manuel Palomar. 2002. A maximum entropy-based word sense disambiguation system. *Proceedings of the 19th International Conference on Computational Linguistics (COLING)*, Taipei, Taiwan, 960–966.

Towell, Geoffrey, Ellen Voorhees & Claudia Leacock. 1998. Disambiguating highly ambiguous words. *Computational Linguistics*, 24(1): 125–146.

Tufiş, Dan, Radu Ion & Nancy Ide. 2004. Fine-grained word sense disambiguation based on parallel corpora, word alignment, word clustering and aligned wordnets. *Proceedings of the 20th International Conference on Computational Linguistics (COLING)*, Geneva, Switzerland, 1312–1318.

Vapnik, Vladimir. 1998. *Statistical Learning Theory*. New York, U.S.A.: John Wiley.

Véronis, Jean. 1998. A study of polysemy judgements and inter-annotator agreement. *Programme and Advanced Papers of Senseval-1: The First International Workshop on the Evaluation of Systems for the Semantic Analysis of Text*, Herstmonceux, England, 2–4.

Vossen, Piek, ed. 1998. *EuroWordNet. A multilingual database with lexical semantic networks*. Dordrecht, Germany: Kluwer Academic Publishers.

Wilks, Yorick, Dan Fass, Cheng-ming Guo, James McDonald, Tony Plate & Brian M. Slator. 1993. Providing machine tractable dictionary tools. *Semantics and the Lexicon*, ed. by James Pustejowsky, 341–401.

Wu, Dekai, Weifeng Su & Marine Carpuat. 2004. A kernel PCA method for superior word sense disambiguation. *Proceedings of the 42nd Annual Meeting of the Association for Computational Linguistics (ACL)*, Barcelona, Spain, 637–644.

Yarowsky, David. 1992. Word-sense disambiguation using statistical models of Roget's categories trained on large corpora. *Proceedings of the 14th International Conference on Computational Linguistics (COLING)*, Nantes, France, 454–460.

Yarowsky, David. 1993. One sense per collocation. *Proceedings of the ARPA Human Language Technology Workshop*, Princeton, U.S.A., 266–271.

Yarowsky, David. 1994. Decision lists for lexical ambiguity resolution: Application to accent restoration in Spanish and French. *Proceedings of the 32nd Annual Meeting of the Association for Computational Linguistics (ACL)*, Las Cruces, U.S.A., 88–95.

Yarowsky, David. 1995a. Unsupervised word sense disambiguation rivaling supervised methods. *Proceedings of the 33rd Annual Meeting of the Association for Computational Linguistics (ACL)*, Cambridge, U.S.A., 189–196.

Yarowsky, David. 1995b. *Three Machine Learning Algorithms for Lexical Ambiguity Resolution*. Ph.D. Thesis, Department of Computer and Information Sciences, University of Pennsylvania.

Yarowsky, David. 2000. Hierarchical decision lists for word sense disambiguation. *Computers and the Humanities*, 34(2): 179–186.

Yarowsky, David, Silviu Cucerzan, Radu Florian, Charles Schafer & Richard Wicentowski. 2001. The Johns Hopkins Senseval-2 system descriptions. *Proceedings of Senseval-2: Second International Workshop on Evaluating Word Sense Disambiguation Systems*, Toulouse, France.

Yarowsky, David & Radu Florian. 2002. Evaluating sense disambiguation performance across diverse parameter spaces. *Natural Language Engineering* 8(4): 293–310.

8 Knowledge Sources for WSD

Eneko Agirre[1] and Mark Stevenson[2]

[1]University of the Basque Country
[2]University of Sheffield

This chapter explores the different sources of linguistic knowledge that can be employed by WSD systems. These are more abstract than the features used by WSD algorithms, which are encoded at the algorithmic level and normally extracted from a lexical resource or corpora. The chapter begins by listing a comprehensive set of knowledge sources with examples of their application and then explains whether this linguistic knowledge may be found in corpora, lexical knowledge bases or machine readable dictionaries. An analysis of knowledge sources used in actual WSD systems is then presented. It has been observed that the best results are often obtained by combining knowledge sources and the chapter concludes by analyzing experiments on the effect of different knowledge sources which have implications about the effectiveness of each.

8.1 Introduction

The long history of research into word sense disambiguation has identified a range of linguistic phenomena, such as selectional preferences and domain information, that are thought to be relevant to resolving word sense ambiguity. We call such linguistic phenomena *knowledge sources*. Reports of WSD systems usually fail to refer to knowledge sources and prefer to focus on lower level features, such as "bag-of-words" or n-grams, used within the disambiguation algorithms. The features employed by a particular approach are relevant at the algorithmic level but there is not necessarily a clear theoretical connection to the more abstract choice of the knowledge source chosen to resolve word sense ambiguity. One reason

217

E. Agirre and P. Edmonds (eds.), Word Sense Disambiguation: Algorithms and Applications, 217–251.
© 2007 Springer.

for this complication is that features may encode more than one linguistic knowledge source, and vice versa. We think an analysis in terms of knowledge sources allows deeper insight into why WSD algorithms work, and ultimately into the phenomenon of polysemy itself.

This chapter aims to clarify the distinctions and relations between linguistic knowledge sources, features, and the lexical resources used for WSD. We first present the terminology used throughout this chapter:

- **Knowledge Sources (KS):** High-level abstract linguistic and semantic phenomena relevant to resolving ambiguity, for example, selectional preferences or the domain of each word sense (sports, military, etc.).
- **Features:** Ways of encoding the context used by systems. For instance, the domain of a word sense can be represented by the words co-occurring often with the word sense (bag-of-words feature) as extracted from sense-tagged corpora, or the domain code assigned to the word sense in a specific machine-readable dictionary (MRD) or lexical knowledge base (LKB). (Chaps. 5–7 give examples of features used by actual WSD algorithms).
- **Lexical Resources:** The specific resources that have been used to extract the features in actual systems. For instance, as just mentioned, bag-of-words features can be extracted from sense-tagged corpora, and domain codes can be found in MRDs or LKBs.

This chapter is organized as follows. In Section 8.2 we describe high level and abstract knowledge sources relevant to WSD. Section 8.3 describes the features used in actual WSD systems and relates them to the knowledge sources they represent and the lexical resources from which they are acquired. Section 8.4 studies knowledge sources as used in a number of relevant systems. Section 8.5 presents some experimental results in the literature regarding the contribution of different knowledge sources and/or features, which are then analyzed in Section 8.6. Finally, Section 8.7 presents the conclusions drawn from this chapter.

8.2 Knowledge Sources Relevant to WSD

The literature has proposed a wide range of knowledge sources related to the WSD problem. In this section we provide a list, and demonstrate, with examples, how each can be used in a WSD system.

Knowledge sources may belong to one of three broad classes: syntactic, semantic, or pragmatic/topical (Stevenson and Wilks 2001). Syntactic knowledge sources have to do with the role of a word within the grammatical structure of sentences; examples are part-of-speech tags and subcategorization information. Semantic knowledge sources relate to properties of the things to which words refer, for example selectional preferences and associations between word meanings. Pragmatic/topical knowledge relates to the role of the word within the wider discourse, for example reasoning with reference to world knowledge or information about the topic of the text under consideration.

The following list elaborates previously presented lists of knowledge sources presented by Hirst (1987), McRoy (1992) and Agirre and Martínez (2001a). This list is an effort to systematize closely related linguistic phenomena, and often there is no clear-cut border among the knowledge sources. Each item is numbered for further reference.

8.2.1 Syntactic

Part of Speech (KS 1)

Part-of-speech (POS) tags indicate the grammatical category of a word and can be a powerful feature to disambiguate words. For example, in the *Longman Dictionary of Contemporary English* (LDOCE) (Procter 1978) the word *fast* has four major senses, each applying to a different part-of-speech category (noun, verb, adjective, and adverb). In this case knowing the relevant part of speech is sufficient information to disambiguate the word. However, this is not the case for all words and, in particular, is not useful for homographs. For example, *bank* has (at least) two senses in which the word can be used as a noun, 'financial institution' and 'edge of river', and knowledge of the part of speech in context will not provide any indication of which of these is being used in a particular context (Wilks and Stevenson 1998).

Morphology (KS 2)

The morphological behavior of a word can be relevant for WSD. Some morphological forms cannot be associated with certain senses, so if a word is used in that form then the sense can be ruled out. For example, *tins* can be either the plural of the noun *tin* or the third person singular form of the verb *to tin*, as in *John tins food for a living*. There are two nominal senses for *tin*, 'small metal container' and 'metal'. The second of these is a mass noun and so cannot be the intended sense when the word is used in plural form.

This knowledge source is often more effective in languages that have richer morphologies than English. In Basque, for instance, certain suffixes can only be composed with animate nouns. For example, the word *lapur* can mean 'electrical appliance' or 'robber', but it can only mean 'robber' in *lapurrarengana* ('to the robber'), because the suffix *arengana* only attaches to animate nouns.

Collocations (KS 3)

Collocations have been defined as "any statistically significant co-occurrence [of words]" (Sag et al. 2002:8). At one end of the scale are collocations that cannot be analyzed by decomposition, for example, *kick the bucket* and *take the biscuit*. This class of collocations can only be disambiguated by explicitly storing the phrase and an associated meaning. At the other end of the scale are collocations that can be analyzed by decomposition into constituent lexemes. However, these may not be completely productive since they block alternative rephrasing using synonyms. For example, *motor car* cannot be rephrased as *engine car* or *motor automobile*. Although it is possible to analyze these collocations without storing an explicit meaning for each, there is a benefit from doing so since their semantics differ from standard productive word combinations and so may cause problems during disambiguation. Besides, collocations have proved to be a useful knowledge source. For example, in the phrase *river bank* the fact that the word *bank* is immediately preceded by *river* indicates that it is used in its 'edge of river' sense.

Subcategorization (KS 4)

Subcategorization information can be a useful knowledge source. For example, the verb *to grow* is intransitive when it is used in the 'become bigger' sense (*John grew quickly*) but transitive in all other senses (*John grew the plants*).

8.2.2 Semantic

Frequency of Senses (KS 5)

The distribution of senses in text is far from uniform (Resnik and Yarowsky 1997). Knowledge about the a priori distribution is useful information for WSD (McCarthy et al. 2004). For example, there are 4 senses of *people* in WordNet 1.6 (Fellbaum 1998) but only one of them accounts for 90% of occurrences in the Semcor sense-tagged corpus (Miller et al. 1993) (see Chap. 4).

Semantic Word Associations (KS 6)

The relationship between the meanings of different words and senses is very valuable for WSD. They can be divided into two main classes: paradigmatic and syntagmatic (Kriedler 1998).

Paradigmatic Relations (KS 6a). Paradigmatic relations are defined as associations between the meanings of words. Examples are hypernymy, the relation between a word and a more general term (e.g., *vehicle* is a hypernym of *car*) and meronymy, the part-whole relationship (e.g., *mast* is a meronym of *ship*). In the sentence *Cherry is a type of tree common in Japan* there is a hypernymy relation between *cherry* and *tree* which implies that in this context *cherry* means 'plant' rather than 'fruit'. Another example in which paradigmatic relations come into play is when the context implies that words are being used in similar meanings. For example, in *The guests may choose between duck or beef* the fact that *duck* and *beef* are coordinated implies that there is a paradigmatic relation between them. In fact, both words have two senses with a common hypernym ('meat') in WordNet, and therefore the 'meat' readings of *duck* and *beef* can be selected.

Syntagmatic Relations (KS 6b). Syntagmatic word relations describe the associations between words in sentences with respect to various syntactic dependency relationships. For example, in *The dog bit the postman* the direct object of *bit* is a strong indicator that the word is being used in the 'attack' sense. These relations can be seen as a restriction of collocations, where the words in the collocation need to be in a syntactic dependency relation. Although these kind of relations could also be classified as syntactic, we would like to stress that such word pairs are also semantically related. Thus, the semantic-word-association knowledge source includes all types of semantic relation.

Selectional Preferences (KS 7)

Verbs and adjectives often expect words of a specific semantic class as the fillers to their argument slots (Cruse 1998). In the ideal scenario these preferences may be used to disambiguate several words at once. For example, two senses of the word *stake* are 'post' and 'bet', which have the semantic types, say, 'implement' and 'abstract', respectively; the verb *drove* expects a direct object of type, say, 'vehicle' (*drive the truck*) or 'implement' (*drive the nail*). There is only one possible combination of noun and verb senses satisfying these preferences in the sentence *John drove the stake into the ground.*

An important aspect of selectional preferences is that the slot fillers are expressed in terms of a set of abstract semantic types that are often organized into a hierarchy (Wilks 1975). The syntagmatic relations (KS 6b) above are similar to selectional preferences (Resnik 1997) but express the constraints in terms of sets of words representing potential slot fillers rather than abstract semantic types that generalize over the set of words.

Semantic Roles (KS 8)

Semantic roles (Fillmore 1971) are closely related to selectional preferences (KS 7) and subcategorization of verbs (KS 4). For example, in the sentence *The bad news will eat him,* the object of eat fills the experiencer role (as opposed to the theme role), and this fact can be used to better constrain the possible senses of *eat*, together with the selectional preferences of *eat*.

8.2.3 Pragmatic/Topical

Domain (KS 9)

Knowledge of the domain of the text in which a word is used can be useful for WSD. For example, if we find the word *bat* in a text known to be about sports, then it is more likely that the 'sports' sense of bat is the one used in the text. In this chapter, we assume that the domain is a label drawn from an externally-defined list. Example domain labels are the metadata manually added to newswire stories, subject codes in LDOCE, or the output of an automatic process such as a text categorization system (see Chap. 10).

Topical Word Association (KS 10)

It is known that words appearing together in text are likely to be linked to a common topic. Also, there may be no explicit representation of the domain (i.e., domain labels) for a collection of texts. Topical word associations refer to the knowledge about which pairs of word senses are likely to appear together in texts on the same topic. By topic we mean here any domain or specialization of a domain, depending on the target application and document collection; it might range from, for example, 'sports' in general to the

'2004 Olympic Games'. For instance, *racket* and *court* are topically related and disambiguate each other without the need for an explicit domain label (KS 9). These word associations are also different from the paradigmatic associations (KS 6a) since the words may be of different ontological types. Topical word associations are also related to syntagmatic word associations (KS 6b), but in the latter the two associated words must be syntactically related, and need not be topically related. The same goes for collocations (KS 3), which may not be associated with any particular topic.

Pragmatics (KS 11)

In some cases, world knowledge, and reasoning with it, is necessary for disambiguation. The ALPAC report (ALPAC 1966) used this as evidence that WSD was too difficult a problem to be solved by computer. Their argument was motivated by an example sentence from Bar-Hillel (1964) (see also Chap. 11 (Sect. 11.2)): *The box was in the pen.* This sentence can only be disambiguated using knowledge of the relative physical sizes of two senses of *pen*: 'writing implement' and 'enclosure'. However, examples like this are unusual and the majority of word occurrences can be disambiguated using more basic knowledge sources (Yarowsky 1996).

Certain knowledge sources provide categorical evidence as to the word sense used or disallowed by a particular context, but most of them provide heuristic knowledge. For example, the word *star* has (at least) two nominal senses ('celestial body' or 'celebrity') and one verbal sense ('to be the star of a performance'). In the sentence, due to Charniak (1983), *The astronomer married the star,* the evidence provided by the part-of-speech information can be used to categorically rule out the verb sense. However, the correct sense cannot be found by choosing the one that is topically related to *astronomer*, a technique that is successful in many other cases. This sentence can be disambiguated via other knowledge sources, such as the selectional preferences of the verb *to marry*.

8.3 Features and Lexical Resources

The knowledge sources outlined in the previous section are all relevant to the disambiguation decisions made by WSD algorithms. However, in order to be applied they need to be coded as features, which need to be identifiable in text. These features need to be derived from lexical resources, such as corpora, MRDs, or LKBs. Corpora used in WSD may be tagged with word senses although they need not be. *Sense-tagged corpora* (as opposed to *untagged corpora*) are far more useful for WSD since it is then easy to examine the behavior of a word used in a particular sense. However, the main disadvantage of tagged text is that it is extremely time-consuming to produce (see Chap. 4). Researchers have also tried to use the information contained in structured lexical resources including LKBs (e.g., WordNet), and MRDs (e.g., LDOCE).

Different lexical resources contain different types of disambiguation information; consequently, WSD methods have often been tailored around the available lexical resources. Chapters 5–7 present a variety of algorithms using structured lexical resources, untagged corpora, and tagged corpora, respectively.

We now present a list of the features which are commonly used in WSD systems. Following each feature is a description of the knowledge source (or sources) and lexical resource from which it may be obtained. According to the scope of the context, the features are grouped into three categories: target-word-specific[1] features, local features, and global features. In the end of this section, Figure 8.1 summarizes the relation among knowledge sources and features, where we can see that the relation is in most cases many-to-many.

8.3.1 Target-Word Specific Features

Word Form of Target Word. This feature may partially encode POS and morphology (KS 1 and KS 2), depending on the language.

Part of Speech of Target Word. A direct encoding of POS (KS 1). The part of speech of a lexeme is one of the most readily identifiable features. It is available in lexicons commonly used for WSD and these can be used to determine the grammatical category for each sense. The part of speech of a word in context can be identified using one of the many taggers (for example, the Brill tagger (Brill 1995)).

Sense Distribution of the Target Word. Directly encodes the frequency of senses (KS 5). In principle this distribution could be found by analyzing a tagged corpus. However, this would suffer from data sparseness problems unless the corpus was extremely large and the annotation of high quality. No appropriate resource is currently available, but some lexical resources attempt to order the senses in terms of their frequency of occurrence, however, the dictionary creators are also limited by the lack

---

[1] "Target word" refers to the word being disambiguated.

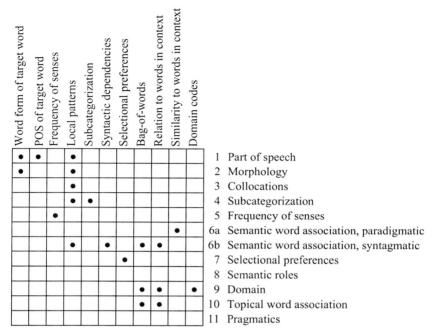

Fig. 8.1. Relation between knowledge sources (rows) and commonly used features (columns). Two of the rows (KS 8 and KS 11) have no related features.

of appropriate sense-tagged corpora and the ordering is often subjective (Kilgarriff 1997).

8.3.2 Local Features

Local Patterns. Some of the most commonly used features in WSD systems are local patterns around the target word. These partially encode several knowledge sources: collocations (KS 3), subcategorization (KS 4) and syntagmatic semantic word associations (KS 6b). The local patterns around the target word have many potential forms that vary in terms of their extent and fillers. Possible extent of patterns include n-grams around the target word, n-th word to the right or left of the target, and n^{th} word with a certain property to the left or right of the target. Several features in the context could be used to fill these patterns such as word forms in text, word lemmas, their part of speech tags, or a mixture of these. Example patterns under this definition include trigrams containing the target word and the two words immediately to the left, bigrams containing POS tags of the first two words to the right of the target, and bigrams composed of the target and the first noun to its right.

These features are most easily extracted from a tagged corpus. In an untagged corpus it is difficult to tell which senses of the word the patterns apply to. Consequently this feature is most commonly used with supervised approaches to WSD (see Chap. 7) where the system has access to tagged training data (Brown et al. 1991, Gale et al. 1993, Ng and Lee 1996).

Subcategorization. Directly encodes KS 4. Details of a word's subcategorization behavior are most easily obtained from tagged corpora using a robust parser (e.g., Minipar (Lin 1993) or RASP (Carroll and Briscoe 2001)). Martínez et al. (2002) used Minipar to derive subcategorization information for verbs from tagged corpora. For instance, from *The unfortunate hiker fell-1 into a crevasse*[2] we can derive that the first sense of the verb *to fall* allows for a subject but no other arguments. Some dictionaries (e.g., LDOCE and WordNet) list information about the syntactic behavior of words although this has not been extensively used in WSD.

Syntactic Dependencies. This feature encodes syntagmatic relations (KS 6b). The dependencies of a particular word sense can be extracted from a corpus which is parsed and tagged with word senses (Lin 1997, Yarowsky and Florian 2002).

Selectional Preferences. A direct encoding of KS 7. This information is not included in all lexicons but may be included in hand-crafted ones such as those used by Wilks (1978) and McRoy (1992). MRDs often include selectional preference information. For example, LDOCE has relatively detailed information based on a set of 36 semantic types that Stevenson (2003) used for disambiguation. WordNet also includes some selectional preference information although it is limited to simple types such as "somebody" and "something" for the arguments of verb senses and these are of little practical use as an information source. Methods have also been devised to acquire selectional preferences automatically from untagged corpora (Resnik 1997, McCarthy et al. 2001) and tagged, parsed corpora (Agirre and Martínez 2001b) (see Chap. 5 (Sect. 5.4) for more details).

---

[2] We use *fell-1* to indicate that *fell* in that sentence has been hand-tagged with the first sense of the verb *to fall* in WordNet.

8.3.3 Global Features

Bag-of-Words. Partially encodes semantic and topical word associations (KS 6b and KS 10), as well as domain information (KS 9). Bag-of-words features consist of a wide context window around the target word. This context is encoded as a simple list of the words in that window and how often they occur there. Other forms of the feature might consist of counts of bigrams in the context. These features can be extracted from text with no linguistic processing other than tokenization. Most WSD systems use this kind of feature.

Relation to Words in Context. Partially encodes semantic and topical word associations (KS 6 and KS 10), as well as domain information (KS 9). This feature has been typically extracted from dictionary definitions. The first proposal for using definitions to identify semantic and topical word associations came from Lesk (1986), who suggested that counting the number of content words shared by the definitions of two senses provided a measure of semantic relatedness. Recent work has looked at combining corpus evidence with dictionary definitions (see Chap. 5).

Similarity to Words in Context. Encodes paradigmatic relations (KS 6a). Taxonomical information such as that contained in WordNet can be used to find the similarity between the senses of the target word and the words in the context (Patwardhan et al. 2003) (see Chap. 5).

Domain Codes. Encodes domain information (KS 9). Some lexical resources list the most likely domain for a sense. For example, LDOCE uses a set of 100 subject codes (and 246 subdivisions), so the 'railway track' sense of *track* is marked with the 'Railway' subject code and the 'album track' sense with 'Music'. A thesaurus, such as *Roget's International Thesaurus* (Chapman 1977), also includes domain codes in the form of the categories into which the words are organized.

The main challenge in using domain codes in WSD is to find a way to accurately identify the domain. In addition, most lexicons are structured in such a way that there is a unique sense for each domain and therefore identifying the domain of the target word is equivalent to disambiguating it. For example, Yarowsky (1992) used bag-of-words features to model Roget categories and disambiguated ambiguous words by comparing their contexts with the model acquired for each category. Domain codes can also be applied more directly, for example Stevenson and Wilks (2001) used LDOCE subject codes by choosing the senses for words in a paragraph that maximize the number of shared codes. (See Chap. 10 (Sect. 10.2.1).)

Note that some of the above features offer overlapping and somehow redundant information. For example, a relevant argument-head relation such as *bit:postman* in *The dog bit the postman* can appear as a local pattern (e.g., the word trigram *bit the postman*), a syntactic dependency, or as a bag-of-words feature (i.e., *postman* in the context of *bit*). This redundancy and overlap is reflected in the mapping in Fig. 8.1.

8.4 Identifying Knowledge Sources in Actual Systems

Different knowledge sources have been favored at different times during the history of WSD research. Some of the early WSD systems enjoyed access to rich sets of, generally hand-crafted, knowledge sources. For example, Wilks's preference semantics (Wilks 1975) relied on extraction patterns which described the relations between content words in a text. Each ambiguous word had a set of senses that listed its selectional preferences (KS 7), the sole knowledge source used for disambiguation. However, Boguraev (1979) found that this approach did not work well for polysemous verbs. Hirst (1987) created a system, called "polaroid words", that contained a grammar, parser, lexicon, and semantic interpreter all based around a specialized knowledge representation language. Small's "word expert" approach (Small 1980) also had access to rich knowledge sources although in this case they were all stored in the lexicon as hand-crafted disambiguators. It is difficult to determine exactly which of the knowledge sources Hirst's and Small's systems had access to although it is clear that a wide range was employed. The above systems each relied on hand-crafted knowledge sources which were restricted by limited lexical coverage to small domains and did not scale up well to larger applications.

McRoy's system (McRoy 1992) was not limited to a particular domain. It used of a system of "core" and "dynamic" (or domain-specific) lexicons, the first applied to all texts while the dynamic lexicons are only used when the text being disambiguated is identified as being on the same topic as the lexicon. These lexicons were bespoke data sources for WSD and were complemented by several others including a concept hierarchy, a library of collocation patterns, semantic classes, selectional preferences, role-related expectations as well as part-of-speech tags and morphological information. These features encode the majority of knowledge sources outlined in Section 8.2. However, her system was not evaluated against a tagged corpus.

We have already mentioned Lesk (1986) (see Sect. 8.3.3), who developed an approach to WSD that has often been duplicated using dictionary definitions as the sole source of disambiguation information (KS 6, 9, and 10). Disambiguation was carried out by computing the overlap of content words in the definitions. Cowie et al. (1992) used the LDOCE subject codes as an additional source of information (KS 9).

A more recent approach has been to make use of large corpora to provide the disambiguation information. For example, Brown et al. (1991) and Gale et al. (1993) used bilingual corpora in which the translation in the parallel text was used as the sense tag, thereby avoiding the need for manual disambiguation (see Chap. 6). Knowledge sources used were simple collocates such as first noun to the left/right, second word to the left/right and so on. These encoded KS 3 and KS 6b. In general supervised systems that learn from sense-tagged text have tended to use quite simple knowledge sources. More complex ones were used by Ng and Lee (1996) who used part-of-speech information (KS 1), morphological form (KS 2), surrounding words and local collocates (KS 3, 6b, and 10) and words in verb-object syntactic relation (KS 6b). Subsequently, richer sets of features have been acquired in the supervised WSD literature (see Section 8.5, below, and Chap. 7).

Early experience with WSD showed that the features that model knowledge sources were difficult to obtain for anything other than limited domains or a handful of words, and that, in general, they had to be encoded by hand. Later, researchers made use of the information in existing lexical resources such as MRDs and LKBs, building systems that were able to cope with large vocabularies and general domain texts, but with limited accuracy. More recently, the features of choice have been the ones extracted from hand-tagged corpora.

8.4.1 Senseval-2 Systems

One important advent in the history of WSD has been Senseval (see Chap. 4). Although an increasing number of tasks are being proposed (some of which go beyond WSD), we will focus on the English WSD tasks in Senseval-2 and Senseval-3.

Senseval-2 was carried out in 2001. The majority of entries relied on information from a small number of knowledge sources, with several sites entering multiple systems in order to compare different aspects of those knowledge sources or different combinations of them.

Supervised systems were the most homogeneous, with only a few knowledge sources being commonly used among the participating entries: first, bag-of-words features where widely used (KS 6b, 9, and 10), second, local patterns such as 2–4 words (also coded as lemmas or POS tags) around the ambiguous token, (KS 3, 4, 6b), and lastly, knowledge sources corresponding to the target word (KS 1, 2, and 5).

Several supervised systems augmented these knowledge sources with additional or more precise information, for example Dang and Palmer (2002) also employed the output from a named entity identifier and relations between WordNet senses (KS 10), while a system entered by Yarowsky et al. (2001) used a richer set of features including subject, object, and prepositions of verbs, and modification relations for nouns and adjectives, which better modeled syntagmatic word associations (KS 6b). Mihalcea and Moldovan (2001) supplemented training instances from Semcor with automatically acquired examples and used a standard set of knowledge sources.

Unsupervised systems based their disambiguation decisions on different knowledge sources. For example, McCarthy et al. (2001) and Preiss (2001) used selectional preferences based on the WordNet hierarchy (KS 7) and the results of an anaphora resolution algorithm to replace anaphoric expressions with their antecedents. The system described in Magnini et al. (2001) based its disambiguation decisions solely on domain information and topical word associations (KS 9 and KS 10) using a version of WordNet augmented with domain labels. Fernández et al. (2002) collected co-occurrence vectors for each word from very large corpora. These co-occurrence vectors were used to build co-occurrence vectors for word senses using definitions in an MRD (KS 6b, 9, and 10).

Montoyo and Suárez (2001) combined two different systems. Disambiguation of nouns was carried out using an unsupervised method relying on information about the structure of the EuroWordNet noun hierarchy and the textual glosses (KS 6a and KS 10). Verbs and adjectives are disambiguated at a later stage using a narrow context of 3 words that records the lemma, part of speech, and collocations (KS 1–3). Pedersen's (2002) analysis of the systems entered in the English and Spanish lexical sample showed that Montoyo and Suárez's system behaved differently from the other seven systems participating in the Spanish task. This system was the only one to make use of the structure of the sense inventory and was able to disambiguate different corpus instances from the others although it was also unable to disambiguate many of the instances covered by the other systems.

The systems entered into Senseval-2 tended to favor the use of a relatively small set of features that encode a wide range of knowledge sources, which is representative of the current trend in WSD research. A small number of systems chose to encode these knowledge sources through features which were different from those used by the majority of entries; analysis of results showed that this had a positive influence on the word instances that systems were able to disambiguate. No supervised systems made use of selectional preferences, subcategorization information, or paradigmatic information. A few systems employed the output from other NLP components such as named entity identification and anaphora resolution.

8.4.2 Senseval-3 Systems

Senseval-3 was carried out in 2004. Overall, most of the systems relied on knowledge sources already used in Senseval-2. There was a more widespread use of richer features such as syntactic features (Lee et al. 2004) and domain information (Strapparava et al. 2004) both in supervised and unsupervised systems. Aside from that, two innovations are worth mentioning.

Mihalcea and Faruque (2004) presented a supervised system which, in addition to a semantic language model not very different from other supervised methods, used semantic generalizations for syntactic dependencies extracted from a parsed version of Semcor. The semantic generalization was done using the WordNet hierarchy. This method implicitly uses selectional preferences (KS 7), but instead of modeling them explicitly they are fed as positive and negative examples into a supervised machine learning algorithm.

McCarthy et al. (2004) proposed an unsupervised system which induced the predominant sense of each word. They observed that the most frequent sense heuristic (KS 5) was successful in the Senseval-2 all-words task, as it performed better than all except two systems, including many supervised systems. In the absence of large quantities of tagged examples the method induces the most predominant sense for any word (see Chap. 6).

8.5 Comparison of Experimental Results

There have been few experiments that have systematically explored the contribution of different knowledge sources to WSD. Systems such as Hirst's (1987) and McRoy's (1992), which combined several knowledge sources, did not report quantitative results either for the entire system or for individual knowledge sources. More recent experiments have studied

Table 8.1. Results of selected all-words systems in Senseval-2. Types S and U refer to supervised and unsupervised. The rank of the systems (according to recall) is shown together with the precision and coverage (as percentage).

System	Type	Knowledge sources used	Rank	Prec.	Cov.
Mihalcea & Moldovan	S	KS 1–5, 6b, 9–10	1	69.0	100.0
MFS baseline	S	Most frequent sense KS 5	3	57.0	100.0
Fernández et al.[a] (2002)	U	Cooc. vectors KS 6b, 9, 10	6	55.6	98.9
Magnini et al. (2001)	U	Domain information KS 9, 10	12	74.8	47.7
McCarthy et al. (2004)	U	Selectional preferences KS 7	17	59.8	23.3

[a]Fernández et al. (2002) proposed two systems, one fully unsupervised and the other relying on word sense frequencies from Semcor (KS 5). We consider here the totally unsupervised system.

the quantitative effects of combining various knowledge sources, usually together with other factors. We summarize the results of these studies below, mentioning also the effect of different algorithms and results on different parts of speech and other factors.

8.5.1 Senseval Results

A common strategy among Senseval participants was to use a combination of knowledge sources although some unsupervised systems used a single knowledge source. The top lines of Table 8.1 show the results in the Senseval-2 all-words task for three such unsupervised systems (presented in Sect. 8.4.1) allowing us to compare the relative performance of their knowledge sources. The winning system is also shown for comparison. It can be seen that domain information and selectional preferences provide reasonable precision but at the expense of coverage while co-occurrence vectors provide full coverage without sacrificing that much precision. The winning system uses a combination of features typical of supervised systems, and thus implicitly captures several knowledge sources.

Table 8.2 shows selected results for Senseval-3. Mihalcea and Faruque's (2004) system attains one of the highest results. Unfortunately they do not provide separate results for their system working on selectional preferences in isolation. McCarthy et al (2004) provide an unsupervised approximation of the most-frequent-sense (MFS) heuristic, with good results on precision, but not full coverage.

Table 8.2. Results of selected all-words systems in Senseval-3. Types S and U refer to supervised and unsupervised. The rank of the systems (according to recall) is shown together with precision and coverage (as percentage).

System	Type	Knowledge sources used	Rank	Prec.	Cov.
Decadt et al. (2004)	S	KS 1–5, 6b, 9–10	1	65.1	100.0
Mihalcea & Faruque	S	KS 1–5, 6b, 7, 9–0	2	65.1	98.6
MFS baseline	S	Most frequent sense KS 5	6	62.4	100.0
McCarthy et al. (2004)	U	Most frequent sense KS 5	22	49.0	88.4

The results on the lexical-sample tasks are more difficult to interpret. All systems (except those already mentioned that participated in both tasks) used a complex combination of algorithms, parameterization, and features, and it is thus very difficult to extract any conclusion regarding knowledge sources. We therefore do not include them here.

8.5.2 Yarowsky and Florian (2002)

Yarowsky and Florian (2002) experimented with the effect of varying a diverse range of knowledge sources and learning algorithms. The following features were used in their experiments:

- **Local context** (KS 1–4, 6b): This includes a diverse set of features (n-grams, small context window) using raw words, lemmas, and part-of-speech tags in a ±2 word window around, and including, the ambiguous word.
- **Syntactic features** (KS 6b): The particular features extracted depend on the part of speech of the ambiguous word. For example, for nouns, the headword of any verb-object, subject-verb, and noun-noun relations were extracted.
- **Bag-of-words** (KS 6b, 9, 10): Sets of words that occur in the context of the ambiguous word regardless of their position.

They tested various aggregative and discriminative supervised machine learning algorithms (see Chap. 7). Aggregative algorithms integrate evidence from all feature sets and then select the sense with the highest combined support whereas discriminative algorithms aim to identify the features that discriminate the candidate sense most efficiently. The aggregative algorithms used were Feature-Enhanced Naïve Bayes (FENBayes), a standard cosine vector model (Cosine), and the Bayes Ratio model (BayesR) (Gale et al. 1993). The discriminative algorithms employed were a transformation-based learning system (TBL) (Florian et al. 2002) and decision lists (DL) (Yarowsky 1996).

Yarowsky and Florian tested their system on the Senseval-2 evaluation data. Table 8.3 shows the results for each of the five algorithms across the entire corpus and each grammatical category. The effect of omitting the syntactic dependency features (KS 6b) is also recorded for each combination. The Feature-Enhanced Naïve Bayes model and Bayes Ratio classifiers are consistently the best performing. Verbs were consistently found to be the most difficult grammatical category to disambiguate. They are also the most affected by the removal of syntactic features. This is probably because verbs, and to a lesser extent adjectives, depend on precise identification of their arguments. The experiments also show that nouns benefit more from information about the wide context and basic collocations, although this is not shown in Table 8.3.

Table 8.4 demonstrates the differences between the performance of aggregative and discriminative models by varying the features presented to each algorithm. Discriminative models are more robust to the removal of features and this is because they attempt to identify the most informative feature. On the other hand aggregative models make their decisions by combining all features and are severely restricted when they only have access to a single feature type. All in all, the best results are obtained using all available knowledge sources.

8.5.3 Lee and Ng (2002)

Lee and Ng (2002) also evaluated a variety of knowledge sources using several different learning algorithms. The following features were used:

- **Part of speech of neighboring words** (KS 1, 4): Part-of-speech tags applied to lexical items in a ±3 word window around, and including, the ambiguous word.
- **Local context** (KS 2–4, 6b): A set of 11 variable length n-grams in a ±3 word window around the ambiguous word.
- **Syntactic relations** (KS 6b): The sentence containing the ambiguous word is parsed. The features extracted depend on the part of speech of the ambiguous word but include the parent headword from the parser, its syntactic category, and relative position to the ambiguous word in the sentence.
- **Single words in surrounding context** (KS 6b, 9, 10): Existence of a set of pre-defined keywords in the context of the ambiguous word.

Table 8.3. Selected results from Yarowsky and Florian (2002) on the Senseval-2 data set expressed as the percentage of word instances correctly disambiguated for each of the learning algorithms on the entire corpus and individual part-of-speech categories. The effect of omitting the syntactic dependency features (KS 6b) is measured for each combination, and shown in parentheses.

Algorithm	All	Noun	Verb	Adjective
Baseline	61.5	59.3	43.5	60.1
FENBayes	72.7 (−1.1)	72.8 (−0.6)	55.6 (−3.0)	71.2 (−1.2)
Cosine	69.7 (−0.8)	70.1 (−0.7)	52.0 (−3.65)	66.7 (+1.35)
BayesR	72.8 (−1.3)	73.2 (−0.5)	54.7 (−2.6)	71.9 (−1.9)
TBL	71.1 (−1.0)	70.4 (−1.6)	56.1 (−7.0)	70.8 (−2.3)
DL	70.1 (−2.3)	67.4 (−0.3)	55.4 (−3.4)	70.8 (−0.7)

Table 8.4. Selected results from Yarowsky and Florian (2002) on the Senseval-2 data set expressed as the difference in the percentage correctness of omitting and including only single features for the five algorithms.

Features used	Aggregative			Discriminative	
	FENB	Cosine	BayesR	TBL	DL
Omit bag-of-words (KS 6b, 9, 10)	−14.7	−8.1	−5.3	−0.5	−2.0
Omit local context (KS 1–4, 6b)	−3.5	−0.8	−2.2	−2.9	−4.5
Omit syntactic features (KS 6b)	−1.1	−0.8	−1.3	−1.0	−2.3
Bag-of-words only (KS 6b, 9, 10)	−6.4	−4.8	−4.8	−6.0	−3.2
Local context only (KS 1–4, 6b)	−18.4	−11.5	−6.1	−1.5	−3.3
Syntactic features only (KS 6b)	−28.1	−14.9	−5.4	−5.4	−4.8

With the exception of the first feature each of these features could be applied with or without feature selection. When feature selection is applied the value of a feature is used only if it is observed at least three times for at least one instance of the ambiguous word in the training data.

Lee and Ng (2002) used this feature set with four different learning algorithms (see Chap. 7 for details): Support Vector Machines (SVM) (Vapnik 1995), AdaBoost (AdB) (Freund and Schapire 1996), Naïve Bayes (NBayes) (Duda and Hart 1973) and Decision Trees (DT) (Quinlan 1993). Each of the learning algorithms was tested on the Senseval-1 and Senseval-2 data sets. The results obtained for the Senseval-2 data are shown in Table 8.5. Results from the Senseval-1 data had similar implications.

Table 8.5. Selected results from Lee and Ng (2002) on the Senseval-2 data set expressed as the percentage of word instances correctly disambiguated. The best binary and multi-class configuration of learning algorithm and knowledge source with or without feature selection is quoted. The best performing configuration for each learning algorithm is shown in bold font.

Algorithm	POS (KS 1, 4)	Surrounding words (KS 6, 10)	Local context (KS 2–4, 6b)	Syntactic relations (KS 6b)	Combined
SVM	54.7	57.7	60.5	54.5	**65.4**
AdB	55.9	55.4	59.3	53.5	**62.8**
NBayes	58.0	56.2	55.8	54.2	**62.7**
DT	55.3	50.9	**57.2**	54.2	56.8

Table 8.6. Selected results from Lee and Ng (2002) showing the results of the best configuration for each learning algorithm analysed by grammatical category.

POS	SVM	AdB	NBayes	DT
Noun	68.8	69.2	66.4	60.0
Verb	61.1	56.1	56.6	51.8
Adjective	68.0	64.3	68.4	63.8
All	65.4	62.8	62.7	57.2

A first observation is that there is not much difference in the performance of the individual knowledge sources. Second, all algorithms benefit from the combination of all knowledge sources, except for Decision Trees, which gets the lowest scores among the four learning algorithms overall.

For completeness, we show in Table 8.6 the results for each learning algorithm calculated across each of the three main grammatical categories. The results are consistent on each of the main grammatical categories across the four learning algorithms in the experiment. Each algorithm finds verbs the most difficult grammatical category to disambiguate. Results for nouns and adjectives are higher than the average.

8.5.4 Martínez et al. (2002)

Martínez et al. (2002) explore the contribution of a broad set of syntactically motivated features that range from the presence of complements and adjuncts, and the detection of subcategorization frames, to grammatical relations instantiated with specific words. Minipar (Lin 1993) was used for parsing with nearly all dependencies returned being used. Two forms of syntactic relation were used:

- **Instantiated grammatical relations (IGR)** (KS 6b): IGRs are coded as (word-sense, relation, value) triples, where the value can be either the word form or the lemma.
- **Grammatical relations (GR)** (KS 4): GRs refer to the grammatical relations themselves. In this case, we collect bigrams *(word-sense, relation)* and also n-grams (word-sense, relation-1, relation-2, relation-3, ...). The relations can refer to any argument, adjunct, or modifier. N-grams are similar to verbal subcategorization frames and were used only for verbs.

The performance of the syntactic features is measured in isolation and in combination with a basic set of local and topical features. Two machine learning algorithms were used: decision lists (DL) and AdaBoost (AdB). DL is a discriminative learning algorithm, as noted earlier, while AdB is an aggregative approach that uses combinations of features and negative evidence, that is, the absence of features.

Table 8.7 shows the percentage correct precision and coverage for each of the grammatical feature sets as used by the DL algorithm. IGRs provide high precision, but low coverage. Uninstantiated GRs provide lower precision but higher coverage. The only exceptions are verbs, which get very similar precision for both kinds of syntactic relations. A combination of both attains the best recall, and is the feature set used in subsequent experiments.

All in all, AdB is able to outperform DL in all cases, except with local features. Syntactic features get worse results than local features, except for verbs. Regarding the contribution of syntactic features to the basic set, DL scarcely profits from the additional syntactic features (only significant for verbs). AdB attains significant improvement, showing that basic and syntactic features are complementary.

Table 8.7. Evaluation of the syntactic features in Martínez et al. (2002) showing the percentage precision (P) and coverage (C) for various combinations of algorithms and knowledge sources. A "+" in an "All" row indicates the difference in the precision over the basic ("local + topical") feature set is significant according to McNemar's test.

Knowledge sources	Alg.	All POS (P/C)	Nouns only (P/C)	Verbs only (P/C)	Adjs. Only (P/C)
Local context (KS 1–4, 6b)	DL	80.3/44.3	90.3/54.2	68.3/32.4	86.2/54.0
GR (KS 4)	DL	67.1/52.1	65.4/57.6	67.3/41.2	70.1/65.4
IGR (KS 6b)	DL	72.9/31.9	74.6/36.0	68.6/32.2	81.6/21.8
All syntax (GR+IGR)	DL	67.7/59.5	67.6/62.5	66.3/52.7	70.7/68.9
Local + global	DL	59.3/97.5	63.2/100	52.6/94.0	65.3/100
All (local+topical+syntax)	DL	59.4/97.7	63.3/100	52.7/94.6+	65.4/100
All syntax (GR+IGR)	AdB	55.2/100	60.0/100	47.5/100	62.6//100
Local + global	AdB	60.7/100	67.9/100	51.6/100	66.2/100
All (local+topical+syntax)	AdB	**62.5/100+**	**69.3/100+**	**53.9/100+**	**67.7/100+**

These results are consistent with those of previous sections: syntactic features allow for a small improvement in the precision, especially for verbs. DL is a discriminative approach and so does not combine information well. Boosting appears to benefit from the addition of local and global syntactic features. Regarding the types of syntactic features, IGRs are best, as expected, but GRs provide very good clues for verbs, comparable to local features and IGRs.

8.5.5 Agirre and Martínez (2001a)

Agirre and Martínez (2001a) present the results of a large number of WSD algorithms making use of a diverse set of knowledge sources. The disambiguation information was derived from a number of sources: corpora, an LKB, and an MRD. WordNet 1.6 was used as the sense inventory and played the role of both the LKB providing taxonomical structure and the MRD. The algorithms used include:

- **First sense** (KS 5): The first sense of the dictionaries is usually the most salient. The word senses in WordNet are ordered according to frequency in Semcor, so first sense in WordNet also means the most frequent sense in Semcor.

- **Dictionary definition overlap** (KS 6b, 10): A simple computation of the overlap between the definitions for the word senses of the target word and the words in the surrounding context is used (Lesk 1986) (see Chap. 5).
- **Conceptual density** (ConDen) (KS 6a): A measure of concept-relatedness based on taxonomies (see Chap. 5).
- **Decision lists on a number of features:** A wide range of features were employed following Martínez et al. (2002) (see Sect. 8.5.4):
  - **Local context (KS 1–4, 6b):** N-grams and small windows of POS tags and lemmas.
  - **Argument-head relations (KS 6b).**
  - **Subcategorization (KS 4).**
  - **Global context (KS 6, 9–10):** Bag-of-words feature for the words in the sentence.
- **Semantic classes** (KS 10): A system that disambiguates word senses at a coarse-grained level combining broad semantic classes with corpora using mutual information (Agirre and Rigau 1996).
- **Selectional preferences** (KS 7): A formalization of selectional preferences that learns preferences for classes of verbs on subject and object relations extracted from Semcor, based on the tagged corpus (Agirre and Martínez 2001b). Note that the coverage of this algorithm is rather low, due to the sparseness of training data.

These algorithms were tested on one or both of two experimental settings. The test corpora include either all occurrences of 8 nouns (*account, age, church, duty, head, interest, member,* and *people*) in Semcor or all polysemous nouns occurring in a set of 4 random files from Semcor (br-a01, br-b20, br-j09, and br-r05). Table 8.8 shows the results of each knowledge source on at least one of the two evaluation corpora.[3] Results of each algorithm were compared against a baseline that assigned a random sense.

From the comparison of the results, it is clear that algorithms based on hand-tagged corpora provide results above the most frequent baseline. This is true for all features (local context, subcategorization, argument-head relations, and global), including the combination of hand-tagged corpora with taxonomical knowledge (selectional preferences), which gets precision close to the most frequent sense on the 4-files task. Other resources

---

[3] Two algorithms (Conceptual Density and Semantic Classes) were tested on the 4-file test set using WordNet 1.4. The results on WordNet 1.6 are expected to be very similar.

Table 8.8. Summary of knowledge sources and results of the algorithms used by Agirre and Martínez (2001a). Scores are given for the two test sets as percentage precision (P) and coverage (C).

Knowledge source	Lexical resources	Algorithm	Results (P/C) 8-nouns	4-files
–	–	Random	19/100	28/100
Main sense (KS 5)	MRD	–	69/100	66/100
Definition (KS 6b, 10)	"	Overlap	42/100	–
Hierarchy (KS 6a)	Ontology	ConDen	–	43/80
Most frequent sense (KS 5)	Corpora	–	69/100	66/100
Subcategorization (KS 4)	"	DL	78/96	–
Local context (KS 1–4, 6b)	"	DL	70/92	–
Arg-head relations (KS 6b)	"	DL	78/69	–
Global context (KS 6, 10)	"	DL	81/87	–
Semantic classes (KS 6, 10)	MRD+Corpora	MI	–	41/100
Selectional pref. (KS 7)	Ontology+Corpora	Probability	63/33	65/31

provide more modest results: conceptual density on ontologies, definition overlap on definitions, or the combination of MRD and corpora.

8.5.6 Stevenson and Wilks (2001)

Another set of experiments comparing different knowledge sources was carried out by Stevenson and Wilks (2001). They assigned senses from the LDOCE dictionary and made use of the rich sources of linguistic knowledge available in that resource. Stevenson and Wilks made use of several knowledge sources:

- **Part of speech** (KS 1): Applied to the target word by the Brill tagger (Brill 1995).
- **Surface form** (KS 2): Surface form of ambiguous word in context.
- **Collocations** (KS 3, 6b): Single words in a ±2 word window, first noun, verb, and adjective to the right and left.
- **Dictionary definitions** (KS 6a, 10): Results of the simulated annealing algorithm (Cowie et al. 1992) used to maximize the overlap of dictionary definitions for LDOCE senses (see Chap. 5 (Sect. 5.2.1)).
- **Selectional preferences** (KS 7): LDOCE lists the semantic class of nouns from a set of 36 possible types as well as the classes expected by adjectives and the arguments of verbs. LDOCE does not contain any

preference information for adverbs. The preferences for all words in a sentence are resolved using a constraint satisfaction algorithm (Stevenson 2003) (see Chap. 5 (Sect. 5.4)).

- **Domain codes** (KS 9): Results of the simulated annealing algorithm used to maximize the number of LDOCE subject codes applied to all words in a paragraph (see Chap. 10 (Sect. 10.2.1)).

These knowledge sources were applied in different ways. First, any senses that did not agree with the one assigned by the part-of-speech tagger were immediately eliminated from consideration. The dictionary definitions, selectional preferences, and subject codes are each applied in their own algorithm, the output of which is used as an element in a feature vector. These vectors are supplemented with the collocations and part-of-speech information and used in a supervised learning approach. The TiMBL (Daelemans et al. 1999) k-nearest neighbor learning algorithm, an aggregative approach, was used to combine the knowledge sources in this experiment.

Semcor was also used as an evaluation corpus. However, content words in Semcor are marked with senses from WordNet and the system assigned meanings from LDOCE. Consequently the WordNet senses were mapped onto their equivalents in LDOCE by means of a mapping derived from LDOCE (created by Bruce and Guthrie (1992)) and the Penman Upper Model from ISI (Bateman et al. 1990)).

Table 8.9 shows the results of each knowledge source and their combination when applied to the adapted Semcor corpus. Results are given for the four main grammatical categories and combined. The knowledge source based on subject codes is the most successful, consistently achieving over 70% correct disambiguation across grammatical categories. The least successful knowledge source is selectional preferences (KS 7), whose limitations have already been noted by Agirre and Martínez (2001a) (see above), McRoy (1992), and Resnik (1997). In addition these experiments confirm the observation of Martínez and Agirre (2002) that semantic and topical word associations (KS 6, 10) are valuable knowledge sources.

The combination of knowledge sources generally performs better than any applied individually for all part-of-speech classes. The one exception is the adverbs in which the combination actually performs worse than the subject-codes disambiguator. This seems to be due to the poor performance of the other knowledge sources on this part-of-speech category, the dictionary definitions achieve just over 50% correct disambiguation and

Table 8.9. Disambiguation precision (as percentage correct) for the different knowledge sources used by Stevenson and Wilks (2001).

Knowledge sources	All POS	Nouns	Verbs	Adjs.	Adverbs
All	90.37	91.24	88.38	91.09	70.61
Dictionary definitions (KS 6b, 10)	65.24	66.50	67.51	49.02	50.61
Selectional preferences (KS 7)	44.85	40.73	75.80	27.56	–
Domain information (KS 9)	79.41	79.18	72.75	73.73	85.50

LDOCE does not contain any selectional preference information for adverbs.

8.6 Discussion

The results mentioned in the previous section, even coming from diverse experimental settings, allow us to analyze and compare different parameters: knowledge sources involved, lexical resources used, features and algorithms used, and part-of-speech of target words.

If the results are analyzed from the perspective of knowledge sources, we can observe the following (all results cited have been given in the previous section):

- **Part of speech (KS 1):** POS has been shown to be a useful knowledge source (Stevenson and Wilks 2001); it can be used to quickly reduce the senses being considered and, when used as the sole knowledge source, provides enough information to accurately perform homograph-level disambiguation (Stevenson 2003).
- **Morphology (KS 2):** No separate analysis is provided, but the word form of the target word is usually included in local features for supervised systems, and is regarded as a useful feature.
- **Collocations (KS 3):** Syntactic collocations are one of the strongest indicators if learned from hand-tagged corpora. Usually they are not encoded as a separate feature, but included in local context features such as word n-grams and small context windows.
- **Subcategorization (KS 4):** Subcategorization can be approximated from hand-tagged corpora using POS n-grams, but the work of Martínez et al. (2002) shows that better results can be achieved for verbs when subcategorization is modeled by explicit syntactic relations extracted from the tagged corpora using a parser.

- **Frequency of word senses (KS 5):** Frequency provides a baseline that is difficult to match. Systems not using tagged corpora often have difficulties reaching this level.
- **Semantic word associations (KS 6):** Regarding semantic word associations, taxonomical information from LKBs is very weak as shown by Martínez et. al. (2002) and Montoyo and Suarez (2001), while argument-head relations extracted from hand-tagged data are strong features.
- **Selectional preferences (KS 7):** Selectional preferences get acceptable accuracy when obtained from the combination of an LKB and an untagged corpus, but the applicability is quite low (Martínez et al. 2002, McCarthy et al. 2001). It seems that selectional preferences as coded in an MRD also have limited effect (Stevenson and Wilks 2001).
- **Semantic roles (KS 8):** To our knowledge, semantic roles have not been applied in any system that has been quantifiably evaluated and so it is difficult to gauge their contribution.
- **Domain knowledge (KS 9):** Magnini et al. (2001) and Stevenson (2003) show that the domain codes in LKBs and MRDs are useful for disambiguation even without tagged corpora.
- **Topical word associations (KS 10):** Such associations are very reliable when acquired from tagged data. Efforts to capture such information using definitions on MRDs have been less successful (Fernández et al. 2001, Stevenson and Wilks 2001).
- **Pragmatics (KS 11):** High-level reasoning is not currently used in WSD systems. Some researchers (e.g., Yarowsky (1996)) believe that simpler knowledge sources are sufficient to disambiguate the vast majority of word instances.

Regarding lexical resources, hand-tagged corpora seem to be the most effective for the automatic acquisition of all the knowledge sources that we considered, although they are very expensive to create. The results from the Senseval exercises indicate that this is true on both the lexical sample and the all-words tasks (see Chap. 4). Supervised systems trained on Semcor (around 500,000 words) outperformed their unsupervised counterparts on the all-words task. However, complex linguistic knowledge can be also extracted from LKBs and MRDs. When combined with untagged corpora they can be very effective for acquiring selectional preferences and domain knowledge, which also provide good results in WSD.

Supervised systems capture knowledge sources with three main kinds of features: local context (n-grams and small windows), syntactic (specific syntactic relations), and large context (bag-of-words). These features mix different knowledge sources (large-context features can capture argument-head semantic associations as well as topical word associations), and they contain overlapping information (the same argument-head relation can be captured by small contexts, large contexts, and syntactic parsing). Sometimes, adding new features, such as syntactic information, does not improve the results dramatically, and a possible reason is overlap: the linguistic information was already present in another form (e.g., subcategorization captured by POS n-grams). Finally, certain knowledge sources (e.g., selectional preferences and domain information) have seldom been used in the context of supervised WSD systems.

The usefulness of various knowledge sources is dependent, to some extent, on the grammatical category of the target word. Bag-of-words features seem to be the most effective for nouns, implying that semantic and topical word associations (KS 6a and KS 10) are the strongest features. Another indication is the high precision obtained by Stevenson and Wilks using subject codes from LDOCE. Verbs benefit most from local knowledge sources like collocations (KS 3), subcategorization (KS 4), argument-head associations (KS 6b), and selectional preferences (KS 7). Verbs are the most difficult to disambiguate, and also tend to be the most polysemous grammatical category. Adjectives benefit from similar knowledge sources to verbs although they do not seem to profit from selectional preferences.

The interaction between knowledge sources and algorithms is the most complex. It appears that aggregative learning models, such as AdaBoost, Naïve Bayes, Support Vector Machines, and Memory-Based Learning, perform better than discriminative models when several knowledge sources are being combined. This is because each knowledge source provides some useful information for the disambiguation process which aggregative models can take advantage of by combining information from several knowledge sources encoded as a range of learning features. Discriminative models attempt to identify the optimal feature for disambiguation which can, at best, represent a restricted set of knowledge sources. However, Yarowsky and Florian (2002) show that Transformation Based Learning, a discriminative model, provides the best results for verbs, while aggregative models perform best for nouns and adjectives. This provides some evidence that disambiguation of verbs may depend on a smaller number of knowledge sources than nouns and adjectives. Aggregative algorithms also seem to be most suitable for bag-of-word features, while discriminative algorithms behave better with local collocations. Lee and Ng (2002) show that Support Vector Machines are best for most of the features they use, except for POS surrounding the target word, for which Naïve Bayes proves best. Unfortunately Lee and Ng do not provide a discriminative algorithm for comparison.

Nevertheless it could well be that different words of the same part of speech exhibit different behavior. Moreover, all knowledge sources seem to be valuable, as the combinations always fare better than using single features in isolation. Feature selection strategies like those applied by Mihalcea and Moldovan (2001) seem to provide ground for fitting the features to each single word (see Chap. 7).

8.7 Conclusions

This chapter has listed a set of knowledge sources of potential interest for WSD. We have shown that these knowledge sources can be acquired from a number of different resources: untagged corpora, sense-tagged corpora, lexical knowledge bases, and machine readable dictionaries. The results show that information from tagged corpora is the most reliable for WSD. Domain information and selectional preferences from untagged corpora also provide reliable clues.

Viewing WSD techniques in terms of the knowledge sources they use provides a solid linguistic motivation for the choice of approach. Focusing on this level, rather than the features used by implementations, gives a more abstract view of the different approaches to the problem. Unfortunately, knowledge sources are rarely represented separately, but are usually mixed in feature groups (e.g., local context features). Current approaches to WSD also tend to favor features that represent several knowledge sources. It is difficult to measure the effectiveness of individual knowledge sources (as well as combinations) because:

• Knowledge sources are hidden behind superficial features,
• Systems seldom present analyses of the contribution of individual knowledge sources, and
• Algorithms and knowledge sources interact in complex ways.

From the results of the systems that participated in the Senseval exercises and of the reported measurements on performance with respect to knowledge sources, we draw the following conclusions:

- All knowledge sources seem to provide useful disambiguation clues.
- Each part of speech profits from different knowledge sources, for example knowledge sources like KS 9 and KS 10 which encode the topic of a text are most useful for disambiguating nouns while those that represent local context benefit verbs and adjectives. However, the combination of all consistently gets the best results across POS categories.
- Some learning algorithms are better suited to certain knowledge sources; those which use an aggregative approach seem suited to combining the information provided by several knowledge sources. There is also evidence that different grammatical categories may benefit from different learning algorithms.

A common theme that runs through research on knowledge sources for WSD is that combinations of knowledge sources provide better results than when they are used alone. Future work in this area should attempt to identify the best combination of knowledge sources for the WSD problem and methods for combining them effectively. One explanation for why combinations of knowledge sources are so successful is that polysemy is a complex phenomenon and that each knowledge source captures some aspect of it but none is enough to describe the semantics of a word in enough detail for disambiguation. It is likely that greater understanding of the relevant knowledge sources and how they interact will allow the development of more detailed theories of polysemy. In turn this may provide a framework for approaching some more advanced problems related to semantics that are not generally tackled in the community at present, for example the identification of when a word is being used in a novel way or sense (not included in the dictionary being used for disambiguation) and the analysis of metaphor.

Acknowledgments

The authors gratefully acknowledge the comments by Philip Edmonds and David Yarowsky. Eneko Agirre was supported by the European Union project MEANING (IST-2001-34460) and the MCYT project HERMES (TIC-2000-0335-C03-03). Mark Stevenson was supported by the European Union Language Engineering project ECRAN (LE-2110) and the EPSRC grants MALT (GR/M73521) and RESULT (GR/T06391).

References

Agirre, Eneko & David Martínez. 2001a. Knowledge sources for word sense disambiguation. *Proceedings of the Fourth International Conference on Text Speech and Dialogue (TSD)*, Plzen, Czech Republic.

Agirre, Eneko & David Martínez. 2001b. Learning class-to-class selectional preferences. *Proceedings of the ACL/EACL Workshop on Computational Natural Language Learning (CoNLL)*, Toulouse, France.

Agirre, Eneko & German Rigau. 1996. Word sense disambiguation using conceptual density. *Proceedings of the 16th International Conference on Computational Linguistics (COLING)*, Copenhagen, Denmark.

ALPAC. 1966. *Languages and Machines: Computers in Translation and Linguistics*. National Research Council Publication 1416, Washington, USA.

Bar-Hillel, Yehoshua. 1964. *Language and Information* Addison-Wesley, New York, USA.

Bateman, John A., Robert Kasper, Johanna Moore & Richard A. Whitney. 1990. *A General Organization of Knowledge for Natural Language Processing: The PENMAN Upper Model*. Technical report, USC/Information Sciences Institute, Marina del Rey, USA.

Boguraev, Branimir. 1979. *Automatic Resolution of Linguistic Ambiguities*. Ph.D. Thesis, Computer Laboratory, University of Cambridge, Cambridge, UK.

Brill, Eric. 1995. Transformation-based error-driven learning and natural language processing: A case study in part of speech tagging. *Computational Linguistics*, 21(4):543–566.

Brown, Peter F., Stephen A. Della Pietra, Vincent J. Della Pietra & Robert L. Mercer. 1991. Word sense disambiguation using statistical methods. *Proceedings of the 29th Annual Meeting of the Association for Computational Linguistics (ACL)*, Berkeley, USA, 264–270.

Bruce, Rebecca & Louise Guthrie. 1992. Genus disambiguation: A study in weighted preference. *Proceedings of the 14th International Conference on Computational Linguistics (COLING)*, Nantes, France, 1187–1191.

Carroll, John & Ted Briscoe. 2001. High precision extraction of grammatical relations. *Proceedings of the 7th ACL/SIGPARSE International Workshop on Parsing Technologies*, Beijing, China, 78–89.

Charniak, Eugene. 1983. *Marker Passing: A Theory of Contextual Influence in Language Comprehension*. Cognitive Science 7.

Chapman, Robert L. 1977. *Roget's International Thesaurus, Fourth Edition*. Harper and Row, New York, USA.

Cowie, Jim, Louise Guthrie & Joe Guthrie. 1992. Lexical disambiguation using simulated annealing. *Proceedings of the 14th International Conference on Computational Linguistics (COLING)*, Nantes, France, 359–365.

Cruse, David. 1998. *Lexical Semantics*. Cambridge University Press, Cambridge, UK.

Daelemans, Walter, Jakub Zavrel, Ko van der Sloot & Antal van den Bosch. 1999. *TiMBL: Tilburg Memory Based Learner, Version 2.0, Reference Guide*. ILK Technical Report 99-01, Tilburg University, The Netherlands.

Decadt, Bart, Véronique Hoste, Walter Daelemans, & Antal van den Bosch. 2004. GAMBL, Genetic Algorithm Optimization of Memory-Based WSD. *Proceedings of the ACL/EACL Senseval-3 Workshop*, Barcelona, Spain, 108–112.

Dang, Hoa Trang & Martha Palmer. 2002. Combining contextual features for word sense disambiguation. *Proceedings of the ACL Workshop on Word Sense Disambiguation: Recent Successes and Future Directions*, Philadelphia, USA.

Duda, Richard & Peter E. Hart. 1973. *Pattern Classification and Scene Analysis*. New York: Wiley.

Elworthy, David. 1994. Does Baum-Welch re-estimation help taggers? *Proceedings of the 4th Conference on Applied Natural Language Processing*, Stuttgart, Germany, 53–58.

Fellbaum, Christiane. 1998. *WordNet: An Electronic Lexical Database*. Massachusetts and London: The MIT Press.

Fernández, David, Julio Gonzalo & Felisa Verdejo. 2001. The UNED systems at Senseval-2. *Proceedings of Senseval-2: Second International Workshop on Evaluating Word Sense Disambiguation Systems*, Toulouse, France, 75–78.

Fillmore, Charles. 1971. Types of lexical information. *Semantics: An interdisciplinary reader in philosophy, linguistics, and psychology*. Cambridge: Cambridge University Press, 370–392.

Florian, Radu, Silviu Cucerzan, Charles Schafer & David Yarowsky. 2002. Classifier combination for word sense disambiguation. *Journal of Natural Language Engineering*, 8(4): 327–341.

Freund, Yoav & Robert E. Schapire. 1996. Experiments with a new boosting algorithm. *Proceedings of the 13th International Conference on Machine Learning*, Bari, Italy, 148–156.

Gale, William, Kenneth W. Church & David Yarowsky. 1993. A method for disambiguating word senses in a large corpus. *Computers and the Humanities,* 26(5): 415–439.

Hirst, Graeme. 1987. *Semantic Interpretation and the Resolution of Ambiguity*. Cambridge, UK: Cambridge University Press.

Kilgarriff, Adam. 1997. Putting frequencies in the dictionary. *International Journal of Lexicography*, 10(2): 135–155

Kriedler, Charles. 1998. *Introducing English Semantics*. London and New York: Routledge.

Lee, Yoong K. & Hwee Tou Ng. 2002. An empirical evaluation of knowledge sources and learning algorithms for word sense disambiguation. *Proceedings of the Conference on Empirical Methods in Natural Language Processing (EMNLP)*, Philadelphia, USA, 41–48.

Lee, Yoong K., Hwee Tou Ng & Tee Kiah Chia. 2004. Supervised word sense disambiguation with support vector machines and multiple knowledge sources. *Proceedings of the ACL/EACL Senseval-3 Workshop*, Barcelona, Spain, 137–140.

Lesk, Michael. 1986. Automatic sense disambiguation using machine readable dictionaries: How to tell a pine cone from an ice cream cone. *Proceedings of SIGDOC-86: 5th International Conference on Systems Documentation*, Toronto, Canada, 24–26.

Lin, Dekang. 1993. Principle based parsing without overgeneration. *Proceedings of the 31st Annual Meeting of the Association for Computational Linguistics (ACL)*, Columbus, USA, 112–120.

Lin, Dekang. 1997. Using syntactic dependency as local context to resolve word sense ambiguity. *Proceedings of the 35th Annual Meeting of the Association for Computational Linguistics (ACL)*, Madrid, 64–71.

Magnini, Bernardo, Carlo Strapparava, Giovani Pezzulo & Alfio Gliozzo. 2001. Using domain information for word sense disambiguation. *Proceedings of Senseval-2: Second International Workshop on Evaluating Word Sense Disambiguation Systems*, France, 111–114.

Martínez, David, Eneko Agirre & Lluis Márquez. 2002. Syntactic features for high precision word sense disambiguation. *Proceedings of the 19th International Conference on Computational Linguistics (COLING)*, Taipei, Taiwan.

McCarthy, Diana, John Carroll & Judita Preiss. 2001. Disambiguating noun and verb senses using automatically acquired selectional preferences. *Proceedings of the ACL/EACL Senseval-2 Workshop*, Toulouse, France.

McCarthy, Diana, Rob Koeling, Julie Weeds & John Carroll. 2004. Using automatically acquired predominant senses for word sense disambiguation. *Proceedings of Senseval-3: Third International Workshop on the Evaluation of Systems for the Semantic Analysis of Text*, Barcelona, Spain, 151–158.

McRoy, Susan W. 1992. Using multiple knowledge sources for word sense disambiguation. *Computational Linguistics*, 18(1): 1–30.

Mihalcea, Rada & Dan Moldovan. 2001. Pattern learning and active feature selection for word sense disambiguation. *Proceedings of Senseval-2: Second Inter-

national Workshop on Evaluating Word Sense Disambiguation Systems, Toulouse, France.

Mihalcea, Rada & Ehsanul Faruque. 2004. SenseLearner: Minimally supervised word sense disambiguation for all words in open text. *Proceedings of Senseval-3: Third International Workshop on the Evaluation of Systems for the Semantic Analysis of Text*, Barcelona, Spain, 155–158.

Miller, George. A., Claudia Leacock, Randee Tengi & Ross. T. Bunker. 1993. A semantic concordance. *Proceedings of the ARPA Workshop on Human Language Technology*, 303–308.

Montoyo, Andres & Armando Suárez. 2001. The University of Alicante word sense disambiguation system. *Proceedings of Senseval-2: Second International Workshop on Evaluating Word Sense Disambiguation Systems*, Toulouse, France.

Ng, Hwee Tou & Hiang B. Lee. 1996. Integrating multiple knowledge sources for word sense disambiguation: An exemplar-based approach. *Proceedings of the 34th Meeting of the Association for Computational Linguistics (ACL)*, Santa Cruz, CA, USA, 40–47.

Patwardhan, Siddharth, Satanjeev Banerjee & Ted Pedersen. 2003. Using measures of semantic relatedness for word sense disambiguation. *Proceedings of the Fourth International Conference on Intelligent Text Processing and Computational Linguistics (CICLing)*, Mexico City, Mexico.

Pedersen, Ted. 2002. Assessing system agreement and instance difficulty in the lexical sample tasks of Senseval-2. *Proceedings of the ACL Workshop on Word Sense Disambiguation: Recent Successes and Future Directions*, Philadelphia, PA, USA.

Preiss, Judita. 2001. Anaphora resolution with word sense disambiguation. *Proceedings of Senseval-2: Second International Workshop on Evaluating Word Sense Disambiguation Systems*, Toulouse, France, 143–146.

Procter, Paul, ed. 1978. *Longman Dictionary of Contemporary English*. Harlow, UK: Longman Group.

Quinlan, J. Ross. 1993. *C4.5: Programs for Machine Learning*. San Francisco: Morgan Kaufmann.

Resnik, Philip. 1997. Selectional preferences and word sense disambiguation. *Proceedings of the ACL/SIGLEX Workshop on Tagging Text with Lexical Semantics: What, Why and How?*, Washington, DC, USA, 52–57.

Resnik, Philip & David Yarowsky. 1997. A perspective on word sense disambiguation algorithms and their evaluation. *Proceedings of the ACL/SIGLEX Workshop Tagging Texts with Lexical Semantics: What, Why and How?*, Washingtonn, DC, USA, 79–86.

Sag, Ivan A., Timothy Baldwin, Francis Bond, Ann Copestake & Dan Flickinger. 2002. Multiword expressions: A pain in the neck for NLP. *Proceedings of the 3rd International Conference on Intelligent Text Processing and Computational Linguistics (CICLing)*, Mexico City, Mexico, 1–15.

Small, Steven L. 1980. *Word Expert Parsing: A Theory of Distributed Word-based Natural Language Understanding.* Ph.D. Thesis, Department of Computer Science, University of Maryland, USA.

Strapparava, Carlo, Alfio Gliozzo, & Claudio Giuliano. 2004. Pattern abstraction and term similarity for word sense disambiguation: IRST at Senseval-3. *Proceedings of Senseval-3: Third International Workshop on the Evaluation of Systems for the Semantic Analysis of Text*, Barcelona, Spain, 229–233.

Stevenson, Mark. 2003. *Word Sense Disambiguation: The Case for Combination of Knowledge Sources.* Stanford, USA: CSLI Publications.

Stevenson, Mark & Yorick Wilks. 2001. The interaction of knowledge sources in word sense disambiguation. *Computational Linguistics*, 27(3): 321–349.

Vapnik, Vladimir. 1995. *The Nature of Statistical Learning Theory.* New York, USA: Springer-Verlag.

Wilks, Yorick. 1975. A preferential pattern-seeking semantics for natural language inference. *Artificial Intelligence*, 6: 53–74.

Wilks, Yorick. 1978. Making preferences more active. *Artificial Intelligence* 11(3): 197–223.

Wilks, Yorick & Mark Stevenson. 1998. The grammar of sense: Using part of speech tags as a first step in semantic disambiguation. *Journal of Natural Language Engineering*, 4(2): 135–144.

Yarowsky, David. 1992. Word-sense disambiguation using statistical models of Roget's categories trained on large corpora. *Proceedings of the 14th International Conference on Computational Linguistics (COLING)*, Nantes, France, 454–460.

Yarowsky, David. 1996. *Three Algorithms for Lexical Ambiguity Resolution*, Ph.D. Thesis, School of Computer and Information Science, University of Pennsylvania, USA.

Yarowsky, David, Silviu Cucerzan, Radu Florian, Charles Schafer & Richard Wicentowski. 2001. The Johns Hopkins Senseval-2 system description. *Proceedings of Senseval-2: Second International Workshop on Evaluating Word Sense Disambiguation Systems*, Toulouse, France, 163–166.

Yarowsky, David & Radu Florian. 2002. Evaluating sense disambiguation across diverse parameter spaces. *Journal of Natural Language Engineering*, 8(2): 293–310.

9 Automatic Acquisition of Lexical Information and Examples

Julio Gonzalo and Felisa Verdejo

Universidad Nacional de Educación a Distancia (UNED)

A possible way of solving the knowledge acquisition bottleneck in word sense disambiguation is mining very large corpora (most prominently the World Wide Web) to automatically acquire lexical information and examples to feed supervised learning methods. Although this area of research remains largely unexplored, it has already revealed a strong potential to improve WSD performance. This chapter reviews the main approaches, initial accomplishments, and open challenges in this topic.

9.1 Introduction

The knowledge acquisition bottleneck is perhaps the major impediment to solving the word sense disambiguation (WSD) problem. Unsupervised methods rely on knowledge about word senses, which is barely formulated in dictionaries and lexical databases. Supervised methods depend crucially on the existence of manually annotated examples for every word sense, a requisite that can so far be met only for a handful of words for testing purposes, as it is done in the Senseval exercises (see Chap. 4).

Therefore, one of the most promising trends in WSD research is using the largest corpus ever accessible, the World Wide Web, to acquire lexical information automatically (Kilgarriff and Grefenstette 2003). WSD has been traditionally understood as an intermediate language engineering technology which could improve applications such as information retrieval (IR). In this case, however, the reverse is also true: Web search engines implement simple and robust IR techniques that can be successfully used when mining the Web for information to be employed in WSD.

E. Agirre and P. Edmonds (eds.), Word Sense Disambiguation: Algorithms and Applications, 253–274.
© 2007 *Springer.*

In this chapter we review the main approaches to acquire lexical information using the Web. We have distinguished two types of research: acquiring topical knowledge about word senses (which is discussed in Sect. 9.2) and acquiring examples for supervised learning (which is discussed in Sect. 9.3). Of course, these two kinds of strategies are not isolated from each other. For instance, the method of Agirre and Martínez (2000) to extract topic signatures associated with word senses (which is described in Sect. 9.2) starts by retrieving examples from the Web for every word sense. In the opposite order, the method of Santamaría et al. (2003) assigns web directories to word senses (also described in Sect. 9.2) and then retrieves examples for supervised learning (described in Sect. 9.3). The above are monolingual techniques; Section 9.3.4 is devoted specifically to cross-lingual techniques.

The chapter is organized as follows. Section 9.2 discusses two kinds of topical knowledge which can be extracted from the Web and have been used in (unsupervised) WSD: topic signatures (lists of words topically related to the word sense) and word sense/web directory associations. Then, Section 9.3 compares existing approaches (both monolingual and cross-lingual) to the acquisition of training examples, which are probably the most valuable resource for WSD as they enable the use of supervised learning algorithms. Because of their relevance, this chapter emphasizes such methods. Finally, Section 9.4 summarizes the accomplishments and main challenges in mining the Web for WSD.

9.2 Mining Topical Knowledge About Word Senses

WordNet, which is the most frequently used sense inventory in WSD, does not incorporate topical or domain information, which is very valuable for sense disambiguation and for many other purposes.[1] We will mention here two strategies to enrich WordNet with domain information from the Web: extraction of topical signatures and association of WordNet senses with Web directories.

---

[1] See Chapter 10 (Sect 10.1) for a brief discussion of the terminology related to topics and domains.

9.2.1 Topic Signatures

Agirre et al. (2000) used the Web to enrich WordNet senses with topic signatures. A *topic signature* is defined as a list of words which are topically related to the word sense, together with a measure of the strength of the association. An example is *waiter* as a person who waits versus a person who serves a table. In the first sense, the topic signature could be made of words such as *hospital, station, airport,* and *cigarette.* In the second sense, the list would include *restaurant, menu, waitress,* and *dinner.*

Such topic signatures are built in two main steps: 1) using the Web search engine (Altavista, in this case) to retrieve sets of documents associated with each word sense, and 2) using the documents to extract and weight the words that form the topic signatures for every sense. In step one, a list of cue words for each sense is extracted from WordNet (including synonyms, words in the gloss and words in related synsets). Then, for each sense, a Boolean query is formed to retrieve documents containing the original word, at least one of the cue words of the intended sense, and none of the cue words for the other senses of the word. Then, in the second step, a weight is assigned to each word in the set of documents for each sense. This weight grows when the frequency of the word is higher than what would be expected from the contrast set made of the documents belonging to the other senses of the word. The words and their weights, in decreasing order of weight, form the topic signature for each word sense. Table 10.3 (in Chap. 10) gives an example for the noun *boy.*

In this work, the topic signatures are used in a straightforward WSD approach (to test the utility of the information provided by the signatures) with encouraging results. They are also used to cluster WordNet senses (two close senses will have close topic signatures; cf. verb grouping in Chap 4. (Sect. 4.6)), which are in turn successfully used in the WSD experiments described in the paper. The authors conclude that the quantitative evidence in favor of topic signatures is high, but a qualitative inspection of the data suggests that more filtering is needed to discard poor quality documents and some topical biases of the Web (e.g., the topic signature for *boy* was biased towards pornography issues).

In Agirre and Lopez de Lacalle (2004) topic signatures for all WordNet nominal senses have been built with similar techniques (using the Google search engine instead of Altavista, and querying with the method of monosemous relatives – described in Section 9.3.2 below – to create the examples). In order to avoid the cost (especially in time) of downloading full Web documents, the authors collect the examples directly from Google snippets (the small pieces of text matching the query, which Google uses

Topic signature extracted from Web data:

circuit (1804.11), electrical (1031.70), panel (714.00), solar (659.35), electric (649.94), plug (606.26), feedback (522.25), control (500.64), battery (462.07), device (343.18), generator (335.51), electrostatic (318.90), system (314.36), loop (272.64), bridge (270.08), distributor (266.72), use (255.84), board (251.91), delay (247.48), resonant (240.84), series (238.49), computer (237.91), instrument (223.26), fuse (189.73), capacitor (184.64), voltage (183.87), strip (183.56), current (173.38), tank (164.29), power (153.42), wire (151.61), resistor (137.76), design (131.88), relay (129.29), output (115.00), switch (115.00), transducer (112.47), transformer (106.25), ...

Topic signature extracted from Senseval-2 training data:

pass (17.42), stage (17.42), delay (13.93), capacitor (10.45), network (9.89), clock (6.96), connection (6.96), control (6.96), neural (6.96), brain (3.48), cause (3.48), churning (3.48), destroy (3.48), device (3.48), disconnect (3.48), due (3.48), equal (3.48), experimental (3.48), frequency (3.48), govern (3.48), input (3.48), line (3.48), missouri (3.48), next (3.48), pattern (3.48), physicist (3.48), practice (3.48), rate (3.48), reliving (3.48), scramble (3.48), second (3.48), semblance (3.48), speed (3.48), part (1.02), process (1.02), produce (1.02), provide (1.02), run (1.02), two (1.02), 2 (0.97), first (0.33), use (0.33), circuit (0.04), ...

Fig. 9.1. Topic signatures for the first sense of *circuit* ('electrical circuit'). The number in parentheses is the weight assigned to the corresponding word.

to describe the content of every URL in the ranked list of results). The problem with Google snippets is that they are often ungrammatical and incoherent as text fragments. The authors apply a number of simple heuristics to filter them, such as discarding fragments shorter than six words, with a number of non-alphanumeric characters greater than half of the words or with more words in uppercase than in lowercase. These filters discard approximately two out of three snippets, retaining an average of 160 examples per word. Fig. 9.1 compares the topic signatures for *circuit-1* ('electrical circuit') obtained from the Web corpus and from the Senseval-2 training corpus. Note that both topic signatures seem equally reasonable, although one of them involves manual annotations (Senseval-2) while the other is obtained in a completely automatic manner (Web data). Of course, the great advantage of the Web corpus is that it can be applied to all WordNet senses, not just to a handful of words. The final corpus[2] contains around 4,500 topic words per word sense.

---

[2] http://ixa.si.ehu.es/Ixa/resources/sensecorpus

9.2.2   Association of Web Directories to Word Senses

Santamaría et al. (2003) developed a system that automatically associates WordNet senses with Web directories. Web directories, such as Yahoo! Directory or the Open Directory Project (ODP)[3] are hierarchical thematic categories that organize the information in the Web so that the information of interest to a user can be located not only by *querying* (as in a search engine), but also by *browsing* the contents of the Web through iterative topic refinement. The most interesting feature of Web directories, from the perspective of the Web as a corpus, is that both the directories and the association of Web pages to directories are manually constructed. Compared to the Web, then, directories should be a much cleaner and balanced source of information. The hypothesis of Santamaría et al. is that one or more assignments of Web directories to a word sense would be an enormously rich and compact source of topical information about the word sense, which includes both the hierarchy of associated subdirectories and the Web pages beneath them.

The approach consists mainly of three stages. First, a query is formed similarly to Agirre et al. (2000), using relevant cue words extracted from WordNet for every word sense, and using cue words from the other senses as negative information. The query is sent to ODP directories, and a set of directories (rather than documents) is retrieved. Then the directories are compared with the word senses, assuming that a relevant directory (represented by the chain of parent directories that lead to it) will have some degree of overlap with the word sense (represented by the chain of hypernyms of the associated synset in WordNet). Then the authors apply a set of additional criteria and filters to end up with possible associations and an empirical confidence measure for each association.

The main result of the algorithm is a set of (word sense, Web directory) associations with a confidence weight. Table 9.1 lists some of the results for the word *circuit*. For instance, the directory "computers/cad/electronic design automation" is assigned to *circuit-1* ('electrical circuit') with a confidence of 0.78. The algorithm also detects some sense specializations (i.e., hyponyms of existing WordNet senses) such as "business/industries/electronics/components/integrated circuits" as a sense specialization (integrated circuit) of *circuit-1*. Using this technique, the authors characterized 27,383 word senses corresponding to 24,558 WordNet nouns with 86% accuracy as measured on the set of nouns used in the Senseval-2 test bed.[4]

---

[3] http://dmoz.org
[4] http://nlp.uned.es/ODP

Table 9.1. Some WordNet-sense/ODP-directory associations for *circuit*. Below each of the senses of *circuit*, the list of associated categories are listed with the confidence weight. In the case of *circuit-1*, a category that is a specialization is also detected.

ODP directories for each sense	Confidence
circuit-1 ('electrical circuit')	
business/industries/electronics and electrical/contract manufacturers	0.98
manufacturers/printed circuit boards/fabrication	0.88
computers/cad/electronic design automation	0.78
sense specialization (hyponym):	
business/industries/electronics and electrical/components/int. circuits	0.98
circuit-2 ('tour', 'journey around a particular area')	
sports/cycling/travel/travelogues/europe/france	0.58
regional/asia/nepal/travel and tourism/travel guides	0.66
circuit-5 ('racing circuit')	
sports/motorsports/auto racing/stock cars/drivers and teams	0.78
sports/motorsports/auto racing/tracks	0.82

These sense/directory associations have been used to automatically acquire sense-tagged examples for supervised WSD; see Section 9.3.3 below.

9.3 Automatic Acquisition of Sense-Tagged Corpora

The most direct way of using the Web (and other corpora) to enhance WSD performance is the automatic acquisition of sense-tagged corpora, the fundamental resource to feed supervised WSD algorithms (see Chap. 7). Although this is far from being commonplace in the WSD literature, a number of different and effective strategies to achieve this goal have already been proposed. We will classify them in five types: acquisition by direct Web searching (Sect. 9.3.1), bootstrapping (Sect. 9.3.2), acquisition via Web directories (Sect. 9.3.3), acquisition via cross-language evidence (Sect. 9.3.4), and Web-based cooperative annotation (Sect. 9.3.5).

9.3.1 Acquisition by Direct Web Searching

Leacock et al. (1998) use the monosemous lexical relatives of a word sense as a key for finding training sentences in a corpus. For instance, looking for *business suit* as a monosemous hyponym of *suit* can give us training sentences for the appropriate sense of suit. Mihalcea and Moldovan (1999) extend this idea and apply it to the Web as the target corpus.

Mihalcea and Moldovan use four ranked procedures to search the Web for instances of a word sense:

1. Monosemous synonyms. For instance, *remember-1* has the monosemous synonym *recollect*. Therefore, "recollect" is used to search the Web for examples.
2. Defining phrases. For instance, *produce-5* is defined as "bring onto the market or release, as of an intellectual creation". The definition is automatically parsed and "bring onto the market" is used as defining phrase (*release* is discarded as ambiguous).
3. In case of failure, a Boolean query is made with synonyms (grouped with OR operators) in conjunction with words from the defining phrases (using the NEAR operator). For instance, "cultivate NEAR growing AND (grow OR raise OR farm OR produce)" retrieves examples for *produce-6*, synonyms, *grow, raise, farm,* and *produce,* and defining phrase, "cultivate by growing".
4. In case of failure, do a similar search but substituting the NEAR operator with the more relaxed AND operator.

Once examples are retrieved, a post-processing phase checks that the part of speech of the word in every example is correct; otherwise, the example is eliminated. This method provides an average of 670 example sentences per word sense, with a reported precision of 91%, clearly indicating the potential of the Web to solve the knowledge acquisition bottleneck. In this work, however, results on the application of the examples to supervised WSD are not presented.

Somewhat surprisingly, using the Web did not quickly become a mainstream approach for WSD. A partial explanation can be found in Agirre and Martínez (2000): they replicated the same strategy to build a sense-tagged corpus and used the results to train a WSD system that was tested against a subset of Semcor. The results were disappointing: only a few words got better than random results. Agirre and Martínez concluded that the examples, being themselves correct, could provide systematically misleading features, and that the unbalanced number of examples (all word senses received basically the same number of training instances) could be misleading for the supervised learning process.

In Agirre and Martínez (2004), the same authors built another Web corpus, focusing on only the monosemous-relatives technique and applying additional filters. Monosemous relatives included in this work are

church-1: *church, Christian church, Christianity* (a group of Christians; any group professing Christian doctrine or belief)
church-2: *church, church building* (a place for public (especially Christian) worship)
church-3: *church service, church* (a service conducted in a church)

Synonyms: *church building* (sense 2), *church service* (sense 3), ...
Direct hyponyms: *Protestant Church* (sense 1), *Coptic Church* (sense 1), ...
Direct hypernyms: *house of prayer* (sense 2), *religious service* (sense 3), ...
Distant hyponyms: *Greek Church* (sense 1), *Western Church* (sense 1), ...
Siblings: *Hebraism* (sense 2), *synagogue* (sense 2), ...

Fig. 9.2. The three synsets (the synonym set and definitions are shown) corresponding to the three senses of *church* in WordNet 1.6, followed by a partial list of monosemous relatives (with the corresponding sense of *church* in parenthesis.

synonyms, hyponyms, hypernyms, and siblings (with different degrees of confidence) (see Fig. 9.2). It is shown that the monosemous relatives technique can be used to extract examples for all nouns in WordNet.

The authors focus on the bias problem, comparing several possibilities:

1. Taking the same number of examples per sense (no bias).
2. Taking all examples found in the Web per sense (Web bias).
3. Using the same proportion of examples per sense as in Semcor (Semcor bias).
4. Using the same proportion of examples as in the Senseval-2 training set (Senseval-2 bias, which is optimal for evaluating with Senseval-2 data).
5. Using the ranking method proposed by McCarthy et al. (2004) (see Chap. 6 (Sect. 6.1.2)) (automatic bias).

Bias is shown to have a strong impact on recall: the worst strategy (no bias) reaches a recall of 38%, while the best possible bias (Senseval-2 bias) reaches 58% (a relative improvement of 53%). The paper does not discuss whether this is a problem of Web data (which can be biased for certain contexts or senses) or an intrinsic feature of supervised learning systems.

Overall, training a supervised WSD system with Web data provides better results than any unsupervised system participating in Senseval-2 (see Table 9.2). Overall, Web data is shown to be very useful for WSD, but still does not match the results obtained with hand-tagged data, or even the most-frequent-sense baseline.

Table 9.2. Web data versus Senseval-2 unsupervised WSD systems (Agirre and Martínez 2004).

Method	Type of method	Senseval-2 recall
Web corpus (Semcor bias)	Minimally supervised	**49.8%**
UNED	"	45.1
Web corpus (automatic bias)	Unsupervised	**43.3**
Litkowski-clr-ls	"	35.8
Haynes-IIT2	"	27.9
Haynes-IIT1	"	26.4

In our opinion, a problem of directly querying the Web to get training samples is that we only capture a fraction of the relevant examples, the ones that co-occur with query terms. This set of examples may be just a fraction of the possible contexts for the word sense. For instance, if we want to find examples for *mother-1* ('a woman who has given birth to a child'), we can use its monosemous relative *female parent* (a synonym of *mother-1* in WordNet 2.0) to search Web examples, obtaining over 10,000 hits in Google. Substituting *female parent* for *mother*, we can certainly obtain a very large set of examples for *mother-1*. But this set is strongly biased: We will find many examples from, say, the domain of law, such as "non custodial female parent support group" or of biology, "the DNA of the female parent plant", but no examples of common contexts for *mother-1* such as "My female parent is coming for dinner tonight". This problem is also correlated with Web bias. In this case, the proportion of examples for *mother-1* will be underestimated from Web data.

One way to alleviate this problem is searching the Web with the widest possible set of queries per word sense. This is more feasible if we have initial examples for every word sense, as in the approach described in the following section.

9.3.2 Bootstrapping from Seed Examples

Mihalcea (2002a) enriches the method described in Mihalcea and Moldovan (1999) with a bootstrapping approach inspired by Yarowsky (1995). Yarowsky's method trains a decision list system using a few tagged seed samples, and the system is then employed to tag new instances (see details in Chap. 7 (Sect 7.2.4)). Mihalcea creates a set of seeds extracted from Semcor, WordNet, and the Web (using the monosemous relatives approach

Table 9.3. Comparison between Senseval-2 training data and Web data (Mihalcea 2002b).

	Senseval-2 training examples		Mihalcea (2002b) Web examples	
	Num. of examples	Precision	Num. of examples	Precision
art	123	65%	265	73%
chair	121	83	179	87
church	81	64	189	58
detention	46	88	163	83
nation	60	73	225	70

described in the previous section). Then, the Web is searched using queries formed with the seed expressions. Finally, the words surrounding the target word (noun phrases and verb/noun constructs) in the documents retrieved are disambiguated using Mihalcea and Moldovan's (2000) algorithm. These expressions serve in turn as new seeds for a new Web search. The sense-tagged corpus generated with this approach (GenCor) was tested in Senseval-2, achieving one of the best scores both in the lexical sample and the all-words tasks, and a good part of the success is due to the Web acquired corpora. For instance, in the all-words task, the first sense heuristic gives a precision of 64%; if only Semcor and WordNet are used for training, the result is 65% (+ 2% relative improvement). The same algorithm, trained with the Web-based corpus, achieves a precision of 69% (+ 6% relative improvement). This additional recall due to the Web corpus boosts the system to the best result among Senseval-2 participants.

Using the same system and test bed, Mihalcea (2002b) compares the quality of Web data (up to seven iteration steps in the bootstrapping process) with hand-tagged data. This comparison is made on a limited number of words: for the noun *channel*, the supervised WSD system using the Web corpus reaches optimal results after 6 iterations (34% precision), matching supervision with the hand tagged data (34% precision as well). For the five additional nouns considered in the experiment, *art, chair, church, detention,* and *nation*, the results with the Web corpus are comparable with the results using hand-tagged data (see Table 9.3).

These are, to our knowledge, the best results reported for WSD using Web data, confirming the potential of the Web to solve the knowledge acquisition bottleneck. They have been obtained, however, using Semcor and other sources as seeds, and such a large initial set of seeds is only available for English. Another pending issue is extending the evaluation to a larger set of words, because inter-word variability in WSD is extremely high, and results obtained on five words cannot be extrapolated to a full language vocabulary.

9.3.3 Acquisition via Web Directories

The word sense to Web directory associations obtained by Santamaría et al. (2003) can be trivially applied to obtain sense-tagged corpora, extracting the occurrences of the word in the Web pages listed under the Web directory entry or in the manually built description of the pages under the directory. For instance, *circuit-2* ('tour', 'journey') is associated with ODP directories such as "sports/cycling/travel/travelogues/Europe/France". The Web page that describes this directory contains a number of examples of *circuit*, such as *the Tour du Mont-Blanc is a circuit of 322km based in the Alps*, which can be automatically assigned the *circuit-2* sense.

Compared to the strategies described above, the use of directories has, a priori, at least three advantages: 1) catalogued Web pages are a cleaner source of information than the Web itself, 2) as the algorithm retrieves directories rather than documents, the occurrences of the word in the documents associated with the directory do not necessarily co-occur with the seed words used in the Web search, permitting a larger variety of training samples, and 3) Web directories can be distributed without copyright problems, and they are more stable over time than individual Web pages. A drawback of the method is that it can only be applied to word senses that can be related to some topical domain; some word senses, however, do not have any domain specificity.

Santamaría et al. (2003) experimented with the above approach, comparing the quality of examples retrieved from ODP pages with the hand-tagged training samples provided in the Senseval-2 English lexical sample task. Only the examples found in the pages that describe the Web categories (rather than the Web pages listed under the category) were used in this experiment. The initial problem is the coverage of the approach: only 10 nouns (out of 29 polysemous nouns) receive characterizations for two or more senses. In order to measure the quality of the data (rather than the coverage), only the senses which are characterized with ODP directories were used in the evaluation. For this subset, the recall obtained with Web data is as good as with the hand-tagged training material, when the number of training instances is comparable (see Table 9.4). Again, the problem is coverage: Web directories provide enough training material for only half of the words included in the experiment.

Table 9.4. WSD with examples retrieved from ODP Web directories (Santamaría et al. 2003).

Senses	Num. of training instances		Test instances	Recall	
	Senseval	ODP	Senseval	Senseval	ODP
bar-1, 10	127, 11	1, 1	62, 6	91%	50%
child-1, 2	39, 78	3, 80	35, 27	57	44
circuit-1, 2, 5	67, 6, 7	229, 2, 5	23, 2, 8	70	70
facility-1, 4	26, 61	4, 18	15, 28	79	67
grip-2, 7	6, 1	17, 6	4, 0	100	100
holiday-1, 2	4, 57	5, 17	26, 2	96	96
material-1, 4	65, 7	63, 10	30, 9	79	79
post-2, 3, 4, 7, 8	1, 64, 20, 11, 7	2, 7, 1, 9, 3	2, 25, 13, 12, 4	45	25
restraint-1, 4, 6	17, 32, 11	2, 2, 2	8, 14, 4	65	50
stress-1, 2	3, 45	8, 50	1, 19	95	95
Total	773	547	379	73%	58%

In summary, this is a promising approach that extracts high-quality examples from a clean, manually-classified subset of the Web. Coverage, however, is low: not every word sense can be associated with a Web directory (some degree of domain specificity is required), and the number of examples found in directory descriptions is limited. The authors conclude that the approach can be especially useful for applications in which only domain disambiguation is required, such as information retrieval.

9.3.4 Acquisition via Cross-Language Evidence

Sometimes choosing a correct translation for a word in context can be easier than disambiguating its sense. This is often the case when there are enough translation statistics extracted from available parallel corpora. In such cases, translation information can be used to partially disambiguate the word, because only a subset of the possible senses can be translated to given term (Gale et al. 1992). For instance, if we know that a particular instance of *bank* is translated into French as *rive*, we can conclude that the correct sense of *bank* is *bank-3* ('riverside'). In this way, word-aligned parallel corpora can be used as a source of examples for supervised WSD.

Of course, this strategy might not lead to full disambiguation (i.e., returning a single word sense, as opposed to returning several word senses) for every aligned word, because there tends to be many cases of parallel polysemy between pairs of languages (especially if they do not belong to distant language families). For instance, most senses of *art* can be translated as *arte* in Spanish; in this case, translation preserves ambiguity. Chapter 3 suggests that this level of disambiguation is sufficient for more applications. Chapter 6 (Sect. 6.4) discusses the early work on using parallel corpora to label word occurrences with their translations as a form of WSD. In the remainder of this section, we will focus on how to exploit parallel corpora for full-fledged disambiguation, and on how to acquire parallel corpora from the Web.

One algorithm that provides full disambiguation is Diab's (2003) unsupervised bootstrapping approach to WSD, which exploits noisy parallel corpora described. Diab's method to annotate a parallel corpus with senses consists of the following steps:

1. Locate words in the source corpus and their corresponding translations in the target corpus.
2. Group source words that translate to the same target word. For instance, target French *rive* produces the source group {*bank, shore, riverside*}, while *banque* produces {*bank, brokerage*}.
3. Measure the similarity among the different senses of the words in the source groups. In Diab's case study, WordNet is used together with the "Noun Groupings" similarity measure (Resnik 1999a) (see Chap. 5 (Sect. 5.3) for other similarity measures).
4. Assign the closest sense tags to the respective word occurrences in the corpus. For instance, the source groups above would disambiguate as {*bank-3, shore-1, riverside-2*} and {*bank-2, brokerage-1*}; these sense assignments are projected to the corpus in the original sentences (e.g., *He has a house by the river bank-3*). Note that at least two words are needed in each source group to make this disambiguation step possible. If a word has always the same (polysemous) translation in the parallel corpus, then no semantic annotation is possible with this algorithm.
5. Project the assigned sense tags from the source language words to the corresponding target language words in the parallel corpus. For instance, if *Il a une maison par la rive du fleuve* is the translation for *He has a house by the river bank-3*, then *rive* receives the sense *bank-3* in that context.

Diab's algorithm shows that parallel corpora can be effectively used for word sense disambiguation, even in languages without appropriate sense inventories (by projecting sense tags from a source language having richer computational resources). Using an English corpus translated into Spanish by a machine translation (MT) system, Diab's algorithm reached a recall of 57% on the Senseval-2 English all-words task. Bhattacharya et al. (2004) recast and refined Diab's approach in a probabilistic framework, achieving 65% recall on the same test bed. Diab (2004) also compares the results of a supervised learning algorithm on the Senseval-2 English lexical sample task, using either examples acquired from the output of an MT system or manual-annotated Senseval-2 examples. The latter gives much better results, but, still, Diab's method gives results comparable to that of the best unsupervised systems that participated in Senseval-2. Note that these results are obtained with a "noisy" data set, because the output of MT systems are not yet of human quality.

An alternative approach is to exploit the multilingual sense alignments in a multilingual wordnet, such as the EuroWordNet (Vossen 1998), BalkaNet (Tufiş et al. 2004a), or from the MEANING project (Vossen et al. 2006). Tufiş et al. (2004b) used BalkaNet to disambiguate word occurrences in parallel corpora following a simple strategy: Given two aligned words, *w1* and *w2*, their senses are mapped to the Interlingual Index (ILI) that links monolingual wordnets together. If there is one ILI record common to the possible pairs of senses of *w1* and *w2*, then this ILI record is the appropriate sense for both words. If the wordnet alignments do not point to the same ILI record, but to semantically close concepts, then a semantic similarity score is used to detect the closest pair of ILI records connecting *w1* and *w2* sense-pairs. If there is more than one ILI record in common between the two words, the ILI record of the most frequent sense of the target word is selected (additional heuristics apply in case of ties). Finally, a sense clustering method is applied, in which a disambiguated occurrence of a word can be propagated to other non-disambiguated instances in a cluster. The method is applied to an annotated version of George Orwell's *1984*, with a best result of 75% accuracy, which is comparable to inter-annotator agreement for the dataset.

More recently, Chan and Ng (2005) have shown that even a direct application of aligned texts as examples for word sense disambiguation reaches state-of-the-art results in an all-words disambiguation task. Chan and Ng start by mapping WordNet 1.7 senses into similar definition entries for two bilingual English-Chinese dictionaries; then the Chinese translations are gathered from the relevant definition entries, and examples are automatically retrieved from word-aligned parallel corpora. The problem of translation ambiguity is ignored, assigning an ambiguous translation to the lowest numbered WordNet sense. Even with this limitation, a state-of-the-art supervised learning system (Lee and Ng 2002) achieves an accuracy of 77% in the Senseval-2 English all-words task, comparable to the accuracy using Semcor as training data (76%), an impressive result.

Again, the problem is the knowledge acquisition bottleneck: parallel corpora are scarce resources – especially when languages other than English are involved – and usually domain-specific, and therefore not suitable for general WSD. And once again, the Web is a potential solution to this problem.

Creating a parallel corpus out of the Web usually involves three steps (Resnik and Smith 2003): 1) locating domains, sites or pages that might have parallel translations, 2) generating candidate URL pairs from such data, and 3) filtering candidate pairs with structural or content-based criteria.

Generation of candidate pairs can be done with relatively simple strategies such as language identification, URL matching (e.g., substituting "esp" with "eng" – Spanish and English – in an existing URL and checking whether the substituted URL also exists), or the comparison of document lengths.

Filtering candidate pairs can be done according to structural criteria (looking for similar document structure) or content criteria (similar content). Some approaches include PTMINER, BITS, and STRAND. PTMINER (Chen and Nie 2000) locates promising sites by querying for pages in a given language that contain links to pages in different languages. Once bilingual sites are located and crawled, filtering criteria include language identification, URL matching and length comparison, without structural or content comparison. Chen and Nie produced an English-French corpus of around 100 megabytes per language using these techniques and improved cross-language information retrieval (CLIR) systems submitted by participants in the CLEF comparative evaluation of multilingual information retrieval.

BITS (Ma and Liberman 1999) uses bilingual dictionaries to compute a content-based similarity score between candidate pairs, with additional filters for document length and similarity of anchors (numbers, acronyms, etc.).

STRAND (Resnik 1999b) uses structural filtering to compare language pairs, linearizing the HTML structure of both documents and aligning the resulting sequences. Four scalar values on the alignment characterize the quality of the alignment, and a machine learning process is used to optimize filtering according to these parameters, to obtain a precision of 97% and a recall of 83% over a set of English-French candidate pairs. Resnik and Smith (2003) enhanced STRAND with content-based similarity measures and applied it over the Internet Archive[5] to obtain an English-Arabic parallel corpus of more than one million tokens per language, with a precision of 95% and a recall of 99% over the extracted candidate pairs. An interesting feature of STRAND, when combined with the Internet Archive, is that it solves legal distribution problems by listing the URLs rather than the documents themselves, and that URLs are stable as part of the Internet Archive.

To our knowledge, these automatically extracted parallel corpora have not been applied to WSD yet, but given the increasing success of WSD based on parallel corpora, it is reasonable to expect results in the near future.

Besides parallel corpora, evidence about translation in context can also be obtained from comparable corpora or even from the Web as a big, comprehensive multilingual corpus. Grefenstette (1999) showed that multiword translation can be done accurately just by using the co-occurrence statistics of the candidate translation pairs for the original words in the multiword expression. For instance, *strong tea* is much more frequent on the Web than *powerful tea* according to the statistics of querying Altavista. In the case of translation ambiguity, a multiword expression can be translated with the collocation that is more frequent in the target language, according to statistics gathered from the Web or a large comparable corpus. Fernández-Amorós (2004) applies this idea using a large scale bilingual noun phrase alignment which was extracted from the CLEF English-Spanish comparable corpus (López-Ostenero et al. 2005). Although the corpus exceeds one gigabyte in size, and the noun phrase alignment contains more than one million phrases in each language, it covers only 5% of the collocations to be disambiguated in the Senseval-2 test bed. This is an indication that perhaps only the Web can provide enough statistical evidence to be useful for WSD.

9.3.5 Web-Based Cooperative Annotation

The Web is not only useful for WSD as a huge corpus, but also as a huge social network of potential volunteers for performing cooperative annotation tasks. This is the approach taken by the Open Mind Word Expert (OMWE)[6] project, in which a Web site collects sense annotations made by

---

[5] www.archive.org
[6] www.teach-computers.org/word-expert.html

Web users (Chklovski and Mihalcea 2002). The system has an active learning component that selects the hardest examples (from an automatic WSD perspective) as the examples to be shown to the volunteers for manual annotation. In order to find such examples, two different classifiers (an instance-based classifier and a constraint-based tagger) are applied to untagged data. The agreement between both systems is very low, leading to a high accuracy in the cases where they agree, and to a low accuracy when they disagree. The cases of disagreement are therefore chosen to be hand tagged.

One potential problem with Web volunteers is how to control the quality of their annotations. In order to control this factor, redundant tagging (from two taggers) is collected for each example, allowing only one tag per example per volunteer. The inter-annotator agreement rate for the English collection is 62.8% (Mihalcea and Chklovski 2003), which is much lower than the 85.5% agreement attained in the Senseval-2 test set (Kilgarriff 2001). In addition, the best systems in Senseval-3, where OMWE was used as the test corpus, inexplicably outperformed the Web volunteers (see Chap. 4 (Sect. 4.7)) by a small margin. The quality of the tagging is thus an open issue.

OMWE is growing daily. At the time of writing, OMWE for English already exceeds the number of annotations in Semcor, thus becoming the largest manually sense-tagged corpus for WSD. At least 70,000 instances of about 230 words are annotated with WordNet 1.7 senses (Edmonds and Kilgariff 2002). The OMWE project is also collecting hand-tagged examples for Romanian, and also translation equivalences for English-Hindi and English-French.

In summary, collecting annotations from anonymous volunteers in the Web has revealed as a surprisingly effective way of alleviating the knowledge acquisition bottleneck. It is more feasible, however, for building test resources (as used in Senseval-3) than to obtain training material for a complete language, which remains a formidable task for humans.

9.4 Discussion

The automatic extraction of examples to train supervised learning algorithms reviewed in Section 9.3 has been, by far, the best explored approach to mine the web for word sense disambiguation. Some results are certainly encouraging:

- In some experiments, the quality of the Web data for WSD equals that of human-tagged examples. This is the case of the monosemous relatives plus bootstrapping with Semcor seeds technique (Mihalcea 2002b) and the examples taken from the ODP Web directories in Santamaría et al. (2003). In the first case, however, Semcor-size example seeds are necessary (and only available for English), and it has only been tested with a very limited set of nouns; in the second case, the coverage is quite limited, and it is not yet clear whether it can be grown without compromising the quality of the examples retrieved.
- It has been shown (Agirre and Martinez 2004) that a mainstream supervised learning technique trained exclusively with web data can obtain better results than all unsupervised WSD systems which participated at Senseval-2.
- Web examples made a significant contribution to the best Senseval-2 English all-words system (Mihalcea 2002a).

There are, however, several open research issues related to the use of Web examples in WSD:

- High precision in the retrieved examples (i.e., correct sense assignments for the examples) does not necessarily lead to good supervised WSD results (i.e., the examples are possibly not useful for training) (Agirre and Martínez 2000).
- The most complete evaluation of Web examples for supervised WSD (Agirre and Martínez 2004) indicates that learning with Web data improves over unsupervised techniques, but the results are nevertheless far from those obtained with hand-tagged data, and do not even beat the most-frequent-sense baseline.
- Results are not always reproducible; the same or similar techniques may lead to different results in different experiments. Compare, for instance, Mihalcea (2002b) with Agirre and Martínez (2004), or Agirre and Martínez (2000) with Mihalcea and Moldovan (1999). Results with Web data seem to be very sensitive to small differences in the learning algorithm, to when the corpus was extracted (search engines change continuously), and on small heuristic issues (e.g., differences in filters to discard part of the retrieved examples).
- Results are strongly dependent on bias (i.e., on the relative frequencies of examples per word sense), as shown in Agirre and Martínez (2004). It is unclear whether this is simply a problem of Web data, or an intrinsic problem of supervised learning techniques, or just a problem of how WSD systems are evaluated (indeed, testing with rather small Senseval

data may overemphasize sense distributions compared to sense distributions obtained from the full Web as corpus).

- In any case, Web data has an intrinsic bias, because queries to search engines directly constrain the context of the examples retrieved. There are approaches that alleviate this problem, such as using several different seeds/queries per sense (Mihalcea 2002b) or assigning senses to Web directories and then scanning directories for examples (Santamaría et al. 2003); but this problem is nevertheless far from being solved.
- Once a Web corpus of examples is built, it is not entirely clear whether its distribution is safe from a legal perspective.

Besides automatic acquisition of examples from the Web, there are some other WSD experiments that have profited from the Web:

- The Web as a social network has been successfully used for cooperative annotation of a corpus (OMWE) (Chklovski and Mihalcea 2002) which has already been used in three Senseval-3 tasks (English, Romanian and Multilingual).
- The Web has been used to enrich WordNet senses with domain information: topic signatures (Agirre et al. 2000) and Web directories (Santamaría et al. 2003), which have in turn been successfully used for WSD.

It is clear, however, that most research opportunities remain largely unexplored. For instance, little is known about how to use lexical information extracted from the Web in knowledge-based WSD systems; and it is also hard to find systems that use Web-mined parallel corpora for WSD, even though there are already efficient algorithms that use parallel corpora in WSD. Therefore, it is reasonable to expect many new, exciting results in this area in the near future.

Acknowledgments

We are indebted to the editors of this volume, Eneko Agirre and Phil Edmonds, for their feedback, support and patience along the whole editorial process. This work has been partially supported by a Spanish government grant (project R2D2, TIC2003-07158-C04).

References

Agirre, Eneko, Olatz Ansa, Eduard H. Hovy & David Martínez. 2000. Enriching very large ontologies using the WWW. *Proceedings of the Ontology Learning Workshop, European Conference on Artificial Intelligence (ECAI)*, Berlin, Germany.

Agirre, Eneko & David Martínez. 2000. Exploring automatic word sense disambiguation with decision lists and the Web. *Proceedings of the COLING Workshop on Semantic Annotation and Intelligent Annotation*, Luxembourg, 11–19.

Agirre, Eneko & Osier López de Lacalle. 2004. Publicly available topic signatures for all WordNet nominal senses. *Proceedings of the Language Resources and Evaluation Conference (LREC)*, Lisbon, Portugal.

Agirre, Eneko & David Martínez. 2004. Unsupervised WSD based on automatically retrieved examples: The importance of bias. *Proceedings of the Conference on Empirical Methods in Natural Language Processing (EMNLP)*, Barcelona, Spain, 25–33.

Bhattacharya, Indrajit, Lise Getoor & Yoshua Bengio. 2004. Unsupervised sense disambiguation using bilingual probabilistic models. *Proceedings of the 42nd meeting of the Association for Computational Linguistics (ACL)*, Barcelona, Spain, 287–295.

Chan, Yee Seng & Hwee Tou Ng. 2005. Scaling up word sense disambiguation via parallel texts. *Proceedings of the 19th International Joint Conference on Artificial Intelligence (IJCAI)*, Edinburgh, U.K., 1010–1015.

Chen, Jiang & Jian-Yun Nie. 2000. Cross-language information retrieval between Chinese and English. *Proceedings of the International Conference on Chinese Language Computing*, Chicago, U.S.A.

Chklovski, Tim & Rada Mihalcea. 2002. Building a sense tagged corpus with Open Mind Word Expert. *Proceedings of the ACL SIGLEX Workshop on Word Sense Disambiguation: Recent Successes and Future Directions*, Philadelphia, U.S.A., 116–122.

Diab, Mona. 2003. *Word Sense Disambiguation within a Multilingual Framework*. Ph.D. Thesis, University of Maryland, U.S.A.

Diab, Mona. 2004. Relieving the data acquisition bottleneck in word sense disambiguation. *Proceedings of the 42nd meeting of the Association for Computational Linguistics (ACL)*, Barcelona, SpaiN, 303–310.

Edmonds, Philip & Adam Kilgarriff. 2002. Introduction to the special issue on evaluating word sense disambiguation systems. *Natural Language Engineering*, 8(4): 279–291.

Fernández-Amorós, David. 2004. *Anotación semántica no supervisada.* Ph.D. Thesis, Universidad Nacional de Educación a Distancia (UNED), Madrid, Spain.

Gale, William, Kenneth W. Church & David Yarowsky. 1992. One sense per discourse. *Proceedings of the DARPA Speech and Natural Language Workshop,* Harriman, U.S.A, 233–237.

Grefenstette, Gregory. 1999. The WWW as a resource for example-based MT tasks. *Proceeedings of the ASLIB Conference on Translating and the Computer 21,* London, U.K.

Kilgarriff, Adam. 2001. English lexical sample task description. *Proceedings of Senseval-2: Second International Workshop on Evaluating Word Sense Disambiguation Systems,* Toulouse, France.

Kilgarriff, Adam & Gregory Grefenstette, eds. 2003. Introduction to the special issue on the Web as corpus. *Computational Linguistics,* 29(3): 333–348.

Leacock, Claudia, Martin Chodorow & George Miller. 1998. Using corpus statistics and WordNet relations for sense identification. *Computational Linguistics,* 24(1): 147–165.

Lee, Yoong K. & Hwee T. Ng. 2002. An empirical evaluation of knowledge sources and learning algorithms for word sense disambiguation. *Proceedings of the 7th Conference on Empirical Methods in Natural Language Processing (EMNLP),* Philadelphia, U.S.A., 41–48.

López-Ostenero, Fernando, Julio Gonzalo & Felisa Verdejo. 2005. Noun phrases as building blocks for cross-language search assistance. *Information Processing and Management,* 41(3): 549–568.

Ma, Xiaoyi & Mark Liberman. 1999. BITS: A method for bilingual text search over the Web. *Proceedings of the Machine Translation Summit VII,* Singapore.

McCarthy, Diana, Rob Koeling, Julie Weeds & John Carroll. 2004. Finding predominant senses in untagged text. *Proceedings of the 42nd Annual Meeting of the Association for Computational Linguistics (ACL),* Barcelona, Spain, 280–287.

Mihalcea, Rada. 2002a. Word sense disambiguation with pattern learning and automatic feature selection. *Natural Language Engineering,* 8(4): 348–358.

Mihalcea, Rada. 2002b. Bootstrapping large sense tagged corpora. *Proceedings of the Language Resources and Evaluation Conference (LREC),* Las Palmas, Spain.

Mihalcea, Rada and Tim Chklovski. 2003. Open Mind Word Expert: Creating large annotated data collections with Web users' help. *Proceedings of the EACL Workshop on Linguistically Annotated Corpora,* Budapest, Hungary.

Mihalcea, Rada & Dan Moldovan. 1999. An automatic method for generating sense tagged corpora. *Proceedings of the American Association for Artificial Intelligence (AAAI)*, Orlando, U.S.A., 461–466.

Mihalcea, Rada & Dan Moldovan. 2000. An iterative approach to word sense disambiguation. *Proceedings of Flairs*, Orlando, U.S.A.

Resnik, Philip. 1999a. Disambiguating noun groupings with respect to Word-Net senses. *Natural Language Processing Using Very Large Corpora*, ed. by S. Armstrong, K. Church, P. Isabelle, S. Manzi, E. Tzoukermann, and D. Yarowsky, 77–98. Dordrecht: Kluwer Academic Publishers.

Resnik, Philip. 1999b. Mining the Web for bilingual text. *Proceedings of the 37th Annual Meeting of the Association for Computational Linguistics (ACL)*, Maryland, U.S.A., 527–534.

Resnik, Philip & Noah Smith. 2003. The Web as a parallel corpus. *Computational Linguistics,* 29(3): 349–380.

Santamaría, Celina, Julio Gonzalo & Felisa Verdejo. 2003. Automatic association of Web directories to word senses. *Computational Linguistics,* 29(3): 485–502.

Tufiş, Dan, Dan Cristea & Sofia Stamou. 2004a. BalkaNet: Aims, methods, results, and perspectives. A general overview. *Romanian Journal of Information Science and Technology*, 7(1–2): 9–43.

Tufiş, Dan, Radu Ion & Nancy Ide. 2004b. Fine-grained word sense disambiguation based on parallel corpora, word alignment, word clustering, and aligned WordNets". *Proceedings of the 20th International Conference on Computational Linguistics (COLING)*, Geneva, Switzerland, 1312–1318.

Vossen, Piek, German Rigau, Iñaki Alegria, Eneko Agirre, David Farwell & Manuel Fuentes. 2006. Meaningful results for information retrieval in the MEANING project. *Proceedings of the 3rd Global Wordnet Conference*, Jeju Island, Korea.

Yarowsky, David. 1995. Unsupervised word sense disambiguation rivalling supervised methods. *Proceedings of the 33rd Meeting of the Association for Computational Linguistics (ACL)*, Cambridge, U.S.A., 189–196.

10 Domain-Specific WSD

Paul Buitelaar,[1] Bernardo Magnini,[2] Carlo Strapparava,[2] Piek Vossen[3]

[1]DFKI GmbH
[2]Istituto per la Ricerca Scientifica e Tecnologica (ITC-irst)
[3]Irion Technologies

This chapter describes a number of approaches to word sense disambiguation, which take the wider "semantic space" of ambiguous words into account. Semantic space may be instantiated by a specific domain, task, or application. Approaches discussed include the use of subject codes as specified in dictionaries or manually added to WordNet and similar semantic resources, the extraction of topic signatures through a combined use of a semantic resource and domain-specific corpora, and domain-specific tuning of semantic resources in a top-down or bottom-up fashion.

10.1 Introduction

An important aspect of word sense disambiguation (WSD) is the wider *semantic space* in which the ambiguous word occurs. Semantic space[1] may be instantiated by a specific domain (e.g., biomedicine), a sub-domain (e.g., anatomy), a specific task (e.g., heart transplantation) or an organization (e.g., biomedicine at Aventis). Researchers have used different terms to indicate semantic space in the context of word sense disambiguation: "subject" (Guthrie et al. 1991), "discourse" (Gale et al. 1992), "domain"

---

[1] "Semantic space" is a technical term used in the context of Latent Semantic Indexing to indicate a "mathematical representation of a large body of text" (Landauer et al. 1998). A similar use of the term goes back to much earlier work, e.g., Rieger (1983). Here the term is not used directly in this formal sense, but most of the methods discussed assume a similar notion of word meaning.

E. Agirre and P. Edmonds (eds.), Word Sense Disambiguation: Algorithms and Applications, 275–298.
© 2007 *Springer.*

(Peh and Ng 1997, Cucchiarelli and Velardi 1998), or "topic" (Agirre et al. 2001). Although there are slight differences among the terms,[2] here we will use them interchangeably to indicate semantic space.

The influence of a particular domain on sense disambiguation can be clearly illustrated with some cross-lingual examples, as they would appear in (machine) translation.[3] Consider for instance the English word *housing*. In a more general sense, this translates into German *Wohnung* ('accommodation, dwelling'). However in engineering it translates into *Gehäuse* ('frame, casing'). Also verbs may be translated differently (i.e., have a different sense) according to the semantic space in which they occur. For instance, English *warming up* translates into *erhitzen* ('broil, heat') in a more general sense, but into *aufwärmen* ('limber up') in the sports domain.

This chapter deals with several aspects of the following two questions. If senses are strongly aligned with specific domains, then:

1. Is it possible to disambiguate between senses in a completely generic way, that is, without reference to a specific domain?
2. Is sense disambiguation (by occurrence) even necessary, as the domain will determine the appropriate sense (of each occurrence)?

The first question is concerned with the influence of domain on the disambiguation process. For instance, it seems theoretically impossible to define a training corpus and sense inventory that is truly generic (i.e., general enough to represent any possible domain). The second question concerns the observation that sense disambiguation is unnecessary if a particular sense can be assigned universally within a certain domain. The disambiguation problem then shifts more towards modeling the role of a particular sense within a domain, for instance by use of such techniques as topic detection and domain modeling.

In summary, it may not be feasible to separate sense disambiguation from the domain in which it operates, which in turn implies that modeling this domain is the first priority for sense disambiguation.

---

[2] "Domain" will be used primarily as "technical domain", whereas a "subject" or "topic" may indicate a more loosely defined semantic space, such as sports, rock climbing, etc. The use of "discourse" to indicate semantic space is more controversial, as this term has a more precise meaning within linguistic theory. However, our use of the term can be paraphrased as "semantically coherent text segment on a particular subject," which corresponds roughly to that of the other terms mentioned.

[3] Examples from: D. Luckhardt, Approaches to Disambiguation (http://is.uni-sb.de/ studium /handbuch/infoling/ambi/sublanguage).

The remainder of this chapter consists of a detailed description of a number of approaches (subject codes, topic signatures, domain tuning) to domain-specific word sense disambiguation, followed by a section that gives some examples of the use of such approaches in applications (user-modeling and cross-lingual information retrieval). The chapter closes with conclusions and some discussion on the pros and cons of a stronger focus on domains in word sense disambiguation.

10.2 Approaches to Domain-Specific WSD

10.2.1 Subject Codes

A semantic space may be indicated in a dictionary by the use of a so-called *subject code*. In the *Longman Dictionary of Contemporary English* (LDOCE) (Procter 1978), subject codes like MD ('Medical domain') or ML ('Meteorology') are used to define which senses of a word are used in which domains. Three of the senses of the word *high,* for instance, correspond to three different domains: Music (a high tone), Drugs (the experience of being high), and Meteorology (a high pressure area).

Subject codes can be used to detect the topic of a text segment by simply counting their frequency over all content words (Walker and Amsler 1986). Or, subject codes can be used in sense disambiguation by constructing topic-specific context models (Guthrie et al. 1991). Such neighborhoods can be constructed by taking into account all words in the definitions and sample sentences of all the dictionary words that share the same subject code.

Given this perspective it seems worthwhile to identify also the semantic space of WordNet synsets more explicitly by the introduction of subject codes. In WordNet Domains (Magnini and Cavaglià 2000)[4] synsets have been annotated with at least one domain label, selected from a set of about two hundred hierarchically organized labels.

Table 10.1 shows the domain distribution over the WordNet 1.6 synsets, considering 43 disjoint domain labels. This set of labels constitutes an intermediate level of the domain hierarchy (i.e., the use of Sport instead of Volleyball or Basketball).

The annotation methodology used for creating WordNet Domains was mainly manual, and based on lexico-semantic criteria, which take advantage of the already existing conceptual relations in WordNet.

---

[4] http://wndomains.itc.it/

Table 10.1. Domain distribution over WordNet 1.6 synsets.

No. of synsets	Domain	No. of synsets	Domain	No. of synsets	Domain
36820	Factotum	1771	Linguistics	532	Publishing
21281	Biology	1491	Military	511	Tourism
4637	Earth	1340	Law	509	Computer-science
3405	Psychology	1264	History	493	Telecommunication
3394	Architecture	1103	Industry	477	Astronomy
3271	Medicine	1033	Politics	381	Philosophy
3039	Economy	1009	Play	334	Agriculture
2998	Alimentation	963	Anthropology	272	Sexuality
2975	Administration	937	Fashion	185	Body-care
2472	Chemistry	861	Mathematics	149	Artisanship
2443	Transport	822	Literature	141	Archaeology
2365	Art	746	Engineering	92	Veterinary
2225	Physics	679	Sociology	90	Astrology
2105	Sport	637	Commerce		
2055	Religion	612	Pedagogy		

Information brought by domains is complementary to what is already in WordNet:

- Domains may include synsets of different syntactic categories. For instance, Medicine groups together senses from nouns, such as *doctor-1* and *hospital-1*, and from verbs such as *operate-7*.
- Domains may include senses from different WordNet sub-hierarchies (i.e., deriving from different unique beginners or from different lexicographer files). For instance, Sport contains senses such as *athlete-1* derived from *life-form-1*, *game-equipment-1* from *physical-object-1*, *sport-1* from *act-2*, and *playing-field-1* from *location-1*.
- Domains may group senses of the same word into semantic clusters, which has the important side effect of reducing the level of ambiguity when we are disambiguating to a domain (cf. verb groups in Chap. 4). For instance, the word *bank* has ten different senses in WordNet 1.6 (see Table 10.2): three of them (senses 1, 3, and 6) can be grouped under the Economy domain, while senses 2 and 7 belong to Geography and Geology, respectively.

Roget's International Thesaurus presents a different map of semantic space; the 1,042 heads under which all words are categorized can be thought of as semantic classes, or subject codes.

Table 10.2. WordNet senses and domains for the word *bank.*

Sense	WordNet synset and gloss	Domains
1	*depository, financial institution, bank,* *banking concern, banking company* (a financial institution)	Economy
2	*bank* (sloping land)	Geography, Geology
3	*bank* (a supply or stock held in reserve)	Economy
4	*bank, bank building* (a building)	Architecture, Economy
5	*bank* (an arrangement of similar objects)	Factotum
6	*savings bank, coin bank, money box, bank* (a container)	Economy
7	*bank* (a long ridge or pile)	Geography, Geology
8	*bank* (the funds held by a gambling house)	Economy, Play
9	*bank, cant, camber* (a slope in the turn of a road)	Architecture
10	*bank* (a flight maneuver)	Transport

Using subject codes in sense disambiguation has been shown to be fruitful, relative to using other sources of knowledge. For instance, Yarowsky (1992) developed a method in which word senses are aligned to semantic classes, such as those provided by Roget's hierarchy, which relied on the observation that a sufficient number of words in a class will be monosemous so that a reliable discriminator can be trained on contexts of all the words in the class. As a consequence, being able to determine the semantic class of a word from its context provides a method for the discrimination of its senses. The approach consists of three steps:

1. For each Roget category, collect words that are typically found in the context of the category (e.g., for the Bird category of *crane* collect words in the context of *heron, grebe,* and *hawk,* and for the Machine category collect words in the context of *jackhammer, drill,* and *bulldozer),*
2. For a given word (e.g., *crane*), train a classifier to separate the two or more categories in which it is a member, based on the context words associated with each category,
3. Given a novel context, apply the classifier.

This unsupervised method has achieved 92% accuracy on homograph distinctions. However, a somewhat weak aspect in the approach is the need to link Roget categories to word senses as provided by a dictionary or lexicon. In fact, Yarowsky treats categories *as* senses, but he suggests one could align categories to senses by using dictionary definitions as context (thereby in effect recreating Lesk's (1986) dictionary algorithm; see Chap. 5 (Sect. 5.2)).

Stevenson and Wilks (2001) adapted the Yarowsky (1992) algorithm to work with the LDOCE subject codes, which brings it closer to WSD with dictionary senses. Experiments were performed on a subset of the British National Corpus (BNC) on the words appearing at least 10 times in the training context of a particular word. In addition, while Yarowsky assumed a uniform prior probability for each Roget category, the probability of each subject category was estimated as the proportion of senses in LDOCE to which a given category was assigned. They report that the performance of using only subject codes (79% precision) was much better than that of using only dictionary definition words (65%), or selectional restrictions (44%) (see Chap. 5 for more discussion on knowledge-based methods).

More recently Escudero et al. (2000) used domain features extracted from WordNet Domains in a supervised approach tested on the Senseval-2 tasks (see Chap. 4 for Senseval). Prior probabilities for each domain were computed considering the frequency of a domain in WordNet Domains. The introduction of such domain features systematically improved system performance, especially for nouns (+3%).

While Escudero et al. (2000) integrated domains within a wider set of features, Magnini et al. (2002) presented at Senseval-2 a system that makes use of only domain information. The underlying hypothesis of the approach, called DDD (Domain Driven Disambiguation), is that information provided by domain labels offers a natural way to establish associations among word senses in a certain text fragment, which can be profitably used during the disambiguation process. In particular, they argued that domains constitute a fundamental feature of text coherence, such that word senses occurring in a coherent portion of text tend to maximize domain similarity. Following from this premise they verified a "one-domain-per-discourse" heuristic[5] on Semcor, the portion of the Brown Corpus semantically annotated with WordNet senses.

The basic idea of DDD is that the disambiguation of a target word w in its context t is mainly a process of comparison between the domain of the context and the domains of the word's senses. The algorithm is in principle quite simple and requires three steps, as shown in Fig. 10.1.

---

[5] Gale et al. (1992) proposed a related one-sense-per-discourse heuristic. See Chap. 5 (Sect. 5.5.2) and Sec. 10.2.2 below.

(1) for the context t of the target word w, compute the domain vector $DV(t)$
(2) for all the senses s_i of w, compute the domain vectors $DV(s_i)$
(3) choose the sense $\hat{s}$, such that

$$\hat{s} = \arg \max_{s_i} \left(similarity \left(DV(s_i), DV(t) \right) \right)$$

Fig. 10.1. Domain driven disambiguation (DDD) algorithm for WSD.

The domain vectors (DV) in the algorithm are data structures that collect the domain information related to both word senses and texts. They are vectors in a multidimensional space in which each domain represents a dimension of the space. The value of each component is the relevance of the corresponding domain with respect to the object described by the vector.

In step (1) the system determines the relevant domain for the context t of the word to be disambiguated (± 50 words around the target word are used). In this phase the system makes use of thresholds, one for each domain considered, that need to be exceeded for a domain to be relevant.

Then, in step (2), a domain vector $DV(s_i)$ is built for each sense s_i of the target word. In an unsupervised setting this is done using the association between words senses and domains provided in WordNet Domains. If training data is available, $DV(s_i)$ is obtained by applying step (1) to each training example.

Finally, in step (3), the sense of w is selected that maximizes the similarity with the relevant domain of the context, computed as the dot product of $DV(s_i)$ and $DV(t)$.

The DDD system was evaluated in the all-words task at Senseval-2 obtaining 75% precision and 36% recall. The low recall was due to the fact that just a subset of the word senses in a document are actually related to the domain of the context. However, the fact that the DDD approach allows one to predict the class of words that can be disambiguated is an appealing feature of the system, which has been exploited in an application scenario (see Sect. 10.3.1 below). Gliozzo et al. (2004b) present an empirical assessment of the potential utilization of domains in WSD in a wide range of comparative settings.

In Magnini et al. (2002), the thresholds used in step (1) were estimated based on the intuition that a domain is relevant to a text if its frequency in that text is significantly higher than in texts unrelated to that domain. Gliozzo et al. (2004a) improved the algorithm by using an unsupervised method, combining the annotations in WordNet Domains and a probabilistic framework that made use of a balanced corpus. More precisely, given a domain D, the "empirical" probability density function (i.e., the frequency distribution of D in the corpus according to WordNet Domains) can be seen as the decomposition of two distinct distributions, the distribution for D and for *non-D*. This decomposition is effectively computed using the Gaussian mixture model and the expectation maximization (EM) algorithm (Redner and Walker 1984), which can represent every smooth probability function as a linear combination of two Gaussian probability density functions. The methodology was applied on the BNC to estimate relevance thresholds for the domains shown in Table 10.1. The DDD system had a significant improvement (+ 3%) with respect to the performance obtained in the all-words task at Senseval-2.

10.2.2 Topic Signatures and Topic Variation

Topic Signatures

The topic-specific context models (i.e., neighborhoods) as constructed by, for instance, Guthrie et al.'s (1991) neighborhoods, above, can be viewed as *topic signatures* of the topic in question. A topic signature can, however, be constructed even without the use of subject codes by generating it (semi-) automatically from a lexical resource and then validating it on topic-specific corpora (Hearst and Schütze 1993).

An extension of this idea is to construct "topics" around individual senses of a word by collecting a number of documents corresponding to this sense. The collected documents then represent a topic out of which a topic signature may be extracted, which in turn corresponds directly to the word sense under investigation.

One such approach is to retrieve relevant documents through Web search engines by defining queries for a particular word sense or WordNet synset (Agirre et al. 2000, 2001). A query consists of a Boolean combination of cue words (extracted from the synset, its gloss, available hypernyms, hyponyms, etc.) that restrict the search to only those documents that are most relevant to the particular word sense.

For instance, the following query can be defined for the first WordNet 1.6 sense of *boy*:

(boy   AND (altar boy OR ball boy OR ... OR male person)
     AND NOT (man OR ... OR broth of a boy OR
          son OR ... OR mama's boy OR black)

Table 10.3. Top ten words for three senses of *boy* in WordNet 1.6.

Sense 1 (*male child, boy, child*)		Sense 2 ('informal reference to a man')		Sense 3 (*son, boy*)	
Score	Word	Score	Word	Score	Word
43.14	*male*	35.00	*exboyfriend*	72.14	*mamma's*
33.47	*sonny*	31.89	*womaniser*	70.76	*esau*
29.41	*ball*	24.23	*womanizer*	69.65	*man-child*
27.85	*laddie*	23.71	*ex-husband*	54.17	*mama's*
25.57	*schoolboy*	23.30	*eunuch*	50.59	*offspring*
21.26	*sirrah*	19.98	*galoot*	49.56	*male*
18.91	*ploughboy*	18.84	*divorced*	29.85	*jnr*
16.35	*adult*	18.02	*philanderer*	27.76	*mother's*
14.23	*altar*	16.88	*strapper*	12.73	*female*
13.61	*bat*	13.98	*geezer*	6.35	*chromosome*

By submitting the query to a search engine, a number of documents are retrieved from which a list of the most relevant words for this word sense is generated. Table 10.3 gives the top ten relevant words for the first three senses of *boy* (using the WordNet 1.6 topic signature web-interface (Agirre and Lopez de Lacalle 2004)).[6] Although results are mixed, a rough signature for the senses can be recognized from this list, corresponding to the use of the word *boy* in different topics.

Topic Variation

Constructing topic signatures corresponding to particular senses assumes that a predominant sense can be identified for a given topic or domain. This may be true for clearly ambiguous words (i.e., in the case of homonymy). For instance, *sentence* will be dominant in the judicial sense in the law domain and in the syntactic sense in the linguistics domain. However, for words with related senses (i.e., in the case of systematic polysemy; see for instance Buitelaar (1998)) the topic signatures will overlap, as with the results on *boy* in sense 1 ('young male person') and sense 3 ('son').

In fact, this idea has also been investigated from a different angle in reaction to Gale et al.'s (1992) one-sense-per-discourse heuristic (see Chap. 5 (Sect. 5.5.2)). Krovetz (1998) demonstrated that many words have overlapping senses that will be used simultaneously throughout one discourse.

---

[6] http://ixa3.si.ehu.es/cgi-bin/signatureak/signature.cgi

The main question that then remains is what exactly constitutes a semantic space?

Some indication of this is given by sense disambiguation results that involve a variation of topic. More specifically, we can observe some effects of topic variation by training a sense disambiguation system on one topic and applying it to another. For instance, training on the *Wall Street Journal* while testing on Semcor and vice versa shows a degradation of 12% and 19% in precision, respectively (Escudero et al. 2000). On the other hand, applying context information (collocations) extracted from the *Wall Street Journal* to a financial text in Semcor shows significantly higher precision than on texts in other domains in Semcor (Martínez and Agirre 2000).These results therefore suggest that a semantic space corresponds to a larger or smaller chunk of text (a corpus, a text, or a text segment) with a homogeneous distribution of senses and corresponding collocations.

10.2.3 Domain Tuning

As shown by the *boy* example (Fig. 10.3), the WordNet senses of this word do not easily line up with an empirically-derived set of topics. In fact, this is indicative of a more fundamental problem of using a general (not domain-specific) sense inventory such as WordNet.

> The usual scenario ... has been that the word senses are taken from a general purpose dictionary, ... whereas the material to be disambiguated is ... Wall Street Journal. ... So, the profiles [signatures] ... will be for general English senses according to the WSJ ... (Kilgarriff 1998:5).

Therefore, a general sense inventory needs to be tuned to the domain at hand, which involves selecting only those senses that are most appropriate to the domain (Basili et al. 1997, Cucchiarelli and Velardi 1998, Turcato et al. 2000, Buitelaar and Sacaleanu 2001), as well as extending the sense inventory with novel terms (Buitelaar and Sacaleanu 2002, Vossen 2001) and novel senses, specific to the domain.

In the next two sections, we will take a closer look at two approaches to the tuning of a general sense inventory to particular domains. The first approach empirically defines the most appropriate set of higher-level synsets in the WordNet hierarchy, which in turn directs the elimination of lower-level synsets (i.e., senses). The second approach instead defines the set of appropriate synsets based on the lowest (i.e., sense) level. Given the difference in direction, we call the first approach top-down and the second bottom-up.

Top-Down Domain Tuning

According to Cucchiarelli and Velardi's (1998) method, a domain-specific sense inventory that is balanced (i.e., that has an even distribution of words to senses) and at the right level of abstraction (i.e., trading off ambiguity versus generalization) can be selected automatically given the following criteria: generality, discrimination power, domain coverage, and average ambiguity.

Applying these criteria in a quantitative way to WordNet and a given domain-specific corpus, the method automatically selects a set of relevant "categories" (i.e., groups of synsets). The method starts by applying the Hearst and Schütze (1993) algorithm for empirically determining alternative balanced sets of synsets, where each set represents a category. This algorithm applies a recursive function that groups synsets into categories according to the inheritance structure of WordNet. The algorithm uses preset upper and lower bounds for category inclusion. As long as a category is small enough (i.e., under the upper-bound) synsets may be assigned to it.

After the categories have been determined, a scoring function is applied in order to decide the alternative set of categories that is the most relevant one for the domain at hand. The scoring function takes the four criteria mentioned above as performance factors into account. For instance, the generality of a higher-level synset C_i can be expressed as $1/DM(C_i)$, in which $DM(C_i)$ represents the average distance between the set C_i and the top-level synsets. Similar performance factors for the other three criteria are defined.

To illustrate the method, consider the set of categories shown in Table 10.4 that was selected for the financial domain on the basis of the *Wall Street Journal* corpus. Given this set of higher-level synsets, only those senses that are subsumed by these will be maintained in the tuned (domain-specific) sense inventory. For instance, for the word *stock*, only 5 out of 16 senses are kept, as shown in Tables 10.5 and 10.6.

Bottom-Up Domain Tuning

The above method uses a top-down approach that propagates the domain relevance of higher-level synsets down through the WordNet hierarchy. A somewhat different approach would be to assign a domain relevance to each word sense directly. Buitelaar and Sacaleanu's (2001) method determines

Table 10.4. Categories for the financial domain, based on the *Wall Street Journal*.

Category	Higher-level synset
C_1	*person, individual, someone, mortal, human, soul*
C_2	*instrumentality, instrumentation*
C_3	*written communication, written language*
C_4	*message, content, subject matter, substance*
C_5	*measure, quantity, amount, quantum*
C_6	*action*
C_7	*activity*
C_8	*group action*
C_9	*organization*
C_{10}	*psychological feature*
C_{11}	*possession*
C_{12}	*state*
C_{13}	*location*

Table 10.5. Senses for stock (kept by domain tuning on the *Wall Street Journal*).

Sense	Synset hierarchy for sense	Top synset for sense
1	*capital > asset*	*possession* (C_{11})
2	*support > device*	*instrumentality* (C_2)
4	*document > writing*	*written communication* (C_3)
5	*accumulation > asset*	*possession* (C_{11})
6	*ancestor > relative*	*person* (C_1)

Table 10.6. Senses for stock (discarded by domain tuning on the *Wall Street Journal*).

Sense	Synset hierarchy for sense
3	*stock, inventory > merchandise, wares >…*
7	*broth, stock > soup > …*
8	*stock, caudex > stalk, stem > …*
9	*stock > plant part > …*
10	*stock, gillyflower > flower > …*
11	*malcolm stock, stock > flower …*
12	*lineage, line of descent > … > genealogy > …*
14	*lumber, timber > …*

(1)   for each word W_1 in WordNet *WN*
(2)   for each synset S of which W_1 is a member
(3)   for each synonym W_2 in synset S, compute domain relevance
               score of W_2 in domain corpus *DC*
(4)   compute domain relevance score for S over all W_2
(5)   assign S with the highest score to each occurrence of W_1 in *DC*
           (or similar corpora in the same domain)

Fig. 10.2. WSD algorithm with bottom-up domain tuning (Buitelaar and Sacaleanu 2001).

the domain-specific relevance of synsets on the basis of the relevance of their constituent synonyms that co-occur within domain-specific corpora. Fig. 10.2 shows the algorithm: first the domain relevance of each of the synonyms in a synset is computed and then this information is used to compute the cumulative relevance of each synset.

The relevance measure used in this process is a slightly adapted version of standard *tf.idf*, as used in vector-space models of information retrieval (Salton and Buckley 1988):

$$relevance(t \mid d) = \log(tf_{t,d}) \log|N/df_t| \qquad (10.2)$$

where t represents the term, d the domain-specific corpus, N the total number of domain-specific corpora taken into account (instead of comparing term frequency between documents as in the traditional use of *tf.idf*, here we compare term frequency between domain-specific corpora; *tf* and *df* are term frequency and document/corpus frequency). This formula gives full weight to terms that occur in just one domain (i.e., domain-specific corpus) and zero to those occurring in all.

Given term relevance, one can now compute the relevance of each synset. This is simply the sum of the relevance of each term in the synset, which may be defined as follows:

$$relevance(c \mid d) = \sum_{t \in c} relevance(t \mid d) \qquad (10.3)$$

where c is a synset.

To increase the number of terms to be found within a domain-specific corpus, a given synset may be extended with its hyponyms as these are often directly related (e.g., *cell* expanded with *dungeon* or *blastomere*). Adding hyponyms changes the relevance formula accordingly:

$$relevance(c'\,|\,d) = \sum_{t \in c'} \frac{T}{|c'|} relevance(t\,|\,d) \qquad (10.4)$$

where c' is the extended synset and T is the number of synonyms in the synset that are found in the domain-specific corpus.

In order to assess the correctness of this method an experiment would need to show two points: 1) How well the method selects domain-specific concepts, and 2) How well the most specific sense (synset) is selected for domain-specific terms. On the first point, Buitelaar and Sacaleanu (2001) report experiments that achieve an accuracy of 80% to 90% for three domains (Financial, Soccer, and Medical). On the second point, different results for different domains were obtained. Out of 24 terms in the Medical domain, 12 had at least one sense that is specific to the domain, all of which were determined correctly. For the Financial domain, 6 out of 17 terms had at least one domain-specific sense, of which 5 were determined correctly. For the Soccer domain, there were 6 out of 8 terms of which 5 were determined correctly. These results indicate a consistently accurate selection of domain-specific senses.

In similar work, McCarthy et al. (2004) report an approach in which they use untagged domain-specific corpora to determine predominant senses for corresponding domains. Their method produced a 64% precision on sense disambiguation of nouns with WordNet on the Senseval-2 English all-word task (see Chap. 6 (Sect. 6.1.2)).

10.3 Domain-Specific Disambiguation in Applications

Sense disambiguation is a subtask within more comprehensive applications, such as machine translation, document classification, and information retrieval. Therefore should evaluate sense disambiguation not only in a standalone fashion, but also as part of such applications, and this especially pertinent for domain-specific WSD. In this section we take a closer look at the use of some of the above approaches to domain-specific WSD in the context of particular applications. See Chapter 10 for a broader discussion of the applications.

10.3.1 User-Modeling for Recommender Systems

Despite its popularity in the computational linguistics community, Word-Net (and many other lexical resources) is still scarcely used in real

NLP-based applications. One reason for this is that the granularity of sense distinctions makes it hard to use in WSD. The problem is being addressed from the following two converging directions. From the resource side, WordNet can be extended, for instance, by adding information on clusters of similar senses (see Sect. 10.2.3 above and Chap. 4 on verb groups). From the application side, it is important to select scenarios where the loss of sense granularity is not crucial, but the benefits of a sense-based approach are still significant.

An attempt in the latter direction is SiteIF (Magnini and Strapparava 2004), a document recommendation, a form of document classification, system for a multilingual news website where the introduction of a sense-based analysis of the documents had positive effects. The system exploits a sense-based document representation as a starting point to build a model of the user's interests. Documents passed over are processed and relevant senses are extracted and then combined to form a semantic network. A filtering procedure dynamically predicts new documents on the basis of the semantic network. There are two main advantages of a sense-based approach: first, the model's predictions, based on senses rather than words, are more accurate; second, the user model is language independent, allowing navigation in multilingual sites.

SiteIF uses the Domain Driven Disambiguation (DDD) algorithm, above, as its WSD component. The sense-based approach was compared against a pure word-based approach, resulting both in better precision (+ 34%) and in better recall (+ 15%) in document prediction. Because of the DDD method, the algorithm shows good performance particularly in the disambiguation of words that are related to the relevant domain of a text. The gain in overall performance shows that achieving high precision on this class of words is important for effective user-modeling systems, where there is a need for high quality (i.e., precision) recommendations. On the other hand, low recall does not seem to be a serious drawback for a pure recommender system, where there is no need to answer an explicit query (as is required, for instance, in a standard information retrieval system).

10.3.2 Cross-Lingual Information Retrieval

Sail-Labs Antwerp applied a domain-based disambiguation to the Hewlett-Packard document collection (Vossen 2001). Sail-Labs had a multilingual semantic network built around WordNet 1.5 and linked to a domain hierarchy of 750 concepts. The domain hierarchy was used to disambiguate the senses, much as described in Section 10.2.1 for the WordNet Domains.

The complete document set was used to calculate the dominant domains. First, only concepts from the dominant domains were accepted and, second, concepts of the hypernyms of these domain concepts were accepted even if these did not have a domain relation. In the latter case, for instance, a particular sense of *system* was preferred because it dominated domain concepts even though it did not have a domain-related meaning. Other words without domain-related senses were not expanded. In doing so, it was assumed that words are used in the same sense throughout the document collection, a much stronger heuristic than one-sense-per-discourse. As this work relies on homogeneous domains, the heuristic may still be valid.

The disambiguation was used to derive a trimmed wordnet from the generic wordnet[7] that only contained the relevant concepts and was extended with all the extracted terminology. This trimmed wordnet was used in a cross-retrieval test environment and compared with the generic wordnet and no wordnet.

The mono- and cross-lingual information retrieval experiments were carried out on the same set of 26,260 English HTML documents from which the terminology was extracted. A set of 100 English queries based on logged user queries was used. The queries were translated into Dutch and French by native speakers. The best matching document was selected manually. The following two types of retrieval runs were carried out.

- **Literal:** Query terms are directly matched with the English index terms.
  - **EN:** Unexpanded English queries to English documents.
  - **FR:** Untranslated French queries to English documents.
  - **NL:** Untranslated Dutch queries to English documents.
- **Query expansion:** Query terms are first expanded to synonyms or translations. Two different methods of expansion have been applied:
  - **All meanings:** The complete wordnet database was used with all word meanings; no disambiguation was applied to trim the database.
  - **Trimmed:** The wordnet database was trimmed after disambiguation and extended with terminology; disambiguation was applied.

Each of the query expansion methods was applied for the three languages, where the amount of expansion differs:

- **EN:** Expanded English queries to English documents; expansion with synonyms.

---

[7] The term "wordnet", in lowercase, indicates any WordNet-like database rather than English WordNet itself.

Table 10.7. Retrieval results with trimmed and general multilingual wordnets.

Retrieval run	EN	FR	NL
Literal queries	89.6%	39.9%	43.6%
Query expansion – All meanings (no WSD)	82.4	54.2	54.3
Query expansion – Trimmed (WSD)	86.4	65.4	61.7

- **NL:** Dutch queries translated to English and expanded with synonyms.
- **FR:** French queries translated to English and expanded with synonyms.

Table 10.7 shows the results. The baseline is represented by the first row, where there is no query expansion or translation. The baseline for mono-lingual retrieval (the EN column) consisted of matching literal English queries to English documents. This resulted in 89.6% recall as an average score, where the intended result in the first ten was considered to be correct. Only a single result was considered correct. We did not evaluate appropriateness of the other results. Using synonyms for all meanings decreases the English monolingual retrieval to 82.4%. This is due to the fact that less precise synonyms were introduced, which tends to have a negative effect in specialized documents. Disambiguation improves this by 4% to 86.4%. This suggests that expansion with synonyms after disambiguation is useful if non-literal queries are expected.

A stronger effect can be seen for cross-lingual retrieval. Here the baseline is to match the French and Dutch queries directly with the English index (the first row, columns FR and NL respectively). Obviously, this gives poor results: 39.9% and 43.6%. It still works a little bit because of the specific terminology that is the same in all three languages. Taking translations for all meanings increases retrieval to about 54% and disambiguation improves on that to 65.4% for French and 61.7% for Dutch.

These experiments clearly showed that WSD has a positive effect in cross-lingual retrieval and only a small negative impact on mono-lingual retrieval. The latter is not as bad as it seems, since the queries were rather technical and did not show much variation in the usage of synonyms. Another advantage of domain disambiguation is that the trimming could be done for the complete domain. A small domain-specific wordnet (about 10% of the size) makes query expansion and index expansion much faster without loss of precision. Finally, we believe that WSD up to the domain level avoids trying to choose between very specific and fine-grained senses that do not make a difference for the application.

10.3.3 The MEANING Project

A more recent and similar study (Vossen et al. 2006) has been carried out in the MEANING project[8] on English and Spanish news collections. For English, part of the Reuters news collection was used (23,307 articles), and for Spanish, a database from the EFE News Agency with news pictures and captions (26,546 articles). Domain-based disambiguation is expected to be more difficult for these databases because the language in news articles is more general.

The project used the TwentyOne retrieval system developed by Irion Technologies (Delft, the Netherlands). Disambiguation was applied in a similar way as above by assigning the proper WordNet domain labels to the text and selecting concepts within the domains, if applicable. All concepts or selected concepts were expanded with synonyms or translations from a multilingual WordNet database. The difference to the Sail-Labs experiment is that here the indexes, instead of the queries, were translated to other languages, with synonym expansion. Furthermore, noun phrases (NPs), automatically extracted from the indexed documents, that showed a clear ambiguity were selected as queries. These English and Spanish queries were translated to the other languages for cross-lingual retrieval and we also generated (English and Spanish) queries with synonyms for non-literal mono-lingual retrieval (e.g., *mobile* to search for *cell phone* and *jail* to search for *police cell*).

The system ran the queries against the corresponding language-indexes, where the English index (Reuters) and Spanish index (EFE) were expanded with synonyms and the other language-indexes with translations (and synonyms). Three variants of the indexes were used:

- Literal indexes based on the literal words in the text,
- Indexes with WordNet expansion and translation based on all meanings, and
- Indexes with WordNet expansion and translation with disambiguated meanings.

Queries were matched against document pages. Retrieval was measured in terms of recall by checking whether the document from which the NP originated was listed in the first 10 results. The results are shown in Table 10.8. As above (Sect. 10.3.2), literal queries applied to the literal index

---

[8] The MEANING project: Developing Multilingual Web-scale Language Technologies, was funded by the European Union's 5th Framework IST Programme as IST-2001-34460.

Table 10.8. Retrieval results on the Reuters news collection in the MEANING project.

Index variant	English Literal queries	English Paraphrased queries	Cross-lingual
Literal	79%	25%	7%
Expansion (no WSD)	64	29	32
Expansion (WSD)	71	31	28

perform the best: 79% recall. Literal queries applied to expanded indexes had a recall of 64% without disambiguation and 71% with disambiguation. For paraphrased queries, the recall for the literal index dropped to 25%, and expanded indexes dropped to 29% (no disambiguation) and 31% (with disambiguation). There was some advantage in the disambiguated index compared to the non-disambiguated index, both for literal (+7%) and paraphrased queries (+2%). In general, we can say that less noise is introduced by the disambiguated indexes.

The project also applied a cross-lingual test using Dutch, German, French, Spanish, and English translations of the queries, applied to the corresponding translated indexes. Column 4 of Table 10.8 gives the average of the results on these languages. Clearly, the results were very poor on the literal index because the English words were copied to the language indexes. Translated indexes without disambiguation gave best results: 32% compared to 28% for the disambiguated expansion. Thus, the advantage of disambiguation disappeared in the cross-lingual context.

A possible explanation for the small differences between the disambiguated and non-disambiguated expansion is that page-retrieval is relatively robust to the noise that is introduced by the synonym/translation expansion. This robustness can be formulated as follows: wrong words are added to the index, but the combination of wrong words is unlikely to be used in a query or is not consistent enough to push out good results from the first 10 results. Apparently, disambiguation does not remove enough noise to show a significant difference.

Based on this analysis, the similarity measurement for matching queries was adapted for the experiments on the Spanish news captions in the EFE corpus. Queries were treated as phrases and compared with the NPs rather than the complete page. It was expected that NPs should be more robust to noisy expansion than pages. Here, the literal indexes were Spanish and MEANING's wordnets were to for the expansion. The languages for the cross-lingual retrieval were English, Catalan, Basque, and Italian.

Table 10.9. Retrieval results on the EFE news collection in the MEANING project.

Index variant	Spanish Literal Queries	Spanish Paraphrased Queries	Cross-lingual
Literal	**94%**	**15%**	**2%**
Precision in first position	57	1	1
Expansion (no WSD)	**91**	**76**	**47**
Precision in first position	52	4	25
Expansion (WSD)	**92**	**65**	**44**
Precision in first position	57	41	28

The results are shown in Table 10.9. In general, we see that the recall for the literal Spanish queries on the literal index was very high: 94%, despite the general news language. We also see that the expanded indexes (both non-disambiguated and disambiguated) did not suffer much compared to the literal index. Both the high recall in general and the fact that the noise is apparently not harmful could be the result of matching queries with NPs instead of queries with pages. The NP context is thus more noise-robust.

In the case of paraphrased Spanish queries, the results for the literal index dropped dramatically, even more than in the Reuters experiment. Again this is due to NP-based retrieval: paraphrases might occur on the same page but not likely in the same NP. We also see that the recall results for expanded indexes are still good for paraphrased indexes but are better for the non-disambiguated index: 76% versus 65%, as expected since NPs are noise-robust. As above, column 4 shows the average cross-lingual result over English, Catalan, Basque, and Italian.

To get a better insight into the precision of the result, the intermediate rows show the proportion of NPs retrieved in the first (i.e., top) position. Disambiguation thus leads to better results than both the literal and the non-disambiguated indexes. This means that the noise reduction is effective.

To corroborate this result, a separate task-oriented evaluation was carried out by EFE, in order to demonstrate the better precision afforded by disambiguated indexes. A number of testers from EFE were asked to use the three systems to find pictures for news articles based on the captions in the database. The task was described using words that exhibit ambiguity or synonymy with the indexed words. The testers were free to use the search engine in their search. The system showed the first 10 results on the direct result page, where the results were ranked by the best matching NP. The experiments showed that pictures were found twice as fast with the disambiguated system compared to the literal index, and 12.5% faster compared to the non-disambiguated system. With all three systems, the testers could find a correct picture but with the disambiguated system they needed fewer searches and they had to verify fewer results.

Concluding, the MEANING project applied domain-based disambiguation to news language, a more general genre of text. Although recall was not improved by disambiguation, precision in the first position had a significant improvement. The problem of retrieval and disambiguation can be defined as a noise-reduction problem, which can be seen as another way of approaching a more well-defined semantic-space.

10.4 Conclusions

In this chapter a number of approaches to sense disambiguation were presented that take the wider semantic space of ambiguous words into account. Taking this idea to an extreme would imply modeling this semantic space as the first priority in word sense disambiguation. Several arguments might be raised against such a view.

First of all, it would drive us back to earlier methods that were not very robust and required major efforts in adapting to new domains. However, as a counter-argument, there are now many robust methods (based on machine-learning) for lexical acquisition, which would allow for a rapid adaptation of semantic resources to a new domain.

A second main issue would be that, from an evaluation point of view, it is important to evaluate the performance of different algorithms, independent of a specific domain or application. As a counter-argument here, one can ask what such an evaluation proves. Sense disambiguation evaluated without a particular (application) domain can only show an artificial result, which is hard to interpret and generalize from (see Chaps. 4 and 11 for more discussion on this point).

In summary, it seems worthwhile to focus WSD research more directly on domain-specific approaches as this is required from an application point of view and at the same time allows for more robust, unsupervised methods. Currently, the most active domain-specific application area for WSD seems to be in bioinformatics (Liu et al. 2004, Schuemie et al. 2005). On the other hand, recent work on general WSD has successfully taken up the idea of using domains as an important feature for disambiguation (Novischi 2004, Montoyo et al. 2005, Koeling et al. 2005, Gliozzo et al. 2005).

References

Agirre, Eneko, Olatz Ansa, Eduard Hovy & David Martínez. 2000. Enriching very large ontologies using the WWW. *Proceedings of the Ontology Learning Workshop, European Conference on Artificial Intelligence (ECAI)*, Berlin, Germany.

Agirre, Eneko, Olatz Ansa, David Martínez & Eduard Hovy. 2001. Enriching WordNet concepts with topic signatures. *Proceedings of the NAACL Workshop on WordNet and Other Lexical Resources*, Pittsburgh, PA.

Agirre, Eneko & Oier Lopez de Lacalle. 2004. Publicly available topic signatures for all WordNet nominal senses. *Proceedings of the 4rd International Conference on Language Resources and Evaluations (LREC)*. Lisbon, Portugal.

Basili, Roberto, Michelangelo Della Rocca & Maria-Theresa Pazienza. 1997. Contextual word sense tuning and disambiguation. *Applied Artificial Intelligence*, 11:235–262.

Buitelaar, Paul. 1998. *CoreLex: Systematic Polysemy and Underspecification.* Ph.D. Thesis, Brandeis University.

Buitelaar, Paul & Bogdan Sacaleanu. 2001. Ranking and selecting synsets by domain relevance. *Proceedings of the Workshop on WordNet and Other Lexical Resources*, Pittsburgh, PA.

Buitelaar, Paul & Bogdan Sacaleanu. 2002. Extending synsets with medical terms. *Proceedings of the First International WordNet Conference*, Mysore, India.

Cucchiarelli, Alessandro & Paola Velardi. 1998. Finding a domain-appropriate sense inventory for semantically tagging a corpus. *Natural Language Engineering*, 4(4): 325–344.

Escudero, Gerard, Lluis Màrquez & German Rigau. 2000. An empirical study of the domain dependence of supervised word sense disambiguation systems. *Proceedings of Joint SIGDAT Conference on Empirical Methods in Natural Language Processing and Very Large Corpora (EMNLP/VLC)*, Hong Kong, China.

Gale, William, Kenneth Church & David Yarowsky. 1992. One sense per discourse. *Proceedings of the 4th DARPA Speech and Natural Language Workshop*, 233–237.

Gliozzo, Alfio, Bernardo Magnini & Carlo Strapparava. 2004a. Unsupervised domain relevance for word sense disambiguation. *Proceedings of the 2004 Conference on Empirical Methods in Natural Language Processing (EMNLP)*, Barcelona, Spain, 380–387.

Gliozzo, Alfio, Carlo Strapparava & Ido Dagan. 2004b. Unsupervised and supervised exploitation of semantic domains in lexical disambiguation. *Computer Speech and Language*, 18(3): 275–299.

Gliozzo, Alfio, Claudio Giuliano & Carlo Strapparava, 2005. Domain kernels for word sense disambiguation, *Proceedings of the 43rd Annual Meeting of the Association for Computational Linguistics (ACL)*, Ann Arbor, Michigan, 403–410.

Hearst, Marti & Hinrich Schütze. 1993. Customizing a lexicon to better suit a computational task. *Proceedings of the ACL SIGLEX Workshop on the Acquisition of Lexical Knowledge from Text.*

Guthrie, Joe A., Louise Guthrie, Yorick Wilks & Homa Aidinejad. 1991. Subject dependent co-occurrence and word sense disambiguation. *Proceedings of the 29th Annual Meeting of the Association for Computational Linguistics*, 146–152.

Kilgarriff, Adam. 1998. Bridging the gap between lexicon and corpus: Convergence of formalisms. *Proceedings of LREC Workshop on Adapting Lexical Resources to Sublanguages and Applications*, Granada, Spain.

Koeling, Rob, Diana McCarthy & John Carroll. 2005. Domain-specific sense distributions and predominant sense acquisition. *Proceedings of the Human Language Technology Conference and Conference on Empirical Methods in Natural Language Processing (HLT/EMNLP)*, 419–426.

Krovetz, Robert. 1998. *More than one sense per discourse.* Research Memorandum, NEC Labs America, Princeton, NJ.

Lesk, Michael. 1986. Automated sense disambiguation using machine-readable dictionaries: How to tell a pine cone from an ice cream cone. *Proceedings of the 1986 ACM SIGDOC Conference*, Toronto, Canada, 24–26.

Liu, H, Teller, V. & Friedman, C. 2004. A multi-aspect comparison study of supervised word sense disambiguation. *Journal of the American Medical Informatics Association*, 11(4): 320–31.

Magnini, Bernardo & Gabriela Cavaglià. 2000. Integrating subject field codes into WordNet. *Proceedings of the Second International Conference Language Resources and Evaluation Conference (LREC)*, Athens, Greece, 1413–1418.

Magnini, Bernardo, Carlo Strapparava, Giovanni Pezzulo & Alfio Gliozzo. 2002. The role of domain information in word sense disambiguation. *Natural Language Engineering*, 8(4): 359–373.

Magnini, Bernardo & Carlo Strapparava. 2004. User modeling for news web sites with word sense based techniques. *User Modeling and User-Adapted Interaction*, 14: (2–3): 239–257.

Martínez, David & Eneko Agirre. 2000. One sense per collocation and genre/topic variations. *Proceedings of Joint SIGDAT Conference on Empirical Methods in Natural Language Processing and Very Large Corpora (EMNLP/VLC)*, Hong Kong, China.

McCarthy, Diana, Rob Koeling, Julie Weeds & John Carroll. 2004. Finding predominant senses in untagged text. *Proceedings of the 42nd Annual Meeting of the Association for Computational Linguistics*. Barcelona, Spain, 280–287.

Montoyo, Andres, Armando Suarez, German Rigau, Manuel Palomar. 2005. Combining knowledge- and corpus-based word sense disambiguation methods. *Journal of Artificial Intelligence Research*, 23: 299–330.

Novischi, Adrian 2004. Combining methods for word sense disambiguation of WordNet glosses. *Proceedings of FLAIRS 2004*, Florida.

Peh, Li Shiuan & Hwee Tou Ng. 1997. Domain-specific semantic class disambiguation using wordNet. *Proceedings of the Fifth Workshop on Very Large Corpora*. Beijing & Hong Kong, 56–64.

Procter, Paul, ed. 1978. *Longman Dictionary of Contemporary English*. London: Longman Group.

Redner, Richard A. & Homer F. Walker, 1984. Mixture densities, maximum likelihood and the EM algorithm. *SIAM Review*, 26(2): 195–236.

Salton, Gerard & Chris Buckley. 1988. Term-weighting approaches in automatic text retrieval. *Information Processing and Management*, 24(5): 513–523.

Schuemie, M. J., Kors, J. A. & Mons, B. 2005. Word sense disambiguation in the biomedical domain: An overview. *Journal Computational Biology*, 12(5): 554–65.

Stevenson, Mark & Yorick Wilks. 2001. The interaction of knowledge sources in word sense disambiguation. *Computational Linguistics*, 27(3): 321–349.

Turcato, David, Fred Popowich, Janine Toole, Dan Fass, Devlan Nicholson & Gordon Tisher. 2002. Adapting a synonym database to specific domains. *Proceedings of the ACL Workshop on Recent Advances in Natural Language Processing and Information Retrieval*, Hong Kong.

Vossen, Piek. 2001. Extending, trimming and fusing WordNet for technical documents. *Proceedings of the Workshop on WordNet and Other Lexical Resources*, Pittsburgh, PA.

Vossen, Piek, German Rigau, Iñaki Alegria, Eneko Agirre, David Farwell & Manuel Fuentes. 2006. Meaningful results for information retrieval in the MEANING project. *Proceedings of the 3rd Global Wordnet Conference*, Jeju Island, Korea.

Yarowsky, David. 1992. Word sense disambiguation using statistical models of Roget's categories trained on large corpora. *Proceedings of the 14th International Conference on Computational Linguistic (COLING)*, Nantes, France, 454–460.

Walker, Don & Robert Amsler. 1986. The use of machine readable dictionaries in sublanguage analysis. *Analyzing Language in Restricted Domains*, ed. by Ralph Grishman & Richard Kittredge, 69–83, Hillsdale, NJ: Erlbaum.

11 WSD in NLP Applications

Philip Resnik

University of Maryland

When is word sense disambiguation useful in practice? This chapter considers applications of word sense disambiguation in language technology, looking at established and emerging applications and at more and less traditional conceptions of the task.

11.1 Introduction

In discussing the role of word sense disambiguation in natural language processing, it is helpful to make the distinction between an *enabling technology* and an *application*. An enabling technology produces a result that is not useful by itself; an application performs a task that has direct value to the end user, to which an enabling technology can contribute. To take an everyday example, an electricity adapter converting between 220 volts and 110 volts is an enabling technology, since by itself it has no direct connection with a user's needs. Its value emerges in combination with a larger application of technology, such as an electric razor that works in both the United States and Europe. As Agirre and Edmonds (Chapter 1) point out, word sense disambiguation (WSD) is an enabling technology, as are other common NLP tasks like part-of-speech tagging and parsing. These can be distinguished from language applications like machine translation and the automatic transcription of speech.

A voltage converter has a well defined task: converting electric current from N volts to M volts within some clearly specified tolerance. This task is the same whether the converter is used with an electric razor, an espresso maker, or a television set. In contrast, there is no universally accepted characterization of the WSD "task", and in fact it has been argued

E. Agirre and P. Edmonds (eds.), Word Sense Disambiguation: Algorithms and Applications, 299–337.
© 2007 *Springer*.

that defining WSD in an application-independent way makes little sense (see Chap. 2). In this chapter on applications, therefore, I begin in Section 11.2 with the basic question of why people believe WSD should matter in applications at all. In Sections 11.3 and 11.4, I consider how different conceptions of word sense relate to a variety of specific applications, and in Section 10.5 I briefly summarize and conclude with prospects for the future.

11.2 Why WSD?

Why *do* so many NLP researchers and developers remain convinced that WSD *should* matter in NLP applications? There seem to be three main species of argument.

Argument from Faith

A belief in the importance of WSD for applications is a part of the canon in natural language processing. It is passed from teacher to student and easily accepted on intuitive grounds – it just seems obvious that if *bank* can refer to either a financial institution or a riverbank, a search engine query *must* be more likely to pull back the wrong documents, an MT system *must* be more likely to arrive at the wrong translation, and so forth, unless the intended meaning of the word is picked from an enumerated list of the meanings it can have. Ide and Véronis (1998:1), in their valuable overview of sense disambiguation and its history, begin by saying that WSD is "obviously essential for language understanding applications such as message understanding, man-machine communication, etc." and "at least helpful, and in some instances required" for applications such as machine translation and information retrieval where deep understanding may not be the goal. Like many firmly held beliefs, this idea is supported by widely quoted scriptural references, most notably Bar-Hillel's (1960) famous "the box is in the pen" example, where it is taken as self evident that accurate translation of this sentence requires distinguishing among explicit senses of *pen* ('writing utensil' versus 'enclosure where small children play').[1]

---

[1] The example is strained for speakers of American English, where the unambiguous *playpen* would have to be used. Surprisingly, given the example's longevity, British informants find it unnatural also.

Common as this argument is, it must be viewed with suspicion. If presented without further support, it is nothing more than a variant of what Dawkins (1986) terms the "argument from personal incredulity", which is to say, a claim that something must be the case because one cannot imagine it being otherwise.[2]

The problem of word sense ambiguity has been a central concern since the earliest days of computing – Hutchins (1997) quotes a 1949 letter from Warren Weaver to Norbert Wiener on the question of machine translation, in which he refers to "the semantic difficulties because of multiple meanings." And yet, central though it still is in many people's minds, the facts remain that (a) explicit word sense disambiguation plays very little role in many current NLP applications, and (b) NLP applications are making fine progress anyway. Those facts suggest that rather than taking the importance of WSD for granted, its role in applications is worth examining.

Although Bar-Hillel refers specifically to machine translation, his example illustrates a common view of sense disambiguation more generally. It is widely believed that ultimate success in language processing – human-quality performance on language-related tasks – will eventually require deeper, explicit semantic interpretation that relies on enumerating and explicitly choosing among the senses of words. While it certainly does seem plausible that *distinguishing* word meanings in context would be a requirement for human-like NLP, it is not clear that this requires a process that presupposes "*determination of* all the different senses for every word" or which needs to "assign each occurrence of a word to *the* appropriate sense" (Ide and Véronis 1998:3, my emphases).

Argument by Analogy

The path of language technology development over the last two decades presents a tremendous challenge to the traditional breakdown of NLP into problems of morphological analysis, syntactic parsing, word sense disambiguation, logical-form semantic representation, discourse analysis, and so forth. Enabling technologies designed to solve those problems have played very little role in the most visible successes of human language technology for end users, such as the commercial viability of automatic speech recognition, the ubiquity of spell checking, or the incorporation of Web text retrieval into everyday life. Those achievements derive largely from

---

[2] Bar-Hillel also makes an argument from personal incredulity when he dismisses the idea of equipping an MT system with "a dictionary [and] also with a universal encyclopedia" as "utterly chimerical" (Bar-Hillel 1960, quoted by Hutchins 1999).

linguistically shallow techniques such as n-gram and Hidden Markov Modeling, stemming, co-occurrence-based feature vector representations, and the like. We have learned that it is possible to accomplish a huge amount using shallow methods rather than creating and manipulating linguistically deeper representations.[3]

On the other hand, the language technology community is discovering that some forms of linguistic depth *can* make a difference, notably syntactic structure, and one could argue by analogy that this bodes well for WSD. As one good example, Chelba and Jelinek (1998) managed to demonstrate (after decades of experience to the contrary) that the use of syntactic structure in stochastic language models can lead to reductions in perplexity and word error rate compared to standard trigram modeling, an advance with potential repercussions for applications such as speech recognition, statistical MT, and optical character recognition. Other examples include Kumar and Byrne (2002), who showed that a syntactic measure of lexical distance can be used to improve the performance of stochastic word-alignment models for machine translation; Microsoft Word, which has for some years incorporated grammar checking based on syntactic parsing; and recent success applying synchronous context-free parsing in machine translation (Chiang 2005).

These developments do provide something of a response to the suggestion that linguistically better-informed methods have little to contribute to applications in general. However, including WSD in this response has two weaknesses. First, the argument really cannot be made without identifying what properties of the linguistic representations had value for the relevant applications, and then making the analogy to WSD clear and explicit. Second, the gains achieved by linguistically better-informed methods have generally not been great enough to change the prevailing wisdom among practitioners – for example, virtually all language modeling in practical applications still uses n-gram models.

Argument from Specific Applications

Ultimately, the value of WSD in applications comes down to a question of specifics: in which applications does it help, and why? Although no application can be cited as an unequivocal success for WSD, there is certainly one widely noted failure: monolingual information retrieval. Given how starkly the results contradict the intuition that word sense disambiguation

---

[3] By "deeper", I mean further removed from the visible surface form, not necessarily more richly elaborated.

should make a difference, monolingual IR is the flagship example for pessimism about WSD's practical potential. WSD is more broadly a focal point for examination of all of NLP's practical utility in IR. Voorhees (1999), for instance, uses negative results involving WSD in IR to illustrate broader insights into problems of exploiting deeper NLP techniques for IR more generally. Voorhees (1999:23) correctly observes that (monolingual) text retrieval "can be viewed as a great success story for natural language processing ... a major industry has been built around the automatic manipulation of unstructured natural language text", but, contrary to Ide and Véronis (1998), this world changing phenomenon has taken place without the use of explicit disambiguation.

Monolingual information retrieval is, however, only one of many applications. Although I have suggested one should be skeptical of the argument from faith and I find the argument by analogy to be of limited value, the argument from specific applications is worth considering more fully. That is the main subject for the remainder of this chapter.

In Sections 11.3 and 11.4, I look in more detail at traditional and less traditional construals of the WSD task, and at current and future NLP applications. Although this exercise does not lead to fresh optimism for traditional WSD in current applications, I will suggest that broader conceptions of the task have potential given the directions in which NLP applications are evolving.

11.3 Traditional WSD in Applications

The most enduring conception of word senses in NLP comes from the lexicographic tradition, where the meanings of words are explicitly enumerated, sometimes being organized into a hierarchical structure, and they are considered to be properties of those words independent of any particular application. In a computational setting, most traditional natural language processing approaches adopt this sort of characterization of word senses as an *a priori* enumeration of discrete (albeit possibly overlapping) meanings, and what I term "traditional WSD" is the problem of selecting one of those meanings.

Kilgarriff (1997) provides an informative discussion of this conceptualization (together with a host of useful references), and his brief synopsis of the traditional conception of the WSD task is worth quoting in its entirety:

> Many words have more than one meaning. When a person understands a sentence with an ambiguous word in it, that understanding is built on the basis of

just one of the meanings. So, as some part of the human language understanding process, the appropriate meaning has been chosen from the range of possibilities. (p. 91)

Although presented as a sub-task of human sentence understanding, rather than a component of language technology, this has been the basic conception of WSD adopted in most NLP applications, as well. Not surprisingly, it has also formed the basis thus far for most tasks in the Senseval evaluation exercises (see Chap. 4).

One might therefore extend Kilgarriff's synopsis of traditional WSD with the following sentence:

> Successful natural language processing applications, therefore, must also pick the correct meaning of a word from that range of possibilities.[4]

11.3.1 WSD in Traditional Information Retrieval

As mentioned above, the traditional characterization of WSD has formed the basis for numerous unsuccessful attempts to gain improvements in IR. The dominant paradigm in IR is based on "bag-of-words" representations: a piece of text is characterized as an unordered collection of terms, and the assessment of a document's relevance in response to a query depends primarily on the terms they have in common. Most intuitively, the terms are the words themselves. In practice, common uninformative words are excluded as terms, and multiple forms of words are mapped down to a single form via stemming – for example, *connect, connects, connecting*, and *connection* would all be stemmed as *connect*. As a result, a query about "connecting my camera" and a document containing "connection of a digital camera" would have terms *connect* and *camera* in common.[5]

Stemming is useful in IR because it helps to treat *connecting* and *connection* as different surface forms for the same essential content. Many attempts to apply WSD in IR have followed from the same basic premise. As an illustrative example, consider Voorhees's (1999) case study investigating WSD in a monolingual IR system. A variant of the usual bag-of-words

---

[4] This is consistent with Ide and Véronis (1998:3), whose characterization of the WSD task "necessarily involves two steps: (1) the determination of all the different senses for every word relevant (at least) to the text or discourse under consideration; and (2) a means to assign each occurrence of a word to the appropriate sense."

[5] See Baeza-Yates & Ribeiro-Neto (1999) for a good introduction to IR.

model for IR, the idea is to go beyond words to a more conceptual representation: for example, if a query or document contains the word *bank*, then its representation contains not only the term *bank* itself, but also the WordNet sense identifier produced by disambiguating *bank* in context. In theory, at least, disambiguating both query and document terms should improve precision by avoiding matches where sense *bank-1* is intended in the query and sense *bank-2* is intended in the document. Disambiguation would also improve recall in cases where the same concept (say, 'a container for holding money') is lexicalized by one word in the query (*bank*) and by a synonym in the document (say, *cash box*). WSD would resolve both to the same sense identifier, and thus it no longer matters that the query and the document express the same idea differently on the surface.

In her study, Voorhees found that WSD hurt quite a bit more than it helped. Her results confirmed Sanderson's (1994) finding that even relatively low error rates for WSD can have fatal effects on information retrieval performance. They also confirmed Krovetz and Croft's (1992) observation that monolingual IR evaluation is a difficult setting in which to seek WSD-based improvements.

Three reasons for this have been widely noted. First, if queries are short, there is extremely limited context available for context-based disambiguation of query terms, which makes WSD difficult. Second, even for words with multiple senses, the most frequent sense often heavily dominates the frequency distribution of the text collection under consideration; in such cases using the word itself is likely to be just as good as correct disambiguation. Third, most document retrieval models exhibit a tendency toward implicit disambiguation of multi-word queries, which helps bag-of-words IR perform well even in the absence of explicit word senses, particularly for longer queries.

As an example of the last of these, consider what happens when the query "*interest bank Fed*" is issued against a document collection where some documents are about finance and others are about rivers. A document about finance is much more likely than a document about riverbanks to contain more than one term from this query. As a result, that document will score higher than a 'riverbank' document in a bag-of-words system, even though no explicit disambiguation of query or document terms has taken place.[6]

---

[6] Sanderson (2000) calls this the "query word collocation effect". See his excellent discussion for a more detailed analysis of word sense disambiguation and IR.

Implicit disambiguation may have less of an effect, opening up possibilities for explicit WSD, when documents are short, providing less opportunity for multiple matches with the query. In the context of retrieving images by their captions, Smeaton and Quigley (1996) show that the potential gains for short documents are significant if WSD can be done accurately (they did it manually). On the other hand, Sanderson (2000) observes that "any type of expansion on these [short] sorts of documents will have been likely to be beneficial."

Krovetz (1997, 2002) has stressed that his often-cited 1992 experiments do support the potential for improved monolingual IR performance using WSD, even though they have often been interpreted as saying the opposite. He points to his empirical finding that, given a query term w used in sense s, relevant documents containing w are indeed more likely to be using the term in sense s rather than in other senses s'. So, for example, if the query contains *bank* used as *bank-1* and a document contains *bank* in a different sense, *bank-2*, then that does predict the document is less likely to be relevant. Sense-based matching therefore has a potential role to play in distinguishing between relevant and irrelevant documents. Moreover, query terms do turn out to be highly ambiguous, even in restricted domains, which means that disambiguation has room to help, whether it occurs implicitly or explicitly. This is still an argument from faith, but it is one grounded in empirical, application-specific investigation.

The operative question, then, is not whether traditional WSD could help in IR, but whether it can provide value over and above the implicit disambiguation effect or other shallow techniques, particularly in the presence of skewed sense frequency distributions, and whether it can be made to help more than it hurts. The discussion is somewhat mixed. On the one hand, researchers with extensive experience investigating NLP in IR have not found explicit WSD to be useful for the reasons discussed above (e.g., Voorhees (1999); Tomek Strzalkowski (personal communication); see also Sparck Jones (1999)). Sanderson (1994) is widely cited for his result showing that a 20–30% error rate is enough to undermine the use of WSD in an IR system, and a corresponding suggestion that 90% accuracy must be obtained before WSD is of practical use. Prospects for obtaining this level of accuracy seem poor for the foreseeable future, at least with regard to making fine-grained sense distinctions in an "all words" task (see Chap. 4). Sanderson (2000) goes on to a further analysis of the factors affecting the success of disambiguation in IR, together with relevant literature, and concludes that in general, attempts "at automatic disambiguation and IR have failed to improve effectiveness".

On the other hand, one can find a few results that might point in a positive direction. Mandala et al. (1998) report favorable results for a WSD technique in IR, evaluating using standard test collections.[7] Gonzalo et al. (1998) created a test collection from a manually-disambiguated corpus (Semcor, the WordNet semantic concordance) to experiment with varying levels of disambiguation accuracy, and found that indexing with WordNet synsets helped in a known-item retrieval task; see also Gonzalo et al. (1999), which revisits the experiments of Sanderson (1994) and Krovetz (1997) using the Semcor test collection.

Moreover, recent results suggest that it is worthwhile to focus on those words that can be disambiguated with high precision, rather than disambiguating all words. Mihalcea and Moldovan (2000) obtained gains in a limited evaluation, using a subset of one standard IR test collection, via a combination of synset-based and word-based indexing; their WSD approach yielded synset accuracy of greater than 92% when applied to approximately 55% of the nouns and verbs. Stokoe et al. (2003) also obtained above-baseline results using an approach explicitly designed to avoid the impact of inaccurate disambiguation, although they qualify these results by observing that their baseline model was below the state of the art. Similarly, Kim et al. (2004) focus on exploiting WSD where it can be accurate and on mitigating the effects of inaccuracy, applying coarse-grained semantic tags to nouns and allowing multiple sense assignment rather than one-best tagging; their approach appears to improve performance against realistic IR baselines. Liu et al. (2004) employ high-precision disambiguation of query terms for selective query expansion.

11.3.2 WSD in Applications Related to Information Retrieval

Traditional IR has been a difficult proving ground for traditional WSD – as one IR researcher put it, when it comes to convincing results, "it's all pretty thin on the ground." As discussed above, the effect of implicit disambiguation, produced by documents matching multiple query terms, is one important reason that monolingual IR performance has been hard to improve upon using WSD techniques. Another is the traditional formalization of the IR task in terms of document-level relevance, which allows bag-of-words approaches to identify relevant documents without a deeper

---

[7] This reference does not seem to be widely cited, perhaps because it is less well known, or perhaps because their evaluation baseline (the SMART system) did not represent state-of-the-art IR system performance.

understanding of the specific information sought by the query. These obstacles for WSD's impact in traditional IR may be less of an issue in two emerging retrieval applications: cross language IR, where translation ambiguity complicates implicit disambiguation, and question answering, where the nature of the task is less likely to reward bag-of-words models. Categorizing (or disambiguating) search-engine queries for advertising purposes may also be bringing new attention to text classification.

Cross-language IR

Cross-language information retrieval (CLIR) is an application developing at a rapid pace, thanks to the increasingly global nature of information seeking on the Web, global commerce, and the needs of the intelligence community. WSD may well have greater potential in CLIR than in IR, owing to the interaction of sense ambiguity with translation ambiguity.

In a CLIR setting, the user presents a query of the usual kind, but some of the relevant documents may be written in a different language – let us call the query language L_Q and imagine seeking documents in language L_D. In one common approach, known as *query translation*, query terms in L_Q are translated into L_D (e.g., using a bilingual dictionary), effectively reducing the problem to monolingual retrieval in L_D. The problem, however, is that in addition to the usual problem of sense ambiguity *within* L_D, the translation from L_Q *into* L_D often is also ambiguous, in that each L_Q query term can typically translate into multiple words in L_D, representing different senses of the L_Q term. In most CLIR systems all the translations are included, though often with different weights. Despite the amelioration of weighting schemes, the noise added by the additional translation "fan out" can interfere with the implicit disambiguation effect.

Consider, for example, a situation where word x in an English query can translate into any of x_1, x_2, and x_3 in, say, Chinese, and where word y in the English query can translate into any of y_1, y_2, y_3, and y_4. Furthermore, suppose that x_1 and y_1 are the correct Chinese translations. As one would hope, Chinese documents containing both x_1 and y_1 will score higher than documents containing only one or the other, yielding the implicit disambiguation effect. But notice that documents containing both of x_1 and y_2 will *also* score higher, even though y_2 is the wrong translation for y in this context, and the same holds for x_2 and y_3, as well as all the other combinations. In practice, for at least some of the eleven unintended x_i, y_j combinations, there will be at least some documents containing both terms, and those documents will be rewarded in their scores even though they may not contain concepts corresponding to the original query terms x and y.

This effect is the reason behind Oard and Dorr's (1996) observation that polysemy appears to be more of a "key limiting factor" in multilingual retrieval than in monolingual retrieval. They note that "polysemy can be reduced using syntactic and semantic information, of which the simplest type is phrase formation." For example, the word *interest* is ambiguous in English between a financial sense and a hobby sense, expressed in Chinese by distinct words, 利息 [li4 xi5] and 興趣 [xing4 qu5], respectively. If an English query contains the words *interest* and *rate*, and the words are considered independently, then the incorrect translation of *interest* as the latter is likely to hurt precision. For example, the system might give a high score to a news article in Chinese that, say, comments on the increasing *rate* at which people in China have taken up an *interest* in browsing the Internet.

In contrast, if linguistic analysis of the English query were to identify *interest rate* as a phrase, translating the phrase would be preferable: being more specific, *interest rate* will likely have fewer translations in Chinese than either *interest* or *rate* alone, leading to fewer chance matches. The benefit of query language phrase formation, then, arises at least in part from the fact that in the query language, phrases will tend to have less sense ambiguity than words. As a result, in CLIR, "word sense disambiguation, which, like phrase formation, has demonstrated limited utility in a monolingual context might be a productive avenue for further investigation" (Oard and Dorr 1996:24; for more discussion of translation granularity in CLIR, see Levow, Oard, and Resnik 2005). And, indeed, a number of results in the CLIR literature suggest the value of improving translation selection (e.g., Ballesteros and Croft 1997, Gao et al. 2001, Qu et al. 2002). The majority of such results do not make use of explicit WSD. Two recent exceptions are Clough and Stevenson (2004) and Vossen et al. (2006), both using EuroWordNet. This latter work presents positive results for domain-specific WSD in CLIR, and is presented in detail in Chapter 10 (Sect. 10.3.3).

Question Answering

In some respects, question answering (QA) is one of the oldest NLP applications: natural language interfaces to databases and knowledge bases date back at least as far as the LUNAR system for answering questions about rock samples that were brought back by the Apollo expeditions (Woods and Kaplan 1971). In its most recent incarnation, the aim of QA is to find answers in open-domain natural language text. Rather than querying an IR system with *"Edison light bulb patent"* – receiving, say, full articles on Edison and the light bulb in response – the goal is to ask a QA system specific questions such as *"When did Edison patent the light bulb?"* and receive back a concise answer rather than a set of relevant documents.[8]

QA has seen a significant increase in research activity, and the first standardized comparison of systems took place at TREC-8 (Voorhees and Tice 2000).[9] Voorhees (1999) suggests that QA might be fertile ground for NLP because "determining the relationships that hold among words in a text is likely to be important in this task" and, similarly, Sparck Jones (1999) mentions extraction of information for question answering as a task that "in general depends on linguistic analysis, even if this may sometimes be done by linguistically shallow means." As an illustration, although parsing to derive the syntactic relationships in the above question – SUBJECT (PATENT, EDISON), OBJECT (PATENT, BULB), and MODIFIER (BULB, LIGHT) – may not be particularly necessary in a model where relevant documents are sought, it is likely to be useful in distinguishing between relevant and irrelevant answers such as *Edison patented the light bulb in 1879* versus *Joseph Swan's earlier light bulb patent in 1878 gave Edison some trouble.*

With syntactically elaborated "terms", the "paraphrase problem" (Oard and Dorr 1996, Woods 1995) is more acute: the bag-of-words system will happily give high marks to a (relevant) document containing *Edison's 1879 patent of the light bulb,* but this text fragment contains syntactic relations that mostly do not match the ones found in the question. Because a noun phrase *patent of the light bulb* is used, for example, the SUBJECT (PATENT, EDISON) relation is not present in the document. Recognizing a match between *Edison's patent* and *Edison patented* suggests taking a step closer to semantics – a step that was less necessary in document-level retrieval, where stemming accounts for the noun/verb divergence and surface co-occurrence is enough to reward the presence of both *Edison* and *patent* regardless of the relationship between them.

There is some reason to believe that in the step toward more use of semantics, explicit sense distinctions are useful in QA. Among NLP practitioners, the LCC-SMU system of Harabagiu and colleagues (Paşca and Harabagiu 2001a) is most often mentioned in this regard, both because it uses NLP more extensively than most other systems and because it has outperformed other systems in community-wide QA evaluations. Among

---

[8] The goals of QA are also evolving beyond "factoid" questions of this kind; e.g., see Harabagiu and Lacutusu (2004), particularly Prange (2004).

[9] TREC (Text REtrieval Conference) is the highly successful series of annual evaluation events for information retrieval systems, organized by NIST (National Institute of Standards and Technology) in the United States.

their techniques, the analysis of questions and possible answers includes syntactic representations at the level of dependencies, and assessing the quality of a match includes using lexical, morphological, and semantic knowledge to "expand the question and answer words to account for as many similarities as possible." For example, their system determines that *maker of greeting cards* is related to *sells greeting cards* because the gloss (i.e., definition) of *make* (in WordNet 1.6, sense 6) is expressed in terms of *manufacture*, whose gloss explicitly identifies that goods are made "for sale", which is morphologically related to *sell*. (See also Moldovan and Rus (2001), who discuss the transformation of WordNet's knowledge into a logical form in order to draw conclusions of this kind.) Sense distinctions are used implicitly in some of their techniques, but explicit WSD does also appear to be used: Paşca and Harabagiu (2001b) discuss a disambiguation process that disambiguates words in the relevant syntactic dependency relationships – for example, *sells:cards* – by taking advantage of both WordNet and the Web (Mihalcea and Moldovan 1999).

An interesting related development, with regard to the role of semantics, is the "Recognising Textual Entailment Challenge" (Dagan, Glickman, and Magnini 2004), an exploratory evaluation exercise designed to focus on paraphrase issues. Participating systems are expected to receive a text snippet such as *Yahoo took over search company Overture Services Inc last year* paired with the snippet *Yahoo bought Overture*, and determine whether the former entails the latter (yes, in this case). In a panel discussion about future evaluations at the Senseval-3 workshop (see Chap. 4 (Sect. 4.7)), Ido Dagan suggested a variation of the textual entailment task designed to focus on word sense issues. The idea would be to specify a word or lexical phrase in each text snippet, and to ask whether the meanings of the specified items are in an entailment relationship; for example, *took over* in the preceding context entails *bought*. Like the snippet entailment task, this lexically-focused task would not require either explicit sense representations or explicit disambiguation, though either might prove helpful.[10] If adopted, the task could form a useful bridge between intrinsic (or *in vitro*) WSD evaluation and system level evaluation in applications like QA where it is important to identify entailment relations.[11]

---

[10] See Resnik (1993:22–26) for an initial foray into formally characterizing WordNet's semantics in terms of entailment.

[11] Textual entailment could also form a bridge between WSD and MT evaluation, since "correct translation" can be thought of as mutual entailment between items in different languages.

Another important consideration in QA is answering the right question. In order to find the right types of answers for a given question type (*who* versus *where* versus *when*, for example), many approaches to QA rely on some variant of named entity tagging: identifying phrases that can be categorized into high-level semantic categories such as Person, Organization, Location, Date, and so forth. For example, Prager et al. (2000) tag text entities with their types as a part of the indexing process, and then extend the query into an IR system with a term designating the expected answer type in order to retrieve text passages containing the right sorts of entities. Thus the sentence *Edison patented the light bulb in 1879* might be indexed as something like *Edison <Person> patented the light bulb in 1879 <Date>*. Given a "*When did ...*" question, their system would add the term "*<Date>*" to the IR query. Other systems do this sort of analysis further downstream in the process. As research on QA continues to develop, the small number of named entity types is giving way to a much larger set of semantic categories (Hovy et al. 2002, Paşca and Harabagiu 2001a). And as the set grows, categorization into entity types more and more closely approaches the general problem of word sense disambiguation.

Document Classification

Most work on classifying texts into predetermined categories (text classification, categorization, or routing) is based on the same bag-of-words representations that are typical in information retrieval. Some attempts to enrich text representations with word sense information have not yielded improvements in performance (e.g., Kehagias et al. 2003, Moschitti and Basili 2004) for reasons similar to those discussed in Section 11.3.1. However, Vossen et al. (2006) present a study using the Reuters news collection in which they obtain improvements for document classification using a WSD technique that emphasizes the importance of topical domains. In similar work, Bloehdorn and Hotho (2004) show that the integration of features into the document representations for text document classification improves the result, achieving highly competitive results on the Reuters-21578 and OHSUMED datasets (for IR and information extraction research). Some improvements can be attributed to the detection of multi-word expressions and to the conflation of synonyms. Further improvements can be achieved by generalizing concepts. In closely related work, Hotho et al. (2003) report improved results in document clustering.

In addition, a particular variety of text classification has become a topic of interest in the context of search engines: categorizing users' queries, for example, in order to do a better job of targeting advertising. To adapt an example from Chris Brew (personal communication), does a user querying with "*duck soup washington d.c.*" want to see pointers to restaurant listings or advertisements for a Marx Brothers film revival? Assessing users' intent is closely related to disambiguating the intended meaning of their queries, and Li and Zheng (2005) report on a competition designed around this task.

11.3.3 WSD in Traditional Machine Translation

Discussions of MT conventionally make a distinction between interlingual systems and transfer systems.[12] In interlingual systems, traditional WSD is necessary in order to identify the correct interlingual or "meaning" representation for a concept expressed in the source language. Translating *The news of the attack broke at 6am*, one might select the communication sense of *broke* rather than the destruction sense (cf. *The glass in the window broke at 6am*). This monolingual analysis task produces an interlingual representation; monolingual generation for the target language then maps from that representation to a surface realization.

Consider Dorr's (1993) interlingual translation framework. The lexicon contains multiple entries for the same English verb, and the syntactic context helps narrow down which entries are viable – for example, the source sentence *I broke the news to Mary* permits only the communication sense (cf. **I broke the glass to Mary*). This filtering during the analysis phase is accomplished by lexical representations that allow a possible goal/recipient argument for the communication sense of *break*, but not for the 'break into pieces' sense. The result of the analysis is a semantic representation built from the component lexical representations of the words in the sentence; crucially, the building blocks for these representations consist of interlingual semantic elements such as CAUSE, BE, and the like. The generation phase proceeds by searching among the combinations of target-language lexical items to find a set that fully covers the sentence's interlingual semantic representation, in a sense reversing the disambiguation process: lexical items are chosen by virtue of their fit to the semantics of the expression being translated. (See also Habash (2003)).

---

[12] "Direct" systems are a third conventional category, but, as the term suggests, they do not use intermediate representations such as word senses. See Dorr et al. (1999) for a good article-length overview of MT that discusses a wide range of ambiguity types.

Transfer systems similarly face the need to determine which source language representation to use for mapping to the target language. In some transfer systems, the link between lexical items is mediated by a mapping between sense inventories in the source and target languages. However, transfer-based systems have an opportunity unavailable to interlingual systems, which eschew (at least in principle) any direct knowledge of how source language expressions map to the target expressions: they can map directly from words to words, in effect treating the set of target-language translations of a word as if it is the word's sense inventory.

However, commenting on the effectiveness of explicit WSD in traditional MT systems is difficult for a number of reasons. First, sense ambiguity is only one of a large variety of forms of ambiguity that challenge MT systems, and perhaps for that reason WSD does not tend to be discussed as a separate component. Second, standardized, community-wide MT evaluations are a fairly recent phenomenon. Explicit WSD does not appear to have played a visible role in any of the systems that participated in the ARPA evaluations of the early 1990s (White and O'Connell 1994), and most participants in more recent comparative evaluations have been either statistical MT systems (discussed below) or commercial systems, for which system details are often kept confidential.[13]

That said, however, Systran, one of the classic transfer-based MT systems, illustrates one way that traditional WSD techniques can be used with target-language terms in the place of sense identifiers. Laurie Gerber (personal communication) comments that for some language pairs, Systran selects the meaning in the target language by first doing monolingual source language disambiguation, and then separately assigning target language meaning, a process akin to what happens in an interlingual framework. However, "word-specific lexical rules", taking linguistic context into account, are also used to assign meaning in the target language; as a result, as for other traditional systems, it is difficult to truly isolate the role of WSD in the translation process.[14]

---

[13] WSD also does not appear to play a role in translation memory systems, one of the more widely used applications of translation technology (Webb 2001).

[14] Zajic and Miller (1998) analyze the errors of two commercial MT systems including word sense issues, in the context of Cybertrans, a fusion of MT technologies widely used by the U.S. National Security Agency "for purposes of document triage, filtering, and pointing to text that may require human skills" (Long 2004).

11.3.4 Sense Ambiguity in Statistical Machine Translation

Explicit WSD generally does not appear to play a role in statistical MT systems. However, lexical choice in statistical models involves many of the same issues as sense disambiguation and it is informative to look at how they address the problem.

Statistical MT originated with the approach of Brown et al. (1990) at IBM. Within IBM-style statistical MT, the disambiguation of word meanings occurs primarily within two component models. The first, dubbed the "Model 1" probability for historical reasons, is the word-to-word conditional probability $\Pr(f|e)$, where f and e are source language and target language words, respectively.[15] Within this model, for example, one would likely find that $\Pr(huile|oil)$ is much greater than $\Pr(vin|oil)$, signifying that *huile* is a much more likely French translation for *oil* than is *vin*. (Or at least one would hope so, since *vin* means *wine!*)

Notice, however, that the Model 1 probabilities do not make use of any contextual information. The role of context in lexical choice appears primarily in a second component model: the language model for the target language. This is typically an n-gram model, that is, one that computes the probability of a word based on the previous $n-1$ words, where typically n is 2 or 3. For example, consider the French word *essence*, which can translate into English as the cognate *essence* (as in essential, the main thing) or as *gas(oline)*. The choice of translation will depend not only on the non-contextual word translation probabilities, but also on the context in the target language. If the statistical model considers *out of* to be most likely as the previous two words in the target sentence, then *gas* will be favored strongly over *essence* as the word that follows.[16]

---

[15] The careful reader may wonder why the relevant probability is $\Pr(f|e)$, not $\Pr(e|f)$, if we are translating *from* the source language *to* the target language. The reversal is explained by the application of Bayes Rule; see Knight (1999) for an extremely lucid statistical MT primer that introduces other component models not covered here, such as the ones that govern word-order differences.

[16] Salim Roukos (personal communication) observes that although the target language model is a primary source of contextual constraint on word choice, the source language can also contribute contextually through the mechanism of summing over multiple alignments. For example, in the training process some credit may have been assigned to the alignment of the word *voiture* 'car' with *gas* (incorrectly), so given a French sentence containing both *voiture* and *essence*, summing over alternative alignments could result in both words supporting the presence of *gas*. This seems like an instance of the right effect for the wrong reason.

Within the past several years, phrase-based models (Och 2002), Koehn et al. 2003) have emerged as the dominant model in statistical MT. Statistical phrase-based translation is similar in spirit to example-based machine translation (EBMT) (Nagao 1984, Brown 1996), in which a target sentence is constructed by covering the source sentence with "chunks" stored in a translation memory. The statistical version employs a probabilistic model of the mapping between "phrases" in the source and target language.[17] For example, it might capture the fact that the English sequence *we have* appears frequently as the translation of French sequence *nous avons*. The translation process can be viewed as segmenting the source sentence into phrases, reordering them, and translating the phrases as units based on the mappings. As in many other statistical approaches, "decoding" is the process of searching for the optimal way to accomplish this, where "optimal" is defined by models learned from training data (Koehn et al. 2003, Koehn 2004).

The move from words in the IBM models to phrases in this approach was motivated in part by the observation that local context in the source language provides strong cues for lexical selection, which word-to-word models do not capture well. In some cases, the problem appears to be related not to word-to-word modeling *per se*, but to its particular realization in the IBM models. To use one of Och's (2002) examples, German *Druckertreiber* is a single word that would translate in English as the two-word phrase *printer driver*; the IBM models fail to account for this because they do not permit many-to-one alignments between target (English) and source (German), and because they analyze complex German words as undivided units. On the other hand, Och points out problems involving non-literal phrase translations (e.g., *that will not be easy* for *das wird schwierig*; Babelfish/Systran translates this as the less natural *that becomes difficult*), as well as the problem of translating of function words such as prepositions, articles, and particles, where "the correct translation depends mainly on the context in the source language." These are cases where target language lexical selection benefits from local context provided by phrase-to-phrase mapping, an effect consistent with Yarowsky's (1993, 2000) widely cited observation that local collocations provide very strong clues for the intended sense.

---

[17] One should note that the term "phrase" is used – misleadingly, for linguists – to describe any contiguous subset of words in a source or target sentence, sometimes generalized to sequences of statistically derived word classes.

Recently, a number of researchers have begun to investigate the relationship between automatic WSD techniques and statistical machine translation. Carpuat and Wu (2005a) attempt to integrate dedicated WSD (using an external sense inventory) into an IBM-style statistical MT system, with negative results. However, in a follow-up paper, Carpuat and Wu (2005b) explore the empirical strengths and weaknesses of statistical MT versus WSD in a Senseval lexical disambiguation task, and in this setting, WSD outperforms statistical MT – which, they argue, supports the claim that statistical MT "should benefit from the better predictions made by the WSD models." Jiménez et al. (2005) demonstrate that lexical translation correspondences extracted from a multilingual sense inventory are useful in improving the statistical translation of dictionary entries. An alternative approach to using WSD in MT is to dissociate WSD techniques from explicit sense inventories entirely; instead, the problem of lexical selection in statistical MT can be cast as a WSD problem in which the "senses" are simply target-language words, and supervised classifiers can be trained using word-aligned parallel text to provide observable word/"sense" training pairs. This idea has been operationalized independently by Cabezas and Resnik (2005), who integrate lexical classification into a statistical phrase-based MT system, and Vickrey et al. (2005), who evaluate on a simplified MT task. We continue this discussion below in Section 11.4.3.

11.3.5 Other Emerging Applications

Beyond cross-language IR and question answering, discussed above, a number of other emerging applications share a need to identify the semantic categories of entities. These include the extraction and mining of information in text, and the acquisition of semantic knowledge.

In information extraction, the goal is to take a natural language text as input and fill in a "template" describing the basic relations that hold, for a particular, domain-specific set of template relations; in text data mining, the goal is to discover patterns of relationships that occur in large bodies of text.

The bioinformatics domain provides a nice illustration. A vast molecular biology literature discusses the relationships between genes, proteins, and enzymatic functions, and enormous databases are under construction tabulating such relationships, but there is a gap between the free text data in articles and the structured data in the databases. The KDD Cup competition for 2002 (Yeh et al. 2002) challenged researchers with the task of analyzing scientific articles in order to extract information useful for human annotators of the *Drosophila* genome – specifically, with identifying all the genes mentioned in an article and determining for each one whether the article reports a relationship between that gene and a gene product (protein and/or RNA). A serious complicating factor in the task, and in the molecular biology literature more generally, is that the same term can often refer to a gene, a protein, or an RNA molecule. Disambiguation of these possibilities in context is therefore valuable, and this specialized problem is amenable to techniques familiar from the WSD literature (Hatzivassiloglou et al. 2001).

Weeber et al. (2001) discuss ambiguity resolution in medical NLP more generally, mentioning such applications as medical decision support, indexing, and literature-based discovery. Other problems of ambiguity include abbreviations, e.g., whether *MG* refers to *milligram* or *magnesium* (Yu et al. 2002, Yu et al. 2004) and the interpretation of acronyms, for example, whether or not *COLD* should be interpreted as *chronic obstructive pulmonary disease*.[18]

One should note that these issues clearly go beyond the medical domain, and affect traditional as well as emerging applications. Readers of this chapter may have searched for NLP on the Web and found pages on neuro-linguistic programming rather than natural language processing, or may have sought information about the Association for Computational Linguistics and found the Association of Catholic Libraries instead. Search engine developers have commented that place names (e.g., whether *New York* refers to the city or the state) and person names (e.g., whether *George Bush* refers to George W. or his father) are a particularly noteworthy problem for which good solutions would be valuable.

These problems may be most severe, and hence disambiguation most valuable, in scenarios where there is a large skew creating rare senses or usages, but where it is important that the rare cases not be missed. For example, Daqing He is a professor at the School of Information Sciences of the University of Pittsburgh. If for some reason it were vitally important to locate documents containing Dr. He's opinion about, say, a new development in Chinese information retrieval, an analyst using current technology either would find that his last name was excluded altogether by a stop list of common words, or buried in false positives (e.g., *He wrote ...*, *He thinks ...*, etc.).

---

[18] The National Library of Medicine has made available a biomedical WSD test collection (http://wsd.nlm.nih.gov/).

Finally, there is one more class of emerging application for which explicit WSD may have particular value: tasks where the goal is to place terms or phrases into an explicit knowledge structure. These include the development of better user interfaces – Hearst (2000) argues for task-oriented search interfaces that more thoroughly integrate metadata, such as topical categories, into the user's experience. Yee et al. (2003) and Stoica and Hearst (2004) illustrate these ideas in an interface searching a collection of fine arts images, creating categories for the collection automatically from image captions using WordNet; however, when faced with sense ambiguity they were forced to either ignore ambiguous terms or choose the first WordNet sense. The MALACH project (Gustman et al. 2002) is similarly concerned with the human-machine interface: it aims to provide access to a very large archive of oral histories related to the Holocaust – 116,000 hours of recorded speech in 32 languages resulting from 52,000 interviews. Beyond transcription of these materials, Gustman et al. are faced with the challenge of mapping from segments of transcribed speech to categories in a thesaurus containing topics, place names, etc. Sawyer et al. (forthcoming) suggest that shallow semantic tagging can be useful for organizing and presenting users with the contents of documents in a new problem domain, during early-phase requirements engineering.

Although it is not really an application *per se*, the Semantic Web is an ambitious effort to give all information on the Web "well-defined meaning, better enabling computers and people to work in cooperation" (Berners-Lee et al. 2001). Semantic Web developers are expending significant effort on the definition of ontological knowledge structures, and there are already efforts to apply automatic semantic tagging to the Web on an enormous scale (Dill et al. 2003). Connections between language technology and resources and the Semantic Web are discussed in Wilcock et al. (2004) and Oltramari et al. (2004).

Pre-dating the Semantic Web, there is, of course, a long tradition of work on building ontologies in support of computational applications. In some cases WSD is an explicit part of the process. For example, Dorr and Jones (2000) employ WSD to improve the creation of large-scale semantic lexicons; Rigau et al. (2002) describe a bootstrapping process including WSD and knowledge acquisition in a multilingual setting; and Basili et al. (2004) discuss the creation of multilingual knowledge sources in the context of ontology-based QA. Knowledge resources for WSD are discussed in Chapter 9.

As a final example of an application involving explicit knowledge structures, consider lexicography: Kilgarriff and Tugwell's (2001) WASP-Bench is an application in which explicit WSD supports lexicographers, rather than the reverse, and Löfberg et al. (2004) discuss coarse-grained semantic tagging for context-sensitive dictionary search. Kilgarriff discusses lexicography in detail in Chapter 2.

11.4 Alternative Conceptions of Word Sense

In this chapter I focus primarily on sense disambiguation with respect to explicitly specified senses, but, as already noted in the discussion of machine translation and cross-language information retrieval, there is significant utility for applications in distinguishing among word meanings even if the alternative meanings are not enumerated explicitly. Giving this topic proper attention would require a much more thorough consideration of the question "what is a word sense?" – I cannot approach that here, though see relevant discussion in Chapters 1, 2, 3, and 6, as well as discussion of subtle sense distinctions in Chapter 4. In this section, I briefly consider several alternative conceptions of word sense including richer representations, patterns of usage, and cross-language relationships.

11.4.1 Richer Linguistic Representations

Kilgarriff (1997; see also Chap. 2) notes that there is a rich variety of theoretical literature, ranging from cognitive linguistics (Lakoff and Johnson 1980) to generative lexicon theory (Pustejovsky 1995), that argues for much richer representations of word meaning than a simple enumeration of senses. This literature is driven to a great extent by two observations. First, word meanings can be extended much more freely than fixed sense enumerations would suggest; for example, it is possible to extend the interpretation of *eat* to a more general notion of 'destroy by consuming' in the process of understanding sentences like *The computer ate my document*. Second, the lexicon contains a variety of systematic relationships between word senses; for *eat*, these include, for example, 'animal' and 'food' meanings (*chicken, lamb, goose*), 'container' and 'amount contained' (*cup, bowl, bottle*), and many others.

Wilks (1997, 1998) points out that such ideas have a long history in the traditional NLP literature, developed and implemented in theories such as preference semantics (Wilks and Fass 1992). Despite the theoretical interest of such models, however, it seems fair to say that these more sophisticated, flexible approaches to word sense have not yet found their way into language technology applications to any great extent, largely because they tend to be knowledge intensive or difficult to formalize and implement on a comprehensive scale. I will therefore not be considering them further here.

11.4.2 Patterns of Usage

Alternative conceptions of lexical organization driven by patterns of usage, on the other hand, have been more influential in language technology applications. Relevant ideas can be traced back at least as far as Firth's (1957) often-quoted pronouncement that "you shall know a word by the company it keeps", to Sparck Jones's (1964) characterization of synonymy in terms of related sentential contexts, and to Harris's (1968:12) distributional hypothesis, which proposed that "the meaning of entities, and the meaning of grammatical relations among them, is related to the restriction of combinations of these entities relative to other entities."

There is an extensive literature on techniques for organizing words and/or word meanings according to distributional patterns in corpora (see Chapter 6). In applications that use them, the underlying semantics of distributionally-derived similarity measures or clusters is usually secondary to whether or not they improve performance. For example, Latent Semantic Indexing (LSI) (Deerwester et al. 1990) is an information retrieval technique in which the vocabulary of a document collection is represented as a matrix V, where element V_{ij} is a weighted function of the frequency with which word w_i appears in document d_j. Words that appear in many of the same documents are therefore represented by similar rows in the matrix. The heart of the technique is a singular value decomposition (SVD) performed on V in order to produce a lower dimensionality matrix; as a result, words with similar patterns of usage wind up closer to each other in the new representation space. Information retrieval performance can improve as a result – if *dentist* and *hygienist* are given similar reduced-dimensionality representations as a result of LSI, a document discussing hygienists can be highly ranked in response to a query that only mentions dentists, even if the query and document have no words in common.

The representational similarity of *dentist* and *hygienist* in the LSI representation space is consistent with the intuition that they mean similar things; both are health care professionals who help take care of teeth. And if, say, *doctor* is represented nearby in the representational space, it may indicate that in this document collection, its 'health care professional' sense is more prevalent than the 'holder of a doctoral degree' sense. LSI, then, would seem to be a technique that uncovers word sense relationships on the basis of noisy distributional patterns of usage.

However, one must be cautious about interpreting the new representation space as possessing a coherent organization in terms of word senses. In addition to *dentist* and *hygienist* moving closer in the LSI representation space, *dentist* and *tooth* will probably also receive more similar representations, as will *dentist* and *cavity*, and many others. What is the semantic relationship between dentists and the teeth they take care of? Between dentists and cavities? When LSI is based on a word/document matrix, greater proximity in the representational space does not correspond to semantic or even conceptual relationships in any obvious way, other than perhaps to say that it identifies words that tend to occur in documents that are about similar things, under some interpretation of "aboutness".

For document retrieval, this matters very little. The conceptual relationships between the words are less important than the effect on performance of the representational choices: when a query contains *dentist*, the words *tooth* and *cavity* in a document are indicators of relevance, and using distributionally-derived representations the documents containing them are more likely to be retrieved. This observation has been borne out in formal evaluations (Schütze and Pedersen 1995; Schütze 1998; Jing and Tzoukermann 1999; see Chap. 6). There is also a related body of research on using distributional representations to improve interactive retrieval on the basis of clustering documents (see discussion in Hearst and Pedersen (1996)) and on the basis of distributional organizations of word meanings (e.g., Véronis (2004)). See Mihalcea, Tarau, and Figa (2004) and Erkan and Radev (2004) for recently introduced techniques, inspired by Google's PageRank algorithm, that take a graph-oriented rather than vector-oriented view of the distributional representation space.

The preceding examples involving *dentist*, *tooth*, and so on illustrate a basic point about distributional patterns of usage: although the distributional techniques can detect patterns that reflect underlying facts about word senses, they can also pick up patterns that bear no obvious relationship to the traditional linguistic conception of word senses. One could argue that the relationship is there, even if it is not obvious; for example, perhaps distributional techniques help because they *approximate* facts about meaning, much as trigram models work partly because they allow a finite-state approximation to "real" grammatical relations, which are often governed by syntactic locality. Or one could argue that one can more closely approximate linguistically relevant word sense distinctions by using a more refined set of distributional features such as syntactic dependency relationships (Lin and Pantel 2001).

Interestingly, one can also argue in the other direction, that the so-called approximations are themselves the more basic phenomenon. Kilgarriff (1997), for example, has suggested a model of word senses in which sense distinctions are defined as "clusters of word usages" that exist "relative to a set of interests" as determined by an NLP application or corpus of interest. He goes so far as to say that "a task-independent set of word senses for a language is not a coherent concept." He is echoed by Krovetz (2002), who suggests that "different natural language applications will need different [sense] distinctions." Schütze's (1998) context group discrimination system implements these ideas in an informational retrieval application (see Chapter 6). Agirre and Edmonds (Chapter 1) categorize task-dependent WSD as one of the most important open issues for WSD.

11.4.3 Cross-Language Relationships

Translation between languages provides a window on word meanings that is not available monolingually. In a monolingual setting, words are observable but meanings are not. In the context of bilingual dictionaries or parallel translations, however, a single "hidden" meaning underlies not one but two observable representations, one in each language (Resnik 2004).

One attempt to exploit this parallelism is cross-language Latent Semantic Indexing (CL-LSI) (Littman et al. 1998). Like LSI, CL-LSI uses dimensionality reduction to construct a "semantic" space for information retrieval in which similar terms are situated more closely to each other. Applying the process to parallel text produces a cross-language LSI space, one in which similarity implies closeness *regardless* of whether the two terms are from the same language or not. To some extent, therefore – bearing in mind the caveats discussed earlier – CL-LSI seeks to induce a space of *language independent* regions of semantic similarity, which are somewhat akin to cross-language word senses. These are then exploited in cross-language retrieval in a manner analogous to monolingual LSI.

Another direction for research is the characterization of discrete knowledge structures using cross-language correspondences. Dyvik (2002) uses bi-directional translations in a bilingual dictionary to derive intuitively plausible WordNet-like word sets and relations between them. Work by Resnik and Yarowsky (2000), extended by Chugur, Gonzalo, and Verdejo (2002), provides an empirical demonstration that the more distinct two monolingual senses are, the more likely those concepts are to be lexicalized with different words in other languages; this fact is then exploited to provide an empirical measure of between-sense distance that gives rise to structures closely corresponding to lexicographic distinctions in a monolingual dictionary. Ide (2000) and colleagues have explored the automation of this idea on a large scale using a multi-way parallel corpus, also applying the approach to sense tagging (Ide et al. 2002, Tufiş et al. 2004). Diab (2003) developed an unsupervised algorithm that uses word-level correspondences in bilingual text to achieve monolingual sense disambiguation in both languages (tagging words with labels from a sense inventory in one of the languages), an approach recently formalized probabilistically and extended by Bhattacharya et al. (2004). Ng et al. (2003) present a related approach in which bilingual corpora are used to obtain training examples for a supervised classifier. See Chapter 6 (Sect. 6.4.) for additional discussion.

A third line of research, dating back to the early 1990s, focuses on the idea of using words in a second language as sense labels. Brown et al. (1991) took advantage of aligned parallel text as training material for tagging source-language words with target language "senses" – for example, in the sentence pair *Me gustan las flores* / *I like the flowers*, a word alignment link between *gustan* and *like*, can be thought of as "sense tagging" the occurrence of *gustar* in the Spanish sentence with the label LIKE. Gale et al. (1992) similarly proposed aligned words as sense labels for WSD, and Dagan and Itai's (1994) exploration of this idea introduced techniques that required only monolingual corpora in the two languages. Li and Li (2004) extend Yarowsky's (1995) WSD bootstrapping technique to a bilingual setting in order to address the problem of lexical selection (word translation disambiguation) using Chinese words in lieu of explicit English senses.

This last approach is regaining currency in the WSD community – it was explored initially in Senseval-2 (Japanese task) and formed the basis for one of the tasks in Senseval-3 (see Chapter 4 (Sect. 4.7), as well as discussion related to statistical MT in Section 11.3.4). Tagging words with words has two very attractive features. First, it has the potential to enormously increase the availability of training data for supervised WSD algorithms, since aligned parallel corpora are more easily obtained than manually sense-tagged text.[19] Second, it connects WSD, and particularly

---

[19] Automatically word-aligned corpora do suffer from noise, however. For a recent look at the state of the art in word alignment for parallel corpora, see Mihalcea and Pedersen (2003) and Martin et al. (2005).

WSD evaluation, to specific end-user applications such as machine translation and cross-language IR where the value of the techniques can be demonstrated.

11.5 Conclusions

In this chapter, I have discussed the relationship between WSD research and NLP applications. Traditional WSD is characterized as the selection of one meaning for a word from a range of possibilities. So conceived, the role of WSD with respect to an explicit sense inventory appears to be questionable in two of the most heavily researched language technology applications, monolingual information retrieval and machine translation. However, there is evidence that traditional WSD and directly analogous techniques are useful in emerging applications such as question answering and biomedical information extraction. In addition, there appears to be a promising argument for the utility of WSD techniques in disambiguating specialized terms such as person and place names, abbreviations, and acronyms. Finally, I discussed several application areas worth watching, including the creation and navigation of metadata, computer-assisted lexicography, and ontology-driven frameworks such as the Semantic Web.

In addition to traditional WSD, I also briefly reviewed some alternative conceptions of word sense. These include distributional characterizations of word meaning, which have been useful in monolingual and cross-language information retrieval, and characterizations based on bilingual correspondences, which show promise in cross-language applications such as CLIR and machine translation. The discussion suggests that focusing on applications provides more than just practical benefit: it is one of the best ways to ensure that, as a community, we are validating our ideas against empirical data. Attention to practical considerations may lead to new and interesting ways to look at word senses and semantics more generally.

Acknowledgments

I would like to acknowledge with gratitude the patience of Phil Edmonds and Eneko Agirre as I wrote, revised, and struggled with this very challenging chapter. Many thanks to Phil, Eneko, Adam Kilgarriff, and an anonymous reviewer for their critiques and comments. I would also like to acknowledge valuable discussion at the Senseval-3 workshop and on the

Senseval e-mail list, and to thank the large number of people who were kind enough to provide me with comments, pointers, or insights about applications of WSD. These include Robert Amsler, Timothy Baldwin, Chris Brew, Chris Callison-Burch, Bill Dolan, Bonnie Dorr, Katrin Erk, Robert Frederking, Laurie Gerber, Gregory Grefenstette, Marti Hearst, Nancy Ide, Jesús Jiménez, Adam Kilgarriff, Bob Krovetz, Gina Levow, Jimmy Lin, Rada Mihalcea, Doug Oard, Paul Rayson, Mark Sanderson, Hinrich Schütze, Karen Sparck Jones, Chris Stokoe, Tomek Strzalkowski, John Tait, Jean Véronis, Luis Villarejo, Ellen Voorhees, Piek Vossen, and Yorick Wilks. The writing of this chapter was supported in part by Department of Defense contract RD-02-5700, DARPA/ITO Cooperative Agreement N660010028910, ONR MURI Contract FCPO.810548265, and National Science Foundation grant EIA0130422.

References

Baeza-Yates, Ricardo & Berthier Ribeiro-Neto. 1999. *Modern Information Retrieval*. Addison-Wesley.

Ballesteros, Lisa & W. Bruce Croft. 1997. Phrasal translation and query expansion techniques for cross-language information retrieval. *Proceedings of the 20th Annual International ACM SIGIR Conference on Research and Development in Information Retrieval*, Philadelphia, PA, 84–91.

Bar-Hillel, Yehoshua. 1960. The present status of automatic translation of languages. *Advances in Computers, Vol. 1* ed. By F. L. Alt, 91–163. New York: Academic Press.

Basili, Roberto, Dorte H. Hansen, Patrizia Paggio, Maria Teresa Pazienza & Fabio Massimo Zanzotto. 2004. Ontological resources and question answering. *Proceedings of the Workshop on Pragmatics of Question Answering at HLT-NAACL 2004*, Boston.

Berners-Lee, Tim, James Hendler & Ora Lassila. 2001. The Semantic Web. *Scientific American*, 284(5): 34–43.

Bhattacharya, Indrajit, Lise Getoor & Yoshua Bengio. 2004. Unsupervised word sense disambiguation using bilingual probabilistic models. *Proceedings of the 42nd Annual Meeting of the Association for Computational Linguistics (ACL)*, Barcelona, Spain, 288–295.

Bloehdorn, Stephan & Andreas Hotho. 2004. Text classification by boosting weak learners based on terms and concepts. *Proceedings of the Fourth IEEE International Conference on Data Mining*, Brighton, UK, 331–334.

Brown, Peter F., John Cocke, Stephen A. Della Pietra, Vincent J. Della Pietra, Fredrick Jelinek, John D. Lafferty, Robert L. Mercer & Paul S. Roossin. 1990. A statistical approach to machine translation. *Computational Linguistics* 16(2): 79–85.

Brown, Peter F., Stephen A. Della Pietra , Vincent J. Della Pietra, Robert L. Mercer. 1991. Word-sense disambiguation using statistical methods, *Proceedings of the 29th Conference of the Association for Computational Linguistics (ACL)*, Berkeley, California, June, 264–270.

Brown, Ralf D. 1996. Example-based machine translation in the Pangloss system. 1996. *Proceedings of the 16th International Conference on Computational Linguistics (COLING)*, Copenhagen, Denmark, 169–174.

Cabezas, Clara & Philip Resnik. 2005. *Using WSD Techniques for Lexical Selection in Statistical Machine Translation*. Technical report CS-TR-4736/LAMP-TR-124/UMIACS-TR-2005-42, July 2005. (http://lampsrv01.umiacs.umd.edu /pubs/TechReports/LAMP_124/LAMP_124.pdf)

Carpuat, Marine & Dekai Wu. 2005a. Word sense disambiguation vs. statistical machine translation. *Proceedings of the 43rd Annual Meeting of the Association for Computational Linguistics (ACL)*, Ann Arbor, MI, June, 387–394.

Carpuat, Marine & Dekai Wu. 2005b. Evaluating the word sense disambiguation performance of statistical machine translation. *Proceedings of Second International Joint Conference on Natural Language Processing (IJCNLP)*. Jeju, Korea, October.

Chelba, Ciprian & Frederick Jelinek. 1998. Exploiting syntactic structure for language modeling. *Proceedings of the 36th Annual Meeting of the Association for Computational Linguistics and 17th International Conference on Computational Linguistics (ACL-COLING)*, Morgan Kaufmann Publishers, San Francisco, California, 225–231.

Chiang, David. 2005. A hierarchical phrase-based model for statistical machine translation. *Proceedings of the 43rd Annual Meeting of the Association for Computational Linguistics (ACL)*, Ann Arbor, MI, 263–270.

Chugur, Irina, Julio Gonzalo & Felisa Verdejo. 2002. Polysemy and sense proximity in the Senseval-2 test suite. *Proceedings of the ACL 2002 Workshop on Word Sense Disambiguation: Recent Successes and Future Directions*, Pennsylvania.

Clough, Paul & Mark Stevenson. 2004. Cross-language information retrieval using EuroWordNet and word sense disambiguation. *Advances in Information Retrieval, 26th European Conference on IR Research (ECIR 2004)*, Sunderland, UK, 327–337.

Dagan, Ido & Alon Itai. 1994. Word sense disambiguation using a second language monolingual corpus. *Computational Linguistics*, 20(4): 563–596.

Dagan, Ido, Oren Glickman & Bernardo Magnini. 2004. *Recognising Textual Entailment Challenge*. (http://www.pascal-network.org/Challenges/RTE/)

Dawkins, Richard. 1986. *The Blind Watchmaker*. W.W. Norton.

Diab, Mona. 2003. *Word Sense Disambiguation within a Multilingual Framework*. Ph.D. Thesis, Department of Linguistics, University of Maryland, College Park, Maryland.

Deerwester, Scott, Susan T. Dumais, George W. Furnas, Thomas K. Landauer & Richard Harshman. 1990. Indexing by latent semantic analysis. *Journal of the American Society for Information Science*, 41(6): 391–407.

Dill, Stephen, Nadav Eiron, David Gibson, Daniel Gruhl, R. Guha, Anant Jhingran, Tapas Kanungo, Sridhar Rajagopalan, Andrew Tomkins, John A. Tomlin & Jason Y. Zien. 2003. SemTag and Seeker: Bootstrapping the Semantic Web via automated semantic annotation. *Proceedings of the Twelfth International Conference on World Wide Web (WWW-2003)*, Budapest, Hungary, 178–186.

Dorr, Bonnie J. 1993. *Machine Translation: A View from the Lexicon*. Cambridge, MA: MIT Press.

Dorr, Bonnie J. & Douglas Jones. 2000. Acquisition of semantic lexicons: using word sense disambiguation to improve precision. *Breadth and Depth of Semantic Lexicons* ed. by Evelyn Viegas, 79–98. Kluwer Academic Publishers, Norwell, MA.

Dorr, Bonnie J., Pamela W. Jordan & John W. Benoit. 1999. A survey of current paradigms in machine translation. *Advances in Computers, Vol. 49* ed. by M. Zelkowitz, 1–69. London: Academic Press.

Dyvik, Helge. 2002. Translations as semantic mirrors: From parallel corpus to wordnet. *Advances in Corpus Linguistics. Papers from the 23rd International Conference on English Language Research on Computerized Corpora (ICAME 23) Göteborg 22–26 May 2002* ed. by Karin Aijmer & Bengt Altenberg, 311–326. Rodopi.

Erkan, Güneş & Dragomir R. Radev. 2004. Lexrank: Graph-based centrality as salience in text summarization. *Journal of Artificial Intelligence Research*, 22: 457–479.

Firth, J. 1957. A synopsis of linguistic theory 1930–1955. *Studies in Linguistic Analysis*, Philological Society, Oxford. Reprinted in *Selected Papers of J. R. Firth 1952–59* ed. by F. Palmer, 168–205, London: Longmans, 1968.

Gale, William, Kenneth Church & David Yarowsky. 1992. Using bilingual materials to develop word sense disambiguation methods. *Fourth International Conference on Theoretical and Methodological Issues in Machine Translation*, Montreal, 101–112.

Gao, Jianfeng, Jian-Yun Nie, Jian Zhang, Endong Xun, Ming Zhou & Changning Huang. 2001. Improving query translation for CLIR using statistical models. *Proceedings of the 24th Annual International ACM SIGIR Conference on Research and Development in Information Retrieval,* New Orleans, Louisiana, USA, 96–104.

Gonzalo, Julio, Felisa Verdejo, Irina Chugur & Juan Cigarran. 1998. Indexing with WordNet synsets can improve text retrieval. *Proceedings of the COLING-ACL 1998 Workshop on Usage of WordNet in Natural Language Processing Systems,* Montreal, Canada.

Gonzalo, Julio, Anselmo Peñas & Felisa Verdejo, 1999. Lexical ambiguity and information retrieval revisited. *Proceedings of the Joint SIGDAT Conference on Empirical Methods in Natural Language Processing and Very Large Corpora (EMNLP/VLC-99),* Maryland.

Gustman, Samuel, Dagobert Soergel, Douglas Oard, William Byrne, Michael Picheny, Bhuvana Ramabhadran & Douglas Greenberg. 2002. Supporting access to large digital oral history archives. *Proceedings of the Joint Conference on Digital Libraries,* 18–27.

Habash, Nizar. 2003. *Generation-Heavy Hybrid Machine Translation.* Ph.D. Thesis, Department of Computer Science, University of Maryland, USA.

Harabagiu, Sanda & Finley Lucatusu, eds. 2004. *Proceedings of the Workshop on Pragmatics of Question Answering at HLT-NAACL 2004,* Boston.

Harris, Zelig. 1968. *Mathematical Structures of Language.* New York: Wiley.

Hatzivassiloglou, Vasileios, Pablo A. Duboué & Andrey Rzhetsky. 2001. Disambiguating proteins, genes, and RNA in text: A machine learning approach. *Proceedings of the Ninth International Conference on Intelligent Systems for Molecular Biology,* Copenhagen, Denmark, 97–106.

Hearst, Marti. 2000. Next generation web search: Setting our sites. *IEEE Data Engineering Bulletin, Special issue on Next Generation Web Search* ed. by Luis Gravano.

Hearst, Marti & Jan Pedersen. 1996. Reexamining the cluster hypothesis: Scatter/Gather on retrieval results. *Proceedings of the 19th Annual International ACM SIGIR Conference on Research and Development in Information Retrieval,* Zurich, 76–84.

Hotho, Andreas, Stephen Staab & Gerd Stumme. 2003. WordNet improves text document clustering. *Proceedings of the Semantic Web Workshop at the 26th Annual International ACM SIGIR Conference on Research and Development in Information Retrieval,* Toronto, Canada.

Hovy, Eduard, Ulf Hermjakob & Deepak Ravichandran. 2002. A question/answer typology with surface text patterns. *Proceedings of the DARPA Human Language Technology Conference (HLT),* San Diego, CA.

Hutchins, John. 1997. Fifty years of the computer and translation. *Machine Translation Review*, 6: 22–24.

Hutchins, John. 1999. Milestones in machine translation, Part 6: Bar-Hillel and the nonfeasibility of FAHQT. *International Journal of Language and Documentation*, 1: 20–21. (http://ourworld.compuserve.com/homepages/WJHutchins/Miles-6.htm)

Ide, Nancy & Jean Véronis. 1998. Word sense disambiguation: The state of the art. *Computational Linguistics*, 24(1): 1–40.

Ide, Nancy. 2000. Cross-lingual sense determination: Can it work? *Computers and the Humanities* 34(1–2): 223–34.

Ide, Nancy, Tomaz Erjavec & Dan Tufiş. 2002. Sense discrimination with parallel corpora. *Proceedings of the ACL-2002 Workshop on Word Sense Disambiguation: Recent Successes and Future Directions*, Philadelphia, 54–60.

Jiménez, Jesús, Lluís Màrquez & German Rigau. 2005. Automatic translation of WordNet glosses. *Proceedings of the EUROLAN'05 Cross-Language Knowledge Induction Workshop*, Cluj-Napoca, Romania, July.

Jing, Hongyan & Evelyne Tzoukermann. 1999. Information retrieval based on context distance and morphology. *Proceedings of the 22nd Annual International ACM SIGIR Conference on Research and Development in Information Retrieval*, Berkeley, CA, USA, 90–96.

Kehagias, Athanasios, Vassilios Petridis, Vassilis Kaburlasos & Pavlina Fragkou. 2003. A comparison of word- and sense-based text categorization using several classification algorithms. *Journal of Intelligent Information Systems*, 21(3): 227–247.

Kilgarriff, Adam. 1997. "I don't believe in word senses". *Computers and the Humanities*, 31(2): 91–113.

Kilgarriff, Adam & David Tugwell. 2001. WASP-Bench: An MT lexicographers' workstation supporting state-of-the-art lexical disambiguation. *Proceedings of MT Summit VIII*, Santiago de Compostela, Spain, 187–190.

Kim, Sang-Bum, Hee-Cheol Seo & Hae-Chang Rim. 2004. Information retrieval using word senses: Root sense tagging approach. *Proceedings of the 27th Annual International ACM SIGIR Conference on Research and Development in Information Retrieval*, Sheffield, UK, 258–265.

Knight, Kevin. 1999. *A Statistical MT Tutorial Workbook*, unpublished, (http://www.isi.edu/natural-language/mt/wkbk.rtf)

Koehn, Philipp. 2004. Pharaoh: A Beam Search decoder for phrase-based statistical machine translation models. *Proceedings of the 6th Conference of the Association for Machine Translation in the Americas (AMTA)*, Georgetown.

Koehn Philipp, Franz Josef Och & Daniel Marcu. 2003. Statistical phrase-based translation. *Proceedings of the Human Language Technology Conference* (HLT-NAACL), Edmonton, Canada, 48–54.

Krovetz, Robert & W. Bruce Croft. 1992. Lexical ambiguity and information retrieval. *ACM Transactions on Information Systems*, 10(2), 115–141.

Krovetz, Robert. 1997. Homonymy and polysemy in information retrieval. *Proceedings of the Eighth conference on European chapter of the Association for Computational Linguistics (EACL)*, Madrid, 72–79.

Krovetz, Robert. 2002. On the importance of word sense disambiguation for information retrieval. *Proceedings of the LREC 2002 Workshop on Creating and Using Semantics for Information Retrieval and Filtering, Third International Conference on Language Resources and Evaluation*, Las Palmas, Canary Islands, Spain, June.

Kumar, Shankar & William Byrne. 2002. Minimum Bayes-risk word alignment of bilingual texts. *Proceedings of the 2002 Conference on Empirical Methods in Natural Language Processing (EMNLP)*, July, Philadelphia, PA.

Lakoff, George & Mark Johnson. 1980. *Metaphors We Live By.* University of Chicago Press.

Levow, Gina-Anne, Douglas W. Oard & Philip Resnik. 2005. Dictionary-based techniques for cross-language information retrieval, *Information Processing and Management*, 41: 523–547.

Li, Hang & Cong Li. 2004. Word translation disambiguation using bilingual bootstrapping. *Computational Linguistics,* 30(1): 1–22.

Li, Ying & Zijan Zheng. 2005. KDD-Cup 2005 presentation, *Eleventh ACM SIGKDD International Conference on Knowledge Discovery and Data Mining (KDD-05)*. (http://kdd05.lac.uic.edu/kddcup.html)

Lin, Dekang & Patrick Pantel. 2001. Induction of semantic classes from natural language text. *Proceedings of ACM SIGKDD Conference on Knowledge Discovery and Data Mining*, 317–322.

Littman, Michael, Susan Dumais & Thomas Landauer. 1998. Automatic cross-language information retrieval using latent semantic indexing. *Cross Language Information Retrieval* ed. by Gregory Grefenstette, 51–62. Kluwer Academic Publishers.

Liu, Shuang, Fang Liu, Clement Yu & Weiyi Meng. 2004. An effective approach to document retrieval via utilizing WordNet and recognizing phrases. *Proceedings of the 27th Annual International ACM SIGIR Conference on Research and Development in Information Retrieval*, Sheffield, UK, 266–272.

Löfberg, Laura, Jukka-Pekka Juntunen, Asko Nykänen, Krysta Varantola, Paul Rayson & Dawn Archer. 2004. Using a semantic tagger as a dictionary search tool. *Proceedings of the 11th EURALEX (European Association for Lexicography) International Congress*, Lorient, France, July, 127–134.

Long, Letitia. 2004. *Statement of Ms. Letitia A. Long, Deputy Under Secretary of Defense for Policy, Requirements and Resources, Office of the Under Secretary of Defense (Intelligence) before the Subcommittee on Intelligence Policy and National Security of the Permanent Select Committee on Intelligence, U.S. House of Representatives, February 26, 2004.* Downloaded from http://www.dod.gov/dodgc/olc/docs/test04-02-26Long.doc, 31 Oct 2005.

Mandala, Rila, Tokunaga Takenobu & Tanaka Hozumi. 1998. The use of WordNet in information retrieval. *Proceedings of the COLING-ACL 1998 Workshop on Usage of WordNet in Natural Language Processing Systems*, Montreal, Canada.

Martin, Joel, Rada Mihalcea & Ted Pedersen. 2005. Word alignment for languages with scarce resources. *Proceedings of the ACL 2005 Workshop on Building and Using Parallel Texts: Data Driven Machine Translation and Beyond*, Ann Arbor, MI, June.

Mihalcea, Rada & Dan Moldovan. 1999. A method for word sense disambiguation of unrestricted text. *Proceedings of the 37th Annual Meeting of the Association for Computational Linguistics (ACL)*, Maryland, NY, 152–158.

Mihalcea, Rada & Dan Moldovan. 2000. Semantic indexing using WordNet senses. *Proceedings of the ACL Workshop on Recent Advances in Natural Language Processing and Information Retrieval*, Hong Kong.

Mihalcea, Rada & Ted Pedersen. An evaluation exercise for word alignment. 2004. *Proceedings of the HLT-NAACL 2004 Workshop on Building and Using Parallel Texts: Data Driven Machine Translation and Beyond*, Edmonton, Canada, May.

Mihalcea, Rada & Philip Edmonds, eds. 2004. *Proceedings of Senseval-3: Third International Workshop on the Evaluation of Systems for the Semantic Analysis of Text*, Barcelona, Spain. (http://www.senseval.org/)

Mihalcea, Rada, Paul Tarau & Elizabeth Figa. 2004. PageRank on semantic networks with application to word sense disambiguation. *Proceedings of the 20th International Conference on Computational Linguistics (COLING)*, Switzerland, Geneva.

Moldovan, Dan & Vasile Rus. 2001. Logic form transformation of WordNet and its applicability to question answering. *Proceedings of 39th Annual Meeting of the Association for Computational Linguistics (ACL)*, Toulouse, France, 394–401.

Moschitti, Alessandro & Roberto Basili. 2004. Complex linguistic features for text classification: a comprehensive study. *Advances in Information Retrieval:*

26th European Conference on IR Research (ECIR 2004), Sunderland, UK, April, 181–196.

Nagao, Makoto. 1984. A framework of a mechanical translation between Japanese and English by analogy principle. *Proceedings of the International NATO Symposium on Artificial and Human Intelligence*, 173–180.

Ng, Hwee Tou, Bin Wang & Yee Seng Chan. 2003. Exploiting parallel texts for word sense disambiguation: An empirical study. *Proceedings of the 41st Annual Meeting of the Association for Computational Linguistics (ACL)*, Sapporo, Japan, 455–462.

Oard, Douglas W. & Bonnie J. Dorr. 1996. *A Survey of Multilingual Text Retrieval*. Computer Science Report CS-TR-3615, University of Maryland, USA.

Och, Franz Joseph. 2002. *Statistical Machine Translation: From Single-Word Models to Alignment Templates*. Ph.D. Thesis, RWTH Aachen, Germany.

Oltramari, Alessandro, Patrizia Paggio, Aldo Gangemi, Maria Teresa Pazienza, Nicoletta Calzolari, Bolette Sandford Pedersen & Kiril Simov, eds. 2004. *OntoLex 2004: Ontologies and Lexical Resources in Distributed Environments*, Workshop in association with the 4th International Conference on Language Resources and Evaluation (LREC), Lisbon, May.

Paşca, Marius & Sanda Harabagiu. 2001a. High performance question/answering. *Proceedings of the 24th Annual International ACM SIGIR Conference on Research and Development in Information Retrieval*, New Orleans LA, 366–374.

Paşca, Marius & Sanda Harabagiu. 2001b. The informative role of WordNet in open-domain question answering. *Proceedings of NAACL-2001 Workshop on WordNet and Other Lexical Resources,* Pittsburgh, PA, 138–143.

Prager, John, Eric Brown, Anni Coden & Dragomir Radev. 2000. Question-answering by predictive annotation. *Proceedings of the 23rd Annual International ACM SIGIR Conference on Research and Development in Information Retrieval*, Athens, Greece, 184–191.

Prange, John. 2004. Making the case for advanced question answering. Keynote presentation. *Workshop on Pragmatics of Question Answering at HLT-NAACL 2004*, Boston.

Pustejovsky, James. 1995. *The Generative Lexicon*. MIT Press.

Qu, Yan, Gregory Grefenstette & David A. Evans. 2002. Resolving translation ambiguity using monolingual corpora. *Advances in Cross-Language Information Retrieval: Third Workshop of the Cross-Language Evaluation Forum (CLEF 2002)*, Rome, Italy, 223–241.

Resnik, Philip. 1993. *Selection and Information: A Class-Based Approach to Lexical Relationships.* Ph.D. Thesis, Department of Computer and Information Science, University of Pennsylvania, USA.

Resnik, Philip. 2004. Exploiting hidden meanings: Using bilingual text for monolingual annotation. *Lecture Notes in Computer Science 2945: Computational Linguistics and Intelligent Text Processing*, ed. by Alexander Gelbukh, 283–299. New York: Springer-Verlag.

Resnik, Philip & David Yarowsky. 2000. Distinguishing systems and distinguishing senses: New evaluation methods for word sense disambiguation. *Natural Language Engineering,* 5(2): 113–133.

Rigau, German, Bernardo Magnini, Eneko Agirre, Piek Vossen & John Carroll. 2002. MEANING: A roadmap to knowledge technologies. *Proceedings of the COLING Workshop on a Roadmap for Computational Linguistics*, Taipei, Taiwan.

Sanderson, Mark. Word sense disambiguation and information retrieval. 1994. *Proceedings of the 17th Annual International ACM SIGIR Conference on Research and Development in Information Retrieval*, Dublin, Ireland, 142–151.

Sanderson, Mark. 2000. Retrieving with good sense. *Information Retrieval*, 2(1): 49–69.

Sawyer, Peter, Paul Rayson, & Ken Cosh. Forthcoming. Shallow knowledge as an aid to deep understanding in early-phase requirements engineering. *IEEE Transactions on Software Engineering.*

Schütze, Hinrich. 1998. Automatic word sense discrimination. *Computational Linguistics*, 24(1): 97–123.

Schütze, Hinrich & Jan Pedersen. 1995. Information retrieval based on word senses. *Fourth Annual Symposium on Document Analysis and Information Retrieval*, Las Vegas, NV, 161–175.

Smeaton, Alan & Ian Quigley. 1996. Experiments on using semantic distances between words in image caption retrieval. *Proceedings of the 19th Annual International ACM SIGIR Conference on Research and Development in Information Retrieval*, Zurich, 174–180.

Sparck Jones, Karen. 1964/1986. *Synonymy and Semantic Classification.* Edinburgh: Edinburgh University Press.

Sparck Jones, Karen. 1999. What is the role of NLP in text retrieval? *Natural Language Information Retrieval*, ed. by Tomek Strzalkowski. New York: Kluwer Academic Publishers.

Stoica, Emilia & Marti Hearst. 2004. Nearly-automated metadata hierarchy creation. *Proceedings of HLT-NAACL 2004: Short Papers*, Boston, MA, USA, 117–120.

Stokoe, Chris M., Michael J. Oakes & John I. Tait. 2003. Word sense disambiguation in information retrieval revisited. *Proceedings of the 26th Annual International ACM SIGIR Conference on Research and Development in Information Retrieval*, Toronto, Canada, 159–166.

Tufiş, Dan, Radu Ion & Nancy Ide. Fine-grained word sense disambiguation based on parallel corpora, word alignment, word clustering, and aligned wordnets. *Proceedings of the Twentieth International Conference on Computational Linguistics (COLING-2004)*. August 2004, Geneva.

Véronis, Jean. 2004. HyperLex: Lexical cartography for information retrieval. *Computer Speech & Language*, 18(3): 223–252.

Vickrey, David, Luke Biewald, Marc Teyssier & Daphne Koller. Word-sense disambiguation for machine translation. 2005. *Proceedings of Human Language Technology Conference/Conference on Empirical Methods in Natural Language Processing (HLT/EMNLP-2005)*. Vancouver, Canada, October.

Voorhees, Ellen M. 1999. Natural language processing and information retrieval. *Information Extraction: Towards Scalable, Adaptable Systems*, ed. by M. T. Pazienza, 32–48. London: Springer-Verlag. (Lecture Notes in Computer Science 1714.)

Voorhees, Ellen M. & Dawn M. Tice. 2000a. Building a question answering test collection. *Proceedings of the 23rd Annual International ACM SIGIR Conference on Research and Development in Information Retrieval*, Athens, Greece, 200–207.

Vossen, Piek, German Rigau, Iñaki Alegria, Eneko Agirre, David Farwell & Manuel Fuentes. 2006. Meaningful results for information retrieval in the MEANING project. *Proceedings of the Third Global WordNet Conference*, Jeju Island, Korea.

Webb, Lynn E. 2001. *Advantages and Disadvantages of Translation Memory: A Cost/Benefit Analysis*. M.A. Thesis, Monterey Institute of International Studies, Monterey, CA, USA.

Weeber, Mark, James Mork & Alan Aronson. 2001. Developing a test collection for biomedical word sense disambiguation. *Proceedings of the AMIA 2001 Symposium*.

White, J. & T. O'Connell. 1994. The ARPA MT evaluation methodologies: Evolution, lessons, and future approaches. *Technology Partnerships for Crossing the Language Barrier: Proceedings of the First Conference of the Association for Machine Translation in the Americas (AMTA)*, Columbia, MD, USA, 193–205.

Wilcock, Graham, Paul Buitelaar, Antonio Pareja-Lora, Barrett Bryant, Jimmy Lin & Nancy Ide. 2004. The roles of natural language and XML in the Semantic Web. *Computational Linguistics and Beyond: Perspectives at the Beginning of the 21st Century*, ed. by Chu-Ren Huang & Winfried Lenders, Frontiers in Linguistics Series, Academia Sinica, Taiwan.

Wilks, Yorick. 1997. Senses and texts. *Computers and the Humanities* 31(2): 77–90.

Wilks, Yorick. 1998. Is word-sense disambiguation just one more NLP task? *Proceedings of the SENSEVAL Conference*, Herstmonceaux, Sussex. Also appears as Technical Report CS-98-12, Department of Computer Science, University of Sheffield.

Wilks, Yorick & Dan Fass. 1992. The preference semantics family. *Computers & Mathematics with Applications,* 23(2–5): 205–221.

Woods, William A. 1995. Finding information on the Web: A knowledge representation approach. Presented at the *Fourth International World Wide Web Conference*, Boston, MA.

Woods, William A. & Ronald Kaplan. 1971. *The Lunar Sciences Natural Language Information System*. Technical Report 2265, Bolt, Beranek and Newman, Cambridge, MA.

Yarowsky, David. 1993. One sense per collocation. *Proceedings of the ARPA Human Language Technology Workshop,* Princeton, 266–271.

Yarowsky, David. 1995. Unsupervised word sense disambiguation rivaling supervised methods. *Proceedings of the 33rd Annual Meeting of the Association for Computational Linguistics*, Cambridge, MA, 189–196.

Yarowsky, David. 2000. Hierarchical decision lists for word sense disambiguation. *Computers and the Humanities*, 34(1–2): 179–186.

Yee, Ping, Kirsten Swearingen, Kevin Li & Marti Hearst. 2003. Faceted metadata for image search and browsing. *Proceedings of the conference on Human Factors in Computing Systems (ACM CHI)*, Ft. Lauderdale, Florida, USA, 401–408.

Yeh, Alexander, Lynette Hirschman & Alexander Morgan. 2002. Background and overview for KDD Cup 2002 Task 1: Information extraction from biomedical articles. *SIGKDD Explorations: Newsletter of the ACM Special Interest Group on Knowledge Discovery and Data Mining*, 4(2): 87–89.

Yu, Hong, George Hripcsak & Carol Friedman. 2002. Mapping abbreviations to full forms in biomedical articles. *Journal of the American Medical Informatics Association*, 9(3): 262–272.

Yu, Hong, Won Kim, Vasileios Hatzivassiloglou & W. John Wilbur. 2004. Using MEDLINE as a knowledge source for disambiguating abbreviations in full-text biomedical journal articles. *Proceedings of the 17th IEEE Symposium on Computer-Based Medical Systems (CBMS 2004)*, Bethesda, MD, USA, 27–33.

Zajic, David M. & Keith J. Miller. 1998. Where interlingua can make a difference. *Proceedings of the AMTA/SIG-IL Second Workshop on Interlinguas*, Langhorne, PA. (Published in technical report MCCS-98-316, Computing Research Laboratory, New Mexico State University.)

A Resources for WSD

Research into WSD has produced and used numerous resources, many of which are freely available on the Internet. This appendix surveys the main resources. It covers sense inventories, including dictionaries, thesauri, and lexical knowledge bases; corpora, including both untagged and sense-tagged corpora; and various other resources such as web sites, software, and data. Lexical resources usually provide additional linguistic information that can be used by WSD systems. Corpora, both untagged and sense-tagged provide examples of words (and word senses) in use.

Many of the resourced below have been discussed in the book, but others are less used or more novel. For each, we give a short description, including its relevance to WSD and information on availability.

In the current world of rapid progress, an appendix such as this is doomed to become outdated. We may also be unaware of some resources. For these reasons, the authors, with the help of the community, will maintain a evolving webpage at http://www.wsdbook.org/.

A.1 Sense Inventories

In this section, we present dictionaries, thesauri and lexical knowledge bases. All WSD systems that use an explicit sense inventory need to make reference to a particular resource. The knowledge-based WSD methods in Chapter 5 also use the linguistic information coded in dictionaries and knowledge bases. Other methods that use the information in dictionaries, thesauri and knowledge bases can be found in Chapters 9 and 10. Many of the knowledge sources referred to in Chapter 8 are also related to these resources.

A.1.1 Dictionaries

Resource	*Longman Dictionary of Contemporary English (LDOCE)*
Description	LDOCE is one of the most widely used dictionaries in language research. It has 55,000 entries or word definitions.

	Definitions are written exclusively in the Longman's Defining Vocabulary, which is a set of approximately 2,000 words (plus derived forms). Another of LDOCE's most characteristic features is the inclusion of subject field labels, which are roughly equivalent to domain tags for each word sense. LDOCE entries also contain so-called box codes, primitives like "abstract", "animate", "human", etc. which are used to represent selectional preference information for verbal word senses.
	Longman has released a version specially suited to NLP called LDOCE3 NLP database, which is based on the 3rd edition of the regular LDOCE. It has been widely used in WSD experiments.
Availability	LDOCE3 NLP Database: freely for research.
Web	http://www.longman.com/ldoce http://www.longman.com/dictionaries/research/dictres.html

Resource	*OED – Oxford English Dictionary – and DIMAP*
Description	The 2nd edition of the *Oxford English Dictionary* (OED) was released in October 2002 and contains 170,000 entries covering all varieties of English. Available in XML and in SGML, this dictionary includes phrases and idioms, semantic relations and subject tags corresponding to nearly 200 major domains. A computer-tractable version of the machine-readable OED was released by CL Research. This version comes along with the DIMAP software, which allows the user to develop computational lexicons by parsing and processing dictionary definitions. It has been used in a number of experiments.
Availability	DIMAP version: available for a fee.
Web	http://www.oed.com http://www.clres.com

Resource	*Hector*
Description	The Hector dictionary was the outcome of the Hector project (1992–1993) and was used as a sense inventory in Senseval-1. It was built by a joint team from Systems Research Centre of Digital Equipment Corporation, Palo Alto, and lexicographers from Oxford Univ. Press. The creation of this dictionary involved the analysis of a 17.3 million word corpus of 80-90s British English. Over 220,000 tokens and 1,400 dictionary entries were manually analyzed and semantically annotated. It was a pilot for the BNC (see below). Senseval-1 used it as the English sense inventory and testing corpus.
Availability	n/a
Web	n/a

A.1.2 Thesauri

Resource	*Roget's Thesaurus*
Description	The older 1911 edition has been made freely available by Project Gutenberg. Although it lacks many new terms, it has been used to derive a number of knowledge bases, including Factotum. In a more recent edition, *Roget's Thesaurus of English Words and Phrases* contains over 250,000 word entries arranged in 6 classes and 990 categories. Jarmasz and Szpakowicz, at the University of Ottawa, developed a lexical knowledge base derived from this thesaurus. The conceptual structures extracted from the thesaurus are combined with some elements of WordNet.
Availability	1911 version and Factotum: freely available.
Web	http://gutenberg.org/etext91/roget15a.txt http://www.cs.nmsu.edu/~tomohara/factotum-roles/node4.html

A.1.3 Lexical Knowledge Bases

Resource	*WordNet*
Description	The Princeton WordNet (WN), one of the lexical resources most used in NLP applications, is a large-scale lexical database for English developed by the Cognitive Science Laboratory at Princeton University. In its latest release (version 2.1), WN covers 155,327 words corresponding to 117,597 lexicalized concepts, including 4 syntactic categories: nouns, verbs, adjectives and adverbs. WN shares some characteristics with monolingual dictionaries. Its glosses and examples provided for word senses resemble dictionary definitions. However, WN is organized by semantic relations, providing a hierarchy and network of word relationships. WordNet has been used to construct or enrich a number of knowledge bases including Omega and the Multilingual Central Repository (see addresses below). The problems posed by the different sense numbering across versions can be overcome using sense mappings, which are freely available (see address below). It has been extensively used in WSD. WordNet was used as the sense inventory in English Senseval-2 and Senseval-3.
Availability	Free for research.
Web	http://wordnet.princeton.edu http://omega.isi.edu http://nipadio.lsi.upc.edu/cgi-bin/wei4/public/wei.consult.perl http://www.lsi.upc.es/~nlp/tools/mapping.html

Resource	*EuroWordNet*
Description	EuroWordNet (EWN) is a multilingual extension of the Princeton WN. The EWN database built in the original projects comprises WordNet-like databases for 8 European languages (English, Spanish, German, Dutch, Italian, French, Estonian and Czech) connected to each other at the concept level via the "Inter-Lingual Index". It is available through ELDA (see below). Beyond the EWN projects, a number of WordNets have been developed following the same structural requirements, such as BalkaNet. The Global WordNet Association is currently endorsing the creation of WordNets in many other languages, and lists the availability information for each WordNet. EWN has been extensively used in WSD.
Availability	Depends on language.
Web	http://www.globalwordnet.org http://www.ceid.upatras.gr/Balkanet

Resource	*WordNet Domains*
Description	WordNet Domains is an extension of the Princeton English WordNet, in which synsets have been annotated by domain labels, such as Medicine, Architecture, and Sport. It has been used in research on domain-specific WSD.
Availability	Free for research.
Web	http://wndomains.itc.it

Resource	*FrameNet (and annotated examples)*
Description	The FrameNet database contains information on lexical units and underlying conceptual structures. A description of a lexical item in FrameNet consists of a list of frames that underlie its meaning and syntactic realizations of the corresponding frame elements and their constellations in structures headed by the word. For each word sense a documented range of semantic and syntactic combinatory possibilities is provided. Hand-annotated examples are provided for each frame. At the time of printing FrameNet contained about 6,000 lexical units and 130,000 annotated sentences. The development of German, Japanese, and Spanish FrameNets has also been undertaken. Although widely used in semantic role disambiguation, it has had a very limited connection to WSD. Still, it has the potential in work to combine the disambiguation of semantic roles and senses.
Availability	Free for research.
Web	http://framenet.icsi.berkeley.edu/

Resource	*UMLS*
Description	The Unified Medical Language System (UMLS) is composed of several knowledge sources. The Metathesaurus is a very large, multi-purpose, and multi-lingual, vocabulary database that contains information about biomedical and health-related concepts, their various names, and the relationships among them. The Semantic Network provides a consistent categorization of all concepts represented in the UMLS Metathesaurus and provides a set of useful relationships between these concepts. The current release of the Semantic Network contains 135 semantic types and 54 relationships. It has been used to develop sense-annotated corpora (see NLM WSD Test Corpus below)
Availability	Free for research.
Web	http://www.nlm.nih.gov/research/umls

A.2 Corpora

Corpora contain direct evidence about the frequency and cooccurrence of linguistic elements that can not be extracted from dictionaries or other sense inventories. We have classified them into three groups: raw corpora without sense annotations, annotated corpora, and automatically acquired corpora. Many corpora now exist for English and other languages. We include below several that have been discussed in the book.

A.2.1 Raw Corpora

By raw corpora, we mean corpora that have no annotation for word meaning, though they may have other annotations, such as part-of-speech tags. Raw corpora are useful for unsupervised WSD systems (Chapter 9).

Resource	*The Brown Corpus*
Description	The Brown Corpus is a million-word "balanced" collection of texts published in United States in 1961. It contains samples of written prose, ranging from a variety of press articles (news, reviews, and reportage), fragments of scientific texts, to fiction, classified into 15 categories. There are 500 documents of about 2,000 words each. Part of the hand-annotated Semcor corpus (see below) is a subset of the Brown Corpus.

	The Brown Corpus is available through ICAME (International Computer Archive of Modern and Medieval English). The corpus can be also accessed on-line at the LDC site (see below).
Availability	Free for research.
Web	http://nora.hd.uib.no/whatis.html

Resource	*The British National Corpus*
Description	The British National Corpus (BNC) is the result of joint work of leading dictionary publishers (Oxford University Press, Longman, and Chambers-Larousse) and academic research centers (Oxford University, Lancaster University, and the British Library). The BNC has been built as a reasonably balanced corpus: for written sources, samples of 45,000 words have been taken from various parts of single-author texts. Shorter texts up to a maximum of 45,000 words, or multi-author texts such as magazines and newspapers, were included in full, avoiding over-representing idiosyncratic texts.
Availability	Available for a fee.
Web	http://www.natcorp.ox.ac.uk

Resource	*The Wall Street Journal Corpus*
Description	This corpus has been widely used in NLP. It is the base of the manually annotated DSO, Penn Treebank, and PropBank corpora. It is not directly available in raw form, but can be accessed through the Penn Treebank.
Availability	Available for a fee at LDC.
Web	http://www.ldc.upenn.edu/Catalog/LDC2000T43.html

Resource	*The New York Times Corpus (English Gigaword Corpus)*
Description	This corpus is not available, but is part of the larger English Gigaword corpus.
Availability	Available for a fee at LDC.
Web	http://www.ldc.upenn.edu/Catalog/LDC2003T05.html

Resource	*The Reuters News Corpus*
Description	This corpus has been widely used in NLP, especially in document categorization. It is currently being used to develop a specialized hand-tagged corpus (see the domain specific Sussex corpus below). An earlier Reuters corpus (for information extraction research) is known as Reuters-21578.
Availability	Freely available.
Web	http://trec.nist.gov/data/reuters/reuters.html

A.2.2 Sense-Tagged Corpora

Sense-tagged corpora are the primary resource for supervised WSD algorithms and the only way of testing and comparing WSD systems in general. We briefly review here the main sense-tagged corpora available, and additional details can be found in Chapter 4. The use of sense-tagged corpora for supervised WSD is discussed in Chapter 7.

Resource	*DSO Corpus*
Description	This corpus was compiled by a team at the Defence Science Organisation (DSO) of Singapore. It contains texts from the Brown and Wall Street Journal corpora. 192,800 sense-tagged tokens of 121 nouns and 70 verbs which, according to the authors, represent some of the most frequently occurring and ambiguous words in English, were manually annotated with WordNet 1.5 synsets by linguistics students at the National University of Singapore.
Availability	Available for a fee at LDC.
Web	http://www.ldc.upenn.edu/Catalog/LDC97T12.html

Resource	*Semcor*
Description	Semcor, created at Princeton University by the same team who created WordNet, is the largest publicly available sense-tagged corpus. It is composed of documents extracted from the Brown Corpus that were tagged both syntactically and semantically. The POS tags were assigned by the Brill tagger, and the semantic tagging was done manually, using WordNet 1.6 senses. Semcor is composed of 352 texts. In 186 texts all of the open class words (192,639 nouns, verbs, adjectives, and adverbs) are annotated with POS, lemma, and WordNet synset, while in the remaining 166 texts only verbs (41,497 occurrences) are annotated with lemma and synset. Although the original Semcor was annotated with WordNet version 1.6, the annotations have been automatically mapped into newer versions (available from the same website below).
Availability	Freely available.
Web	http://www.cs.unt.edu/~rada/downloads.html

Resource	*Open Mind Word Expert*
Description	This corpus has been annotated with WordNet 1.7 senses by regular Web users, in a collaborative annotation effort.
Availability	Freely available.
Web	http://teach-computers.org/word-expert.html http://www.cs.unt.edu/~rada/downloads.html

Resource	*Senseval Test Suites*
Description	The various Senseval competitions have produced training and test data for lexical sample evaluation in a considerable number of languages.
Availability	Freely available.
Web	http://www.senseval.org/

Resource	*MultiSemCor*
Description	MultiSemCor is an English/Italian parallel corpus, aligned at the word level and annotated with POS, lemma and word sense. The corpus was built aligning the Italian translation of Semcor at word level and transferring the word sense annotations from English to the aligned Italian words.
Availability	Free for research.
Web	http://multisemcor.itc.it

Resource	*Line-Hard-Serve Corpus*
Description	This corpus contains around 4,000 sense-tagged examples of each of the words *line* (noun), *hard* (adjective), and *serve* (verb) with subsets of their WordNet 1.5 senses. Examples are drawn from the WSJ corpus, the American Printing House for the Blind, and the San Jose Mercury.
Availability	Freely available.
Web	http://www.d.umn.edu/~tpederse/data.html

Resource	*Interest Corpus*
Description	This corpus contains 2,396 sense-tagged examples from the WSJ corpus of the noun *interest* according to 6 LDOCE senses
Availability	Freely available.
Web	http://www.d.umn.edu/~tpederse/data.html

Resource	*National Library of Medicine WSD Test Collection*
Description	The NLM WSD Test Corpus consists of 50 ambiguous words that occur in medical journal abstracts (from Medline) that have been manually sense tagged with UMLS concepts (see above).
Availability	Freely available.
Web	http://wsd.nlm.nih.gov

Resource	*Domain-Specific Sussex Corpus*
Description	Koeling et al. built a domain-specific sense-tagged corpus based on the BNC and Reuters corpus.
Availability	Contact authors (robk@sussex.ac.uk).
Web	n/a

Resource	*Orwell's 1984 Test Data*
Description	Tufis et al. describe a hand-tagged portion of the multilingual *1984* corpus, comprising Bulgarian, Czech, Greek, Romanian, Serbian, and Turkish translations and the English original aligned at word level. Wordnet was used as the inventory.
Availability	Contact authors (tufis@racai.ro).
Web	n/a

Resource	*PropBank*
Description	PropBank is an annotation of the Wall Street Journal portion of the Penn Treebank II with dependency structures (or "predicate-argument" structures), using sense tags for each word and argument labels for each dependency. The sense tags are related to the VerbNet lexical knowledge base (see above). Although widely used in semantic role disambiguation, it has had a very limited connection to WSD as yet.
Availability	Available for a fee from the LDC.
Web	http://www.cis.upenn.edu/~mpalmer/project_pages/ACE.htm

Resource	*FrameNet Examples*
Description	See FrameNeet entry above.
Availability	Free for research.
Web	http://framenet.icsi.berkeley.edu/

A.2.3 Automatically Tagged Corpora

Only a few automatically-tagged corpora exist. We briefly mention two, which are publicly available.

Resource	*Sensecorpus*
Description	This corpus, containing thousands of examples of WordNet 1.6 nominal senses, constructed using the monosemous relatives method.
Availability	Freely available.
Web	http://ixa.si.ehu.es/Ixa/resources/sensecorpus

Resource	*ODP Corpus*
Description	The ODP corpus contains WordNet 1.7 nominal senses constructed by associating Open Directory Project (ODP) categories to synsets.
Availability	Freely available.
Web	http://nlp.uned.es/ODP http://dmoz.org

A.3 Other Resources

In this section we list a variety of resources related to WSD, many of which have been mentioned in the book, including software, miscellaneous data, and language providers.

A.3.1 Software

Resource	*Sense Learner*
Description	All-words minimally-supervised WSD implementation.
Availability	Freely available.
Web	http://www.cs.unt.edu/~rada/downloads.html

Resource	*WSD Shell*
Description	All-words supervised WSD implementation.
Availability	Freely available.
Web	http://www.d.umn.edu/~tpederse/wsdshell.html

Resource	*WordNet::Sense Relate*
Description	All-words knowledge-based WSD implementation, based on WordNet::Similarity (below).
Availability	Freely available.
Web	http://www.d.umn.edu/~tpederse/senserelate.html

Resource	*WordNet::Similarity*
Description	This Perl package provides a number of word-sense similarity measures based on WordNet.
Availability	Freely available.
Web	http://www.d.umn.edu/~tpederse/similarity.html

Resource	*Senseclusters*
Description	This software clusters similar contexts together using unsupervised knowledge-lean methods. These techniques have been applied to word sense discrimination, email categorization, and name discrimination.
Availability	Freely available.
Web	http://www.d.umn.edu/~tpederse/senseclusters.html

A.3.2 Utilities, Demos, and Data

Resource	*Ted Pedersen's Page*
Description	This webpage includes various corpora and pieces of software. Apart from those already mentioned above, it includes several useful utilities, e.g., for format changing.
Availability	Freely available.
Web	http://www.d.umn.edu/~tpederse

Resource	*Rada Mihalcea's Page*
Description	This webpage includes various corpora and useful utilities.
Availability	Freely available.
Web	http://www.cs.unt.edu/~rada

Resource	*Topic Signatures*
Description	Topic signatures are context vectors built for word senses and concepts. This webpage provides topic signatures for all nominal senses in WordNet 1.6. They were built on the Sensecorpus data (see above).
Availability	Freely available.
Web	http://ixa.si.ehu.es/Ixa/resources/sensecorpus

Resource	*Selectional Preferences from Semcor*
Description	Downloadable selectional preferences for WordNet 1.6 verb senses built from Semcor
Availability	Freely available.
Web	http://ixa.si.ehu.es/Ixa/resources/selprefs

Resource	*Clustering By Committee Online Demo*
Description	Online demo of Clustering By Committee (CBC) for inducing concepts.
Availability	Freely available.
Web	http://www.isi.edu/~pantel/Content/Demos/LexSem/cbc.htm

A.3.3 Language Data Providers

Resource	*Linguistic Data Consortium*
Description	The Linguistic Data Consortium (LDC) is an open consortium of more than 100 universities, companies, and government research laboratories, founded in 1992. Its main objective is to create, collect, and distribute speech and text databases, lexicons, and other linguistic resources for research and development purposes.
Availability	n/a
Web	http://www.ldc.upenn.edu

Resource	*Evaluation and Language Resources Distribution Agency*
Description	The Evaluation and Language Resources Distribution Agency (ELDA) is the operational body of the European Language Resources Association (ELRA), a non-profit organization founded in Luxembourg in 1995 with the purpose of providing language resources for research and development. Its activities include the collection and distribution of linguistic resources, their evaluation and standardization.
Availability	n/a
Web	http://www.elda.fr

A.3.4 Organizations and Mailing Lists

Resource	*Senseval Organization*
Description	Senseval runs competitions to evaluation WSD systems. The website provides data from the competitions, a program to score WSD systems, and the proceedings of the Senseval workshops.
Availability	Freely available
Web	http://www.senseval.org

Resource	*Senseval Mailing List*
Description	This is a low-traffic list, primarily for competition issues
Availability	n/a
Web	http://listserv.hum.gu.se/mailman/listinfo/senseval-discuss

Resource	*SIGLEX*
Description	SIGLEX, the Special Interest Group on the Lexicon of the Association for Computational Linguistics (ACL), provides an umbrella for research interests on lexical issues ranging from lexicography and the use of online dictionaries to computational lexical semantics. SIGLEX is also the umbrella organization for SENSEVAL, evaluation exercises for Word Sense Disambiguation.
Availability	n/a
Web	http://www.clres.com/siglex.html

Index of Terms

A

abbreviations/acronyms, resolving, 318

accuracy, defined, 79

acquisition of examples, automatic, 198, 253–74, *See also* monosemous relatives method

active learning, 195, 199

AdaBoost, 179, 187, 235, 237

advertising, targeting, 312

aggregative method, 233, 244

agreement. *See* inter-tagger agreement

AI. *See* artificial intelligence

AI-complete, 1

all-words task, defined, 76

ALPAC, 5, 223

Altavista, 255

application, 10–12, 18, 55, 58, *See also specific applications*
  positive impact. *See* positive impact
  WSD as enabling technology for, 2, 299–303

artificial intelligence, 6, 48

B

bag of words, 190, 227, 233, 304, 310, 312

BalkaNet, 81

Bar-Hillel, Y., 5, 223, 300

baseline, 14, 79, 88, 91, 291, *See also* most frequent sense
  Lesk, 112

most frequent sense, 123

bias problem, 260, *See also* word sense, skewed frequency distribution

bioinformatics, 11, 295, 317

BITS, 267

BNC. *See* British National Corpus

bootstrapping method, 201, 324

box-in-the-pen example, Bar-Hillel, 5, 223, 300

British National Corpus, 87, 90, 139, 280

Brown Corpus, 82, 84, 173, 197, 280

C

CANDIDE, 57

CBC. *See* Clustering By Committee

CLEF, 268

CLIR. *See* cross-lingual information retrieval

clustering, 134, 137, 140, 148, 150, 153, 278, 321, *See also* word sense, clustering of

Clustering By Committee, 148

collapsing. *See* word sense, clustering of

collocation. *See* feature, local collocation

combination method, 179, 203

combinatorial explosion, 110

conceptual density, 116, 239

concordance, 137, *See also* Key Word in Context

context, 5, 17, 170, *See also* feature

local, 3, 5, 175, 190, 225–26,
  233, 234, 240
  local collocation, 3, 182, 220,
    225, 242, 316
  syntactic, 3, 175, 233, 234, 237
  topical, 190
feature selection, 202
Firth, J. R., 321
Frege, G., 33, 34

G

GenCor, 198, 262
gold standard, 77, 80, 90
Google, 255
graph-based algorithm, 119, 322
Grice, H. P., 32, 34
Grolier's Encyclopedia, 147

H

HAL. *See* Hyperspace Analogue to
  Language
Hector dictionary and corpus, 9,
  87– 88, 92, 173
homograph, 14, 48, 56, 58–64, 58,
  279, S*ee also* word sense, coarse-
  grained
  defined, 8, 60
Hyperspace Analogue to Language,
  147

I

implicit disambiguation. *See* word
  sense disambiguation, implicit
information extraction, 11, 317
information retrieval, 10, 55, 56,
  139, 162, 179, 253, 304–13, *See
  also* cross-lingual information
  retrieval
  explicit WSD, argument against,
    305
  failure of WSD, 302
  implicit disambiguation. *See*
    implicit disambiguation

query ambiguity, 305, 306, 308,
  312
information theory, 120
inter-annotator agreement. *See* inter-
  tagger agreement
interest corpus, 83
inter-tagger agreement, 14, 52, 54,
  194
  defined, 79
  disagreement, 92
  in Senseval-2, 90, 93, 97
  unrealistic goal, 95
IR. *See* information retrieval
ITA. *See* inter-tagger agreement

K

kappa coefficient, 80, 90, 194
kernel-based method, 180
Key Word In Context (KWIC), 30
k-nearest neighbor, 176, 186
knowledge acquisition bottleneck, 6,
  12, 133, 172, 197, 253
knowledge source, 204, 217–51
knowledge-based method, 6, 12,
  107–31, 134
knowledge-intensive method. *See*
  knowledge-based method
knowledge-lean method, 134, *See
  also* minimally supervised
  method

L

Latent Semantic Analysis/Indexing,
  146, 152, 321
  cross-language, 323
LDOCE. *See Longman Dictionary
  of Contemporary English*
learning curve, 195
Lesk algorithm, 6, 88, 108, 239, 240
  adapted, 113
  corpus-based, 112
  simplified, 111
lexical chain, 118
lexical knowledge base, 12, 107,

Index of Authors and Algorithms

A

Agirre and Martínez 2001, 121, 238, domain effect in WSD
Agirre and Martínez 2004, 259, automatic acquisition of examples
Agirre and Rigau 1996, 116, conceptual density, semantic similarity method
Agirre, Ansa, Martínez, and Hovy 2001, 282, topic signatures, sense clustering
Agirre, de Lacalle, and Martínez 2005, 204, supervised kNN method

B

Banerjee and Pedersen 2002/2003, 113, 138, dictionary-based method
Bar-Hillel 1960, 5, 300, WSD and MT
Bhattacharya, Getoor, and Bengio 2004, 324, cross-lingual method
Bloehdorn and Hotho 2004, 312, WSD in document classification
Brown et al. 1991, 7, 159, 324, WSD in statistical MT
Buitelaar and Sacaleanu 2001, 285, domain tuning

C

Cabezas and Resnik 2005, 317, domain tuning
Carpuat and Wu 2005, 317, WSD and MT
Chan and Ng 2005, 266, cross-lingual method
Chklovski and Mihalcea 2002, 85, 269, OMWE
Chugur, Gonzalo, and Verdejo 2002, 323, sense proximity
Clough and Stevenson 2004, 309, WSD in CLIR
Cowie, Guthrie, and Guthrie 1992, 110, dictionary based method
Cucchiarelli and Velardi 1998, 285, domain tuning

D

Dagan and Itai 1994, 324, using second language corpus
Decadt, Hoste, Daelemans, and van den Bosch 2004, 177, 203, 233, supervised kNN method
Diab 2003, 265, 324, cross-lingual method
Dill et al. 2003, 319, SemTag, tagging the Web
Dorr and Jones 2000, 319, acquiring semantic lexicons

Text, Speech and Language Technology

Text, Speech and Language Technology

24. G. Fant: *Speech Acoustics and Phonetics.* Selected Writings. 2004
     ISBN 1-4020-2373-1; Pb 1-4020-2789-3
25. W.J. Barry and W.A. Van Dommelen (eds.): *The Integration of Phonetic Knowledge in Speech Technology.* 2005   ISBN 1-4020-2635-8; Pb 1-4020-2636-6
26. D. Dahl (ed.): *Practical Spoken Dialog Systems.* 2004
     ISBN 1-4020-2674-9; Pb 1-4020-2675-7
27. O. Stock and M. Zancanaro (eds.): *Multimodal Intelligent Information Presentation.* 2005   ISBN 1-4020-3049-5; Pb 1-4020-3050-9
28. W. Minker, D. Bühler and L. Dybkjaer (eds.): *Spoken Multimodal Human-Computer Dialogue in Mobile Environments.* 2004   ISBN 1-4020-3073-8; Pb 1-4020-3074-6
29. P. Saint-Dizier (ed.): *Syntax and Semantics of Prepositions.* 2005
     ISBN 1-4020-3849-6
30. J. C. J. van Kuppevelt, L. Dybkjaer, N. O. Bernsen (eds.): *Advances in natural Multimodal Dialogue Systems.* 2005   ISBN 1-4020-3932-8
31. P. Grzybek (ed.): *Contributions to the Science of Text and Language.* Word Length Studies and Related Issues. 2006   ISBN 1-4020-4067-9
32. T. Strzalkowski and S. Harabagiu (eds.): *Advances in Open Domain Question Answering.* 2006   ISBN 1-4020-4744-4
33. E. Agirre and P. Edmonds (eds.): *Word Sense Disambiguation.* Algorithms and Applications. 2006/2007   ISBN 978-4020-4808-4; Pb 978-4020-6870-6

Printed in the United Kingdom
by Lightning Source UK Ltd.
129249UK00001B/38/A